IMPORTANT

P9-BIG-489

HERE IS YOUR REGISTRATION CODE TO ACCESS MCGRAW-HILL
PREMIUM CONTENT AND MCGRAW-HILL ONLINE RESOURCES

For key premium online resources you need THIS CODE to
gain access. Once the code is entered, you will be able to
use the web resources for the length of your course.

Access is provided only if you have purchased a new book.

If the registration code is missing from this book, the registration screen on our
website, and within your WebCT or Blackboard course will tell you how to obtain
your new code. Your registration code can be used only once to establish access.
It is not transferable.

To gain access to these online resources

1. USE your web browser to go to: **www.mhhe.com/power**

2. CLICK on "First Time User"

3. ENTER the Registration Code printed on the tear-off bookmark on the right

4. After you have entered your registration code, click on "Register"

5. FOLLOW the instructions to setup your personal UserID and Password

6. WRITE your UserID and Password down for future reference. Keep it in a safe place.

If your course is using WebCT or Blackboard, you'll be able to use this code to
access the McGraw-Hill content within your instructor's online course.

To gain access to the McGraw-Hill content in your instructor's WebCT or
Blackboard course simply log into the course with the user ID and Password provided by your instructor. Enter the registration code exactly as it appears to the
right when prompted by the system. You will only need to use this code the first
time you click on McGraw-Hill content.

These instructions are specifically for student access. Instructors are not required
to register via the above instructions.

The McGraw-Hill Companies

Mc Graw Hill **Higher Education**

Thank you, and welcome to your
McGraw-Hill Online Resources.

13-Digit: 978-0-07-312644-9
10-Digit: 0-07-312644-6
t/a Power Learning, 3/e

E4NY-QQ3K-X6NK-XCM3-WA38

REGISTRATION CODE
REGISTRATION CODE

The McGraw-Hill Companies

Mc Graw Hill **Higher Education**

POWER

Learning

Annotated Instructor's Edition

THIRD EDITION

Strategies for Success in College and Life

Robert S. Feldman
University of Massachusetts–Amherst

 **Higher Education**

Boston   Burr Ridge, IL   Dubuque, IA   Madison, WI   New York
San Francisco   St. Louis   Bangkok   Bogotá   Caracas   Kuala Lumpur
Lisbon   London   Madrid   Mexico City   Milan   Montreal   New Delhi
Santiago   Seoul   Singapore   Sydney   Taipei   Toronto

To my students, who make teaching a joy.

Higher Education

P.O.W.E.R. LEARNING: STRATEGIES FOR SUCCESS IN COLLEGE AND LIFE
Published by McGraw-Hill, a business unit of The McGraw-Hill Companies, Inc., 1221 Avenue of
the Americas, New York, NY, 10020. Copyright © 2007, 2005, 2004, 2003, 2000 by The McGraw-Hill
Companies, Inc. All rights reserved. No part of this publication may be reproduced or distributed
in any form or by any means, or stored in a database or retrieval system, without the prior written
consent of The McGraw-Hill Companies, Inc., including, but not limited to, in any network or other
electronic storage or transmission, or broadcast for distance learning.
Some ancillaries, including electronic and print components, may not be available to customers
outside the United States.

This book is printed on acid-free paper.

1 2 3 4 5 6 7 8 9 0 QPD/QPD 0 9 8 7 6 5

ISBN-13: 978-0-07-312640-1
ISBN-10:   0-07-312640-3
AIE ISBN-13: 978-0-07-312643-2
AIE ISBN-10:   0-07-312643-8

Editor in Chief: *Emily Barrosse*
Publisher: *Beth Mejia*
Executive Editor: *David S. Patterson*
Freelance Developmental Editor: *Vicki Malinee, Van Brien & Associates*
Senior Marketing Manager: *Leslie Oberhuber*
Managing Editor: *Jean Dal Porto*
Lead Project Manager: *Susan Trentacosti*
Production Service: *Electronic Publishing Services Inc., NYC, Lake Lloyd*
Art Director: *Jeanne Schreiber*
Art Manager: *Robin Mouat*
Design Manager: *Laurie J. Entringer*
Text Designer: *Amanda Kavanagh*
Cover Design and Illustration: *Asylum Studios*
Photo Research Coordinator: *Nora Agbayani*
Photo Researcher: *Nancy Null, Van Brien & Associates*
Senior Supplement Producer: *Louis Swaim*
Production Supervisor: *Jason I. Huls*
Senior Media Project Manager: *Ron Nelms*
Media Producer: *Michele Borrelli*
Composition: *Electronic Publishing Services Inc., NYC*
Printing: *45# Pub Matte Plus, Quebecor World Dubuque Inc.*
Credits: The credits section for this book begins on page 420 and is considered an extension of the
copyright page.

Library of Congress Cataloging-in-Publication Data

Feldman, Robert S. (Robert Stephen), 1947–
        P.O.W.E.R. learning : strategies for success in college and life / Robert S. Feldman. -- 3rd ed.
        p. cm.
        Includes bibliographical references and index.
        ISBN-13: 978-0-07-312640-1 (softcover : alk. paper)
        ISBN-10: 0-07-312640-3 (softcover : alk. paper)
        ISBN-13: 978-0-07-312643-2 (annotated instructor's edition : soft cover : alk. paper)
        ISBN-10: 0-07-312643-8 (annotated instructor's edition : softcover : alk. paper)
        1. College student orientation. 2. Study skills. 3. Life skills. 4. Success I. Title:
POWER learning. II. Title.
LB2343.3.F44 2007
378.1'98--dc22   2005054489

The Internet addresses listed in the text were accurate at the time of publication. The inclusion of a
Web site does not indicate an endorsement by the authors of McGraw-Hill, and McGraw-Hill does
not guarantee the accuracy of the information presented at these sites.
www.mhhe.com

Let the McGraw-Hill Student Success Team support your course with our workshop program

- Planning to develop a First-Year Experience course from scratch?
- Reenergizing your First-Year Experience course?
- Trying to integrate technology in your class?
- Exploring the concept of learning communities?

We offer a range of author- and consultant-led workshops that can be tailored to meet the needs of your institution.

Our team of experts, led by *P.O.W.E.R. Learning* author Robert Feldman, can address issues of course management, assessment, organization, and implementation. How do you get students to commit to your program? How do you achieve support from your institution? How can you evaluate and demonstrate the effectiveness of your first-year experience course? These are questions that every program faces. Let us help you to find an answer that works for you.

Other workshop topics may include:

- Classroom Strategies for Enhancing Cultural Competence: The P.O.W.E.R. of Diversity
- Using Learning Styles in the Classroom
- Creating Student Success Courses Online
- Motivating Your Students

To schedule a workshop, please contact your local McGraw-Hill representative. Alternately, contact us directly at **fye@mcgraw-hill.com** to begin the process of bringing a P.O.W.E.R. Learning workshop to you.

The POWER to Create Your Own Text!

Do you want to:

- Only cover select chapters?
- Personalize your book with campus information (maps, schedules, registration materials, etc.)?
- Add your own materials including exercises or assignments?
- Address specific student populations, such as student athletes and transferring students?

P.O.W.E.R. Learning can be customized to suit your needs.*

Why Customize?

Perhaps your course focuses on study skills and you prefer that your text not cover life issues such as money matters, health and wellness, or information on choosing a major. Whatever the reason, we can make it happen, easily. McGraw-Hill Custom Publishing can deliver a book that perfectly meets your needs.

What Will My Custom Book Look Like?

Any chapters from the P.O.W.E.R. Learning book that you include will be in full color. Additional materials can be added between chapters or at the beginning or end of the book in black and white. Binding (paperback, three-hole punch, you name it) is up to you. You can even add your own custom cover to reflect your school image.

What Can I Add?

Anything! Here are some ideas to get you started:

- **Campus map** or anything specific to your school: academic regulations or requirements, syllabi, important phone numbers or dates, library hours.
- **Calendars** for the school year, for local theater groups, for a concert series.
- **Interviews** with local businesspeople or your school's graduates in which they describe their own challenges and successes.
- **Your course syllabus or homework assignments** so your students have everything they need for your course under one cover and you don't have to make copies to hand out.

*Orders must meet our minimum sales unit requirements.

Special Chapters Designed for the Unique Needs of Your Students!

Three additional chapters are available for your customized text and have been designed to address the needs of specific student populations.

- *Strategies for Success for Student Athletes.* This chapter discusses the unique challenges of student athletes, such as managing school and team pressures, using resources and understanding eligibility, and knowing when and how to ask for help. It also addresses special concerns such as burnout, dealing with injury, and hazing.
- *Taking Charge of Your Career.* This chapter helps students determine the best career choices that fit personal goals. It provides important tips on how to develop a career portfolio, prepare a résumé and cover letters, and have a successful interview, including follow-up strategies.
- *Transfer Strategies: Making the Leap from Community College to a Four-Year School.* Designed for the potential transfer student, this chapter looks at the pros and cons of moving beyond a two-year degree and what personal decisions to make. It guides students through the transfer process, including applications, credit transfer, financial assistance, and transfer shock.

How Do I Create a Custom Book?

The secret to custom publishing is this: *Custom Publishing Is Simple!*
  Here are the basic steps:

- You select the chapters you would like to use from *P.O.W.E.R. Learning* with your McGraw-Hill sales representative.
- Together, we discuss your preferences for the binding, the cover, etc., and provide you with information on costs.
- We assign your customized text an ISBN and your project goes into production. A custom text will typically publish within 6–8 weeks of the order.
- Your book is manufactured and it is put into inventory in the McGraw-Hill distribution center.
- You are sent a free desk copy of your custom publication.
- Your bookstore calls McGraw-Hill's customer service department and orders the text.

You select what you want—we handle the details!
Contact us:

www.mhhe.com/power

Canada: 1-905-430-5034

United States: 1-800-446-8979

E-mail: **fye@mcgraw-hill.com**

Brief Contents

Contents

3   Recognizing How You Learn, Who You Are, and What You Value   59

7 Writing and Speaking   175

8 Memory   209

9 Choosing Your Courses and Major   233

13   Money Matters   353

14   Stress, Health, and Wellness   383

A   Strategies for Success for Student Athletes   A-1

C   Taking Charge of Your Career   C-1

T   Transfer Strategies: Making the Leap from Community College to a Four-Year School   T-1

Changes That Make a Difference: New Features in the Third Edition

Consistent with the extensive classroom testing and reviewing that shaped the previous editions, each chapter in this third edition has been reviewed and honed by no fewer than thirty first-year experience instructors. Their responses, in addition to feedback from the tens of thousands of students, the hundreds of instructors who used the prior editions, and classroom testing, have resulted in significant additions to the text:

P.O.W.E.R. Profile Assessment. Because students need to know where they are coming from before they can determine where they are going and how to get there, Chapter 1 now contains a major addition: an assessment tool that provides students with a profile of where they stand—both numerically and graphically—in terms of the key topics of the book. The *P.O.W.E.R. Profile* (pages 20–23), which is keyed to the major topics covered in *P.O.W.E.R. Learning,* presents students an opportunity to objectively understand their strengths and weaknesses. By completing the *P.O.W.E.R. Profile* (which they can do in the book or online) at the start of the term and then again at the end of the course, they can clearly see the progress they have made.

Course Connections. Every chapter includes a new Course Connections feature. These boxes take the subject matter of a chapter directly into the classroom, showing how students can use the information to maximize their success in particular classes. For example, the time management chapter addresses how much time students should devote to studying (page 39); the Course Connections in the chapter on recognizing learning styles shows how students can connect their learning style to that of their instructor (page 72); the memory chapter discusses special memorization techniques for specific courses such as foreign languages, math, and science (page 225); and the chapter on decision making addresses ways of demonstrating critical thinking while in class (page 314).

Service Learning and Community Service. Several chapters address service learning and community service. For example, Chapter 1 discusses the rationale for service learning and community service (page 5), and Chapter 12 discusses them as a way to increase cultural competence (page 334).

Academic Honesty and Plagiarism. Discussions with many first-year experience course instructors—as well as instructors across the spectrum of disciplines—revealed increasing concern with academic honesty and plagiarism. In response, the new edition discusses the topic in several places and contexts, including Chapters 5 (page 138), 7 (page 193), and 10 (page 291).

Technology and Information Competency. The increasing emphasis on instructional technology—and the rapid changes in the field—resulted in extensive updating of this chapter. From distance learning to using e-mail effectively, the chapter provides new coverage of working and studying online, developing information competency, blogs (page 292), instant messages (page 272), and locating and evaluating information on the Web and in libraries.

Speaking of Success Interviews. These informative and inspiring profiles have been refreshed with several new faces, including Lev Sviridov (City College of New York) in Chapter 1 (page 24); Jasmine Rosario (Vassar College) in Chapter 2 (page 55); Kate Endress (Ball State University) in Chapter 4 (page 117); Francine Sanchez (Lehman College) in Chapter 9 (page 258); and Edmund Fixico (Fort Berthold Community College) in Chapter 13 (page 378). Additional Speaking of Success interviews are included on the *P.O.W.E.R. Learning* Web site.

Journal Reflections. The Journal Reflections feature found in every chapter, which facilitates the creation of student journals, now concludes with a question specifically designed to elicit critical thinking (see, for example, page 6).

An Overall Streamlining and Tightening of Textual Material. Every sentence has been reassessed with the goal of making the text even more readable and the vocabulary appropriate for first-year students.

Additions of New and Updated Material. This edition incorporates a significant amount of new and updated information, reflecting advances in our understanding of what makes students successful, changes in college instruction, and the suggestions of reviewers. The following sample of new and revised topics provides a good indication of the book's currency.

Chapter 1—*P.O.W.E.R. Learning:* Becoming an Expert Student

- New *P.O.W.E.R. Profile* assessment tool (pages 20–23)
- New discussion of community service (page 5)
- Additional material on service learning (page 5)
- Expanded critical thinking discussion (page 17)
- Reference to orientation programs (page 25)
- Course Connections feature on preparing and organizing for the first day of class (page 11)
- New Speaking of Success interview with Lev Sviridov, City College of New York (page 24)

Chapter 2—Making the Most of Your Time

- Cell phones and text messages as sources of interruptions (page 48)
- Weekly timetable includes 24-hour format (page 44)
- Expanded section on scheduling enjoyable tasks (page 43)
- Revised procrastination scale (page 50)
- Importance of reexamination of priorities (page 53)
- Emphasizes that time management skills are important not just for college, but for future life as well (page 51)
- Course Connections feature on number of hours instructors expect students to prepare for class (page 39)
- "Take an e-break" as a time management strategy (page 48)
- Specific examples in Career Connections illustrating different career paths (page 52)
- New Speaking of Success interview with Jasmine Rosario (page 55)

Chapter 3—Recognizing How You Learn, Who You Are, and What You Value

- More positive self-esteem material (page 77)
- Cycle of Success graphic (page 77)

- Strengthened warning about the importance of time management in distance learning courses and other advantages/disadvantages of distance learning (page 277)
- New information on online databases (page 282)
- Need to establish separate college e-mail account if required by college (page 274)
- New section on dealing with spam (page 275)
- Added cautions regarding plagiarism of Web sources (page 291)
- Discussion of blogs (page 292)

Chapter 11—Making Good Decisions

- New Try It activity on correlation/causation (page 318)
- Added that the college to which a student is transferring is the controlling entity (page 308)
- Importance of asking others for advice in decision making (page 306)
- Course Connections feature on critical thinking in class (page 305)

Chapter 12—Diversity and Your Relationships with Others

- New title emphasizes the importance of diversity
- Expanded rationale for importance of diversity in students' *future* lives (page 329)
- Additional dimensions of diversity and Diversity Wheel (page 327)
- More material applicable to nontraditional students (page 342)
- Importance of participation in community service as a way to increase cultural competence (page 334)
- Course Connections feature on diversity in the classroom (page 336)
- Material on political correctness (page 336)

Chapter 13—Money Matters

- Cautions about dangers of too much work (page 364)
- Idea that taking out loans sometimes can be a better strategy than working at jobs excessively (page 364)
- New statistics on credit card debt among college students (page 366)
- Updated and additional information about FAFSA and Financial Aid Profile online (page 374)
- New Course Connections feature on cost of cutting class (page 370)
- Indebtedness and post-college income (page 366)
- New Speaking of Success interview with Edmund Fixico, Fort Berthold Community College (page 378)

Chapter 14—Stress, Health, and Wellness

- New section on dealing with loss and grief (page 409)
- Rape hotline number (page 408)
- Importance of family social support in fighting stress (page 370)
- Updated terminology (including sexually transmitted infections—STIs) (page 405)
- Course Connections feature on staying alert in class (page 397)

Achieving the Goals of P.O.W.E.R. Learning

The goals of *P.O.W.E.R. Learning: Strategies for Success in College and Life* are achieved through a consistent, carefully devised set of features common to every chapter. Students and faculty endorsed each of these elements. They include the following (see pages xxvii–xxxi for a visual tour):

- **Chapter-opening scenarios.** Each chapter begins with a short vignette, describing an individual grappling with a situation that is relevant to the subject matter of the chapter. Readers will be able to relate to these vignettes, which feature students running behind schedule (Chapter 2, page 30), figuring out a way to keep up with reading assignments (Chapter 6, page 150), or facing a long list of French vocabulary words to memorize (Chapter 8, page 210).

- **Looking Ahead sections.** These sections provide a bridge between the opening vignettes and the remainder of the chapter and include orienting questions that lay out the chapter's objectives.

- **Try It activities.** These sections, interspersed throughout the chapter, include written exercises of all types. There are at least five Try It activities in every chapter, and at least one of these is designated as an in-class, group exercise. Examples of Try It exercises include "Assessing Your Analytical and Relational Learning Style" (Chapter 3, page 67), "Practice Your Notetaking Skills" (Chapter 4, page 114), "Complete a Test Preparation Checklist" (Chapter 5, page 128), "Summarize, Don't Plagiarize" (Chapter 7, page 196), "Work the Web" (Chapter 10, page 290); and "Determine the Diversity of Your Campus Community" (Chapter 12, page 328).

- **Journal Reflections.** This feature provides students with the opportunity to keep an ongoing journal, making entries relevant to the chapter content. Students are asked to reflect and think critically about related prior experiences. For example, the Journal Reflections in Chapter 7, page 177, "How I Feel about Writing," asks students to reflect on their feelings about the writing process, and the one in Chapter 10, page 266, "How I Feel about Computers," asks for students' reactions to technology and computers.

- **Speaking of Success.** Every chapter includes interviews with individuals who exemplify academic success. Some of these individuals are well-known figures such as comedian Bill Cosby (page 86) and writer John Irving (page 170); others are current students or recent graduates. Many of these individuals have struggled to overcome difficulties in their personal lives or in school before achieving academic or career success. Students will be able to relate to or identify with the stories told by the people profiled in these sections; some accounts may inspire readers to work harder to realize their goals and aspirations.

- **Course Connections.** New to this edition, these boxes found in every chapter connect chapter material to students' courses, showing how the information can be applied directly and immediately to what they are doing in their classes. Topics include studying for specific subject areas such as math and science (page 225), considering the amount of study time instructors expect (page 39), matching student and instructor learning styles (page 72), and the real cost of cutting classes (page 370).

P.O.W.E.R. *Learning* offers a wide range of skill-building opportunities.

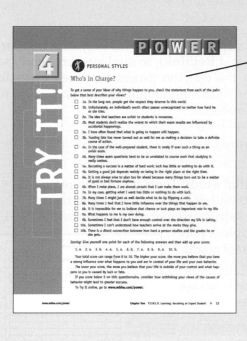

Every chapter offers numerous **Try It** activities for gaining hands-on experience with the material covered in the chapter. These include questionnaires, self-assessments, and group exercises to do with classmates. The Try It activities, along with other assessment opportunities, are also available on the text's website at www.mhhe.com/power.

Every chapter includes an updated list of the three types of **resources** that are useful in finding and utilizing information relevant to the chapter: a list of on-campus resources; books; and websites. There are also exercises in using the web, called **Taking It to the Net.** This material helps students study and retain important concepts presented in chapter, as as guiding future inquiry.

Every chapter includes a new **Course Connections** box that shows students how to use the chapter's content to maximize their success in particular classes.

P.O.W.E.R. Learning demonstrates the connection between academic success and success beyond the classroom.

The **Career Connections** feature links the material in the chapter to the world of work, demonstrating how the strategies discussed in the chapter are related to career choices and success in the workplace.

Due to increasing concern with **academic honesty and plagiarism**, this new edition addresses the topic in several places and contexts, including acknowledging sources in writing papers and giving speeches and crediting material accessed online.

Many new **Speaking of Success** articles have been added that profile real-life success stories. Some of these people are well-known individuals, whereas others are current students or recent graduates who have overcome academic difficulties to achieve success.

Several chapters now address **service learning and community service**—including a rationale for these programs and ways to use them to increase cultural competence.

P.O.W.E.R. Learning helps you develop critical thinking skills.

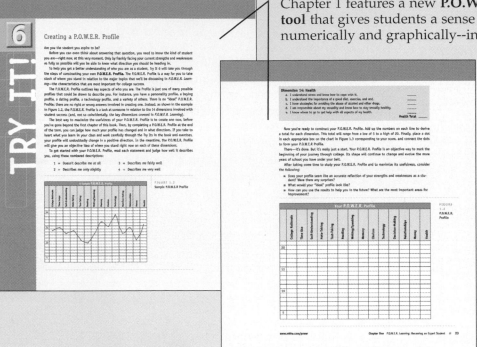

Chapter 1 features a new **P.O.W.E.R. Profile Assessment tool** that gives students a sense of where they stand--both numerically and graphically--in relation to the key topics addressed in the book. The "P.O.W.E.R. Profile" helps students identify their strengths and weaknesses and determine how they want to improve. Students can return to the P.O.W.E.R. Profile at the end of the course to assess and chart their progress.

The **Journal Reflections** feature provides students with the opportunity to keep an ongoing journal, making entries relevant to the chapter content. Students are asked to reflect and think critically about related prior experiences. These now conclude with questions designed to elicit critical thinking and exploration.

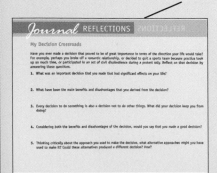

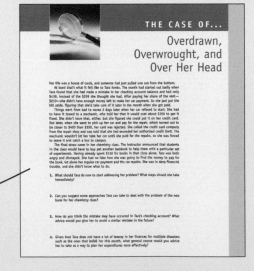

Each chapter ends with a **case study** ("The Case of...") to which the principles described in the chapter can be applied.

Case studies are based on situations that students might themselves encounter. Each case provides a series of questions that encourage students to consider what they've learned and to use critical thinking skills in responding to these questions.

P.O.W.E.R. Learning provides an engaging, accessible, and meaningful presentation.

A **new design and visual presentation** highlight large, clear photos carefully selected to show the diversity of students as well as the latest in technological aids and devices.

Chapter-opening scenarios describe an individual grappling with a situation that is relevant to the subject matter of the chapter. Readers will be able to relate to these vignettes, which feature students running behind schedule, figuring out a way to keep up with reading assignments, or facing a long list of French vocabulary words to memorize.

Key terms appear in boldface in the text and are defined in the margins. In addition, they are listed in a **"Key Terms and Concepts"** section at the end of the chapter, with accompanying page references.

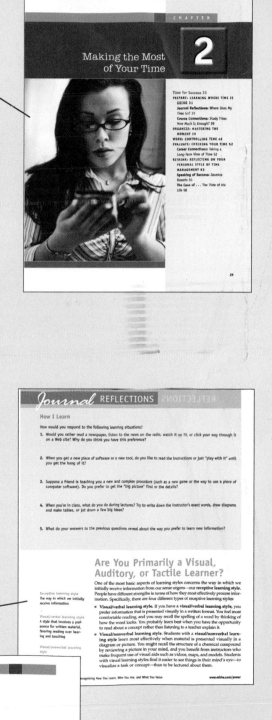

P.O.W.E.R. Tools for Instructors and Students

The same philosophy and goals that guided the writing of *P.O.W.E.R. Learning: Strategies for Success in College and Life* led to the development of a comprehensive, first-rate set of teaching aids. Through a series of focus groups, questionnaires, and surveys, we asked instructors what they needed to optimize their courses. We also analyzed what other publishers provided in the way of teaching aids to make sure that the ancillary materials accompanying *P.O.W.E.R. Learning* would surpass the level of support to which instructors are accustomed. As a result of the extensive research that went into devising the teaching aids, we are confident that whether you are an instructor with years of experience or are teaching the course for the first time, this book's instructional package will enhance classroom instruction and provide guidance as you prepare for and teach the course.

Print Resources

Annotated Instructor's Edition (AIE)

(0-07-312643-8): The AIE, prepared by Joni Webb Petschauer and Cindy Wallace of Appalachian State University, contains the full text of the student edition of the book with the addition of marginal notes that provide a rich variety of teaching strategies, discussion prompts, and helpful cross-references to the Instructor's Resource Manual. The third edition also includes three additional chapters on student athletes, transferring students, and career preparation that can be included in custom versions of *P.O.W.E.R. Learning*.

Instructor's Resource Manual and Testbank

(0-07-326093-2): Written by Joni Webb Petschauer and Cindy Wallace of Appalachian State University with additional contributions from experienced instructors across the country, this manual provides specific suggestions for teaching each topic, tips on implementing a first-year experience program, handouts to generate creative classroom activities, transparency masters, audiovisual resources, sample syllabi, tips on incorporating the Internet into the course, and a bank of chapter quizzes.

Customize Your Text

P.O.W.E.R. Learning can be customized to suit your needs. The text can be abbreviated for shorter courses and can be expanded to include semester schedules, campus maps, additional essays, activities, or exercises, along with other materials specific to your curriculum or situation. Chapters designed for student athletes, transferring students, and career preparation are also available.

Distance Learning Faculty Guide: Designing and Teaching a Distance Learning Course with *P.O.W.E.R. Learning*

(0-07-256298-6): Written by Christopher Poirier and Robert Feldman, this guide provides instructors with an overview of distance learning, an introduction to the most popular distance learning platforms, and detailed instructions on how to design and teach a distance learning course with *P.O.W.E.R. Learning*.

Human Resources

Workshops with Author and Author Team

Are you faced with the challenge of launching a first-year experience course on your campus? Would you like to invigorate your college success program, incorporating the most recent pedagogical and technological innovations? Is faculty recruitment an obstacle to the success of your program? Are you interested in learning more about the P.O.W.E.R. system?

Workshops are available on these and many other subjects for anyone conducting or even just considering a first-year experience program. Led by author Robert Feldman, *P.O.W.E.R. Learning* Instructor's Resource Manual authors Joni Webb Petschauer and Cindy Wallace, or one of the McGraw-Hill *P.O.W.E.R. Learning* consultants, each workshop is tailored to the needs of individual campuses or programs. For more information, contact your local representative, or drop us a line at **fye@mcgraw-hill.com**.

Digital Resources

Instructor's Resource CD-ROM

(0-07-312641-1): All the core supplements are conveniently provided on this CD. Included are the EZ Test computerized test bank, Instructor's Resource Manual, and PowerPoint presentations.

New! Implementing a Student Success Course CD-ROM

(0-07-310690-9): This innovative CD assists you in developing and sustaining your Student Success course. Features include a "how to" guide for designing and proposing a new course, with easy-to-use templates for determining budget needs and resources. Examples of model programs are provided from two-year, four-year, and career schools. The CD explores course goals, such as orientation and retention, and provides research data to support your proposal. Also included are materials to help sustain your course, such as faculty development programs and online resources.

New! LASSI: Learning and Study Strategies Inventory

The LASSI is a ten-scale, 80-item assessment of students' awareness about and use of learning and study strategies related to skill, will, and self-regulation components of strategic learning. The focus is on both covert and overt thoughts, behaviors, attitudes, and beliefs that relate to successful learning and that can be altered through educational interventions. Research has repeatedly demonstrated that these factors contribute significantly to success in college and that they can be learned or enhanced through educational interventions such as learning and study skills courses.

The LASSI provides standardized scores and national norms for ten different scales. The LASSI is both diagnostic and prescriptive. It provides students with a diagnosis of their strengths and weaknesses compared to other college students in the areas covered by the ten scales, and it is prescriptive in that it provides feedback about areas where students may be weak and need to improve their knowledge, attitudes, beliefs, and skills.

The LASSI is available in print or online at **www.hhpublishing.com**. Ask your McGraw-Hill sales representative for more details.

P.O.W.E.R. Learning Web site

(**www.mhhe.com/power**): Instructors and students will find resources such as downloadable resources, self-quizzes, on-line journal activities and assessments, case study assignments, Web exercises, and a rich bank of links for college success.

PageOut, WebCT, Blackboard, and more

The online content of *P.O.W.E.R. Learning* is supported by WebCT, eCollege.com, and Blackboard. Additionally, our PageOut service, free to qualified adopters, is available to get you and your course up and running online in a matter of hours! To find out more contact your local McGraw-Hill representative or visit **www.pageout.net**.

Video Resource

(0-07-236710-5): Real People Talk about Real Success: Filmed expressly for *P.O.W.E.R. Learning* on various campus locations and real world settings, this documentary-style video features a variety of inspiring people, both professionals and students, describing life challenges and how the elements of the P.O.W.E.R. system help them achieve success. Designed for use during the early part of the semester, this video is ideal for helping to break the ice and stimulating discussion. Ask your McGraw-Hill representative for details.

Robert S. Feldman still remembers those moments of being overwhelmed when he started college at Wesleyan University. "I wondered whether I was up to the challenges that faced me," he recalls, "and—although I never would have admitted it at the time—I really had no idea what it took to be successful at college."

That experience, along with his encounters with many students during his own teaching career, led to a lifelong interest in helping students navigate the critical transition that they face at the start of their own college careers. Professor Feldman, who went on to receive a doctorate in psychology from the University of Wisconsin–Madison, teaches at the University of Massachusetts at Amherst, where he is Director of Undergraduate Studies and faculty member in the Department of Psychology. As Director of Undergraduate Studies, he initiated the Minority Mentoring Program, and he directs the UMass first-year experience course for incoming students, *POWER Up for Student Success.*

Professor Feldman's proudest professional accomplishment is winning the College Outstanding Teaching Award at UMass. He also has been named a Hewlett Teaching Fellow and was Senior Online Instruction Fellow. He has taught courses at Mount Holyoke College, Wesleyan University, and Virginia Commonwealth University.

Professor Feldman is a Fellow of both the American Psychological Association and the American Psychological Society. He is a winner of a Fulbright Senior Research Scholar and Lecturer award and has written some 100 scientific articles, book chapters, and books. His books, some of which have been translated into Spanish, French, Portuguese, and Chinese, include *Improving the First Year of College: Research and Practice, Understanding Psychology, 8/e,* and *Development Across the Life Span, 4/e.* His research interests encompass the study of honesty and truthfulness in everyday life, development of nonverbal behavior in children, and the social psychology of education. His research has been supported by grants from the National Institute of Mental Health and the National Institute on Disabilities and Rehabilitation Research.

With the last of his three children completing college last spring, Professor Feldman occupies his spare time with serious cooking and earnest, but admittedly unpolished, piano playing. He loves to travel with his wife, who is also a college professor. He lives with her in a home overlooking the Holyoke mountain range in western Massachusetts.

Acknowledgments

I am indebted to the many reviewers of *P.O.W.E.R. Learning* who provided input at every step of development of the book. These dedicated instructors and administrators provided thoughtful, detailed advice, and I am very grateful for their help and insight. For this edition, they include the following:

Francesco Ancona, Sussex County Community College; Phyllis Arias, Long Beach City College; Barry Armstrong, Liberty University; Erskine Ausbrooks, Dyersburg State Community College; Leslie Barnes-Young, Francis Marion University; Wendy Beck, Utah State University; Kathleen Bryan, Daytona Beach Community College; Mary Carstens, Wayne State College; Joel Corley, Edison Community College; Janet Cutshall, Sussex County Community College; Georgia Davis, Southwest Tennessee Community College; Denise Farley, Sussex County Community College; Sabryna Hamilton, Mid-South Community College; Heather Happ, Loyola University; Jill Hughes, Casper College; Richard Kirk, Central Florida Community College; Pamela Love, Collin County Community College; Phil Mikita, Lorain Community College; Leslie Mitchell, Palm Beach Community College; Holly Morris, Lehigh Carbon Community College; Robin Musselman, Lehigh Carbon Community College; Jennifer Robb, Scott Community College; Ryan Ruda, Garden City Community College; Melissa St. Amour, Eisenhower Middle School; Juliet Scherer, St. Louis Community College–Meramec; Stephen Snyder, Baker College–Muskegon; Rheva Thomason, Palm Beach Community College; Mary Thompson, Sussex County Community College; Kim Titus, Daytona Beach Community College; Phil Van Loon, Cabrillo College; Jan Weis, Scott Community College; Kathie Wentworth, Tri-State University; Evelyn Young, Brevard Community College

The students in my own first-year experience courses (some of whom are shown below) provided thoughtful and wise advice. I thank them for their enthusiasm and eager willingness to provide constructive feedback.

Professors Cindy Wallace and Joni Webb Petschauer of Appalachian State University wrote the Instructor's Resource Manual and provided marginal notes and tips for the Annotated Instructor's Edition. I thank both of them for their enthusiasm, good ideas, dedication, and friendship.

Edward Murphy, Ed.D., an educational testing expert, helped develop the exercises in the book, and I'm grateful for his excellent work. The developmental editor on this edition,

P.O.W.E.R. Learning author Bob Feldman and some of his first-year experience program participants.

Vicki Malinee, made many contributions to the text, and I thank her for her superb creativity and input into every aspect of the book.

John Graiff was a great help on every level in putting this book together, and I thank him for his willingness to go the extra mile. I could not have written this book without his unflagging support.

I am proud to be part of an extraordinary McGraw-Hill editorial, marketing, and sales team. David Patterson, sponsoring editor and chief P.O.W.E.R.-meister, has brought enthusiasm and intelligence to the project, and I welcome his good work. Marketing Manager Leslie Oberhuber, who juggles many balls with a grace that makes everything look easy, is a font of good ideas, and Field Publisher Lisa Berry has brought energy and passion to the Student Success program. I also am grateful to Publisher Beth Mejia, who has brought new vigor to the student success program, and to Editor-in-Chief Emily Barrosse, whose considerable savvy supports *P.O.W.E.R. Learning*. Finally, Steve Debow, President of Social Sciences and Humanities, continues to give strong and imaginative support to this project, and I am grateful for his ongoing personal involvement.

There are several folks who, while no longer officially working on the project, still patiently answer my queries and offer their advice, for which I am extremely grateful. Andy Watts made superb contributions in extending the reach of *P.O.W.E.R. Learning,* and I'm very grateful for his work and even more for his friendship. Phil Butcher, Thalia Dorwick, Allison McNamara, and Alexis Walker were part of the editorial team that developed the book, and I'm ever thankful for their efforts. Above all, I'm grateful to Rhona Robbin, first development editor on the book, and sponsoring editor Sarah Touborg, who provided the impetus for the book. Certainly, the pages of *P.O.W.E.R. Learning* continue to reflect their many contributions.

Without a doubt, there is no better publishing group in the business than the one that worked on *P.O.W.E.R. Learning.* I count myself extremely lucky not only to have found myself a part of this world-class team, but to count each of them as friends.

In the end, I am eternally indebted to my family, both extended and immediate. Sarah, Josh, Jon, Leigh, and of course Kathy, thank you for everything.

Dear Student,

Do you find that there's not enough time to accomplish all the things you want to do? Do you put off studying for tests until the last minute? Do you sometimes have trouble making decisions?

If so, you're not alone. *Every* first-year college student encounters challenges such as these, and many others. That's where *P.O.W.E.R. Learning: Strategies for Success in College and Life* comes in. It is designed to help you to master the challenges you'll face in college as well as in life after college. The *P.O.W.E.R. Learning* system—which is based on five key steps embodied in the word *P.O.W.E.R.* (*P*repare, *O*rganize, *W*ork, *E*valuate, and *R*ethink)—teaches strategies that will help you become a more successful student and that will give you an edge in attaining what you want to accomplish in life.

But it's up to you to make use of the book. By familiarizing yourself with its features and using the built-in learning aids, you'll maximize it usefulness and be more likely to get the most out of it.

Familiarize yourself with the scope of *P.O.W.E.R. Learning*

Begin by skimming the Table of Contents, which provides an overview of the book. By reading the chapter titles, you'll get a sense of the topics that are covered and the logic of the sequence of chapters.

Then, take some time to flip through the book

Choose a chapter that sounds interesting to you, skim a few pages, and see for yourself the kinds of practical information the book provides. Note that every chapter has the same diamond-shaped pattern:

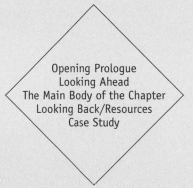

Opening Prologue
Looking Ahead
The Main Body of the Chapter
Looking Back/Resources
Case Study

Use the Built-In Learning Aids

Now that you have a broad overview of *P.O.W.E.R. Learning*, you're ready to consider each of the book's different components.

Opening Prologue

This is a brief account of a student confronting a challenge, of the kind you are likely to face, that is relevant to the chapter topic.

Looking Ahead

This opening section orients you to the topics covered in each chapter, providing a link between the opening situation and the rest of the chapter. It also includes a list of key questions that are addressed—and answered—within the chapter.

Journal Reflections

This feature allows you to keep an ongoing journal, making entries relevant to the chapter content.

Try It

Every chapter offers at least five opportunities for you to gain hands-on experience with the material covered in the chapter. These activities include questionnaires, self-assessments, and group exercises that you can do with your classmates. The name says it all: Try It!

Speaking of Success

Every chapter includes an interview with someone who has achieved academic success. Some of these people are well-known individuals, whereas others are current students or recent graduates who have overcome academic difficulties to achieve success.

Course Connections

The Course Connections features found in every chapter give you an immediate boost in the classes in which you are now enrolled. They will show you how to address the specific content areas of your courses to maximize your success.

Career Connections

Linking college success strategies to the workplace, Career Connections features illustrate how the strategies and skills discussed in the chapter can help you on the job—and to find a job in the first place.

Running Glossary

Key terms appear in boldface in the text and are defined in the margins. In addition, they are listed in the Key Terms and Concepts section at the end of the chapter, where they are referenced by page number, and are identified in the index in color.

Looking Back

Looking Back is a summary organized around the questions featured in the Looking Ahead section that lists the key points discussed in the chapter.

Key Terms and Concepts

This list of important terms you should know is listed in order of appearance, and the page numbers refer back to the point in the chapter where the term was introduced.

Resources

Every chapter includes a list of the three types of resources that can help you find information relevant to the chapter: a list of on-campus resources, books, and Web sites. There are also exercises in using the Web, called Taking It to the Net.

Case Study

Every chapter ends with a case study (The Case of . . .) and accompanying questions. These cases are designed to provide you with an opportunity to apply the principles in the chapter.

Every chapter contains these features, which will serve as familiar guideposts as you make your way through the book. The structure will help you in organizing the book's content, as well as in learning and remembering the material.

Online Learning Center

With a purchase of a new text, you also gain access to an accompanying Web site (**www.mhhe.com/power**) that provides additional practice of the main principles and assessments explored in the text. Many of the handy forms are also available in downloadable templates you can then customize. If you purchased a new text, you will find the password located at the front of the text.

Get in Touch

I welcome your comments and suggestions about *P.O.W.E.R. Learning*, as well as the Web site and CD-ROM that accompanies the book. You can write me at the Department of Psychology at the University of Massachusetts, Amherst, Massachusetts 01003. Even easier, send me an e-mail message at **feldman@psych. umass.edu**. I will write back!

A final word: *P.O.W.E.R. Learning* presents the tools that can maximize your chances for academic and life success. But remember that they're only tools, and their effectiveness depends on the way in which they are used. Ultimately, you are the one who is in charge of your future.

The start of college offers a wonderful point of departure. Make the journey a rewarding, exciting, and enlightening one!

ROBERT S. FELDMAN

P.O.W.E.R. Learning: Becoming an Expert Student

The day has started off with a bang. Literally. As Jessie Trevant struggles sleepily to turn off her clock radio's continual buzzing at 8:35 a.m., she knocks it off the desk next to her bed. The loud bang it makes not only wakes her fully but also rouses her roommate, who grumbles resentfully.

Struggling out of bed, Jessie reflects on the day ahead. It's one of her most intense class days—four different classes, scattered across the campus. She also must put in several hours of work in the college bookstore, where she has a 15-hour-a-week job, and she knows she'd better get started on her history paper, due next week. And then there's that biology test that she must take this morning.

After a quick shower, Jessie joins the flood of students making their way to classes. She glances at her biology textbook and feels a wave of anxiety flood over her: Will I do well enough? How will I manage to hold down a job and have enough time to study? Will I make friends here? Will it ever feel like home? Will I make my family proud? . . . *And underlying them all is a single challenge: Will I be successful in college?*

LOOKING AHEAD >>>

Whether academic pursuits are a struggle or come easily to you . . . whether you live on campus or commute . . . whether you are fresh out of high school or are returning to school many years after high school graduation—college is a challenge. Every one of us has concerns about our capabilities and motivation, and new situations—like starting college—make us wonder how well we'll succeed.

That's where this book comes in. It is designed to help you learn the most effective ways to approach the challenges you encounter, not just in college, but outside the classroom, too. It will teach you practical strategies, hints, and tips that can lead you to success, all centered around an approach to achieving college success: P.O.W.E.R. Learning.

This book is designed to be useful in a way that is different from other college texts. It presents information in a hands-on format. It's meant to be used—not just read. Write on it, underline words and sentences, use a highlighter, circle key points, and complete the questionnaires right in the book. The more exercises you do, the more you'll get from the book. Remember, this is a book to help you with your coursework throughout college, so it's a good idea to invest your time here and now. If the learning techniques you master here become second nature, the payoff will be enormous.

This first chapter lays out the basics of P.O.W.E.R. Learning. By the time you finish this chapter, you'll be able to answer these questions:

- **What are the benefits of a college education?**
- **What are the basic principles of P.O.W.E.R. Learning?**
- **How do expert students use P.O.W.E.R. Learning?**

▪ Why Go to College?

Congratulations. You're in college.

But *why?* Although it seems as if it should be easy to answer why you're continuing your education, for most students it's not so simple. The reasons that people go to college vary from the practical ("I want to get a good job"), to the lofty ("I want to learn about people and the world"), to the unreflective ("Why not?—I don't have anything better to do"). Consider your own reasons for attending college, as you complete Try It 1 on page 4.

Surveys of first-year college students show that almost three-quarters say they want to get training for a specific career, land a better job, and make more money (see Figure 1.1). And, in fact, it's not wrong to expect that a college

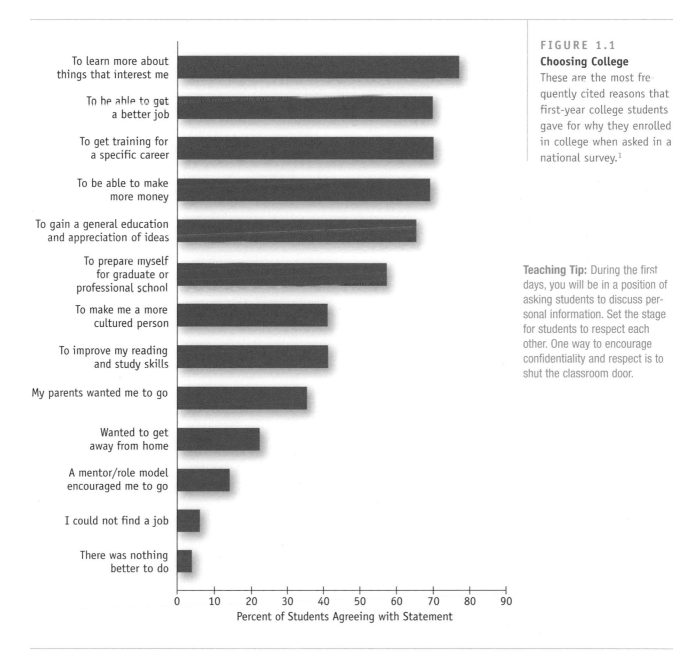

FIGURE 1.1
Choosing College
These are the most frequently cited reasons that first-year college students gave for why they enrolled in college when asked in a national survey.[1]

Teaching Tip: During the first days, you will be in a position of asking students to discuss personal information. Set the stage for students to respect each other. One way to encourage confidentiality and respect is to shut the classroom door.

1

Why Am I Going to College?

Place a 1, 2, and 3 by the three most important reasons that you have for attending college:

_____ I want to get a good job when I graduate.

_____ My parents want me to go.

_____ I couldn't find a job.

_____ I want to get away from home.

_____ I want to get a better job.

_____ I want to gain a general education and appreciation of ideas.

_____ I want to improve my reading and study skills.

_____ I want to become a more cultured person.

_____ I want to make more money.

_____ I want to learn more about things that interest me.

_____ A mentor or role model encouraged me to go.

_____ I want to prove to others that I can succeed.

Now consider the following:

- What do your answers tell you about yourself?
- Did you think about these reasons when you were applying to college?
- How do you think your reasons compare with those of other first-year students who are starting college with you?

To Try It online, go to **www.mhhe.com/power**.

P.O.W.E.R. UP: Use these questions as a Forced Choice exercise that will have your students on their feet and talking during class. See the IRM, Teaching the Text, Chapter 1, Sections IV and VIII.

education helps people find better jobs. The average person with a college degree earns about 50 percent more each year than the average person with only a high school education. That difference adds up: Over the course of their working lifetimes, college graduates earn close to a million dollars more than those with only a high school degree. Furthermore, as jobs become increasingly complex and technologically sophisticated, college will become more and more of a necessity.

But the value of college extends far beyond dollars and cents. Consider these added reasons for pursuing a college education:

- **You'll learn to think and communicate better.** Here's what one student said about his college experience after he graduated: "It's not about what you major in or which classes you take. . . . It's really about learning to think and to communicate. Wherever you end up, you'll need to be able to analyze and solve problems—to figure out what needs to be done and do it."[2]

  Education improves your ability to understand the world—to understand it as it now is, and to prepare to understand it as it will be.

- **You'll be able to better deal with advances in knowledge and technology that are changing the world.** Genetic engineering . . . drugs to reduce forgetfulness . . . computers that respond to our voices. . . . No one knows what the future will hold, but you can prepare for it through a college education. Education can provide you with the intellectual tools that you can apply regardless of the specific situation in which you find yourself.

- **You'll learn to adapt to new situations.** College is a different world from high school. It presents new experiences and new challenges. Your adjustment to the college culture will prepare you for future encounters with new situations.

- **You'll be better prepared to live in a world of diversity.** The racial and ethnic composition of the United States is changing rapidly. Whatever your ethnicity, chances are you'll be working and living with people whose backgrounds, lifestyles, and ways of thinking may be entirely different from your own.

  You won't be prepared for the future unless you understand others and their cultural backgrounds—as well as how your own cultural background affects you.

- **You'll learn to lead a life of community service.** In its broadest sense, **community service** involves making contributions to the society and community in which you live. College provides you with the opportunity to become involved in community service activities, in some cases even getting course credit for it—a process called **service learning.** College also allows you to develop the skills involved in acting towards others with *civility*, respectful, courteous behavior.

Student Alert: Your students' goals for being in college will likely be different than yours are for them. Be prepared to start where they are and take them to where you want them to go.

Teaching Tip: Ask your students to identify their expectations for respectful discussion within your classroom.

Community service
Making contributions to the society and community in which you live

> "Civilization is the making of civil persons."
>
> John Ruskin, author,
> *The Crown of Wild Olive*, 1866

- **You'll make learning a lifelong habit.** Higher education isn't the end of your education. Education will build upon your natural curiosity about the world, and it will make you aware that learning is a rewarding and never-ending journey.

- **You'll understand the meaning of your own contributions to the world.** No matter who you are, you are poised to make your own contributions to society and the world. Higher education provides you with a window to the past, present, and future, and it allows you to understand the significance of your own contributions. Your college education provides you with a compass to discover who you are, where you've been, and where you're going.

In short, there are numerous benefits for attending college. To help you attain these benefits, it's time to introduce you to a process that will help you achieve success, both in college and in life beyond: P.O.W.E.R. Learning.

Service learning
Courses that allow a student to engage in community service activities while getting course credit for the experience

Discussion Prompt: Ask your students how many courses they are taking that have a service learning component?

My School Experiences

Throughout this book, you will be given opportunities to write out your thoughts. These opportunities—called Journal Reflections—offer a chance to think critically about the chapter topics and record your personal reactions to them. As you create your reflections, be honest, to yourself and to your instructor.

Completing these Journal Reflections provides a variety of benefits. Not only will you be able to mull over your past and present academic experiences, you'll begin to see patterns in the kind of difficulties—and successes!—you encounter. You'll be able to apply solutions that worked in one situation to others. And one added benefit: you'll get practice in writing.

If you save these entries and return to them later, you may be surprised at the changes they record over the course of the term. You can either write them out and keep an actual journal, or create your journal electronically at the P.O.W.E.R. Learning Web site at **www.mhhe.com/power**.

1. Think of one of the successful experiences you've had so far in all your years in school. What was it?

2. What made the experience successful? What did you learn from your success?

3. Think of an unsuccessful experience or failure you had in school. Why did it occur?

4. How could you have prevented it? What did you learn from it?

5. Based on these experiences of academic success and failure, what general lessons did you learn that could help you to be a more successful student in the future?

P.O.W.E.R. Learning
A system designed to help people achieve their goals, based on five steps: *Prepare, Organize, Work, Evaluate,* and *Rethink*

◾ P.O.W.E.R. Learning: The Five Key Steps to Achieving Success

P.O.W.E.R. Learning itself is merely an acronym—a word formed from the first letters of a series of steps—that will help you take in, process, and make use of the information you'll acquire in college. It will help you to achieve your goals, both while you are in college and later after you graduate.

Prepare, Organize, Work, Evaluate, and Rethink. That's it. It's a simple framework, but an effective one. Using the systematic framework that P.O.W.E.R.

Learning provides (and which is illustrated in the P.O.W.E.R. Plan diagram) will increase your chances of success at any task, from writing a college paper to purchasing the weekly groceries.

Keep this in mind: P.O.W.E.R. Learning isn't a product that you can simply pull down off the bookshelf and use without thinking. P.O.W.E.R. Learning is a process, and you are the only one who can make it succeed. Without your personal investment in the process, P.O.W.E.R. Learning consists of just words on paper.

Relax, though. You already know each of the elements of P.O.W.E.R. Learning, and you may discover that you are already putting this process, or parts of it, to work for you. You've graduated from high school and been accepted into college. You may have also held down a job, had a first date, and registered to vote. Each of these accomplishments required that you use strategies of P.O.W.E.R. Learning. What you'll be doing throughout this book is becoming more aware of these strategies and how they can be used to help you in situations you will encounter in college and beyond.

P.O.W.E.R. Plan

REPARE

Chinese philosopher Lao Tzu said that travelers taking a long journey must begin with a single step.

But before they even take that first step, travelers need to know several things: what their destination is, how they're going to get there, how they'll know when they reach the destination, and what they'll do if they have trouble along the way. In the same way, you need to know where you're headed as you embark on the intellectual journeys involved in college. Whether it be a major, long-term task, such as college attendance, or a more limited activity, such as getting ready to complete a paper due in the near future, you'll need to prepare for the journey. To see this for yourself, complete Try It 2, "How I Enrolled in College" on page 8.

Setting Goals

Before we seek to accomplish any task, all of us do some form of planning. The trouble is that most of the time such planning is done without conscious thinking, as if we are on autopilot. However, the key to success is to make sure that planning is systematic.

The best way to plan systematically is to use goal-setting strategies. In many cases, goals are clear and direct. It's obvious that our goal in washing dishes is to have the dishes end up clean. We know that our goal at the gas station is to fill the car's tank with gas. We go to the post office to buy stamps and mail letters.

Other goals are not so clear-cut. In fact, often the more important the task—such as going to college—the more complicated may be our goals.

What's the best way to set appropriate goals? Here are some guidelines:

■ **Set both long-term and short-term goals. Long-term goals** are aims relating to major accomplishments that take some time to achieve. **Short-term goals** are relatively limited steps you would take on the road to accomplishing your long-term goals. For example, one of the primary reasons you're in college is to achieve the long-term goal of getting a degree. But in order to reach that goal, you have to accomplish a series of short-term goals, such as completing a set of required courses, taking a series of elective courses, and choosing a major. Even these short-term goals can be broken down into shorter-term goals. In order to

Student Alert: Some of your students will report that they have done goal setting exercises before. Encourage your students to plan anew as they begin their college experience.

Long-term goals
Aims relating to major accomplishments that take some time to achieve

Short-term goals
Relatively limited steps toward the accomplishment of long-term goals

2

TRY IT!

How I Enrolled in College

Academic journeys are similar to other major trips you may have taken, and they require a significant amount of preparation. Consider, for instance, the steps you needed to take to enroll in the college you're now attending. Think back to how you proceeded, and write in the first column below as many of the preparatory steps as you can think of, in the order you did them:

Actual Order of Steps I Took to Enroll in College   **Ideal Order**

_____   _____

_____   _____

_____   _____

_____   _____

_____   _____

_____   _____

_____   _____

_____   _____

Now go back and use the second column to number the steps in the most ideal, logical order.

- How closely does this numbering match the order in which you actually accomplished them?
- If you actually did some of the steps in a less-than-ideal order, how did it hinder or help your attainment of the goal of enrolling in college?

To Try It online, go to **www.mhhe.com/power**.

Teaching Tip: Students will begin to discover differences in each classmate's learning styles as they share the way they set goals.

> **"Goal setting, as far as I can see it, is simply a state of mind, a way of thinking about things. A goal setter makes sure he accomplishes what he needs to accomplish."**
>
> Greg Gottesman, Stanford University[3]

complete a required course, for instance, you have to accomplish short-term goals, such as completing a paper, taking several tests, and so on.

- **Recognize that who you are determines your goals.** Goal setting starts with knowing yourself. As you'll see when we focus on understanding yourself in Chapter 3, it is self-knowledge that tells you what is and is not important to you, and this knowledge will help you keep your goals in focus and your motivation up when things get tough.

- **Make goals realistic and attainable.** Someone once said, "A goal without a plan is but a dream." We'd all like to win gold medals at the Olympics or star in rock videos or write best-selling novels. Few of us are likely to achieve such goals.

Be honest with yourself. There is nothing wrong with having big dreams. But it is important to be realistically aware of all that it takes to achieve them. If our long-term goals are unrealistic and we don't achieve them, the big danger is that we may wrongly reason that we are inept and lack ability and use this as an excuse for giving up. If goals are realistic we can develop a plan to attain them, spurring us on to attain more.

- **State goals in terms of behavior that can be measured against current accomplishments.** Goals should represent some measurable change from a current set of circumstances. We want our behavior to change in some way that can usually be expressed in terms of numbers—to show an increase ("raise my grade point average 10 percent") or a decrease ("reduce wasted time by two hours each week"); or to be maintained ("keep in touch with my out-of-town friends by writing four e-mail messages each month"), developed ("participate in one workshop on critical thinking"), or restricted ("reduce my phone expenses 10 percent by speaking less on the telephone").

- **Goals should involve behavior over which you have control.** We all want world peace and an end to poverty. Few of us have the resources or capabilities to bring either about. On the other hand, it is realistic to want to work in small ways to help others, such as by becoming a Big Brother or Big Sister or by volunteering at a local food bank.

- **Take ownership of your goals.** Make sure that the goals you choose are your goals, and not the goals of your parents, teachers, brothers and sisters, or friends. If you're attending college only because others have told you to, and you have no commitment of your own, you'll find it hard to maintain the enthusiasm—not to mention the hard work—required to succeed.

- **Identify how your short-term goals fit with your long-term goals.** Your goals should not be independent of one another. Instead, they should fit together into a larger dream of who you want to be. Every once in a while step back and consider how what you're doing today relates to the kind of person that you would ultimately like to be.

College is not an end point, but part of a lifelong educational journey.

To get practice in using these goal-setting principles, consider the goals that underlie taking a particular college class in which you are currently enrolled. You probably have several goals for each course you are taking this term. Completing Try It 3 on page 10 will give you a chance to evaluate them.

ORGANIZE

By determining where you want to go and expressing your goals in terms that can be measured, you have already made a lot of progress. But there's another step you must take on the road to success.

The second step in P.O.W.E.R. Learning is to organize the tools you'll need to accomplish your goals. Building upon the goal-setting work you've undertaken in the preparation stage, it's time to determine the best way to accomplish the goals you've identified.

Student Alert: Students have difficulty writing specific, measurable goals. Give them direct feedback about their goals.

success comes not from a trial-and-error approach, but from following a systematic plan for achievement. Of course, this does not mean that there will be no surprises along the way, nor that simple luck is never a factor in great accomplishments. But it does mean that we often can make our own luck through careful preparation and organization.

W ORK

You're ready. The preliminaries are out of the way. You've prepared and you've organized. Now it's time to get started actually doing the work.

In some ways work is the easy part, because—if you conscientiously carried out the preparation and organization stage—you should know exactly where you're headed and what you need to do to get there.

It's not quite so easy, of course. How effectively you'll get down to the business at hand depends on many factors. Some may be out of your control. There may be a power outage that closes down the library or a massive traffic jam that delays your getting to campus. But most factors are—or should be—under your control. Instead of getting down to work, you may find yourself thinking up "useful" things to do—like finally hanging that poster that's been rolled up in a corner for three months—or simply sitting captive in front of the TV. This kind of obstacle to work relates to motivation.

Finding the Motivation to Work

"If only I could get more motivated, I'd do so much better with my _____" (insert *schoolwork, diet, exercising,* or the like—you fill in the blank).

All of us have said something like this at one time or another. We use the concept of **motivation**—or its lack—to explain why we just don't work hard at a task. But when we do that, we're fooling ourselves. We all have some motivation, that inner power and psychological energy that directs and fuels our behavior. Without any motivation, we'd never get out of bed in the morning.

We've all seen evidence of how strong our motivation can be. Perhaps you're an avid runner and you love to jog in the morning and compete in weekend races. Or maybe your love of music helped you learn to play the guitar, making practicing for hours a pleasure rather than a chore. Or perhaps you're a single mother, juggling work, school, and family, and you get up early every morning to make breakfast for your kids before they go off to school.

All of us are motivated. The key to success in and out of the classroom is to tap into, harness, and direct that motivation.

If we assume that we already have all the motivation we need, P.O.W.E.R. Learning becomes a matter of turning the skills we already possess into a habit. It becomes a matter of redirecting our psychological energies toward the work we wish to accomplish.

In a sense, everything you'll encounter in this book will help you to improve your use of the motivation that you already have. But there's a key concept that underlies the control of motivation—viewing success as a consequence of effort:

Effort produces success.

Suppose, for example, you've gotten a good grade on your midterm. The instructor beams at you as she hands back your test. How do you feel?

You will undoubtedly be pleased, of course. But at the same time you might think to yourself, "Better not get a swollen head about it. It was just luck. If

Motivation
The inner power and psychological energy that directs and fuels behavior

Teaching Tip: Using 3 x 5 cards, have your students answer the question "If only I could get more motivated, I'd do so much better with my _____" (insert *schoolwork, diet, exercising,* or the like). Have students work in pairs and come up with possible solutions for each other.

4

TRY IT!

 PERSONAL STYLES

Who's in Charge?

To get a sense of your ideas of why things happen to you, check the statement from each of the pairs below that best describes your views:[4]

☐ 1a. In the long run, people get the respect they deserve in this world.

☐ 1b. Unfortunately, an individual's worth often passes unrecognized no matter how hard he or she tries.

☐ 2a. The idea that teachers are unfair to students is nonsense.

☐ 2b. Most students don't realize the extent to which their exam results are influenced by accidental happenings.

☐ 3a. I have often found that what is going to happen will happen.

☐ 3b. Trusting fate has never turned out as well for me as making a decision to take a definite course of action.

☐ 4a. In the case of the well-prepared student, there is rarely if ever such a thing as an unfair exam.

☐ 4b. Many times exam questions tend to be so unrelated to course work that studying is really useless.

☐ 5a. Becoming a success is a matter of hard work; luck has little or nothing to do with it.

☐ 5b. Getting a good job depends mainly on being in the right place at the right time.

☐ 6a. It is not always wise to plan too far ahead because many things turn out to be a matter of good or bad fortune anyhow.

☐ 6b. When I make plans, I am almost certain that I can make them work.

☐ 7a. In my case, getting what I want has little or nothing to do with luck.

☐ 7b. Many times I might just as well decide what to do by flipping a coin.

☐ 8a. Many times I feel that I have little influence over the things that happen to me.

☐ 8b. It is impossible for me to believe that chance or luck plays an important role in my life.

☐ 9a. What happens to me is my own doing.

☐ 9b. Sometimes I feel that I don't have enough control over the direction my life is taking.

☐ 10a. Sometimes I can't understand how teachers arrive at the marks they give.

☐ 10b. There is a direct connection between how hard a person studies and the grades he or she gets.

Scoring: Give yourself one point for each of the following answers and then add up your score:

  1. a. 2. a. 3. b. 4. a. 5. a. 6. b. 7. a. 8. b. 9. a. 10. b.

Your total score can range from 0 to 10. The higher your score, the more you believe that you have a strong influence over what happens to you and are in control of your life and your own behavior.

The lower your score, the more you believe that your life is outside of your control and what happens to you is caused by luck or fate.

If you score below 5 on this questionnaire, consider how rethinking your views of the causes of behavior might lead to greater success.

To Try It online, go to **www.mhhe.com/power**.

she'd asked other questions I would have been in trouble." Or perhaps you explain your success by thinking, "Pretty easy test."

If you often think this way—and you can find out if you do by completing Try It 4—you're cheating yourself. Using this kind of reasoning when you succeed, instead of patting yourself on the back and thinking with satisfaction, "All my hard work really paid off," is sure to undermine your future success.

A great deal of psychological research has shown that thinking you have no control over what happens to you sends a powerful and damaging message to your self-esteem—that you are powerless to change things. Just think of how different it feels to say to yourself, "Wow, I worked at it and did it," as compared with "I lucked out" or "It was so easy that anybody could have done well."

> "The function of the university is not simply to teach bread-winning, or to furnish teachers for the public schools or to be a center of polite society; it is, above all, to be the organ of that fine adjustment between real life and the growing knowledge of life, an adjustment which forms the secret of civilization."
>
> W.E.B. DuBois, author,
> *The Souls of Black Folk,* 1903

In the same way, we can delude ourselves when we try to explain our failures. People who see themselves as the victims of circumstance may tell themselves, "I'm just not smart enough" when they don't do well on an academic task. Or they might say, "Those other students don't have to work five hours a day."

The way in which we view the causes of success and failure is, in fact, directly related to our success. Students who generally see effort and hard work as the reason behind their performance usually do better in college. It's not hard to see why: When they are working on an assignment, they feel that the greater the effort they put forth, the greater their chances of success. So they work harder. They believe that they have control over their success, and if they fail, they believe they can do better in the future.

Here are some tips for keeping your motivation alive, so you can work with your full energy behind you:

Teaching Tip: Have students use "I" statements in their goals to reinforce personal responsibility.

- **Take responsibility for your failures—and successes.** When you do poorly on a test, don't blame the teacher, the textbook, or a job that kept you from studying. Analyze the situation, and see how you could have changed what you did to be more successful in the future. At the same time, when you're successful, think of the things you did to bring about that success.

- **Think positively.** Assume that the strengths that you have will allow you to succeed and that, if you have difficulty, you can figure out what to do.

- **Accept that you can't control everything.** Seek to understand which things can be changed and which cannot. You might be able to get an extension on a paper due date, but you are probably not going to be excused from a college-wide requirement.

Discussion Prompt: Ask students to share their best ideas for staying motivated.

To further explore the causes of academic success, consider the questions in Try It 5, discussing them with your classmates.

E VALUATE

"Great, I'm done with the work. Now I can move on."

It's natural to feel relief when you've finished the work necessary to fulfill the basic requirements of an assignment. After all, if you've written the five

5

TRY IT!

WORKING IN A GROUP

Examining the Causes of Success and Failure

Complete this Try It while working in a group. First, consider the following situations:

1. Although he studied for a few hours the night before the test, Jack gets a D on a midterm. When he finds out his grade, he is disgusted and says to himself, "I'll probably never do any better in this course. I'd better just blow it off for the rest of the term and put my energies into my other classes."

2. Anne gets an A– on her history exam. She is happy, but when her instructor tells the class that they did well as a group and that the average grade was B+, she decides that she did well only because the test was so easy.

3. Chen gets a C on his first math quiz. Because he didn't do as well as he expected, he vows to perform better the next time. He doubles the amount of time he studies for the next quiz, but still his grade is only slightly higher. Distressed, he considers dropping the class because he thinks that he'll never be successful in math.

Now consider the following questions about each of the situations:

1. What did each student conclude was the main cause of his or her performance?

2. What effect does this conclusion seem to have on the student?

3. Taking an outsider's point of view, what would *you* think was probably the main cause of the student's performance?

4. What advice would you give each student?

Now consider these broader questions:

1. What are the most important reasons why some students are more academically successful in college than others?

2. How much does ability determine success? How much does luck determine success? How much do circumstances determine success?

3. If someone performs poorly on an exam, what are the possible reasons for his or her performance? If someone performs well on an exam, what are the possible reasons for his or her performance? Is it harder to find reasons for good compared with poor performance? Why?

To Try It online, go to **www.mhhe.com/power.**

double-spaced pages required for an assignment, why shouldn't you heave a sigh of relief and just hand your paper in to the instructor?

The answer is that if you stop at this point, you'll almost be guaranteed a mediocre grade. Did Shakespeare dash off the first draft of *Hamlet* and, without another glance, send it off to the Globe Theater for production? Do professional athletes just put in the bare minimum of practice to get ready for a big game? Think of one of your favorite songs. Do you think the composer wrote it in one sitting and then performed it in a concert?

In every case, the answer is no. Even the greatest work does not spring forth as the embodiment of perfection, immediately meeting all the goals of

Evaluation
An assessment of the match
between a product or activity and the goals it was
intended to meet

its producer. Consequently, the fourth step in the P.O.W.E.R. process is **evaluation,** which consists of determining how well the work we have produced matches our goals for it. Let's consider some steps to follow in evaluating what you've accomplished:

- **Take a moment to congratulate yourself and feel some satisfaction.** Whether it's been studying for a test, writing a paper, preparing a review sheet, or reading an assignment, you've done something important. You've moved from ground zero to a spot that's closer to your goal.

- **Compare what you've accomplished with the goals you're seeking to achieve.** Think back to the goals, both short-term and long-term, that you're seeking to achieve. How closely does what you've done match what you're aiming to do? For instance, if your short-term goal is to complete a statistics problem set with no errors, you'll need to check over the paper carefully to make sure you've made no mistakes.

- **Have an out-of-body experience: Evaluate your accomplishments as if you were a respected teacher from your past.** If you've written a paper, reread it from the perspective of that teacher. If you've completed a worksheet, think about what comments you'd write across the top if you were that teacher.

- **Evaluate what you've done as if you were your current instructor.** Now exchange bodies and minds again. This time, consider what you're doing from the perspective of the instructor who gave you the assignment. How would he or she react to what you've done? Have you followed the assignment to the letter? Is there anything you've missed?

- **Be fair to yourself.** The guidelines for evaluation will help you to determine just how much further work is necessary and, even more important, what work is necessary. Don't go too far, though: It's as counterproductive to be too hard on yourself as it is to be too easy. Stick to a middle ground, always keeping your final goal in mind.

- **Based on your evaluation, revise your work.** If you're honest with yourself, it's unlikely that your first work will satisfy you. So go back to *Work* and revise what you've done. But don't think of it as a step back: Revisions you make as a consequence of your evaluation bring you closer to your final goal. This is a case where going back moves you forward.

R ETHINK

They thought they had it perfect. But they were wrong.

In fact, it was a $1.5 billion mistake—a blunder on a grand scale. The finely ground mirror of the Hubble space telescope, designed to provide an unprecedented glimpse into the vast reaches of the universe, was not so finely ground after all.

Despite an elaborate system of evaluation designed to catch any flaws, there was a tiny blemish in the mirror that was not detected until the telescope had been launched into space and started to send back blurry photographs. By then, it seemed too late to fix the mirror.

Or was it? NASA engineers rethought the problem for months, devising, and then discarding, one potential fix after another. Finally, after bringing a fresh eye to the situation, they formulated a daring solution that involved sending a team of astronauts into space. Once there, a space-walking Mr. Goodwrench would install several new mirrors in the telescope, which could refocus the light and compensate for the original flawed mirror.

Although the engineers could not be certain that the $629 million plan would work, it seemed like a good solution, at least on paper. It was not until the first photos were beamed back to Earth, though, that NASA knew their solution was A-OK. These photos were spectacular.

The daring mission to repair the Hubble space telescope was the culmination of months of rethinking how to fix the flaw in the telescope. It worked: A new time-lapse movie of images taken by the telescope showed the seasonal changes on Uranus, as well as other celestial wonders.

It took months of reconsideration before NASA scientists could figure out what went wrong and devise a solution to the problem they faced. Their approach exemplifies—on a grand scale—the final step in P.O.W.E.R. Learning: rethinking.

To *rethink* what you've accomplished earlier means bringing a fresh eye to what you've done. It involves using **critical thinking,** thinking that involves reanalyzing, questioning, and challenging our underlying assumptions. While evaluation means considering how well what we have done matches our initial goals, rethinking means reconsidering not just the outcome of our efforts, but the ideas and the process we've used to get there. Critically rethinking what you've done involves analyzing and synthesizing ideas, and seeing the connections between different concepts.

We'll be considering critical thinking throughout this book, examining specific strategies in every chapter. For the moment, the following steps provide a general framework for using critical thinking to rethink what you've accomplished:

Critical thinking
A process involving reanalysis, questioning, and challenge of underlying assumptions

- **Reanalyze, reviewing how you've accomplished the task.** Consider the approach and strategies you've used. What seemed to work best? Do they suggest any alternatives that might work better the next time?

- **Question the outcome.** Take a "big picture" look at what you have accomplished. Are you pleased and satisfied? Is there something you've somehow missed?

- **Identify your underlying assumptions; then challenge them.** Consider the assumptions you made in initially approaching the task. Are these underlying assumptions reasonable? If you had used different assumptions, would the result have been similar or different?

- **Consider alternatives rejected earlier.** You've likely discarded possible strategies and approaches prior to completing your task. Now's the time to think about those approaches once more and determine if they might have been more appropriate than the road you've followed. It's still not too late to change course.

Discussion Prompt: When have students seen the idea of "rethinking" used by their parents? Their local, state or national governments?

Completing the Process

The rethinking step of P.O.W.E.R. Learning is meant to help you understand your process of work and to improve the final product if necessary. But mostly

Creating a P.O.W.E.R. Profile

Are you the student you aspire to be?

Before you can even think about answering that question, you need to know the kind of student you are—right now, at this very moment. Only by frankly facing your current strengths and weaknesses as fully as possible will you be able to know what direction you should be heading in.

To help you get a better understanding of who you are as a student, Try It 6 will take you through the steps of constructing your own **P.O.W.E.R. Profile.** The P.O.W.E.R. Profile is a way for you to take stock of where you stand in relation to the major topics that we'll be discussing in *P.O.W.E.R. Learning*—the characteristics that are most important for college success.

The P.O.W.E.R. Profile outlines key aspects of who you are. The Profile is just one of many possible profiles that could be drawn to describe you. For instance, you have a personality profile, a buying profile, a dating profile, a technology profile, and a variety of others. There is no "ideal" P.O.W.E.R. Profile; there are no right or wrong answers involved in creating one. Instead, as shown in the example in Figure 1.2, the P.O.W.E.R. Profile is a look at someone in relation to the 14 dimensions involved with student success (and, not so coincidentally, the key dimensions covered in *P.O.W.E.R. Learning*).

The best way to maximize the usefulness of your P.O.W.E.R. Profile is to create one now, before you've gone beyond the first chapter of this book. Then, by completing a P.O.W.E.R. Profile at the end of the term, you can judge how much your profile has changed and in what directions. If you take to heart what you learn in your class and work carefully through the Try Its in the book and exercises, your profile will undoubtedly change in a positive direction. In the meantime, the P.O.W.E.R. Profile will give you an objective idea of where you stand right now on each of these dimensions.

To get started with your P.O.W.E.R. Profile, read each statement and judge how well it describes you, using these numbered descriptions:

1 = Doesn't describe me at all		3 = Describes me fairly well	
2 = Describes me only slightly		4 = Describes me very well	

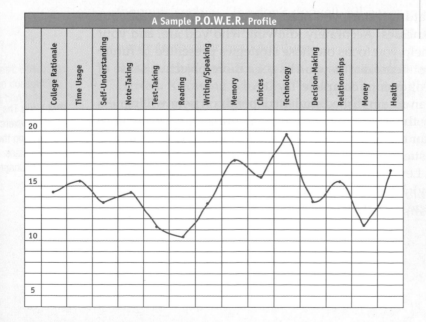

FIGURE 1.2
Sample P.O.W.E.R Profile

Place your response on the line next to each of the questions. Take your time, answer the questions thoughtfully and, above all, truthfully. There are no right or wrong answers. Remember that the profile is not a test; it is for your own enlightenment only.

Dimension 1: College Rationale
a. I understand why attending college is important to me. _____
b. I have clear short-term and long-term goals. _____
c. My course selections are related to my goals. _____
d. I know how to organize myself and get my work done. _____
e. I accept that success or failure is in my own hands. _____

College Rationale Total _____

Dimension 2: Time Use
a. I know how to manage my time effectively. _____
b. I understand how to set priorities for my time. _____
c. I know how to say no to time wasters. _____
d. I understand how to avoid procrastination. _____
e. I consider myself to be a good time organizer. _____

Time Use Total _____

Dimension 3: Self-Understanding
a. I understand how I learn most effectively. _____
b. I know how learning styles can affect academic success. _____
c. I have a clear self-concept and understand who I am. _____
d. I have a good sense of self-esteem. _____
e. I know how to use a personal mission statement to guide important decisions. _____

Self-Understanding Total _____

Dimension 4: Notetaking
a. I take good notes during class lectures and discussions. _____
b. My notes capture the speaker's main points, not side points. _____
c. I know how to use active listening to focus in class. _____
d. I can take good notes on what I read for my courses. _____
e. I review my notes soon after I have written them. _____

Notetaking Total _____

Dimension 5: Test-Taking
a. I generally go to tests well prepared and reasonably calm. _____
b. I understand how to tackle different kinds of test questions. _____
c. I know how to control anxiety before and during testing. _____
d. I usually leave time at the end of a test to check my work. _____
e. I know how to use test results to improve my future test-taking. _____

Test-Taking Total _____

Dimension 6: Reading
a. I know my personal reading style and understand how it affects my reading. _____
b. I understand how to use advance organizers in my reading. _____
c. I know my attention span and understand how to stay focused. _____
d. I know how to check for understanding while I read. _____
e. I understand the importance of rereading and rethinking. _____

Reading Total _____

(continued)

Creating a P.O.W.E.R. Profile (continued)

Dimension 7: Writing & Speaking

a. I know how to use the writing process to start and maintain the flow of my writing. _____

b. I understand the importance of audience in writing. _____

c. I know how to outline, write a first draft, and revise my writing. _____

d. I have strategies to overcome my fear of speaking in public. _____

e. I have a good system for speaking extemporaneously. _____

Writing & Speaking Total _____

Dimension 8: Memory

a. I know my preferred memory style and use it to help me study. _____

b. I know about rehearsal and overlearning and use them in my studies. _____

c. I know how to link new information to information that I already possess. _____

d. I am familiar with several memorization techniques. _____

e. I know how to consolidate my memories to improve test performance. _____

Memory Total _____

Dimension 9: Choices

a. I understand the options and choices available to me at my college. _____

b. I know where I stand in terms of completing my course requirements. _____

c. I know exactly what to do if there's a problem with my course selections or records. _____

d. I am satisfied that my course choices are moving me in the right direction. _____

e. I am confident that I will choose a major that makes sense in terms of my life goals. _____

Choices Total _____

Dimension 10: Technology

a. I understand how to use computer applications effectively for my college work. _____

b. I know how to use the Internet for communication, staying up to date, and research. _____

c. I understand distance learning and know whether or not it's right for me. _____

d. I know how to use library resources and the World Wide Web to gather information. _____

e. I know how to evaluate the accuracy and reliability of information I have found. _____

Technology Total _____

Dimension 11: Decision Making

a. I use a structured process for making important decisions. _____

b. I know how to identify my goals and generate alternatives. _____

c. I am good at assessing alternatives and making decisions I am happy with. _____

d. I use an array of strategies for solving problems. _____

e. I understand the most common obstacles to effective critical thinking. _____

Decision-Making Total _____

Dimension 12: Relationships

a. I understand the importance of diversity on campus and in the broader society. _____

b. I have good relationships with people of many different backgrounds. _____

c. I understand cultural competence and consider myself culturally competent. _____

d. I know what it takes to build good relationships. _____

e. I know how to handle conflict in my relationships. _____

Relationships Total _____

Dimension 13: Money

a. I know my short- and long-term financial goals. _____

b. I understand where my money comes from and where it goes. _____

c. I know how to prepare a realistic budget and stick to it. _____

d. I am realistic about the advantages and disadvantages of credit cards. _____

e. I know where to go if I need financial aid for college. _____

Money Total _____

Dimension 14: Health

a. I understand stress and know how to cope with it. _____
b. I understand the importance of a good diet, exercise, and rest. _____
c. I have strategies for avoiding the abuse of alcohol and other drugs. _____
d. I am responsible about my sexuality and know how to stay sexually healthy. _____
e. I know where to go to get help with all aspects of my health. _____

Health Total _____

Now you're ready to construct your P.O.W.E.R. Profile. Add up the numbers on each line to derive a total for each dimension. This total will range from a low of 5 to a high of 20. Finally, place a dot in each appropriate box on the chart in Figure 1.3 corresponding to your score, and connect the dots to form your P.O.W.E.R Profile.

There—it's done. But it's really just a start. Your P.O.W.E.R. Profile is an objective way to mark the beginning of your journey through college. Its shape will continue to change and evolve the more years of school you have under your belt.

After taking some time to study your P.O.W.E.R. Profile and to maximize its usefulness, consider the following:

- Does your profile seem like an accurate reflection of your strengths and weaknesses as a student? Were there any surprises?
- What would your "ideal" profile look like?
- How can you use the results to help you in the future? What are the most important areas for improvement?

Your P.O.W.E.R. Profile

	College Rationale	Time Use	Self-Understanding	Note-Taking	Test-Taking	Reading	Writing/Speaking	Memory	Choices	Technology	Decision-Making	Relationships	Money	Health
20														
15														
10														
5														

FIGURE 1.3
P.O.W.E.R. Profile

SPEAKING OF
Success

Name: Lev Sviridov

School: The City College of New York,
New York, NY

For Lev Sviridov, a senior at the City College of New York, the road to success was a roundabout one. In one sense it began after the Chernobyl nuclear power plant exploded when he was a young boy in the former Soviet Union. The accident triggered a deep interest in science and research.

Sviridov and his mother fled the Soviet Union in 1993, fearful of arrest because his mother, a journalist, had exposed some government officials as KGB agents. Coming to the United States with no money, Sviridov needed not only to learn a new language, but to help support himself. In the early years, he picked through garbage cans to find bottles and cans, and he was homeless for a time. But he credits his poverty with creating motivation to succeed.

"The fact that I was broke and working at so many jobs—gardening, moving furniture, tutoring, working in the laboratory—paved the way for having great credentials," said Sviridov.[6]

Sviridov not only became successful academically in college, earning extraordinary grades, but he was involved in a variety of activities. He served as president of his college student government and was a member of a Russian human rights organization. He also conducted research in computational biophysical chemistry. His academic credentials were so strong that he won one of the highest of academic awards: a Rhodes Scholarship that will support graduate school study.

But even for an excellent student like Sviridov, studying presents challenges. For example, he says, "I consider myself to be a slow reader, so I have to compensate for that."

In addition, it is easier for him to absorb information through the spoken word. "I feel that study groups are important," he said. "The only time you really know something is when you can explain it to somebody else. I'm always putting together study groups for this purpose."

How does he maintain his busy schedule and remain successful academically? Sviridov follows a basic strategy.

"My approach is that if you do the work that is required of you at a steady pace through the semester, you will be fine," he said. "I just pace myself, go slowly, and make sure I understand the material."

What are the benefits of a college education?

- The reason first-year college students most often cite for attending college is to get a better job, and college graduates do earn more on average than nongraduates.

- College also provides many other benefits. These include becoming well-educated, understanding the interconnections between different areas of knowledge and our place in history and the world, practicing community service, and understanding diversity.

Teaching Tip: Use these questions as an open-ended review of the chapter material.

What are the basic principles of P.O.W.E.R. Learning?

- P.O.W.E.R. Learning is a systematic approach people can easily learn, using abilities they already possess, to acquire successful habits for learning and achieving personal goals.

- P.O.W.E.R. Learning involves **p**reparation, **o**rganization, **w**ork, **e**valuation, and **r**ethinking.

How do expert students use P.O.W.E.R. Learning?

- To *prepare,* learners set both long-term and short-term goals, making sure that their goals are realistic, measurable, and under their control—and will lead to their final destination.

- They *organize* the tools they will need to accomplish those goals.

- They get down to *work* on the task at hand. Using their goals as motivation, expert learners also understand that success depends on effort.

- They *evaluate* the work they've done, considering what they have accomplished in comparison with the goals they set for themselves during the preparation stage.

- Finally, they *rethink,* reflecting on the process they've used and taking a fresh look at what they have done.

KEY TERMS AND CONCEPTS

Community service (p. 5)
Service learning (p. 5)
P.O.W.E.R. Learning (p. 6)
Long-term goals (p. 7)

Short-term goals (p. 7)
Motivation (p. 12)
Evaluation (p. 16)
Critical thinking (p. 17)

RESOURCES

On Campus

If you are commuting to school, your first "official" encounters on campus are likely to be with representatives of the college's Student Affairs Office or its equivalent. The Student Affairs Office has the goal of maintaining the quality of student life, helping to ensure that students receive the help they need. Student Affairs personnel often are in charge of student orientation programs that help new students familiarize themselves with their new institution.

If you are living on campus, your first encounter will more likely be with representatives of the residence halls, often called the Residential Life Office. Their job is to help you settle in and orient you to campus. Your residence hall also probably has student residential advisors living on every floor; they can give you an insider's view of college life.

Whomever you encounter during your first days of college, remember that they're there to help you. Don't feel shy about asking questions about what you may expect, how to find things, and what you should be doing. Be sure to seek them out if you are experiencing any difficulties.

Making the Most of Your Time

As Meadow Baresi stands in the long line at the cafeteria, she mentally goes over the things she needs to get done during the day: *Review notes for the 8:30 a.m. management quiz . . . work on philosophy paper . . . computer sci class at 11:15 a.m . . . pick up ticket receipts from last night's game . . . work at student affairs office from 1:00 to 4:00 . . . go to library to research philosophy paper.* She has the nagging feeling that there's something else she needs to do, but she can't put her finger on it.

She finally gets to the head of the line to pay for her bagel, which she's already half devoured. Glancing at a clock as she leaves the Commons, she gives up the thought of getting in some last-minute studying for her management quiz. It will be a minor miracle if she even makes it to class on time.

She's been up less than an hour, and already Meadow is running behind schedule.

P.O.W.E.R. UP: Ask students to bring all class syllabi and a calendar with them to class. Have them predict the busiest weeks in their first semester on campus using these tools. How can they use this knowledge?

LOOKING AHEAD > > >

Are your days like Meadow's? Are you constantly trying to cram more activities into less time? Do you feel as if you never have enough time?

You're not alone: Most of us wish we had more time to accomplish the things we need to do. However, some people are a lot better at juggling their time than others. What's their secret?

There is no secret. No one has more than 168 hours a week. The key to success lies in figuring out our priorities and using our time better.

Time management is like juggling a bunch of tennis balls: for most of us, juggling doesn't come naturally, but it is a skill that can be learned. Not all of us will end up perfect jugglers (whether we are juggling tennis balls or time), but, with practice, we can become a lot better at it.

This chapter will give you strategies for improving your time management skills. After first helping you learn to account for the ways you currently use—and misuse—time, it gives you strategies for planning your time, including some ways to deal with the inevitable interruptions and counterproductive personal habits that can sabotage your best intentions. It will provide you with skills that are not only important for success in college, but for your future life as well.

We also consider techniques for dealing with competing goals. There are special challenges involved in juggling the priorities of college work with other aspects of life, such as child rearing or holding a job.

After reading this chapter, you'll be able to answer these questions:

- **How can I manage my time most effectively?**
- **How can I deal better with surprises and distractions?**
- **How can I balance competing priorities?**

Time for Success

Without looking up from the page, answer this question: What time is it?

Most people are pretty accurate in their answer. And if you don't know for sure, it's very likely that you can find out. There may be a watch on your wrist; there may be a clock on the wall, desk, or computer screen; or maybe you're riding in a car that has a clock in the dashboard.

Even if you don't have a timepiece of some sort nearby, your body keeps its own beat. Humans have an internal clock that regulates the beating of our heart, the pace of our breathing, the discharge of chemicals within our bloodstream, and myriad other bodily functions.

Time is something from which we can't escape. Even if we ignore it, it's still going by, ticking away, second by second, minute by minute, hour by hour. So the main issue in using your time well is, "Who's in charge?" We can allow time to slip by and let it be our enemy. Or we can take control of it and make it our ally.

By taking control of how you spend your time, you'll increase your chances of becoming a more successful student. Perhaps more importantly, the better you are at managing the time you devote to your studies, the more time you will have to spend on your outside interests. (You can get a sense of your own personal time style by completing Try It 1 on page 32.)

The goal of time management is not to schedule every moment so we become pawns of a timetable that governs every waking moment of the day. Instead, the goal is to permit us to make informed choices as to how we use our time. Rather than letting the day slip by, largely without our awareness, the time management procedures we'll discuss can make us better able to harness time for our own ends.

PREPARE
Learn where time is going

ORGANIZE
Use a master calendar, weekly timetable, and daily to-do list

WORK
Follow the schedules you've put together

EVALUATE
Keep track of your short-term and long-term accomplishments

RETHINK
Reflect on your personal style of time management

P.O.W.E.R. Plan

> **"Time ripens all things. No man's born wise."**
>
> Cervantes, author, *Don Quixote*, 2.4.33, tr. John Ozell

P REPARE: Learning Where Time Is Going

Before you get somewhere, you need to know where you're starting from and where you want to go. So the first step in improving your time management skills is figuring out how you're managing your time now.

Discussion Prompt: Ask students to share the phrases that they associate with the use of time (i.e.; "24-7"; "time flies when you are having fun") and discuss how these words shape our understanding of time.

Create a Time Log

"Where did the day go?" If you've ever said this to yourself, one way of figuring out where you've spent your time is to create a time log. A time log is the most essential tool for improving your use of time.

A **time log** is simply a record of how you actually have spent your time—including interruptions. It doesn't have to be a second-by-second record of every waking moment. But it should account for blocks of time in increments as short as 15 minutes.

Time log
A record of how one spends one's time

POWER

 **PERSONAL STYLES**

Find Your Time Style

Rate how well each of the statements below describes you. Use this rating scale:

1 = Doesn't describe me at all
2 = Describes me only slightly
3 = Describes me fairly well
4 = Describes me very well

	1	2	3	4
1. I often wake up later than I should.				
2. I am usually late for classes and appointments.				
3. I am always in a rush getting places.				
4. I put off big tasks and assignments till the last minute.				
5. My friends often comment on my lateness.				
6. I am easily interrupted, putting aside what I'm doing for something new.				
7. When I look at a clock, I'm often surprised at how late it is.				
8. I often forget appointments and have to reschedule them.				
9. When faced with a big task, I feel overwhelmed and turn my mind away from it until later.				
10. At the end of the day, I have no idea where the time went.				

Rate yourself by adding up the points you assigned. Use this scale to assess your time style:

10–15 = Very efficient time user
16–20 = Efficient time user
21–30 = Time use needs work
31–40 = Victim of time

To Try It online, go to **www.mhhe.com/power**.

TRY IT!

1

Where Does My Time Go?

1. On the typical weekday, what time do you wake up? When would you prefer to wake up if you had the choice?

2. When do you typically go to bed on a typical weekday night? When would you prefer to go to bed if you had the choice?

3. Would you characterize yourself as a "morning person," who accomplishes the most in the early morning, or more as a "night person," who is most comfortable doing work in the evenings? What implications does this have for your scheduling of classes and when you do the most work?

4. If a day suddenly contained more than 24 hours, how would it change your life? What would you do with the extra time? Do you think you would accomplish more?

5. Generally speaking, how would you characterize your time management skills? What would be the benefit to you personally if you could manage time more effectively? What goals might you accomplish if you had more time at your disposal?

Look at the blank time log in Try It 2 on page 34. As you fill out the log, be specific, indicating not only what you were doing at a given time (for example, "reading history assignment") but also the interruptions that occurred (such as "answered cell phone twice" or "switched to Internet for 10 minutes").

By looking at how much time you spend doing various activities, you now know where your time goes. How does it match with your perceptions of how you spend your time? Be prepared to be surprised, because most people find that they're spending time on a lot of activities that just don't matter very much.

Identify the "Black Holes" That Eat up Your Time

Do you feel like your time often is sucked into a black hole, disappearing without a trace?

We all waste time, spending it on unimportant activities that keep us from doing the things that we should be doing or really want to do. For example,

Student Alert: The issue of "balance" is introduced here. Many freshmen will challenge you to tell them "one right way" to manage time and then come up with lots of reasons why *that* particular way will not work for them. Emphasize that effective time management is based on identifying priorities, making appropriate choices and understanding one's learning style preference.

TRY IT!

Identify the Black Holes of Time Management

The first 20 items on this list are common problems that prevent us from getting things done.[1] Check off the ones that are problems for you, and indicate whether you have control over them (controllable problems) or they are out of your control (uncontrollable problems).

	Big Problem for Me	Often a Problem	Seldom a Problem	Controllable (C) or Uncontrollable (U)?
1. Phone interruptions				
2. Drop-in visitors				
3. E-mail interruptions				
4. Hobbies				
5. Text messaging				
6. Inability to say no				
7. Socializing				
8. Snacking				
9. Errands and shopping				
10. Meals				
11. Children's interruptions				
12. Perfectionism				
13. Family appointments				

(continued)

	Big Problem for Me	Often a Problem	Seldom a Problem	Controllable (C) or Uncontrollable (U)?
14. Looking for lost items				
15. Redoing mistakes				
16. Jumping from task to task				
17. Surfing the Web				
18. Reading newspapers, magazines, recreational books				
19. Car trouble				
20. Waiting for public transportation				
21. Other				
22. Other				
23. Other				
24. Other				
25. Other				

Working in a Group:

Examine the problems that affect each group member and then discuss these questions: Do time management problems fall into any patterns? Are there problems that at first seem uncontrollable that can actually be controlled? What strategies for dealing with such problems have you used in the past?

To Try It online, go to **www.mhhe.com/power**.

spending time on your studies is most important to you, or maybe your top priority is spending time with your family. Only you can decide. Furthermore, what's important to you at this moment may be less of a priority to you next month, next year, or five years from now.

"Hello and welcome to the game that'll be put off until tomorrow, but should've been played today."

For the purpose of effective time management in college, the best procedure is to start off by identifying priorities for an entire term. What do you need to accomplish? Don't just choose obvious, general goals, such as "passing all my classes." Instead, think about your priorities in terms of specific, measurable activities, such as "studying ten hours before each chemistry exam." (Look at the example of a priority list in Figure 2.1 and also the *Course Connections* feature.)

Write your priorities on the chart in Try It 4 on pages 40 and 41. After you've filled out the chart, organize it by giving each priority a ranking from 1 to 3. A "1" represents a priority that absolutely must be done; without it you'll suffer a major setback. For instance, a paper with a fixed due date should receive a "1" for a priority ranking; carving out time to take those guitar lessons you always wanted to take might be ranked a "3" in terms of priority. The important point is to rank-order your priorities to reveal what is and is not important to accomplish during the term.

Setting priorities will help you to determine how to make best use of your time. No one has enough time to complete everything; prioritizing will help you make informed decisions about what you can do to maximize your success.

Priority	Ranking
Study for each class at least 30 minutes/day	1
Start each major paper 1 week in advance of due date	2
Hand in each paper on time	1
Review for test starting a week before test date	2
Be on time for job	2
Check in with Mom once a week	3
Work out 3 x/week	3

FIGURE 2.1
List of Priorities

Study Time: How Much Is Enough?

What would you guess is the average number of hours instructors think you should be studying each week? In the view of instructors queried in a national survey, students should spend, on average, 6 hours per week preparing for *each* class in which they're enrolled. And if they're taking courses in the sciences and engineering, instructors expect their students to put in even more hours.[2]

Keep in mind that study time does not include actual class time. If you add that in, someone taking four classes would need 24 hours of outside class preparation and would be in class for 16 hours—for a total of 40 hours, or the equivalent of full-time employment.

If you've underestimated the amount of time instructors believe is necessary to devote to class preparation, you may need to rethink the amount of time you'll need to allocate to studying. You might also speak to your individual instructors to see what they believe is an appropriate amount of preparation. Although they may not be able to give exact figures, their estimates will help you to prioritize what you need to do to be a successful student.

Identify Your Prime Time

Take a look inward. Do you enthusiastically bound out of bed in the morning, ready to start the day and take on the world? Or is the alarm clock a hated and unwelcome sound that jars you out of pleasant slumber? Are you the kind of person who is zombielike by ten at night, or a person who is just beginning to rev up at midnight?

Each of us has our own style based on some inborn body clock. Some of us are at our best in the morning, while others do considerably better at night. Being aware of the time or times of day when you can accomplish your best work will help you plan and schedule your time most effectively. If you're at your worst in the morning, try to schedule easier, less-involving activities for those earlier hours. On the other hand, if morning is the best time for you, schedule activities that require the greatest concentration at that time.

> **"Time moves slowly, but passes quickly."**
>
> Alice Walker, author, *The Color Purple*

IRM Link: Teaching the Text, Chapter 2, Sections IV and VIII; use the "168 Hours in a Week" activity.

But don't be a slave to your internal time clock. Even night people can function effectively in the morning, just as morning people can accomplish quite a bit in the evening. Don't let your concerns become a self-fulfilling prophecy.

O RGANIZE: Mastering the Moment

You now know where you've lost time in the past, and your priority list is telling you where you need to head in the future.

Now for the present. You've reached the point where you can organize yourself to take control of your time. Here's what you'll need:

- A **master calendar** that shows all the weeks of the term on one page. You don't need to buy one; you can make it easily enough yourself. It need not

Master calendar
A schedule showing the weeks of a longer time period, such as a college term, with all assignments and important activities noted on it

Set Priorities

Set your priorities for the term. They may include getting to class on time, finishing papers and assignments by their due dates, finding a part-time job that fits your schedule, and reading every assignment before the class for which it is due. To get started, list priorities in any order. Be sure to consider priorities relating to your school work, other work, family, social obligations, and health. After you list them, assign a number to each one indicating its level—giving a "1" to the highest priority items, a "2" to medium priority items, and a "3" to the items with the lowest priority.

List of Priorities	
Priority	**Priority Index**

Now redo your list, putting your number 1s first, followed by as many of your number 2s and 3s to which you feel you can reasonably commit.

IRM Link: Teaching the Text, Chapter 2, Sections IV and VIII; the "Planning Backwards" activity can be used here.

Weekly timetable
A schedule showing all regular, prescheduled activities due to occur in the week, together with one-time events and commitments

be great art; a rough version will do. The important point is that it must include every week of the term and seven days per week. (See the example of a master calendar in Figure 2.2 on page 42.)

■ A weekly timetable. The **weekly timetable** is a master grid with the days of the week across the top and the hours, from 6:00 a.m. to midnight, along the side. This will permit you to write in all your regularly scheduled activities, as well as one-time appointments when they arise. (A blank weekly

Final List of Priorities	
Priority	
1.	
2.	
3.	
4.	
5.	
6.	
7.	
8.	
9.	
10.	
11.	
12.	

Now consider the following:

- What does this list tell you about your greatest priorities? Are they centered around school, friends and family, jobs, or some other aspect of your life?
- Do you have so many "1" priorities that they will be difficult or impossible to accomplish successfully? How could you go back to your list and trim it down even more?
- What does this listing of priorities suggest about how successful you'll be during the upcoming term?

To Try It online, go to **www.mhhe.com/power**.

timetable is provided in Figure 2.3 on page 44. You can also find it online at **www.mhhe.com/power**.)

- A daily to-do list. Finally, you'll need a **daily to-do list.** The daily to-do list can be written on a small, portable calendar that includes a separate page for each day of the week. Or it can simply be a small notebook, with a separate sheet of paper for every day of the week. Whatever form your daily to-do list takes, make sure it's portable, because you'll need to keep it with you all the time.

Daily to-do list
A schedule showing the tasks, activities, and appointments due to occur during the day

FIGURE 2.3

Weekly Timetable

Make a single copy of this blank timetable or go to the *P.O.W.E.R. Learning* Web site (**www.mhhe.com/power**) and use the online version. Then fill in your regular, predictable time commitments.

Next, make as many copies as you need to cover each week of the term. Then, for each week, fill in the date on the left and the number of the week in the term on the right, and add in your irregular commitments.

Teaching Tip: Have students make copies of this chart or place it on their personal computers, PDAs, etc.

Weekly Timetable

Week of: _____   Week # _____

	Mon	Tues	Wed	Thurs	Fri	Sat	Sun
6–7 a.m.							
7–8 a.m.							
8–9 a.m.							
9–10 a.m.							
10–11 a.m.							
11–12 (noon)							
12 (noon)–1 p.m.							
1–2 p.m.							
2–3 p.m.							
3–4 p.m.							
4–5 p.m.							
5–6 p.m.							
6–7 p.m.							
7–8 p.m.							
8–9 p.m.							
9–10 p.m.							
10–11 p.m.							
11 p.m.–12 (midnight)							
12 (midnight)–1 a.m.							
1–2 a.m.							
2–3 a.m.							
3–4 a.m.							
4–5 a.m.							
5–6 a.m.							

To move from your "average" week to specific weeks, make photocopies of the weekly timetable that now contains your fixed appointments. Make enough copies for every week of the term. On each copy write the week number of the term and the specific dates it covers.

Using your master calendar, add assignment due dates, tests, and any other activities on the appropriate days of the week. Then pencil in blocks of time necessary to prepare for those events. (See a sample in Figure 2.4.)

How much time should you allocate for schoolwork? One very rough rule of thumb holds that every one hour that you spend in class requires, on average, two hours of study outside of class to earn a B and three hours of study outside of class to earn an A. Do the arithmetic: If you are taking 15 credits (with each credit equivalent to an hour of class per week), you'll need to plan for 30 hours of studying each week to earn a B average—an intimidating amount of time. Of course, the amount of time you must allocate to a specific class will vary from week to week, depending on what is happening in the class.

For example, if you estimate that you'll need five hours of study for a midterm exam in a certain class, pencil in those hours. Don't set up a single block of five hours. People remember best when their studying is spread out over shorter periods rather than attempted in one long block of time.

Teaching Tip: Do this activity during class. Ask students to make out a daily to-do list for two weeks. Check for it at the beginning of each class. This is how new habits are created.

Weekly Timetable

Week of: __9/28__   Week # __3__

	Mon	Tues	Wed	Thurs	Fri	Sat	Sun
6–7 a.m.							
7–8 a.m.							
8–9 a.m.							
9–10 a.m.	9:05 Psych	9:05 Music	9:05 Psych	9:05 Music	9:05 Psych		
10–11 a.m.		↓		↓			
11–12 (noon)		11:15 English		11:15 English			
12 (noon)–1 p.m.	12:20 Theater	↓	12:20 Theater	↓	12:20 Theater		
1–2 p.m.	↓		↓				
2–3 p.m.							
3–4 p.m.	3:00 Russian		3:00 Russian		3:00 Russian		
4–5 p.m.	First-year seminar	Work		Work			
5–6 p.m.	↓						
6–7 p.m.		↓		↓			
7–8 p.m.							
8–9 p.m.							
9–10 p.m.							
10–11 p.m.							
11 p.m.–12 (midnight)							
12 (midnight)–1 a.m.							
1–2 a.m.							
2–3 a.m.							
3–4 a.m.							
4–5 a.m.							
5–6 a.m.							

FIGURE 2.4
A Sample Weekly Timetable

Discussion Prompt: After completing this exercise, have your students exchange charts and look at life from someone else's perspective.

Besides, it will probably be hard to find a block of five straight hours on your weekly calendar.

Similarly, if you need to write a paper that's due on a certain date, you can block out the different stages of the writing process that we'll describe in Chapter 7. You'll need to estimate how much time each stage will take, but you probably have a pretty good idea from previous papers you've written.

Some classes may need only a few hours of study in a given week. With good luck, heavy weeks in one class will be compensated for by lighter weeks in others.

Keep in mind that estimates are just that: estimates. Don't think of them as set in stone. Mark them on your weekly calendar in pencil, not pen, so you can adjust them if necessary.

But remember: It's also crucial not to overschedule yourself. You'll still need time to eat, to talk with your friends, to spend time with your family, and to enjoy yourself in general. If you find that your life is completely filled with things that you feel you must do in order to survive and that there is no room for fun, then take a step back and cut out something to make some time for yourself in your daily schedule. Finding time for yourself is as important as carving out time for what others want you to do. Besides, if you are overworked, you're likely to "find" the time by guiltily goofing off without really setting aside the time and enjoying it.

■ **If you've taken each of the previous steps, you're now in a position to work on the final step of organization for successful time management: completing your daily to-do list.**

Unlike the master calendar and weekly timetable—both of which you develop at the beginning of the term—complete your daily to-do list just one day ahead of time, preferably at the end of the day.

List all the things that you intend to do during the next day, and their priority. Start with the things you know you *must* do and which have fixed times, such as classes, work schedules, and appointments. These are your first priority items. Then add in the other things that you *should* accomplish, such as an hour of study for an upcoming test, working on research for an upcoming paper, or finishing up a lab report. Finally, list things that are lower priority but enjoyable, setting aside time for a run or a walk, for example.

Don't schedule every single minute of the day. That would be counterproductive, and you'd end up feeling like you'd failed if you deviated from your schedule. Instead, think of your daily to-do list as a path through a forest. If you were hiking, you would allow yourself to deviate from the path, occasionally venturing onto side tracks when they looked interesting. But you'd also be keeping tabs on your direction so you end up where you need to be at the end and not miles away from your car or home.

Like the sample daily to-do list in Figure 2.5, include a column to check or cross off after you've completed an activity. There's something very satisfying in acknowledging what you have accomplished.

W ORK: Controlling Time

You're in luck: There is no work to time management—or at least not much more than you've already done. The work of time management is to follow the schedules that you've prepared and organized. But that doesn't mean it will be easy. Our lives are filled with surprises: Things take longer than we've

FIGURE 2.5
Sample To-Do List

To-Do List for _____ (date)		
Item		**✔ Completed**
Call Chris to get English notes	1	✓
Meet with Prof. Hernandez	1	✓
Review Russian	1	✓
Work on outline for psych paper	2	✓
Return books to library	2	
Call Nettie	2	✓
Set up meeting with music group	2	
Meet Deena	2	
Do laundry	3	

Teaching Tip: Encourage your students to mark or check items off their lists. This is a visual reminder of "getting things done" and can create a sense of accomplishment when the list seems overwhelming.

planned. A friend we haven't spoken to in a while calls to chat, and it seems rude to say that we don't have time to talk. A crisis occurs; buses are late; computers break down; kids get sick.

The difference between effective time management and time management that doesn't work lies in how well you deal with the inevitable surprises.

There are several ways to take control of your days and permit yourself to follow your intended schedule:

- **Just say no.** You don't have to agree to every request and every favor that others ask of you. You're not a bad person if you refuse to do something that will eat up your time and prevent you from accomplishing your goals.

    Suppose, for example, a friend sees you in the library and asks to borrow the notes from a class that she missed yesterday and that you attended. It's not an unreasonable request. Here's the problem, though: You don't have your notebook with you, and you'd have to stop by your house to pick it up.

    Think through what the request entails. *It may be only 10 minutes to your house, but it's another 10 minutes back. That's 20 minutes. And then there's the time that you'll spend meeting her to give her the notes. And then the time it takes to meet her again, once she's copied the notes. Or suppose you decide to wait while she copies them. Overall, you may end up losing an hour.*

    The solution? You should probably say no to the immediate request. It's not unreasonable to tell your friend that you don't have the time today to get your notebook. You don't have to refuse her completely. She could stop by your house in the evening to pick up the notes, or you could bring them with you the next day. In short, there are ways to accomplish the goal of helping out your friend without wasting time and sabotaging your schedule.

- **Get away from it all.** Go to the library. Lock yourself into your bedroom. Find an out-of-the-way unused classroom.

Discussion Prompt: Saying "no" is a perfect example of being able to accept personal responsibility for one's actions. Choices and consequences are a theme you should discuss throughout this course.

Any of these places can serve to isolate you from everyday distractions and thereby permit you to work on the tasks that you wish to complete. Try to adopt a particular spot as your own, such as a corner desk in a secluded nook in the library. If you use it enough, your body and mind will automatically get into study mode as soon as you seat yourself at it.

■ **Enjoy the sounds of silence.** Although many students insist they accomplish most while a television, radio, or CD is playing, scientific studies suggest otherwise: We are able to concentrate most when our environment is silent. So even if you're sure you work best with a soundtrack playing, experiment and work in silence for a few days. You may find that you get more done in less time than you would in a more distracting environment.

■ **Take an e-break.** Phone calls, text messages, instant messages, e-mail. Who doesn't love to get them?

We may not control when communications arrive, but we can make the message wait until we are ready to receive it. Take an e-break and shut down your communication sources for some period of time. Phone calls can be stored on voicemail systems, and text messages, IMs, and e-mail can be saved on a phone or computer. They'll wait.

■ **Let your fingers do the walking.** As an old telephone company advertisement for the yellow pages says, Let your fingers do the walking. Many things can be done over the phone—or via e-mail or voicemail—rather than in person.

■ **Expect the unexpected.** Interruptions and crises, minor and major, can't be eliminated. However, they can be prepared for.

How is it possible to plan for surprises? Though it may still be too early in the term to get a clear picture of what sorts of unanticipated events you'll encounter, you should keep an eye out for patterns. Perhaps one instructor routinely makes surprise assignments that aren't listed on the syllabus. Maybe you're asked to work extra hours on the weekends because someone doesn't show up and you have to work overtime.

You'll never be able to escape from unexpected interruptions and surprises that require your attention. But by trying to anticipate them in advance, and thinking about how you'll react to them, you'll be positioning yourself to react more effectively when they do occur.

■ **Combat procrastination.** Procrastination is like a microscopic parasite on your day, invisible to the naked eye, but eating up your time nonetheless.

It's 10:30 a.m. You've just come out of your German class. You know that there's going to be a test next week, and you've planned to go over the flash cards you made up last night. It's right there in your schedule: "10:30 a.m.—study German vocabulary." But you're thirsty after sitting in class, so you decide to go and buy yourself something to drink.

As you head into the snack bar, you pass by the campus store, and you think about how you need to buy a couple of pens. After finding the kind of pen you like, you go to the checkout line. You pass by a rack of magazines, and, after leafing through a few, decide to purchase one. You can read it while you have your drink. You make your way to the snack bar, buy your soda, and sip it as you read the magazine.

Suddenly, a half hour has gone by. Because so much time has passed, you decide that it won't be worth it to start studying your German vocabulary. So you spend a little more time reading the magazine and then head off to your next class, which is at 11:00 a.m.

You can't control interruptions and crises that are imposed upon you by others. But even when no one else is throwing interruptions at us, we make up our own. **Procrastination,** the habit of putting off and delaying tasks that are to be accomplished, is a problem that many of us face. To identify whether you are a procrastinator, find your "Procrastination Quotient" (see Try It 5, page 50).

If you find yourself procrastinating, several steps can help you:

Break large tasks into small ones. People often procrastinate because a task they're seeking to accomplish appears overwhelming. If writing a 15-page paper seems nearly impossible, think about writing a series of five 3-page papers. If reading a 750-page book seems impossible, think of it as reading several 250-page books.

Start with the easiest and simplest part of a task, and then do the harder parts. Succeeding initially on the easy parts can make the harder parts of a task less daunting—and make you less apt to procrastinate in completing the task.

Work with others. Just being in the same physical location with others can motivate you sufficiently to accomplish tasks that you consider unpleasant and on which you might be tempted to procrastinate. For instance, studying vocabulary words can be made easier if you plan a study session with several of your classmates. Beware, though—if you spend too much time socializing, you lower the likelihood of success.

One antidote to procrastination is working in a study group. You'll be motivated by the presence of others who face the same challenges and assignments that you do.

Keep the costs of procrastination in mind. Procrastination doesn't just result in delay; it may also make the task harder than it would have been if you hadn't procrastinated. Not only will you ultimately have less time to complete the task, but you may have to do it so quickly that its quality may be diminished. In the worst scenario, you won't even be able to finish it at all.

■ **Balancing school and family demands.** If you are a full-time student and full-time caregiver for children, time management is especially challenging. Not only do children demand—and deserve—substantial quantities of time, but juggling school and family obligations can prove to be more than a full-time job. There are some specific strategies that can help, however:

Provide activities for your children. Kids enjoy doing things on their own for part of the day. Plan activities that will keep them happily occupied while you're doing schoolwork.

Make spending time with your children a priority. Carve out "free play" time for your kids. Even 20 minutes of good time devoted to your children will give all of you—you and them—a lift. No matter how busy you are, you owe it to your children—and yourself—to spend time as a family.

Enlist your child's help. Children love to play adult and, if they're old enough, ask them to help you study. Maybe they can help you clear a space to study. Perhaps you can give them "assignments" that they can work on while you're working on your assignments.

to continue in the job once you're done with school, then accepting new responsibilities may be more reasonable.

Always keep in mind why you're working. If you're working because it's your sole means of support, you're in a very different position from someone who is working to earn a bit of extra money for luxuries. Remember what your priorities are. In some cases, school should always come first; in others, your job may have to come first, at least some of the time. Whatever you decide, make sure it's a thoughtful decision, based on an evaluation of your long-term priorities.

EVALUATE: Checking Your Time

Evaluating how you use your time is pretty straightforward: You either accomplished what you intended to do in a given period, or you didn't. Did you check off all the items on your daily to-do list? If you go over your list at the end of every day, not only will you know how successful your time management efforts have been, but you will be able to incorporate any activities you missed into the next day's to-do list.

IRM Link: Teaching the Text, Chapter 2, Sections IV and VIII; "The Cost of a College Education" activity is relevant here.

The check-off is important because it provides an objective record of what you have accomplished on a given day. Just as important, it provides you with concrete reinforcement for completing the task. As we have noted, there are few things more satisfying than gazing at a to-do list with a significant number of check marks.

Of course, you won't always accomplish every item on your to-do list. That's not surprising, nor even particularly bad, especially if you've included some second- and third-level priorities that you don't absolutely have to accomplish and that you may not really have expected you'd have time for anyway.

 CAREER CONNECTIONS

Taking a Long-Term View of Time

In considering different careers, it is important to consider the length of time it takes to prepare for them. Every profession has a different set of educational and other preparatory requirements, and in order to have informed career goals, you need to determine the kind of things you need to do in order to prepare.

For example, someone who aspires to go into elementary education must complete a period of student teaching, and many states require new teachers to take an exam that is only offered a few times year. Future lawyers must not only complete four years of college, but then an additional three years of law school, along with summer internships. After that's finished, they need to take the bar exam in order to practice law. And some physicians must have eight to ten years of train-

ing *after* they complete their undergraduate education, depending on their specialty.

An effective way to compare careers that you may be considering is to construct a career timeline that lists the steps you'll need to take to prepare for the careers that interest you. Start off by considering what (if anything) you'll need to do in the first year of college. Take into account the preparatory steps for each career you wish to compare, including the kind of courses you'll need to take, the educational and professional requirements that you'll need to fulfill, and any internships or residencies you will need. Different careers will have very different timelines.

Obviously your plan will change as your interests become more firm. The idea is not to identify a rigid path for yourself but to begin the process of understanding what it takes to enter various professions. The more knowledge you have, the greater your ability to make wise choices.

Give yourself a virtual pat on the back for completing the things that you've accomplished. Successful time management is not easy, and if you've improved at all, you deserve to feel some personal satisfaction.

R ETHINK: Reflecting on Your Personal Style of Time Management

At the end of the day, after you've evaluated how well you've followed your time management plan and how much you've accomplished, it's time to rethink where you are. Maybe you've accomplished everything you set out to do, and every task for the day is completed, and every item on your to-do list has a check mark next to it.

Or maybe you have the opposite result. Your day has been a shambles, and you feel as if nothing has been accomplished. Because of a constant series of interruptions and chance events, you've been unable to make headway on your list.

Or—most likely—you find yourself somewhere in between these two extremes. Some tasks got done, while others are still hanging over you. Now is the time to rethink in a broad sense how you manage your time by doing the following:

- **Reassess Your Priorities.** Are your long- and short-term goals appropriate? Are you expecting too much of yourself, given the constraints in your life? Reassess your priorities in order to be sure you're attempting to do what is most important to you.

- **Reconsider Your Personal Style of Time Management.** We've outlined one method of time management. Although it works well for most people, it isn't for everyone. Some people just can't bring themselves to be so structured and scheduled. They feel hemmed in by to-do lists.

  If you're one of those people, fine. You don't need to follow the suggestions presented in this chapter exactly. In fact, if you go to any office supply store or even your college bookstore, you'll find lots of other aids to manage your time. Publishing companies produce elaborate planners, such as Day-Timer, and software companies produce computerized time management software, such as Microsoft's Outlook, that reside on a computer or the Web (see the Resources section at the end of this chapter). Many people use PDA (Personal Data Assistant) handhelds to organize themselves, and some cell phones have built-in calendar systems.

  However you choose to manage your time, the important thing is to do so consistently. And remember that whatever approach to time management you take, it will work best if it is compatible with your own personal

IRM Link: Teaching the Text, Chapter 2, Section VII; Refer to the ideas in "Connect the course to the individual student's life."

Managing your time effectively will allow you to make the most of every moment, helping you to accomplish the things that are most important to you.

values and strengths. Keep experimenting until you find an approach that works for you.

- **Consider Doing Less.** If you keep falling behind, do less. There are only 24 hours in the day, and we need to sleep for about a third of the time. In the remaining hours, it is simply impossible to carry a full load of classes and work full-time and care for a child and still have some time left to have a normal life.

  Consequently, if you consistently fall behind in your work, it may be that you are just doing too much. Reassess your goals and your priorities, and make choices. Determine what is most important to you. It's better to accomplish less, if it is accomplished well, than to accomplish more, but poorly.

- **Do More.** Although it is a problem that many of us would envy, some people have too much time on their hands. Their classes may not be too demanding, or work demands may suddenly slacken off. If this happens to you, take advantage of your time. For example, you might use the extra time to simply relax and enjoy your more unhurried existence. There is a good bit to be said for having time to let your thoughts wander. We need to take time out to enjoy our friends, admire the flowers in the park, exercise, consider the spiritual side of our lives, and the like.

  On the other hand, if you consistently have more time than you know what to do with, reflect on what you want to accomplish and add some activities that help you reach your goals. For example, consider becoming involved in a service-learning activity. Volunteer your time to the community. Consider taking an extra course during the next term.

  But whatever you decide to do, make a real decision. Don't let the time slip away. Once it's gone, it's gone forever.

Teaching Tip: Refer back to the "168 Hours in a Week" activity done earlier to assess whether there is time to "do more." Just as important, discuss the difference between engagement and simply scheduling activities. The energy needed for success is entirely different.

A major goal of time management is to give you the opportunity to do more of the things that are important to you.

SPEAKING OF Success

Name: Jasmine Rosario

School: Vassar College, Poughkeepsie, New York

Jasmine Rosario, who will be the first person in her family to graduate from college, has developed a philosophy that makes time management a number one priority.

"I think that some of the biggest rewards of college don't just involve academics, but come from the opportunities to be involved in a lot of other things," Rosario said.

A psychology major and art history minor, Rosario has taken that philosophy to heart. She is involved in numerous extracurricular activities, holds a campus job, and still maintains high grades.

However, her demanding schedule requires careful time management. "As a result of my involvement outside the classroom," she said, "I have to stay on top of my work, scheduling myself carefully.

"From the very beginning of the semester I'm already making a schedule and immediately know if I'm going to have two finals the same week or papers due on the same day," she added.

Rosario says that as soon as she gets class assignments, she writes them down. In addition, she also prepares weekly and monthly calendars and makes sure to prioritize her obligations.

"I always prioritize my commitments. Academics come first, followed by extracurricular activities and my campus job as a Wellness Peer Educator," she explained.

During periods of intense study, Rosario relieves stress by taking breaks, as well as socializing with other students and talking about anything other than academics.

"It's easy to get overwhelmed with all the work, so I think it's important to take breaks," she said. "For me the number one priority is to take care of myself. Work is work, but your health comes before everything else."

As a Wellness Peer Educator, Rosario has learned that it's important for students to know their limitations.

"Some students stress out and feel like they're in a box by giving too much to extracurricular activities. From the beginning, they have to know how much to give and to be very clear about it," she said.

How can I manage my time most effectively?

- Decide to take control of your time.
- Become aware of the way you use your time now.
- Set clear priorities.
- Use such time management tools as a master calendar, weekly timetable, and a daily to-do list.

Teaching Tip: Ask students these same questions at mid-term.

How can I deal better with surprises and distractions?

- Deal with surprises by saying no, getting away from it all, working in silence, taking control of communications, using the phone to conduct transactions, and leaving slack in your schedule to accommodate the unexpected.
- Avoid procrastination by breaking large tasks into smaller ones, starting with the easiest parts of a task first; working with other people; and calculating the true costs of procrastination.

How can I balance competing priorities?

- Consider how your competing priorities relate to one another.
- Manage work time carefully, use slack time on the job to perform school assignments, use flextime, accept new responsibilities thoughtfully, and assign the proper priority to work.

KEY TERMS AND CONCEPTS

Time log (p. 31)
Priorities (p. 35)
Master calendar (p. 39)

Weekly timetable (p. 40)
Daily to-do list (p. 41)
Procrastination (p. 49)

RESOURCES

On Campus

The college official that schedules classes on campus is known as the Registrar. If you are having difficulty in scheduling your classes, the registrar's office may be helpful. In addition, your academic advisor can help you work out problems in enrolling in the classes you want.

In Print

Stephen Covey's *The Seven Habits of Highly Successful People* (Fireside, 1990) and Alan Axelrod and Brian Tracy's *Eat That Frog! 21 Great Ways to Stop Procrastinating and Get More Done in Less Time* (Berrett-Kohler, 2002) offer practical, hands-on guides to time management.

How to Do Everything with Microsoft Outlook (Osborne-McGraw-Hill, 2000), by Julia Kelly and Megg Bonar, provides a quick, hands-on introduction to Microsoft's Outlook software, a popular time management program that is part of the Microsoft Office Suite.

Finally, Veronique Vienne and Erica Lennard's *The Art of the Moment: Simple Ways to Get the Most Out of Life* (Clarkson Potter, 2002) is an antidote to the impulse to schedule every minute of our days. The book celebrates taking time out and devoting it to oneself, providing a practical guide to rest and relaxation.

On the Web

The *P.O.W.E.R. Learning* Web site at **www.mhhe.com/power** provides online versions of all the time management forms presented in this chapter. You can complete the forms online or download them and print out as many copies as you need. Although the Web addresses were accurate at the time the book was printed, check the P.O.W.E.R. Learning Web site [**www.mhhe.com/power**] for any changes that may have occurred.

The University of Victoria's Office of Counseling Services provides two useful sites:

- Effective hints on how to plan study time, ideas about when to study, as well as tips on how to study (**www.coun.uvic.ca/learn/Planning%20Study%20Time.html**).

- A handy self-management checklist that allows visitors to better achieve their goals with the time that they have (**www.coun.uvic.ca/learn/program/hndouts/slfman.html**). It also provides effective techniques for avoiding procrastination and digression, two major obstacles to effective time management.

- Mind Tools Book Store sponsors a site (**www.mindtools.com/page5.html**) with useful information on how to get the most out of one's time. Topics covered include analyzing what time is really worth, prioritizing goals, and planning effective use of the time that one actually has.

TAKING IT TO THE NET

1 Complete a weekly organizer online. Find a site on the Web that offers shareware or freeware featuring a weekly planner (for example, **www.studygs.net/schedule/Weekly.html** or **www.printablecalendar.ca/**). Create a weekly schedule sheet for yourself based on this design. Be sure to write in all of your classes and any other regular obligations that you have. Be sure to set specific times in your daily schedule to study and do homework. (If you already use Outlook or another kind of communications software, use its calendar function to do the same thing.)

2 Make a master calendar for the term, using the same software you used for the exercise above. If your calendar does not provide this information automatically, you can go to Yahoo! (**dir.yahoo.com**), click on "Reference," then again on "Calendars." Here you'll find many links to different calendar-related information such as when holidays occur. Be sure to indicate dates when important assignments are due and when exams occur.

The transformation began when Shaniqua Turner got her first paper back from her English literature instructor. It wasn't the grade—which was good—that mattered so much, but what her instructor uttered, almost as an afterthought, as she handed the paper back to Shaniqua: "Nice job. Your insights were good, and you have great potential as a writer."

Shaniqua was thrilled. She had always thought of herself as having only modest talent in English and, although at one point she had harbored the fantasy of being a newspaper reporter, she had never felt she was good enough to make it.

But now something clicked: Maybe she did have the ability to succeed in a career involving writing.

P.O.W.E.R. UP: Illustrate the concept of preferences by asking students to write their name on a sheet of paper. Then, ask them to write their name again but this time to use their other hand. Ask the students to discuss their observations about this activity. More is included in the IRM about this activity. See Teaching the Text, Chapter 3, Sections IV and VIII.

LOOKING AHEAD >>>

Through the experiences we have in life, we build up a sense of our strengths and weaknesses, what we like and dislike about ourselves. In the process, the sense of who we are also affects the choices we make and the things that we do.

In this chapter you will be asked to consider various aspects of yourself. First you'll look at the ways in which you learn and how you can use your personal learning style to study more effectively.

You'll then explore who you are more broadly, considering the various aspects of your personality. You'll see how your self-esteem—the way you perceive your strengths and weaknesses—can lead to success or failure.

Finally, the chapter helps you investigate where you are headed. By creating your own personal mission state-ment, you'll begin to solidify the knowledge of who you are and where you would be happiest and most productive in the future.

After reading this chapter, you'll be able to answer these questions:

■ **What are my learning styles, and how have they affected my academic success?**

■ **What is self-concept and how does it affect me?**

■ **How does my level of self-esteem affect my behavior?**

■ **How can I make wise personal decisions throughout life?**

Teaching Tip and IRM Link: Read this entire chapter and IRM Teaching the Text, Chapter 3 information prior to teaching this chapter. It is the heart of the course.

Discovering Your Learning Styles

Student Alert: This chapter provides multiple ways to discuss the same information with your students; begin to agree on a common language for discussing learning issues. You will return to this topic repeatedly throughout the semester.

Consider what it would be like to be a member of the Trukese people, a small group of islanders in the South Pacific.

Trukese sailors often sail hundreds of miles on the open sea. They manage this feat with none of the navigational equipment used by Western sailors. No compass. No chronometer. No sextant. They don't even sail in a straight line. Instead, they zigzag back and forth, at the mercy of the winds and tides. Yet they make few mistakes. Almost always they are able to reach their destination with precision. How do they do it?

They can't really explain it. They say it has to do with following the rising and setting of the stars at night. During the day, they take in the appearance, sound, and feel of the waves against the side of the boat. But they don't really have any idea of where they are at any given moment, nor do they care. They just know that ultimately they'll reach their final destination.

It would be foolhardy to suggest that the Trukese don't have what it takes to be successful sailors. The fact that they don't use traditional Western navigational equipment when they're sailing does not mean that they are any less able than Western navigators.

What about academic success? Isn't it reasonable to assume that there are different ways to reach academic goals? Wouldn't it be surprising if everyone learned in exactly the same way?

Each of us has preferred ways of learning, approaches that work best for us. And our success is not just dependent on how well we learn, but on how we learn.

Learning styles reflect our preferred manner of acquiring, using, and thinking about knowledge. We don't have just one learning style, but a variety of styles. Even though our ability may be identical to someone else's, our learning styles might be quite different.

You probably already know quite a lot about your learning styles. Maybe you do particularly well in your biology classes while struggling with English literature. Or it may be the other way around. Because biology tends to be about natural processes, teachers present the subject as a series of related facts. English literature, however, requires you to think more abstractly, analyzing and synthesizing ideas.

Though we may have general preferences for fact-based learning or learning that requires more abstract thinking, we all use a variety of learning styles. Some involve our preferences regarding the way information is presented to us, some relate to how we think and learn most readily, and some relate to how our personality traits affect our performance. We'll start by considering the preferences we have for how we initially perceive information.

Trukese sailors, who live on a small group of islands in the South Pacific, are able to navigate with considerable accuracy across great expanses of open seas, and they do so without the use of any of the standard navigation tools used by sailors in Western cultures. The navigational achievements of the Trukese sailors illustrate that there are multiple ways to attain our goals and that there is no single route to success.

Learning style
One's preferred manner of acquiring, using, and thinking about knowledge

How I Learn

How would you respond to the following learning situations?

1. Would you rather read a newspaper, listen to the news on the radio, watch it on TV, or click your way through it on a Web site? Why do you think you have this preference?

2. When you get a new piece of software or a new tool, do you like to read the instructions or just "play with it" until you get the hang of it?

3. Suppose a friend is teaching you a new and complex procedure (such as a new game or the way to use a piece of computer software). Do you prefer to get the "big picture" first or the details?

4. When you're in class, what do you do during lectures? Try to write down the instructor's exact words, draw diagrams and make tables, or jot down a few big ideas?

5. What do your answers to the previous questions reveal about the way you prefer to learn new information?

Teaching Tip: Every college campus has someone who understands and works with this information. Call on your colleagues to help you.

Receptive learning style
The way in which we initially receive information

Visual/verbal learning style
A style that involves a preference for written material, favoring reading over hearing and touching

Visual/nonverbal learning style
A style that favors material presented visually in a diagram or picture

Are You Primarily a Visual, Auditory, or Tactile Learner?

One of the most basic aspects of learning styles concerns the way in which we initially receive information from our sense organs—our **receptive learning style.** People have different strengths in terms of how they most effectively process information. Specifically, there are four different types of receptive learning styles:

■ **Visual/verbal learning style.** If you have a **visual/verbal learning style,** you prefer information that is presented visually in a written format. You feel most comfortable reading, and you may recall the spelling of a word by thinking of how the word looks. You probably learn best when you have the opportunity to read about a concept rather than listening to a teacher explain it.

■ **Visual/nonverbal learning style.** Students with a **visual/nonverbal learning style** learn most effectively when material is presented visually in a diagram or picture. You might recall the structure of a chemical compound by reviewing a picture in your mind, and you benefit from instructors who make frequent use of visual aids such as videos, maps, and models. Students with visual learning styles find it easier to see things in their mind's eye—to visualize a task or concept—than to be lectured about them.

- **Auditory/verbal learning style.** Have you ever asked a friend to help you put something together by having her read the directions to you while you worked? If you did, you may have an auditory/verbal learning style. People with **auditory/verbal learning styles** prefer listening to explanations rather than reading them. They love class lectures and discussions, because they can easily take in the information that is being talked about.

- **Tactile/kinesthetic learning style.** Students with a **tactile/kinesthetic learning style** prefer to learn by doing—touching, manipulating objects, and doing things. For instance, some people enjoy the act of writing because of the feel of a pencil or a computer keyboard—the tactile equivalent of thinking out loud. Or they may find that it helps them to make a three-dimensional model to understand a new idea.

Learning styles reflect our preferred manner of acquiring, using, and thinking about knowledge. Tactile learners prefer hands-on learning that comes about through touching, manipulating, and doing things.

To get a sense of your own receptive learning style, complete Try It 1 on page 64. But remember, having a particular receptive learning style simply means that it will be easier to learn material that is presented in that style. It does not mean you cannot learn any other way!

Receptive learning styles have implications for effective studying:

If you have a visual/verbal style, consider writing out summaries of information, highlighting and underlining written material, and using flashcards. Transform diagrams and math formulas into words.

If you have a visual/nonverbal style, devise diagrams and charts. Translate words into symbols and figures.

If you have an auditory/verbal style, recite material out loud when studying. Work with others in a group, talking through the material, and consider tape recording lectures.

If you have a tactile/kinesthetic style, incorporate movement into your study. Trace diagrams, build models, arrange flash cards and move them around. Keep yourself active during class, taking notes, drawing charts, and jotting down key concepts.

Auditory/verbal learning style
A style that favors listening as the best approach to learning

Tactile/kinesthetic learning style
A style that involves learning by touching, manipulating objects, and doing things

> **"To be fond of learning is to be near to knowledge."**
>
> Tze-Sze, philosopher

Teaching Tip: Ask students to circle all of the words and phrases that best describe their own learning styles and preferences. Ask them to write a paper or talk with a classmate about the words they selected to describe themselves.

Handling Information: Do You Focus on Pieces or the Whole?

When you are putting a jigsaw puzzle together, do you focus more on the individual pieces and how each one fits together with the one next to it, or is your strategy to concentrate on the whole picture, keeping the finished product in mind?

The way you approach a jigsaw puzzle provides a clue to the process by which you fit together bits of information. Specifically, the strategy

PERSONAL STYLES

What's Your Receptive Learning Style?

Read each of the following statements and rank them in terms of their usefulness to you as learning approaches. Base your ratings on your personal experiences and preferences, using the following scale:

1 = Not at all useful

2 = Not very useful

3 = Neutral

4 = Somewhat useful

5 = Very useful

	1	2	3	4	5
1. Studying alone					
2. Studying pictures and diagrams to understand complex ideas					
3. Listening to class lectures					
4. Performing a process myself rather than reading or hearing about it					
5. Learning a complex procedure by reading written directions					
6. Watching and listening to film, computer, or video presentations					
7. Listening to a book or lecture on tape					
8. Doing lab work					
9. Studying teachers' handouts and lecture notes					
10. Studying in a quiet room					
11. Taking part in group discussions					
12. Taking part in hands-on classroom demonstrations					
13. Taking notes and studying them later					
14. Creating flash cards and using them as a study and review tool					
15. Memorizing and recalling how words are spelled by spelling them "out loud" in my head					

(continued)

	1	2	3	4	5
16. Writing key facts and important points down as a tool for remembering them					
17. Recalling how to spell a word by seeing it in my head					
18. Underlining or highlighting important facts or passages in my reading					
19. Saying things out loud when I'm studying					
20. Recalling how to spell a word by "writing" it invisibly in the air or on a surface					
21. Learning new information by reading about it in a textbook					
22. Using a map to find an unknown place					
23. Working in a study group					
24. Finding a place I've been to once by just going there without directions					

Scoring:

The statements cycle through the four receptive learning styles in this order: (1) visual/verbal; (2) visual/nonverbal; (3) auditory/verbal; and (4) tactile/kinesthetic.

To find your primary learning style, disregard your 1, 2, and 3 ratings. Add up your 4 and 5 ratings for each learning style (i.e., a "4" equals 4 points and a "5" equals 5 points). Use the following chart to link the statements to the learning styles and to write down your summed ratings:

Learning Style	Statements	Total (Sum) of Rating Points
Visual/verbal	1, 5, 9, 13, 17, and 21	
Visual/nonverbal	2, 6, 10, 14, 18, and 22	
Auditory/verbal	3, 7, 11, 15, 19, and 23	
Tactile/kinesthetic	4, 8, 12, 16, 20, and 24	

The total of your rating points for any given style will range from a low of 0 to a high of 30. The highest total indicates your main receptive learning style. Don't be surprised if you have a mixed style, in which two or more styles receive similar ratings.

To Try It online, go to **www.mhhe.com/power**.

you use suggests which of the following two learning styles you are more comfortable with:

Analytic learning style
A style that starts with small pieces of information and uses them to build the big picture

Relational learning style
A style that starts with the big picture and breaks it down into its individual components

People with **analytic learning styles** learn most easily if first exposed to the individual components and principles behind a phenomenon or situation. Once they have identified the underlying components involved, they find it easier to figure out and grasp the broad picture and determine whether particular cases exemplify the principle.

■ Those with **relational learning styles** learn most readily if exposed to the full range of material that they are aiming to learn. Rather than focusing on the individual components of a problem, as those with analytic styles prefer to do, people with relational learning styles do best when they are first given the full picture. They can then take this broad view and break it down into its individual components.

For example, consider trying to understand the way that food is converted to energy in a cell. A more analytic learner would approach the task by learning each individual step in the process, first to last. In contrast, a more relational learner would consider the big picture, focusing on the general, overall process and its purpose.

Students who use an analytic style study most effectively by focusing on facts and specific principles, for they excel at organizing information. They often work best on their own, and science and math may come particularly easy to them. On the other hand, students with a relational style perceive concepts globally, thinking in terms of the big picture. They may be drawn to subject areas that demand the ability to forge a broad overview of material, such as English and history.

You probably already have a good idea of whether you have an analytic or relational learning style, but Try It 2, "Assessing Your Analytical and Relational Learning Styles," will help you understand your learning style further. In addition, you can find out more about how you process information and use learning and study strategies from the *Learning and Assessment Strategies Inventory*, or *LASSI*, an 80-item questionnaire developed by researchers at the University of Texas. You can take the *LASSI* online by going to the *P.O.W.E.R. Learning* Web site at **www.mhhe.com/power**.

Personality Styles

Our learning styles are also influenced by our personality. Are you likely to try out for school productions? Or is the idea of getting on a stage totally lacking in appeal (if not completely terrifying)? Do you relate to the world around you primarily through careful planning or by spontaneously reacting?

Teaching Tip: The combination of individual personality and learning is a captivating concept for students. Tap into this.

According to the rationale of the *Myers-Briggs Type Indicator*, a questionnaire frequently used in business and organizational settings to place people in one of 16 categories, personality type plays a key role in determining how we react to different situations. Specifically, we work best in situations in which others—both students and instructors—share our preferences and in which our personality is most suited to the particular task on which we are working.

Four major personality dimensions are critical. Although we'll describe the extremes of each dimension, keep in mind that most of us fall somewhere between the end points of each dimension.

■ **Introverts versus extraverts.** A key difference between introverts and extraverts is whether they enjoy working with others. Independence is a key characteristic of introverted learners. They enjoy working alone and they are less affected by how others think and behave. In contrast, extraverts are outgoing and more affected by the behavior and thinking of others. They enjoy working with others, and they are energized by having other people around.

Assessing Your Analytical and Relational Learning Styles

Consider the following pairs of statements. Place a check next to the statement in each pair that more closely describes your style.

- ☐ 1a. Before tackling a complex task that I'm unfamiliar with, I prefer to have detailed instructions on how to do it.
- ☐ 1b. I prefer to dive into a new task, trying things out to see what happens and finding my way as I go.
- ☐ 2a. I like watching movies a second time because then I know where they're going.
- ☐ 2b. I generally don't like watching movies a second time because I know their plots already.
- ☐ 3a. I prefer to solve math or science problems using formulas and directions.
- ☐ 3b. I prefer to figure out why formulas work.
- ☐ 4a. When I read mystery stories, I usually let the author tell the story and reveal the mystery.
- ☐ 4b. When I read mystery stories, I like to try figuring out the mystery before the author reveals it.
- ☐ 5a. I usually read the instruction booklet before trying out a new piece of software.
- ☐ 5b. I never read the instruction booklet before trying out a new piece of software.
- ☐ 6a. I prefer to have someone who knows about a subject explain it to me before I try my hand at it.
- ☐ 6b. I'm impatient when others try to explain things to me, preferring to get involved in them myself without much explanation.
- ☐ 7a. Whenever I see a really amazing special effect in a movie, I like to sit back and enjoy it.
- ☐ 7b. Whenever I see a really amazing special effect in a movie, I try to figure out how they did it.

If you tended to prefer the "a" statements in most pairs, you probably have a relational style. If you preferred the "b" statements, you probably have a more analytic style. Remember that no one is purely analytical or purely relational.

To Try It online, go to **www.mhhe.com/power**.

- **Intuitors versus sensors.** Intuitors enjoy solving problems and being creative. They get impatient with details, preferring to make leaps of judgment, and they enjoy the challenge of solving problems and taking a big-picture approach. People categorized as sensors, on the other hand, prefer a concrete, logical approach in which they can carefully analyze the facts of the situation. Although they are good with details, they sometimes miss the big picture.

- **Thinkers versus feelers.** Thinkers prefer logic over emotion. They reach decisions and solve problems by systematically analyzing a situation. In contrast, feeling types rely more on their emotional responses. They are aware of others and their feelings, and they are influenced by their personal values and attachments to others.

- **Perceivers and judgers.** Before drawing a conclusion, perceivers attempt to gather as much information as they can. Because they are open to multiple perspectives and appreciate all sides of an issue, they sometimes have dificulty completing a task. Judgers, in comparison, are quick and decisive. They like to set goals, accomplish them, and then move on to the next task.

The Origins of Our Learning Styles

For many of us, our learning style preferences result from the kind of processing our brain "specializes" in. **Left-brain processing** concentrates more on tasks requiring verbal competence, such as speaking, reading, thinking, and reasoning. Information is processed sequentially, one bit at a time. For instance, people who are naturally inclined to use left-brain processing might be more likely to prefer analytic learning styles, because they first like to look at individual bits of information and then put them together.

On the other hand, **right-brain processing** tends to concentrate more on the processing of information in nonverbal domains, such as the understanding of spatial relationships, recognition of patterns and drawings, music, and

TABLE 3.1 Learning, Personality, and Processing Styles

All of us have particular learning, personality, and processing styles that we tend to rely on. At the same time, we also have capabilities in less-preferred styles. So, for example, although you may be primarily a visual/verbal learner, you have the capacity to use auditory/verbal and tactile/kinesthetic approaches. Note in particular that the four categories of personality styles are considered independent of each other. For instance, you may be an extrovert and at the same time a sensor, a feeler, and a judger. Furthermore, although the "Using the Style" column suggests ways that students with a particular style can make the most of that style, you should also try strategies that work for styles different from your own.

Category	Type	Description	Using the Style[1]
Receptive Learning Styles	Visual/verbal	A style that involves a preference for material in a written format, favoring reading over hearing and touching.	Read and rewrite material, take notes and rewrite them; organize material in charts and tables; transform diagrams and math formulas into words.
	Visual/ nonverbal	A style that favors material presented visually in a diagram or picture.	Use figures and drawings; replay classes and discussions in your mind's eye; visualize material; translate words into symbols and figures.
	Auditory/ verbal	A style in which the learner favors listening as the best approach.	Recite material out loud when studying; consider how words sound; study different languages; tape record lectures; work with others, talking through the material.
	Tactile/ kinesthetic	A style that involves learning by touching, manipulating objects, and doing things.	Incorporate movement into studying; trace figures and drawings with your finger; create models; make flash cards and move them around; keep active during class, taking notes, drawing charts, jotting down key concepts.
Information Processing Styles	Analytic	A style in which the learner starts with small pieces of information and uses them to build the big picture.	Consider the sequence of material; organize information into logical patterns.
	Relational	A style in which the learner starts with the big picture and breaks it down into its individual components.	Build models and break them down; split written material into its components.

(continued)

emotional expression. Furthermore, the right hemisphere tends to process information globally, considering it as a whole. Consequently, people who naturally tend toward right-brain processing might prefer relational learning styles.

Here are some key facts to remember about learning, personality, and processing styles:

■ **You have a variety of styles.** As you can see in the summary of different categories of styles in Table 3.1, there are several types of styles. For any given task or challenge, some types of styles may be more relevant than others. Furthermore, success is possible even when there is a mismatch

TABLE 3.1		Learning, Personality, and Processing Styles	*(continued)*
Category	**Type**	**Description**	**Using the Style**
Personality Styles	Introvert versus extrovert	Independence is a key characteristic of introverted learners, who enjoy working alone and are less affected by how others think and behave. In contrast, extroverts are outgoing and more affected by the behavior and thinking of others. They enjoy working with others.	Experiment with studying in groups compared with working alone, consider your performance in class discussions compared with working on your own.
	Intuitors versus sensors	Intuitive people enjoy solving problems and being creative, often taking a big-picture approach. Sensors, on the other hand, prefer a concrete, logical approach in which they can carefully analyze the facts of the situation.	For intuitors, reflect on the personal meaning of material and seek out tasks that involve creativity. For sensors, seek out concrete tasks that involve the application of logical principles.
	Thinker versus feeler	Thinkers prefer logic over emotion, reaching decisions through rational analysis. In contrast, feelers rely more on their emotions and are influenced by their personal values and attachments to others.	Thinkers should seek to systematically analyze situations, attempting to identify patterns. For feelers, use emotional responses to reflect on material.
	Perceiver versus judger	Before drawing a conclusion, perceivers attempt to gather as much information as they can and are open to multiple perspectives. Judgers, in comparison, are quick and decisive, enjoying setting goals and accomplishing them.	Perceivers organize material sequentially and into component parts; for judgers, using goal-setting preferences facilitates learning.
Brain Processing Styles	Left-brain processing	Information processing that focuses on tasks requiring verbal competence, such as speaking, reading, thinking, and reasoning; information is processed sequentially, one bit at a time.	Organize material logically; identify patterns; make tables of key information; break material into component parts.
	Right-brain processing	Information processing that focuses on information in nonverbal domains, such as the understanding of spatial relationships, recognition of patterns and drawings, music, and emotional expression.	Identify patterns; use graphs and drawings; read aloud; create models.

Connecting Your Learning Style with Your Instructor's Learning Style

Having a sense of your own learning style, and how it matches up with that of your instructor, can help maximize your success in a course. It can give you insight into the kind of test questions your instructor may favor and help you strategize about what to pay particular attention to when you're reading course material.

For example, you should take the instructor's learning styles into account when studying. If your natural tendency is to stick to the facts, and your instructor appears to prefer broad, conceptual views of the material, then be sure to consider the material from the instructor's broader view.

In contrast, if your instructor's learning preferences lean toward factual views of material, pay special attention to the details that your instructor will likely be more interested in. For example, an instructor who focuses on the broad view is not likely to ask you to repeat a detailed series of dates of particular events during the French Revolution. Yet this may be exactly what another instructor, more focused on the details, is interested in.

What if there is a total mismatch between your and your instructor's learning styles? Then keep in mind that there are benefits to the discomfort that you may experience when your instructor emphasizes activities that don't match your own learning styles. Remember that real learning is often difficult and uncomfortable, and the practice you get with less-preferred learning styles in the end will make you a more accomplished student.

Self-concept
People's view of themselves that forms over time, comprising three components: the physical self, the social self, and the personal self

IRM Link: Teaching the Text, Chapter 3, Section VII. Ask the students to write a letter to themselves as outlined in the first activity about connecting this information to the individual student's life.

Our view of ourselves—our **self-concept**—has three parts:

1. Our physical self is both who we are physically—the color of our eyes or the curliness of our hair—and how we feel about our physical form. We all have our blemishes, protruding stomachs, long noses, or other physical quirks, but we don't all feel the same way about them.

2. Our social self is made up of the roles we play in our social interactions with others. As you're reading these words, you're not only a student but you're also a son or daughter, a friend, a citizen, and possibly an employee, a spouse, a lover, and/or a parent. Each of these roles plays an important part in defining your self-concept. Each also helps to determine how you behave while acting in that particular role.

3. Finally, our self-concept also contains a personal self—our inner core, which is that private part of ourselves that no one knows about except us. It consists of the innermost thoughts and experiences that we may or may not choose to share with others.

Self Concept and Self-Fulfilling Prophecies

The way we view ourselves determines how we interact with others, what challenges we feel ready to take on, and our expectations for future success. If you see yourself as a successful student, you are likely to expect that you'll continue to be a successful student. On the other hand, if you see yourself as an incapable, inept student, your chances for future success are diminished.

In short, our self-concept can act as a self-fulfilling prophecy. A **self-fulfilling prophecy** occurs when we hold a belief or expectation that affects our behavior, thereby increasing the likelihood that our beliefs or expectations will come true. For instance, a person who views herself as a poor student may find herself thinking: "Why bother working hard? I'm no good as a student; that's just the way I am." It's easy to see how such a view could lead to a self-fulfilling prophecy: By not working hard, the student guarantees that the prophecy of poor performance comes true.

On the other hand, self-fulfilling prophecies can have positive effects. A person who sees herself as a good student will probably be motivated to study and complete assignments enthusiastically. Her view of herself can therefore bring about the expected behavior—in this case, success.

To get a clearer picture of your own self-concept:

- **Examine the roles you play.** To understand who we are, we need to understand the different roles that we play in life. Consider which of these roles are central to who you are—and who you want to be. Consider how an outsider might look at your actions, beliefs, and interests. How would that person characterize you?

- **Identify your strengths and weaknesses.** Look at yourself with a clear and objective eye, and consider what you do particularly well and what you don't do particularly well. If you're honest, you'll come up with several areas in which you need work—and many other areas in which you're already quite strong. Use Table 3.2 to help you organize your thoughts and build an initial inventory of your strengths and weaknesses.

As you consider your strengths and weaknesses, don't place a value on them. The fact that you procrastinate and put off tasks doesn't make you a bad person, just as the fact that you're a good student doesn't necessarily make you a good person. The point in seeking to identify who you are is to determine your self-concept with accuracy, not to determine how good (or bad) a human being you are.

- **Construct your own definition of who you are.** Don't let what you believe others think about you determine what you think you're good at and bad at. See yourself through your own eyes, not someone else's.

- **Accept your entire self-concept.** If you're being honest with yourself, you'll find that there are parts of yourself that you like more than others. That's OK. Don't disown the parts you don't like; they're also part of who you are. Instead, accept that some parts of yourself need work, while others are the source of justifiable pride.

Self-fulfilling prophecy
A phenomenon that occurs when we hold a belief or expectation that affects our behavior, thereby increasing the likelihood that our beliefs or expectations *will* come true

"Know Thyself."

Discussion Prompt: Expect your students to take over the class with their need to spend time talking about self-concept and self-esteem issues. Let them! It will be time well spent.

Make Sure Your Self-Concept Is Yours

Our own perceptions are not the only source of self-fulfilling prophecies. We sometimes permit others' views of who we are and their expectations about us to determine our behavior.

Measuring Your Self-Esteem

To get an informal estimate of your self-esteem, complete the following scale.[2]

Statement	Strongly Agree	Agree	Disagree	Strongly Disagree
1. On the whole, I am satisfied with myself.				
2. At times I think I am no good at all.				
3. I feel that I have a number of good qualities.				
4. I am able to do things as well as most other people.				
5. I feel I do not have much to be proud of.				
6. I certainly feel useless at times.				
7. I feel that I am a person of worth, at least the equal of others.				
8. I wish I could have more respect for myself.				
9. All in all, I am inclined to feel that I am a failure.				
10. I take a positive attitude toward myself.				

Scoring: For statements 1, 3, 4, 7 and 10, score as follows:

Strongly agree	= 4 points
Agree	= 3 points
Disagree	= 2 points
Strongly disagree	= 1 point

For statements 2, 5, 6, 8, and 9, score as follows:

Strongly agree	= 1 point
Agree	= 2 points
Disagree	= 3 points
Strongly disagree	= 4 points

Add your points together, and interpret the total as follows:

The highest possible score (i.e., an apparently very high level of self-esteem) is 40 points, and the minimum score (i.e., an apparently very low level of self-esteem) is 10. Most people score in the 30- to 40-point range. A much smaller number of people score in the 20s. A score of 10 to 20 is often found in people who suffer from chronic depression; those who score at this level should consider consulting a health care provider or call a 24-hour hotline at 800-448-3000. Keep in mind that this is a very rough gauge of self-esteem and that scores will vary depending on a number of factors, including your mood when you complete the questionnaire.

Now consider the following:

- Do the results of the questionnaire match your own gut feelings about yourself?
- Do you think your self-esteem has changed? Do you have any ideas as to why?

To Try It online, go to **www.mhhe.com/power**.

goals in many different kinds of situations. High self-esteem can also give people a sense of purpose and the belief that they are productive members of society.

In contrast, individuals lacking in self-esteem are more insecure, and their belief in their ability to reach their goals is weak. They feel less tied to others, and their sense of purpose is not firm. And when others are successful, people with low self-esteem may feel jealousy and envy.

Low self-esteem can produce a cycle of failure in which low self-esteem leads to low expectations, reduced effort, elevated anxiety, poor performance, and, finally, an affirmation of the low self-esteem that began the cycle in the first place. Such a cycle can be difficult to break (see Figure 3.1).

If a student with low self-esteem begins studying for a test believing that he is likely to do badly, he may put forth relatively little effort. Moreover, because he is virtually sure he is going to do poorly on the test, he may experience extremes of anxiety, feeling that (another) failure is lurking just ahead.

Ultimately, the combination of lack of effort and anxiety produced by his low self-esteem does him in, and he actually does do poorly on the test. But the cycle of failure is not yet complete: Rather than telling himself that low effort and elevated anxiety caused his poor test performance, he views it as an affirmation of his inferior ability. In turn, this misperception serves to reinforce his low self-esteem.

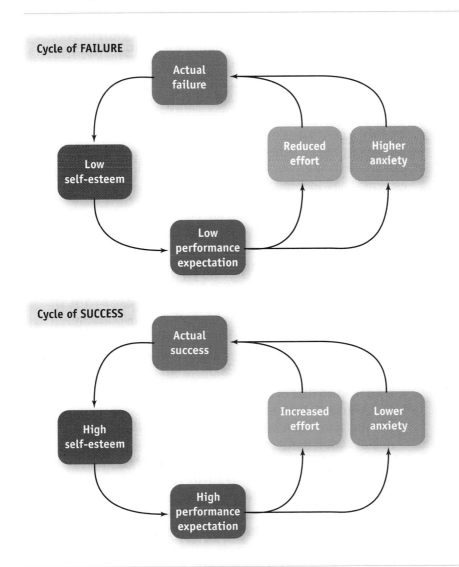

FIGURE 3.1

The Cycle of Failure and the Cycle of Success
Low self-esteem can lead to low performance expectations. In turn, low performance expectations can produce reduced effort and high anxiety, both of which can lead to failure—and ultimately reinforce the low self-esteem that started the cycle. In contrast, those with high self-esteem expect success, and that expectation leads to greater effort and lower anxiety, thereby increasing the likelihood of actual success. Ultimately, this success boosts self-esteem.

Discussion Prompt: Ask students to think about how this information is relevant to their own lives. Have they experienced a *cycle of failure* with activities or courses? How did they break the cycle?

PREPARE
Identify your values

ORGANIZE
Impose order on what
motivates you

WORK
Create a personal
mission statement

EVALUATE
Assess your personal
mission statement

RETHINK
Reconsider your options

P.O.W.E.R. Plan

Teaching Tip: The P.O.W.E.R. process in this chapter culminates in TRY IT! 5 which will be a personal mission statement and reference point for each student that you should refer back to throughout the semester.

P REPARE: Identifying Your Values

The first step toward understanding ourselves is to assess our underlying values systematically. To do this, work through the following steps:

1. Choose the five values that you hold most dear. Here are some examples, but don't necessarily restrict yourself to these: a comfortable life, an exciting life, a sense of accomplishment, world peace, beauty, equality, security, freedom, happiness, inner harmony, love, national security, pleasure, religion, self-respect, fame, friendship, wisdom, work, financial security, risk taking, being challenged.

2. For each value, answer each of these questions below: why is it important to you, who taught it to you, how has it affected your behavior in the past, and in what ways can you affirm it through your future behavior?

Value #1 _____

Why it is important:
Who taught it to you:
How it has affected your past behavior:
In what ways you can affirm it through future behavior:

Value #2 _____

Why it is important:
Who taught it to you:
How it has affected your past behavior:
In what ways you can affirm it through future behavior:

Value #3 _____

Why it is important:
Who taught it to you:
How it has affected your past behavior:
In what ways you can affirm it through future behavior:

Value #4 _____

Why it is important:
Who taught it to you:
How it has affected your past behavior:
In what ways you can affirm it through future behavior:

Value #5 _____

Why it is important:
Who taught it to you:
How it has affected your past behavior:
In what ways you can affirm it through future behavior:

After you've identified your most important values, you'll be ready to move onto the organize step in developing a Mission Statement: determining what motivates you.

ORGANIZE: Imposing Order on What Motivates You

Abraham Lincoln. Albert Einstein. Eleanor Roosevelt.

What is the common link among these three people? According to psychologist Abraham Maslow, each of them achieved **self-actualization,** a state of self-fulfillment in which people realize their highest potential in their own unique way.[3]

According to Maslow, self-actualization is the highest of the various needs that motivate our behavior. As you can see in the illustration in Figure 3.2, our underlying needs form a pyramid. At the bottom of the pyramid are our most basic needs, such as the biological needs that drive our behavior, including food, water, sleep, and sex. The basic needs are not much different from those that drive the behavior of nonhuman animals. The needs on the next higher level of the pyramid are safety needs; we need a safe, secure environment to function effectively.

But as humans are able to meet their more-basic survival needs, they have a chance to become acquainted with levels of need that relate to more-advanced qualities, such as the need for love. As the pyramid indicates, our love and belongingness needs come next: our need to form relationships with others and to look outside ourselves. We seek to give affection and to be contributing members of groups within society.

After these needs are fulfilled, we strive for the esteem of others. Esteem relates to the desire to develop a sense of self-worth. We want others to be aware of our competence and worth and to acknowledge our value in the world.

Only after we meet these physiological, safety, love and belongingness, and esteem needs can we strive for self-actualization. Although early views of self-actualization restricted this quality to a few well-known individuals, self-actualization is now generally regarded as a concept that can apply to any of us.

For instance, a parent with excellent nurturing skills who raises a family, a teacher who year after year creates an environment that maximizes students'

Self-actualization
A state of self-fulfillment in which people realize their highest potential in their own unique way

> "Authentic values are those by which a life can be lived."
> Allan Bloom, author

Teaching Tip: Don't forget to constantly link the information about values, motivation, self concept, etc. to learning preferences and the goal of academic success.

Discussion Prompt: Connect a discussion on motivation to the goals students set for themselves in Chapter 1, i.e.; "Why am I going to college?"

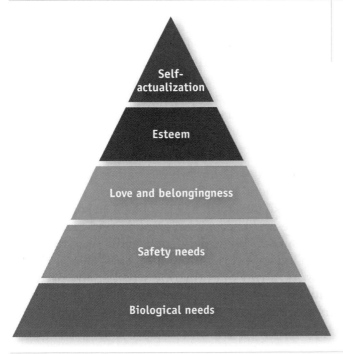

FIGURE 3.2
Pyramid of Motivational Needs

5

TRY IT!

Write a Mission Statement

1. What are your most important values (e.g., comfort, environmental awareness, kindness to others, inner harmony, challenge, etc.)?

2. What are your motivational needs (e.g., love and belonging, esteem, self-actualization)?

3. In what general area or career do you wish to work?

4. What will be your most important "product," for which you want to be known and remembered (e.g., good deeds, wealth, power, prestige, artistic creations, business acumen, etc.)?

5. What kind of person do you want to be (helpful, kind, solitary, powerful, wealthy, etc.)?

6. In what sort of community do you want to live (large city, small city, small town, suburbs, country, woods, farm, etc.)?

7. With whom do you want to live (e.g., spouse, friends, children, etc.)?

8. What words describe your ideal lifestyle (e.g., sophisticated, woodsy, agricultural, down-home, laid back, ambitious, etc.)?

Now write your mission statement. You might, for example, state how you plan to achieve your motivational needs and realize your values through your chosen career. Next you might describe the sort of person you want to be and the "product" you plan to contribute to the world. Finally, you might describe your intended lifestyle, including the type of community you would like to live in and the nature of your ideal family.

To Try It online, go to **www.mhhe.com/power**.

Personal Mission Statement

Prepared by: _____

Date: _____

Identifying Your Interests

Creating a personal mission statement can help you think more productively about one the most important decisions of your college career: identifying your profession. One way to jump-start this process is to systematically identify your current interests, a critical step in determining what kind of work will be most fulfilling and satisfying for you.

However, few of us are fully aware of the complete range of our interests, primarily because we don't take the time to systematically inventory them. Consequently, career advisor Richard Bolles[5] suggests answering the following questions in order to identify the scope of your interests:

■ What are your favorite subjects and hobbies?

■ What do you like to talk about most?

■ When you go to a newsstand, what are the subjects of magazines that you are attracted to?

■ When you read a newspaper, what section do you read first?

■ If you're wandering around a bookstore, what kinds of books do you spend the most time looking at?

■ When you surf the World Wide Web, what sites do you find yourself returning to regularly?

■ When you watch TV game shows, what categories would you choose?

■ If you were to write a book, what would you write about?

■ When you get so engrossed in thought that you lose track of time, what is it you are thinking about?

Once you've got a better grip on your interests after answering each of these questions, the next step is to prioritize them, rank-ordering them from most interesting to least interesting. You can then use this rank-ordered list to investigate careers, seeking out work involving interests similar to your own. For example, if you have strong interests in the visual arts, you might explore careers involving graphic design, computer-assisted graphics, or architecture. If you avidly keep up with the news of the day, you might consider journalism or television news production. The critical point is to try to match what you like to do (as well as your learning and personality style strengths) with what you'll be doing when you're on the job. The closer the match, the happier and more successful you'll be.

Sound familiar? Many of us have heard suggestions like these proposed by parents or others close to us. Such comments often sound quite reasonable.

Why, then, should suggestions like these be taken with great caution? The reason is they relate to decisions that you, and only you, should make. You are the one who must live with their consequences. You are the one who must live with yourself.

One of the worst reasons to follow a particular path in life is that other people want you to. Decisions that affect your life should be your decisions—decisions you make after you've considered various alternatives and chosen the path that suits you best.

Making your own decisions does not mean that you should ignore the suggestions of others. For instance, your parents do have their own unique experiences that may make their advice helpful, and having participated in a great deal of your personal history, they may have a clear view of your strengths and weaknesses. Still, their views are not necessarily accurate. They may still see you as a child, in need of care and protection. Or they may see only your strengths. Or, in some unfortunate cases, they may focus only on your flaws and shortcomings.

People will always be giving you advice. Ultimately, though, you have to make your own judgments about what's right for you, following your head—and your heart.

Discussion Prompt: Recreate a childhood moment. Have students share a dream for the future. Ask them to respond to "if I could be anything I want to be" or a speech they might give in 10-20 years as the graduation speaker.

SPEAKING OF
Success

Name: Bill Cosby

School: B.A., Temple University;
Ed.D., University of Massachusetts

When comedian Bill Cosby received his Doctor of Education degree at the age of 40, he recounts that his mother was the happiest person at the graduation ceremony. According to Cosby, "She said to me, 'You finally got something that you can fall back on.' "[6]

Whether or not Cosby's mother actually believed what she said, it is clear that Cosby thinks that educational success has been a key part of his life. "I feel that school, achieving education and going higher, is something that I wanted to do for myself," he said.

He didn't start out in life as an educational success story. Attending school in the Philadelphia ghetto with friends Fat Albert, Old Weird Harold, Dumb Donald, and others who were later immortalized in his comedy routines, Cosby performed so poorly in the classroom that he was forced to repeat the 10th grade. He dropped out of high school and joined the Navy. Eventually, he finished high school through a correspondence course, realizing that he had to "use the intelligence I was born with."[7]

Cosby became determined to further his education. After completing his stint in the Navy, he enrolled at Temple University, supported by a football scholarship. His goal was to become a physical education teacher.

At Temple, Cosby's schedule was hectic; he was a member of several sports teams, and he also had a number of part-time jobs. His most serious commitment, however, was to academics, and he maintained a B average. He commented, "If I didn't make good at Temple, I knew what waited for me was a lifetime as a busboy or factory hand. I was so afraid that I made myself do well. On an evening when all I wanted was to go out with the boys, the specter of what might happen to me reared up, and boom, I was right back in my room studying."[8]

Cosby's life took another turn when, while in college, he began to work as a part-time bartender. Customers found him hilarious, and they encouraged him to take his brand of comedy on the road. The rest is legend: After graduating from Temple, he became one of the most successful comedians of our era.

Cosby has remained committed to education even after achieving fame and riches as an entertainer. Years after completing his undergraduate degree, he enrolled in a graduate program at the University of Massachusetts, where he received both a master's and a doctoral degree in education.

Cosby has supported various educational institutions with huge gifts, including $20 million to Spelman College in Atlanta. He sees education as a noble enterprise, saying, "Things are not all that hard as long as someone is there to explain it to you, and we should not be afraid of those things."

What are my learning styles, and how have they affected my academic success?

- People have patterns of diverse learning styles—characteristic ways of acquiring and using knowledge.

- Learning styles include visual/verbal, visual/nonverbal, auditory/verbal, and tactile/kinesthetic styles (the receptive learning styles), and analytic and relational styles (information-processing styles).

- Personality styles that influence learning are classified along dimensions of introversion/extraversion, intuition/sensing, thinking/feeling, and perceiving/judging.

What is self-concept and how does it affect me?

- Self-concept is the understanding of the self that a person forms over time. Its major components are the physical, social, and personal selves.

- Self-concept is important because of the effects it has on people's attitudes and behavior. Self-concept can act as a self-fulfilling prophecy, in that people act in accordance with their self-concepts.

How does my level of self-esteem affect my behavior?

- Self-esteem is the overall evaluation we give ourselves as individuals.

- High self-esteem can lead to greater happiness, an enhanced ability to cope with adversity, a sense of security and confidence, and a sense of self-efficacy.

- Low self-esteem can lead to insecurity, low self-efficacy, and a cycle of failure.

How can I make wise personal decisions throughout life?

- A personal mission statement can be used to determine important values and to state the principles by which we intend to lead our lives.

- People's needs can be organized into a hierarchy in which the most basic and fundamental needs form the base of a pyramid and higher-order needs sit atop the basic needs.

- Although we should consider the ideas and opinions of others, we need to make our own decisions and choose our own path.

KEY TERMS AND CONCEPTS

Learning style (p. 61)
Receptive learning style (p. 62)
Visual/verbal learning style (p. 62)
Visual/nonverbal learning style (p. 62)
Auditory/verbal learning style (p. 63)
Tactile/kinesthetic learning style (p. 63)
Analytic learning style (p. 66)
Relational learning style (p. 66)

Left-brain processing (p. 70)
Right-brain processing (p. 70)
Self-concept (p. 72)
Self-fulfilling prophecy (p. 73)
Self-esteem (p. 75)
Self-efficacy (p. 75)
Personal Mission Statement (p. 79)
Self-actualization (p. 81)

On Campus

If you are interested in learning more about your pattern of learning styles, visit your campus counseling center or career center, where you may be able to take special assessment tests that can pinpoint your learning preferences and offer study strategies based on those preferences.

When dealing with the uncertainties of life and establishing your own sense of direction, it may help to speak to someone who has perspective and experience with college students. Here, too, a good place to start on campus is either a general counseling center or one that is designed to help students choose career paths. Mental health offices can also be helpful in putting you in touch with a therapist with whom you can explore issues revolving around your self-concept and self-esteem. Don't hesitate to get help. You are doing it for yourself.

In Print

Gail Wood's book *How to Study: Use Your Personal Learning Style to Help You Succeed When It Counts* (Learning Express Press, 2000) provides an introduction to learning styles, offering tips and suggestions for making use of the way that you learn.

In addition, David Keirsey's *Please Understand Me II* (Prometheus Nemesis, 1998) and Linda Beren's *Understanding Yourself and Others* (Telos, 2000) offer insight into different personality types.

Don't Sweat the Small Stuff . . . and It's All Small Stuff (Hyperion, 1997), written by Richard Carlson, is a down-to-earth guide that is meant to help you sort out what is—and is not—important in your life.

On the Web

Many sites on the World Wide Web provide the opportunity to extend your learning about the material in this chapter. (Although the Web addresses were accurate at the time the book was printed, check the P.O.W.E.R. Learning Web site [**www.mhhe.com/power**] for any changes that may have occurred.)

- Greg Kearsley, an instructional designer and online course developer at Walden Institute, has developed a useful site called "Explorations in Learning & Instruction: The Theory into Practice Database" (**tip.psychology.org/index.html**). This database contains short summaries of 50 major theories of learning and instruction.

- Bulls Eye Consultancy (a human resources firm) provides a basic self-assessment process (**www.bulls-eye.nl/self_1.php**) to help you clarify your values or beliefs. Use this to help you write a personal mission statement.

- The Barksdale Foundation, a nonprofit organization offering "self-esteem and stress control materials and programs," hosts a detailed, online self-esteem evaluation (**barksdale.org/Evaluation/eval69.html**). Simply click which response best describes how you feel about each statement. When you're done, click the submit button and your score will be automatically calculated.

1   To help you write your own mission statement, Mental Help Net (an online guide to mental health, psychology, and psychiatry) offers a Web site entitled "Writing Your Own Philosophy of Life" (**www.mentalhelp.net/psyhelp/chap3/chap3k.htm**), in which a list of goals is grouped in three categories. Use your responses to help you create a mission statement.

2   Go to the University of South Florida's Counseling Center Web site entitled "Building Self-Esteem" (**www.usfweb2.usf.edu/counsel/self-hlp/self-est.htm**). Write down the six strategies listed there for enhancing your self-esteem. How do these suggestions compare to the suggestions offered in this book? Now use a search engine to locate other sources of information about raising self-esteem. (Possible search term: the phrase "raising self-esteem," in quotes.) Did you locate any other suggestions for raising self-esteem? How do they compare to the suggestions in this book?

When he sat himself down in the front row of his biology class at the start of his second semester in college, Hill Taylor realized that something fundamental had changed.

In the past, Hill would have sat as far back in the classroom as he could. That's what he had done all through high school and the beginning of his first semester.

But then he received C's on three midterms.

In a notetaking workshop Hill enrolled in afterward, he learned the importance of active listening and taking good notes in class. He also learned that one way to become more engaged in class is to sit close to the instructor.

Trying out the strategies he was taught in the workshop, Hill found—a bit to his surprise—that they helped. By the end of the semester, he'd pulled his grades way up.

LOOKING AHEAD >>>

Hill Taylor's move from the back to the front of the classroom was both a source and a symbol of his academic success. Hill's ability to take good notes is also likely to pay future dividends, because notetaking skills not only help produce academic success in college but also contribute to career success.

In this chapter we discuss effective strategies for taking notes during class lectures, during other kinds of oral presentations, and from written sources such as textbooks. There's a lot more to good notetaking than you probably think—and a lot less if you view notetaking as essentially "getting everything down on paper." As we explore the ins

and outs of notetaking, we'll pause along the way to discuss the tools of the notetaking trade, how to be an active learner, how to think your way to good notes, and how to deal with disorganized instructors.

After reading this chapter, you'll be able to answer these questions:

■ **What is effective notetaking?**

■ **How can I take good notes in class?**

■ **What techniques apply to taking notes from written materials?**

Taking Notes in Class

You know the type: the student who desperately tries to write down everything the instructor says—no spoken word goes unwritten. And you know what you think to yourself: "If only I took such painstaking notes—I'd do much better in my classes."

Contrary to what many students think, good notetaking does not mean writing down every word that an instructor utters. With notetaking, less is often more. We'll see why as we consider the basic steps in P.O.W.E.R. notetaking.

P REPARE: Considering Your Goals

As with other academic activities, preparation is a critical component of notetaking. The following steps will prepare you for action:

■ **Identify the instructor's—and your—goals for the course.** On the first day of class, most instructors talk about their objectives, what they hope you'll get out of the class, and what you'll know when it's over. Most restate the information on the class syllabus, the written document that explains the assignments for the semester. For example, they may say that they want you to "develop an appreciation for the ways that statistics are used in everyday life."

The information you get during that first session and through the syllabus is critical. If the instructor's goals aren't stated explicitly, you should attempt to figure them out. In addition to those "external" goals, you should have your own goals. What is it you want to learn from the course? How will the information from the course help you to enhance your knowledge, achieve your dreams, improve yourself as a person?

■ **Complete assignments before coming to class.** Your instructor enthusiastically describes the structure of the neuron, recounting excitedly how neurons don't physically touch one another and how electrons flow across neurons, changing their electrical charge. One problem: You have only the vaguest idea what a neuron is. And the reason you don't know is that you haven't read the assignment.

Chances are you have found yourself in this situation at least a few times, so you know firsthand that sinking feeling as you become more and more confused. Because you can't follow the discussion, you can't get interested either, so the class seems boring, and you end up thinking about what you'll have for lunch or the movie you saw last night.

The moral: Always go to class prepared. Do all of your assignments beforehand. Instructors assume that their students have done what they've assigned, and their lectures are based upon that assumption. It's virtually impossible to catch on to the gist of a lecture if you haven't completed the assignments.

■ **Accept the instructor, warts and all.** Not every instructor is a brilliant lecturer. Accept the fact that, just as there are differences in skills among students, some instructors are more adept at lecturing than others. Ultimately, it's your responsibility to overcome a lecturer's flaws. A bad lecturer is not an excuse to do poorly or to give up. Don't let a miserable lecture style—or the fact that the instructor has a bad haircut or a mouth that droops to one side or

PREPARE
Consider your goals

ORGANIZE
Get the tools of notetaking together

WORK
Process—don't copy—information

EVALUATE
Think critically about your notes

RETHINK
Review your notes shortly after class to activate your memory

P.O.W.E.R. Plan

> **"The highest result of education is tolerance."**
>
> Helen Keller, author

	3 ways to store information
	sensory memory—everything sensed
aka working memory (like	short term memory—15-25 sec.
Computer RAM)	Stored as meaning
	5-9 chunks
(like hard disk)	long-term memory—unlimited
Rehearsal: STM to LTM	rehearsal
	visualization
Chunking	Organize information into chunks:
	birds, instruments, body parts, etc.
	Mnemonics
Roy G. Biv	acronyms
Every good boy deserves fun	acrostics
30 days hath September	rhyming
Unfinished Symphony	jingles
pato, caballo	keyword technique
room and furniture	loci technique
sun, zoo, me, store . . .	peg method
	Using senses
	moving
	draw, diagram
	visualize
	Overlearning

FIGURE 4.1

A Notetaking Sample

In this example of a student's notes on a lecture about memory, she has written the material in the larger right-hand column during class. Later, when reviewing her notes, she wrote down key pieces of information in the left-hand column.

Teaching Tip: Point out that not needing the text during class does not mean that students are not expected to read it prior to class.

- **Consider taking a laptop to class.** If you have a laptop and you're comfortable with computers, you might want to use it for taking notes in class. There are several advantages: Legibility problems are avoided, and it's easy to go back and revise or add material after you've taken the notes.

   There are also potential pitfalls. If you do intend to use a laptop for taking notes—and you've checked with your instructor to make sure that you have permission to bring it—remember these guidelines:

   1. Make sure your computer battery is fully charged.

   2. Use a computer that has a quiet keyboard so you don't annoy your follow students, and make sure the built-in speaker is turned off. A tablet PC, which allows you to write on the screen in the same way you write with paper and pencil, may be the best choice.

   3. If the classroom is equipped with wireless Internet reception, avoid the temptation to surf the Web or check your e-mail.

   4. Finally, have an alternative, low-tech notetaking backup. Sometimes instructors present graphical material or formulas that are hard to input into a computer via a keyboard. And sometimes your computer may fail.

Using a laptop to take class notes ensures that they will be legible and that it will be easy to revise them after class. On the other hand, it's difficult to input graphical material, such as complex formulas, and there's also a danger that you'll be tempted to take too many notes.

W ORK: Processing—Not Copying—Information

With pen poised, you're ready to begin the work of notetaking. The instructor begins to speak, and you start to write as quickly as you can, taking down as many of the instructor's words as possible.

Stop! You've made your first mistake. The central act in taking notes is not writing; listening and thinking are far more important. The key to effective notetaking is to write down the right amount of information—not too much and not too little.

Successful notetaking involves not just *hearing* what the instructor says, but *listening actively.* **Hearing** is the involuntary act of sensing sounds. The annoying drip of a faucet or the grating sound of a roommate's voice speaking on the phone in the next room are two examples of how hearing is both involuntary and often meaningless. In contrast, **active listening** is the voluntary act of focusing on what is being said, making sense of it, and thinking about it in a way that permits it to be recalled accurately. Listening involves concentration. And it requires shutting out competing thoughts, such as what we need to pick up at the grocery store or why our date last night was so terrific. (To get a sense of your own listening skills, complete Try It 1 on page 98.)

Keeping the importance of active listening in mind, consider the following recommendations for taking notes:

- **Listen for the key ideas.** Not every sentence in a lecture is equally important, and one of the most useful skills you can develop is separating the key

Hearing
The involuntary act of sensing sounds

Active listening
The voluntary act of focusing on what is being said, making sense of it, and thinking about it in a way that permits it to be recalled accurately

Student Alert: The outline form works best with instructors who use it to create their lectures. It is generally not a useful format for discussion classes.

Note how the lecturer used almost 120 words, while the notes used only around 35 words—less than a third of the lecture.

- **Use abbreviations.** One way to speed up the notetaking process is through the use of abbreviations. Among the most common:

and	& or +	with	w/	without	w/o
care of	c/o	leads to; resulting in	→	as a result of	←
percent	%	change	Δ	number	#
that is	i.e.	for example	e.g.	and so forth	etc.
no good	n.g.	question	?	compared with	c/w
page	p.	important!	!!	less than	<
more than	>	equals, same as	=	versus	vs.

- **Take notes in outline form.** It's often useful to take notes in the form of an outline. An outline summarizes ideas in short phrases and indicates the relationship among concepts through the use of indentations.

  When outlining, it's best to be formal about it, using roman numerals, regular numbers, and capital and small letters (see the example in Figure 4.2). Or, if

FIGURE 4.2
A Sample Outline

I. Difficulties faced by college students seeking affordable housing
  A. Students subjected to high rents close to campus
    1. Forced to share apartments
    2. Sometimes must live far from campus
  B. Made to sign harsh leases
II. Possible solutions
  A. College offers subsidized housing
    1. Advantage: Housing costs can be lowered
    2. Potential problems
      a. College becomes students' landlord
      b. College uses funds for housing instead of investing in education
  B. Rent control
    1. Advantage: Can provide fixed, reasonably priced rents
    2. Disadvantages
      a. Creates permanent expensive rent-control bureaucracy
      b. Landlords may neglect rent-control property
      c. Little incentive for owners to increase the number of rental units
      d. Strong competition for rent-fixed units
III. Summary
  A. Advantages and disadvantages to both solutions
  B. May need new, creative solutions

you prefer, you can also simply use outlining indentations without assigning numbers and letters.

Outlining serves a number of functions. It forces you to try to determine the structure of the lecture. Organizing the key points and noting the connections among them helps you remember the material better because you have processed it more. The effort involved in outlining also keeps your mind from drifting away from the lecture.

Use Try It 2 on pages 102 and 103, "Outline a Lecture," to practice your outlining skills.

Teaching Tip: Ask students to take notes on a chapter in this text using the outline format.

■ **Copy information written on the board or projected from overheads or PowerPoint Slides.** If your instructor takes the time to write something out to be displayed in class, you should take the time to copy it. This goes for definitions, quotations, phrases, and formulas—if you see them in writing, they're quite likely important enough to include in your notes. In fact, material displayed prominently has "test item" written all over it. You might want to highlight such material in some way in your notes.

■ **Use different notetaking techniques for class discussions.** Not every course is structured as a lecture. Classes that are based less on lectures and more on class discussion pose greater challenges for notetaking.

Asking questions in class does more than just provide you with the opportunity to clarify points you don't understand. It often will make you feel more a part of the class, and it will encourage other students to participate.

Discussion Prompt: What do your students do about information presented on an overhead or through a PowerPoint presentation that they missed? Can they request copies of this information from their faculty members? Why or why not?

Take Notes during Discussions

Take notes on the following class discussion about the growth of English as a global language. Use cues from the instructor about the importance and accuracy of each point, and record in your notes only the key points that shed light on the topic.

Instructor: OK, so why is English so important globally, not just in English-speaking countries?

Alicia: Um, well, English is spoken by a lot of people. When I was in Denmark last summer, everyone spoke it. It just seems to be everywhere.

Instructor: OK. It's certainly a very widely used language. But we're trying to figure out why. We're looking for causes, not just symptoms, right? Anyone else? Bart?

Bart: Yeah, English is becoming, like, everyone's second language simply because it has established a good base. Not only did the *English* English people—you know, the British—spread the language all over through colonizing the world—you know, the sun never sets on the British Empire and all—but now America is everywhere, too. I mean, we're cool—our culture is cool and very influencing.

Instructor: Good, good. Yes, you've given two good reasons why English is widespread. The British Empire spread the language through parts of Asia, Africa, and the Caribbean in the 18th and 19th centuries, and modern U.S. culture is highly influential, which causes many people worldwide to welcome English. What else?

Catherine: Well, the way in which the American culture is spreading is very much language-centered. It's American movies and music that are everywhere, and these involve the language, not just the style. I mean, people know a lot more than how to say Coca-Cola and Nike, don't they? They listen to American CDs and movies, and they even produce songs and movies in English. So it's not just culture we're spreading, it's our language too.

Instructor: Exactly! The language is perhaps the most important aspect of the culture that we're distributing. Damon?

Damon: Yeah, I was just going to say, another thing that's caused the language to spread is global communications, which are just about always in English. Look at the language of aviation—pilots talk to each other in English, don't they? And the Internet. The universal language of the Internet is English. So if you want to communicate globally, and now everyone does because for the first time everyone *can,* you've got to pick up some English.

Rosario: Right. It's the universal second language. And it will only get more universal as American culture spreads further and other cultures develop to the point of being able to join the party—communicating, and buying stuff and listening to our music and so on. I mean, it's the biggest game in town, and it's spoken by the people with the biggest wallets. Money talks, you know. And now it talks American English.

Instructor: You've really hit it now. Language has always gone where the resources are. If someone has what you want, you'd better speak their language. Money speaks American English. Very well put, Rosario! Excellent discussion, folks.

Write your notes here:

Were you able to identify the information that was most important? How would actually seeing the instructor's nonverbal reactions to the students' comments be helpful?

Working in a Group:

Compare your notes on the discussion with these of your classmates. As a group, try to create an optimal set of notes, reflecting the most important points.

To Try It online, go to **www.mhhe.com/power**.

There's another option: Many instructors teach multiple sections of the same course. If this is the case, you might, schedule permitting, sit in on an additional section of the course. The second time around the information may become much clearer.

6. *Talk with the instructor after class.* If you feel totally lost after a lecture, or even if you've missed only a few points, speak with the instructor after class. Ask for clarification and get him or her to reexplain points that you missed. Such a dialogue will help you to understand the material better. But it will also do something more: help build your relationship with your instructor.

   In the very rare case in which an instructor oversteps the bounds of decency, either by harshly putting students down, making discriminatory racial, ethnic, or religious remarks, or acting in a sexually harrassing manner, immediately report the matter to someone in the college administration. The appropriate person might be a department chair or dean of students. Such behavior is not only offensive, but in many cases illegal.

Keep a Balance between Too Many Notes and Too Few Notes

The key to effective notetaking is to keep a balance between too many and too few notes.

The best way to achieve this balance is by paying close attention in class. By being alert, engaged, and involved in class, you'll be able to make the most of the techniques we've discussed. The result: notes that capture the most important points raised in class and that will optimize your recall and mastery of the course subject matter (see a sample of two students' notes in Figure 4.3).

E VALUATE: Thinking Critically about Your Notes

IRM Link: Teaching the Text, Chapter 4, Section VII, see the ideas in connection to the individual student's life.

Toward the end of class, take a moment to look over your notes. Now's the time—before the class has ended—to evaluate what you've written.

After being sure you can answer "yes" to the most basic question—can I read what I've written?—ask yourself these questions:

- Do my notes do a good job of representing what was covered in class?
- Do they reflect the emphases of the instructor?
- Are there any key points that are not entirely clear?
- Do I need help clarifying any of the points my instructor made?

Evaluating your notes is a critical part of the notetaking process. You can get a sense of how effective your notetaking has been while you still have a chance to ask your instructor to clarify anything that is still not clear.

Perhaps, for example, you've left out a keyword in a definition. Maybe you don't understand a concept fully, even though you've written about it in your notes. Possibly you've left out the third step in a list of six steps necessary to accomplish something.

If you look over your notes while you're still in class, you have time to ask your instructor for clarification. Or you can wait till the end of class and raise your question privately. Most instructors will be happy to answer questions from students who have obviously been actively listening. Just make sure that you add what they tell you to your notes so you'll be able to refer to them later. (To practice evaluating your notes, complete Try It 4 on page 110.)

Here is an instructor's introductory lecture on Toni Morrison's *Beloved*. At the bottom of the page are two students' notes. Which student—A or B—did a better job of capturing the important points in the lecture?

FIGURE 4.3
Notes on a Lecture

Instructor: In today's class, we'll discuss Toni Morrison's *Beloved*. As I'm sure you all know, Morrison is both a popular and an acclaimed author—and it's not easy to be both. Born Chloe Anthony Wofford in 1931, Morrison has written some of the most affecting and intelligent works on the African- American experience ever written by anyone, and yet to call her an "African-American writer" doesn't seem to do her justice. In many ways, she is simply an American writer—and certainly one of our best.

Beloved is a truly remarkable work. It was nominated for nearly every major literary prize, including the National Book Award and the National Book Critics Circle Award, and it in fact won the Pulitzer Prize for fiction in 1988. Morrison herself is distinguished for having won the Nobel Prize for literature in 1993.

What makes *Beloved* unique is the skillful, sure way in which Morrison blends intensely personal storytelling and American history, racial themes and gender themes, the experience of Blacks with the experience of all people everywhere, the gritty down-to-earth reality of slavery with a sense of mystical spirituality.

We will be paying special attention to these themes as we discuss this work. I am particularly interested in your views on the relative importance of race and gender in this book. Is it more important that Sethe, the main character, is black or that she's a woman? Which contributes more to her being? How does Morrison use both race and gender to drive her plot? What does she tell us about both?

Student A Notes

Toni Morrison's *Beloved*

— Morrison popular and acclaimed author, not easy to be both
— Cloe Anthony?
— effective and intelligent African American writer
— *Beloved* won National Book Award, Pulitzer 1988, Nobel Prize 1993
— gritty reality of spirituality and slavery
— Seth a black woman—what does this tell us?

Student B Notes

Toni Morrison's *Beloved*

— M. both popular and respected; many awards
— more than "Afr. Amer. writer"—a great
— Amer. writer
Beloved:
   blend of personal and historical,
   race and gender themes,
   Black experience and universal experience,
   reality and spirituality
— Is it more imp. that Sethe is Black or female? (race/gender?)
— How race & gender move plot?

Taking notes helps prevent daydreaming during class, because it gives you something to do besides listening passively to an instructor.

POWER

4
TRY IT!

Evaluate Your Class Notes

Take a set of notes you made recently during one of your classes and evaluate it on the following criteria.

Statement	Not Even Slightly	Slightly	Moderately	Pretty Well	Very Well
1. I can read my notes (i.e., they are legible).					
2. Someone else can read my notes.					
3. My notes are complete; I missed nothing important.					
4. My notes represent the key points that were covered in class.					
5. My notes reflect the instructor's emphases.					
6. The instructor's key points are clear and understandable.					
7. The notes contain only important points, with no extraneous material.					
8. I understand not only the notes but also the class content they reflect.					
9. Using only the notes, I will be able to reconstruct the essential content of the class in 3 months.					

🚶 Working in a Group:

What do your answers tell you about the effectiveness of your notetaking skills? What might you do differently the next time you take notes?

Evaluate and compare the notes you took during the previous 20 minutes of the class you are in now. How do your notes compare with those of the other members of your group?

To Try It online, go to **www.mhhe.com/power**.

RETHINK: Activating Your Memory

The lecture has ended and class is over. You put the top on your pen, close your notebook, stash everything in your backpack, and head out for a cup of coffee before your next class.

Wait! Before you close up your notebook, finish the P.O.W.E.R. process. Rethink what you've heard. Spending 5 or 10 minutes reconsidering what you've written right now can save you *hours* of work later. The reason: Rethinking promotes the transfer of information into long-term memory (something discussed more in Chapter 8). As you link the new information you've taken down to what you already know and then integrate it, you essentially plug this information into your memory in a much more meaningful way, which means you can remember it better and more easily.

> **"I'd think to myself 'I don't need to write that down, I'll remember it.' A few days later, it was like, "*what* did he say . . . ?"**
>
> Student, Duke University[4]

If you looked over your notes to clarify and evaluate the information in them in class, you've already begun the process. But once class is over, you need to review the material more formally. Here's how to do it:

- **Rethink as soon as possible.** Time is of the essence! The rethinking phase of notetaking doesn't have to take long; 5 to 10 minutes are usually sufficient. The more critical issue is *when* you do it. The longer you wait before reviewing your notes, the less effective the process will be.

  There's no doubt that the best approach is to review the material just after the class has ended. As everyone else is leaving, just stay seated and go over your notes. This works fine for classes late in the day, when no other class is scheduled in the room. But what if you must vacate the room immediately after class? The next best thing is to find a quiet space somewhere nearby and do your rethinking there.

  In any case, don't let the day end without examining your notes. In fact, reconsidering material just before you go to sleep can be particularly effective.

- **Make rethinking an active process.** Some people feel the notes they take in class are akin to historical documents in a museum, with Do Not Touch! signs hanging on them. On the contrary, think of your notes as a construction project and yourself as the person in charge of the project.

  When you review your notes, do so with an eye to improving them. If any information is not entirely clear, change the wording in your notes, adding to or amending what's there. If certain words are hard to read, fix them; it won't be any easier to read them the night before a test—in fact, chances are you'll have even more trouble.

  If, on rethinking the material, you don't understand something, ask your instructor or a friend to clarify it. And when you receive an explanation, add it to your notes so you won't forget it. (You might want to use a different-colored pen for additions to your notes, so you'll know they came later.)

- **Think critically about the material in your notes.** As you review the information, think about the material from a critical point of view. Go beyond the facts and pieces of information, integrating and evaluating the material.

  In addition, as you rethink your notes, don't think of them only in terms of a single lecture or a single class. Instead, take a longer view. Ask yourself how they fit into the broader themes of the class and the goals that you and the instructor have for the semester. How will the information be useful to you? Why did the instructor emphasize a particular point?

If you've configured your notes by leaving a 2½-inch column on the left-hand side of the page, now is the time to make use of that blank column. Write down keywords, significant points, major concepts, controversies, and questions. The process of adding this information will not only help you to rethink the material now, it will also provide guideposts when you study before a test.

Concept mapping
A method of structuring written material by graphically grouping and connecting key ideas and themes

■ **Create concept maps. Concept mapping** (Sometimes called "mind mapping") is a method of structuring written material by graphically grouping and connecting key ideas and themes. In contrast to an outline, a concept map visually illustrates how related ideas fit together. The pictorial summary gives you another handle to store the information in memory, and it focuses your thinking on the key ideas from the lecture.

In a concept map, each key idea is placed in a different part of the map, and related ideas are placed near it—above, below, or beside it. What emerges does not have the rigid structure of an outline. Instead, a "finished" concept map looks something like a map of the solar system, with the largest and most central idea in the center (the "sun" position), and related ideas surrounding it at various distances. It has also been compared to a large tree, with numerous branches and subbranches radiating out from a central trunk. (Figure 4.4 presents a sample concept map.)

Student Alert: Notetaking is like time management. There are daily notes that support the overall course goals just like daily to-do lists support the semester (and lifetime) plan. Help students to make the connection between daily habits and "the bigger picture."

Building a concept map has several advantages. It forces you to rethink the material in your notes in a new style—particularly important if you used traditional outlining while taking the notes. In addition, it helps you to tie together the material for a given class session. Finally, it will help you to build a master concept map later, when you're studying the material for a final exam. (To practice in the techniques we've been discussing, see Try It 5 on page 114, "Practice Your Notetaking Skills.")

IRM Link: Teaching the Text, Chapter 4, Section IV and VIII; see the film activity.

Taking Notes as You Study

Weighing as much as five pounds, bulky and awkward, and filled with more information than you think anyone could ever need to know, it's the meat-and-potatoes of college life: your course textbook. You might feel intimidated by its size; you might be annoyed at its cost; you might think you'll never be able to read it, let alone understand, learn, and recall the material in it. How will you manage?

Study notes
Notes taken for the purpose of reviewing material

The answer involves taking **study notes,** notes taken for the purpose of reviewing material. They are the kind of notes that you take now to study from later. (We'll consider research notes, notes that you take to write a paper or prepare a report, in Chapter 7 when we discuss writing papers.)

Several strategies are useful for taking study notes from written material such as magazines, books, journals, and Web sites. Which approach works best depends on whether you're able to write on the material you wish to take notes on.

Taking Notes on Material You Can Write On

Here are some suggestions for creating study notes for material you own, on which you're free to annotate the text directly by underlining, highlighting, or writing in the margins:

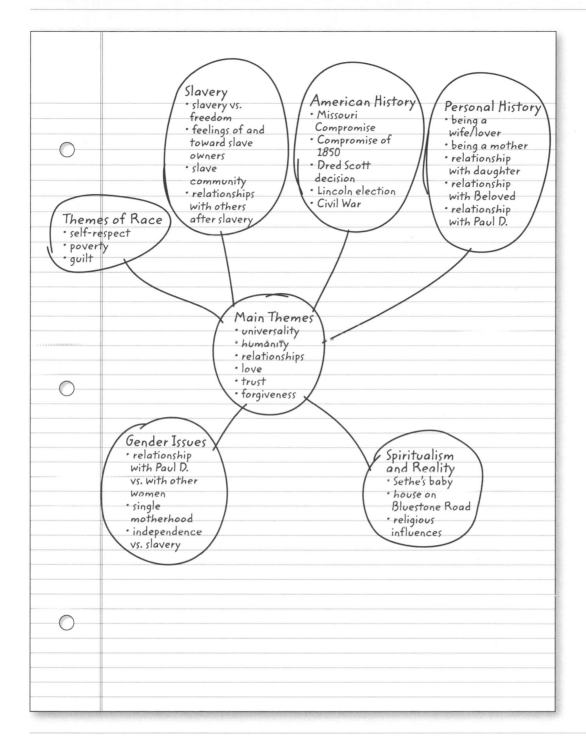

FIGURE 4.4

A Concept Map of Toni Morrison's *Beloved*

■ **Integrate your text notes into your study notes.** Start by annotating the pages, using the techniques that work best for you: highlighting, underlining, circling, making marginal notes. (These techniques are discussed in detail in Chapter 7; you may want to look ahead to that discussion.) Keep in mind that writing on the text, by itself, is not sufficient to promote learning—it's what you do next that counts.

Specifically, after you've finished reading and annotating the material, create study notes. The study notes should provide a summary of

Teaching Tip: Encourage students to argue with the author, create questions, circle new or important words, and/or write their own ideas as they read. Point out that it is important to own the book.

5

Practice Your Notetaking Skills

Practice your notetaking skills, using any techniques you find helpful, in one of the classes in which you are enrolled this term. Use these notes to answer these questions:

1. Which specific techniques did I use in taking notes?

2. Which of the notetaking techniques detailed in this chapter was I unable to use, and why?

3. Could I take the notes I made in class and redo them, using one of the techniques in this chapter, such as creating a concept map?

After you have taken notes, use the techniques discussed in this chapter to evaluate and rethink them. Creating a concept map on a separate sheet of paper may be particularly helpful.

To Try It online, go to **www.mhhe.com/power**.

Student Alert: Encourage students to review their notes each day before class.

Flash cards
Index cards that contain key pieces of information to be remembered

the key points, in outline form or in the form of concept maps. Either form of summary should supplement the annotations you've made on the printed page.

Furthermore, any notes you take should stand on their own. For instance, they should include enough information to be useful whether or not you have the book or article on hand.

■ **Use flash cards.** If you feel confident that the annotations you've written in the book are sufficiently comprehensive, you might consider taking notes on flash cards. **Flash cards** are simply index cards that contain key pieces of information that you need to remember.

Taking Notes on the Job: Meetings of the Minds

For many people, meetings take up a good part of their professional workdays and being able to take effective notes can provide a significant career advantage.

Meetings are similar to class discussions. During a meeting you will want to look for key topics and make note of the ideas that receive the most emphasis or enthusiastic response. Note these areas and keep them in mind as likely priorities.

During meetings, tasks are often assigned. Not only do you want to clearly note what you are to do and when you are supposed to do it, but keeping track of what others are doing will also be helpful, because you may need to get information from them or otherwise coordinate efforts. For instance, if you are assigned the task of managing the development of your company's Web site, you'll want to clarify in your notes who has agreed to do what portion of the task.

Taking notes when others are speaking also shows that you are paying attention to what the speaker is saying. It's a kind of compliment that suggests you find what the speaker is saying to be so important that you will want to refer to it later.

Finally, notetaking plays another role: It can make seemingly interminable meetings appear to proceed faster by providing something for you to do that's more active than simply listening. In short, not only can notetaking provide you with a clear record of what occurred in a meeting, but it can also keep you engaged in what is going on.

Flash cards are particularly useful in subjects that present many small bits of information to remember, such as foreign language vocabulary words or scientific formulas. When you need to learn a list of foreign words, for instance, you can write a foreign word on one side of a card and its English meaning on the other side.

One of the greatest virtues of flash cards is their portability. Because they are small, they can fit into your pocket or handbag, and you can look at them at odd times when you have a spare moment.

Taking Notes on Material You Can Write On

Taking notes on material that can't be written on is a different story. Library books, magazines, journal articles, and materials on library reserve that are shared with others require a different approach.

- **Approach the written material as you would a class lecture.** The techniques we discussed earlier for taking notes in class can all be adapted for taking notes from written material. In fact, the task is often easier, because, as is not the case with the spoken word, you'll be able to refer back to what was said earlier—it's in black and white in front of you.

- **Laptops can be especially helpful in creating study notes.** If you're a good keyboarder, it's often easier and quicker to take notes using a word-processing program. On the other hand, don't be lured into typing too much. You need to be just as selective in what you input into your computer as you would be in taking notes during a class lecture.

Student Alert: Make certain that your students understand that notes can and should be taken on print materials as well as lectures.

IRM Link: Teaching the Text, Chapter 4, Section V; EVALUATE. Make a direct connection between your students' evaluation of their notetaking and the grades they receive. If students are not satisfied with their grades, they might consider changing their notetaking style.

■ **Use the tricks of the trade we discussed earlier for taking notes from a class lecture.** Look for key ideas, definitions, quotations, and formulas, and include them in your notes. Use the headings that are included in the text, such as chapter and section titles. Bold or italic type is also a clue that an important point is being made. Graphs and charts often provide critical information.

■ **Use the same form of notetaking that you use in class lectures.** If you take notes in class using the two-column method (in which you reserve a 2½-inch column on the left-hand side of your paper for adding comments during later review of the notes), use that technique here as well. If you write your notes in outline form, create an outline based on the written material. If you often create graphics such as concept maps, create them now. The point is to produce notes that are consistent with those you take during class lectures.

SPEAKING OF
Success

Name: Kate Endress

School: Ball State University, Muncie, Indiana

Succeeding In college is hard work, but being successful both academically and outside the classroom takes exceptional commitment and work.

Kate Endress, a senior at Ball State University, knows this firsthand. She has been named an Academic All-American by earning nearly all A's and, at the same time, being a starter on her college basketball team.

It hasn't been easy juggling studies and athletics. But during her four years of college she developed a number of approaches that helped her meet the challenge.

"I try to make the most of my class time, including taking notes efficiently," she said. "Because I usually find the first test hardest, I often end up taking more notes than probably necessary.

"After that I try to get a feel for the kinds of questions the professor asks, be it definitions, lists, or conceptual questions," Endress added. "Then for the remaining tests, I star or highlight all sections of my notes that I think are potential test questions. I also fill my margins with little tidbits to help me remember certain sections, such as a story the professor told about a subject or an acronym."

Organization is also an important factor in Endress's academic success.

"I have a to-do list that I go over every night before I go to bed," she said. "I write down everything I need to do the next day and then prioritize it. This makes me very productive and I can get a lot of things done quickly. I also schedule down time for myself. For example, some days I'll schedule a long lunch."

Endress attributes her success to hard work and thoughtful preparation. "Although I thought I was fairly prepared when I went into college, college was much more of a challenge," she noted. "During my first semester I was forced to come up with ways for me to be more productive in class so I didn't have to spend every waking minute studying."

She added, "For me, taking good notes and actually learning the material in class cuts down on the amount of time I have to study outside of class."

What is effective notetaking?

■ The central feature of good notetaking is listening and distilling important information—not writing down everything that is said.

How can I take good notes in class?

■ Prepare for taking notes by identifying the instructor's and your own goals for the course, completing all assignments before arriving in class, and "warming up" for class by reviewing the notes and assignments from the previous class.

■ Before writing notes, listen and think, processing the information that the instructor is attempting to deliver.

■ Notes should be brief phrases rather than full sentences and, if possible, in outline form to reveal the structure of the lecture. Material written on the board should usually be copied word-for-word.

■ Before leaving class, evaluate your notes, verifying that they are complete and understandable while there is still time to correct them. As soon as possible after class, actively rethink your notes.

What techniques apply to taking notes from written materials?

■ Taking good study notes from written materials involves many of the principles that apply to taking good notes from oral presentations, although the source material can be consulted repeatedly, making it easier to get the information down accurately.

■ Concept maps and flash cards can be helpful tools for notetaking from textbooks.

KEY TERMS AND CONCEPTS

Hearing (p. 97)
Active listening (p. 97)
Meta-message (p. 98)

Concept mapping (p. 112)
Study notes (p. 112)
Flash cards (p. 114)

RESOURCES

On Campus

If you are having difficulty taking class notes effectively, talk with your course instructor. Bring your notes with you soon after a class has ended, and let the instructor assess what you are doing correctly and what could stand improvement.

If your problems persist, and you have great difficulty translating the spoken word into notes, then there's a small possibility that you suffer from an auditory learning disability. Be tested by your college learning disabilities office or counseling office to rule this out.

In Print

Judy Kesselman-Turkel and Franklynn Peterson's *Note-Taking Made Easy* (University of Wisconsin Press, 2003) provides a broad overview of how to take good notes in class, as does Bobbi DePorter and Mike Hernacki's *Quantum Notes* (Learning Forum, 2000).

In addition, Ron Fry's *Taking Notes* (Career Press, 1994) and *Noteworthy: Listening and Notetaking Skills* (2nd ed.), by Phyllis Lim and William Smalzer (William S. Hein & Co., 1996) provide a fine overview of strategies for increasing your listening and notetaking expertise.

On the Web

The following sites on the World Wide Web provide the opportunity to extend your learning about the material in this chapter. (Although the Web addresses were accurate at the time the book was printed, check the P.O.W.E.R. Learning Web site [**mhhe.com/power**] for any changes that may have occurred.)

- Brigham Young University's Career and Counseling Center offers this page (**www.byu.edu/stlife/cdc/learning/note-tak.php**) on the Cornell Notetaking System. This notetaking system can help you improve the organization of your notes, while allowing you to make use of your existing strengths as a notetaker.

- The University of Victoria's Learning Skills Program offers a tutorial in concept mapping at **www.coun.uvic.ca/learn/program/hndouts/class1.html**. (Other useful online information from this program can be found at **www.coun.uvic.ca/learn/**.)

- Take Note: How to Take Notes for a Student with a Disability (**www.stlcc.edu/fp/access/Stu/NoteHandout.html**) is a site offered by St. Louis Community College and presents a comprehensive outline on how to help a disabled student take notes. Also contains information on general notetaking as well.

TAKING IT TO THE NET

1 The best way to improve notetaking skills is to practice. Locate a current news story of interest on the Internet and take notes while reading it. Remember to leave the left margin large enough to add key points and summary information. One possible strategy is to go to the "News" section of the Yahoo! home page (**www.yahoo.com/**). Click on one of the news categories (e.g., Sports, Politics, Business, etc.) and look for a story that sounds interesting.

2 Taking notes during lectures is an important part of classroom learning, but keeping up with a speaker for an entire hour can be difficult. You can improve your notetaking skills for lectures by taking notes while listening to recorded speeches on the Internet. For example, go to an Internet site containing audio recordings of speeches (e.g., **www.pbs.org/newshour/vote2004/demconvention/speeches/obama.html**) and take notes while listening to a speech. Afterwards, go back and indicate the key points and terms in the left margin of your notes. You can check your comprehension by comparing the speech to news articles reporting on it. (You can also check the articles for bias!)

Teaching Tip: Ask students to review (and take notes on) the sites indicated and to report back to class their opinion of the usefulness of each one. Ask them to bring their notes to class.

THE CASE OF...

The Human Dictation Machine

Everyone wanted to borrow Lila Bauman's notes.

If they missed a class, or even if they had been there but had just spaced out, other students in Lila's classes knew that they could find out what had happened in class by borrowing her notes. It was all there in black and white. The woman was virtually a human dictation machine. She spent her time in class in a whirlwind of notetaking, writing down seemingly every word her instructor uttered in a clear, meticulous script. By the end of a term, her notebooks were so lengthy that they approached the size of telephone books from a small city.

The strange thing, though, was that—despite her copious notes—Lila was only a mediocre student. Before tests she studied her notes thoroughly, but she never seemed to get grades higher than a C+. She didn't know why, especially in light of what she saw as her notetaking expertise.

1. How do you think Lila defines "good notetaking"?

2. Why does Lila's method of notetaking produce such poor results? What is she missing?

3. If you asked Lila to summarize the instructor's main ideas after a class lecture, how successful do you think she would be? Why?

4. Do you think it would be easy or hard to study for a final exam using Lila's notes? Why?

5. Do you think Lila evaluates her notes during or after class? Do you think she ever rethinks them? What questions would you ask to help her perform these steps?

6. In general, what advice would you give Lila on notetaking?

Taking Tests

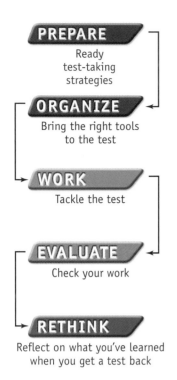

PREPARE
Ready test-taking strategies

ORGANIZE
Bring the right tools to the test

WORK
Tackle the test

EVALUATE
Check your work

RETHINK
Reflect on what you've learned when you get a test back

P.O.W.E.R. Plan

better again, and that your life is ruined. If you don't do well on a test, you're the same person you were before you took the test—no better, no worse. You just did badly on a test. Period.

In short, tests are not a measure of your value as an individual. They are only a measure of how well (and how much) you studied, and your test-taking skills. Tests are tools; they are indirect and imperfect measures of what we know. Someone with a great deal of knowledge can do poorly on a test; tension or going at too slow a pace can lead to unwelcome results in some cases. Another person may know considerably less and still do better on the test simply because he or she may have learned some test-taking skills along the way.

How we do on a test depends on a number of considerations: the kind of test it is, the subject matter involved, our understanding of test-taking strategies, and, above all, how well we prepare for it. Let's turn, then, to the first step in test-taking: preparation. (The five steps are summarized in the P.O.W.E.R. Plan on the left.)

P REPARE: Readying Your Test-Taking Strategies

Preparation for tests requires a number of strategies. Among the most important are the following:

Remember: Everything You Do in a Course Is Preparation for a Test

All the things you do during a course help to prepare you for a test. There is no surer way to get good grades on tests than to attend class faithfully and to complete all class assignments seriously and on time.

Preparing for tests is a long-term proposition. It's not a matter of "giving your all" the night before the test. Instead, it's a matter of giving your all to every aspect of the course.

Know What You Are Preparing For

Determine as much as you can about the test before you begin to study for it. The more you know about a test beforehand, the more efficient your studying will be.

To find out about an upcoming test, ask these questions:

- Is the test called a "test," "exam," "quiz," or something else? As you can see in Table 5.1, the names imply different things. For simplicity's sake, we'll use the term test throughout this chapter, but know that these distinctions exist, and they should affect the way you prepare.
- What material will the test cover?
- How many questions will be on it?
- How much time is it expected to take? A full class period? Only part of a period?
- What kinds of questions will be on the test?
- How will it be graded?
- Will sample questions be provided?
- Are tests from previous terms available?

TABLE 5.1 Quizzes, Tests, Exams . . . What's in a Name?

Although they may vary from one instructor to another, the following definitions are most commonly used:

Quizzes. A **quiz** is a brief assessment, usually covering a relatively small amount of material. Some quizzes cover as little as one class's worth of reading. Although a single quiz usually doesn't count very much, instructors often add quiz scores together, and collectively they can become a significant part of your final course grade.

Tests. A **test** is a more extensive, more heavily weighted assessment than a quiz, covering more material. A test may come every few weeks of the term, often after each third or quarter of the term has passed, but this varies with the instructor and the course.

Exams. An **exam** is the most substantial kind of assessment. In many classes, just one exam is given—a final exam at the end of the term. Sometimes there are two exams, one at the midpoint of the term (called, of course, a midterm) and the second at the end. Exams are usually weighted quite heavily because they are meant to assess your knowledge of all the course material covered up to that point.

Match Test Preparation to Question Types

Test questions come in different types (see Table 5.2 on page 126), and each requires a somewhat different style of preparation.

- **Essay questions.** Essay tests focus on the big picture—ways in which the various pieces of information being tested fit together. You'll need to know not just a series of facts, but also the connections between them, and you will have to be able to discuss these ideas in an organized and logical way.

  The best approach to studying for an essay test involves four steps:

  1. Carefully reread your class notes and any notes you've made on assigned readings that will be covered on the upcoming exam. Also go through the readings themselves, reviewing underlined or highlighted material and marginal notes.

  2. Play professor: Think of likely exam questions. To do this, you can use the key words, phrases, concepts, and questions that come up in your class notes or in your text. Some instructors give out lists of possible essay topics; if yours does, focus on this list, but don't ignore other possibilities.

  3. Without looking at your notes or your readings, answer each potential essay question—aloud. Don't feel embarrassed about doing this. Talking aloud is often more useful than answering the question in your head.

     You can also write down the main points that any answer should cover. (Don't write out *complete* answers to the questions unless your instructor tells you in advance exactly what is going to be on the test. Your time is probably better spent learning the material than rehearsing precisely formulated responses.)

Student Alert: Do your students agree with this quote or do they believe their high school provided more rigorous preparation for college?

> "High school is memorization and regurgitation. Here you have to think."
>
> Junior, Engineering Student, Notre Dame University[1]

1

Complete a Test Preparation Checklist

Before taking your next test, complete the following test preparation checklist.

Test Preparation Checklist

☐ I checked whether it's a quiz, test, or exam.

☐ I began preparation long before the test (e.g., by taking notes in class).

☐ I understand what material will be covered.

☐ I know how many questions will be on the test.

☐ I know how long it will take.

☐ I know what kinds of questions will be on the test.

☐ I know how it will be graded.

☐ I obtained sample questions and/or previous tests, if available.

☐ I formed or participated in a study group.

☐ I used different and appropriate preparation strategies for different types of questions.

☐ I read my class notes.

☐ I composed some essay questions.

☐ I answered essay questions aloud.

☐ I actively memorized facts and details.

☐ I made and used index cards.

☐ I created and used a test like the real test.

To Try It online, go to **www.mhhe.com/power**.

Like any competitive event, testing can motivate us to do our best. You might think of moderate test anxiety as a desire to perform at your peak—a useful quality at test time.

On the other hand, for some, anxiety can spiral into the kind of paralyzing fear that makes their minds go blank. There are several ways to keep this from happening to you:

1. *Prepare thoroughly.* The more you prepare, the less test anxiety you'll feel. Good preparation can give you a sense of control and mastery, and it will prevent test anxiety from overwhelming you.

2. *Take a realistic view of the test.* Remember that your future success does not hinge on your performance on any single exam. Think of the big picture: put the task ahead in context, and remind yourself of all the hurdles you've passed so far.

3. *Learn relaxation techniques.* You can learn to reduce or even eliminate the jittery physical symptoms of test anxiety by using relaxation tech-

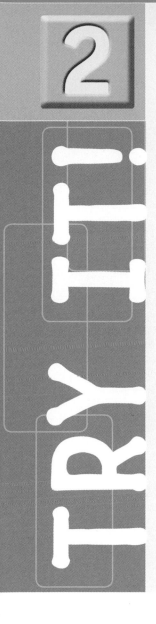

 **PERSONAL STYLES**

Measure Your Test-Taking Style

Do you feel anxious at the very thought of a test, or are you cool and calm in the face of testing situations? Get a sense of your test-taking style by checking off every statement below that applies to you.

- ☐ 1. The closer a test date approaches, the more nervous I get.
- ☐ 2. I am sometimes unable to sleep on the night before a test.
- ☐ 3. I have "frozen up" during a test, finding myself unable to think or respond.
- ☐ 4. I can feel my hands shaking as I pick up my pencil to begin a test.
- ☐ 5. The minute I read a tough test question, all the facts I ever knew about the subject abandon me and I can't get them back no matter how hard I try.
- ☐ 6. I have become physically ill before or during a test.
- ☐ 7. Nervousness prevents me from studying immediately before a test.
- ☐ 8. I often dream about an upcoming test.
- ☐ 9. Even if I successfully answer a number of questions, my anxiety stays with me throughout the test.
- ☐ 10. I'm reluctant to turn in my test paper for fear that I can do better if I continue to work on it.

If you checked off more than four statements, you have experienced fairly serious test anxiety. If you checked off more than six statements, your anxiety is probably interfering with your test performance. In particular, statements 3, 5, 6, 7, and 10 may indicate serious test anxiety.

If, based on your responses to this questionnaire and your previous experience, your level of test anxiety is high, what are some of the steps described in this chapter that might be helpful to you?

To Try It online, go to **www.mhhe.com/power**.

---

niques. These techniques are covered in Chapter 14, but the basic process is straightforward: Breathe evenly, gently inhaling and exhaling. Focus your mind on a pleasant, relaxing scene such as a beautiful forest or a peaceful farm, or on a restful sound such as that of ocean waves breaking on the beach.

4. *Visualize success.* Think of an image of your instructor handing back your test marked with a big fat "A." Or imagine your instructor congratulating you on your fine performance the day after the test. Positive visualizations that highlight your potential success can help replace images of failure that may fuel test anxiety.

What if these strategies don't work? If your test anxiety is so great that it's getting in the way of your success, make use of your college's resources. Most provide a learning resource center or a counseling center that can provide you with personalized help. (For more on dealing with test anxiety, see the Course Connections feature.)

Teaching Tip: Visualization is used more and more in a variety of areas such as athletics and wellness. Model this activity with your class.

Special Techniques for Dealing with Math Anxiety

For many students, the greatest test anxiety comes when they're taking a math test. Math seems to bring out the worst fears in some people, perhaps because it's seen as a discipline in which answers are either totally right or totally wrong, or because they've felt they've "hit the wall" and they'll never be able to understand a concept, no matter how hard they try.

Such feelings about math can be devastating, because they can prevent you from doing well even if you know the material. If you suffer from math anxiety, keep these things in mind:

- Math is like any other subject: the greatest component of success is the effort you put in, not whether you have a "math gene" that makes you naturally good at math.

- It's a false stereotype that women are not as good at math as men, but it's a stereotype that many women buy into. Research has shown that when men do badly on a math test, they're most likely to think that they haven't put in enough effort. But when women don't do well on a math test, they're three times more likely than men to feel that they don't have enough ability to be successful.[2] That's an erroneous view of the world. Don't become a prisoner of stereotypes.

- Remember that math has practical uses. Some people are afraid of math because they view it as theoretical, with no practical value. But if you want to figure out the size of a room, how to calculate a tip in a restaurant, or how much interest you'll pay on a loan, you'll need to make use of geometry, arithmetic, and algebra.

- Finally, use these special strategies to deal with math problems on exams:

  1. Analyze math problems carefully. What are the known quantities or constants, and what pieces of information are missing? What formula(s) or theorem(s) apply?

  2. For word problems, consider if they are similar to word problems that you've studied and mastered.

  3. Consider drawing a diagram, graph, or probability tree.

  4. Break down calculations into their component parts.

  5. Check your math carefully.

  6. Be neat and logical in your presentation. Your instructor may give you partial credit if you lay out every step you're going through.

Teaching Tip: Test anxiety is a good topic for guest speakers to address. Many campuses have experts in this area and since you test and evaluate your students, someone outside that relationship provides a valuable, and possibly different, perspective.

Form a Study Group

Study groups
Small, informal groups of students whose purpose is to help members work together and study for a test

Study groups are small, informal groups of students who work together to learn course material and study for a test. Forming such a group can be an excellent way to prepare for any kind of test. Some study groups are formed for particular tests, while others meet consistently throughout the term.

The typical study group meets a week or two before a test and plans a strategy for studying. Members share their understanding of what will be on the test, based on what an instructor has said in class and on their review of notes and text material. Together, they develop a list of review questions to guide their individual study. The group then breaks up, and the members study on their own.

A few days before the test, members of the study group meet again. They discuss answers to the review questions, go over the material, and share any new insights they may have about the upcoming test. They may also quiz one another about the material to identify any weaknesses or gaps in their knowledge.

Study groups can be extremely powerful tools because they help accomplish several things:

- They help members organize and structure the material to approach their studying in a systematic and logical way.

- They allow students to share different perspectives on the material.

- They make it more likely that students will not overlook any potentially important information.

- They force members to rethink the course material, explaining it in words that other group members will understand. As we will discuss in Chapter 9, this helps both understanding and recall of the information when it is needed on the test.

- Finally, they help motivate members to do their best. When you're part of a study group, you're no longer working just for yourself; your studying also benefits the other study group members. Not wanting to let down your classmates in a study group may encourage you to put in your best effort.

Study groups, made up of a few students who study together for a test, can help organize material, provide new perspectives, and motivate members to do their best.

There are some potential drawbacks to keep in mind. Study groups don't always work well for students with learning styles that favor working independently. In addition, "problem" members—those who don't pull their weight—may cause difficulties for the group. In general, though, the advantages of study groups far outweigh their disadvantages. (To set up your own study group, see Try It 3 on page 132.)

Use Your Campus Learning or Tutorial Center Resources

Many colleges have a learning center, tutorial center, or other office that can help you study for a test. Often they are staffed by advanced students who have already taken courses that you're studying for. Take advantage of any opportunities you have to get the advice of such "expert" students. Not only can they provide you with general study strategies, but they can give you tips on a particular instructor's tests.

Don't wait until after you do badly on a test to visit your campus learning or tutorial centers. A visit prior to your first test is a good use of your time, even if you feel it's not essential. Just knowing what resources are available can boost your confidence.

Cramming: You Shouldn't, But . . .

You know, of course, that **cramming,** hurried, last-minute studying, is not the way to go. You know that you're likely to forget the material the moment the

Cramming
Hurried, last-minute studying

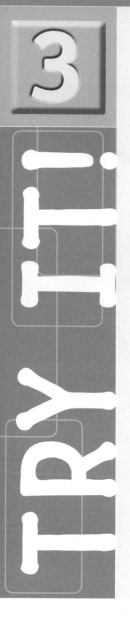

WORKING IN A GROUP

Form a Study Group

The next time you have to prepare for a test, form a study group with three to five classmates. They may have a variety of study habits and skills, but all must be willing to take the group seriously.

The first time you meet, compare notes about what is likely to be on the test and brainstorm to come up with possible test questions. If the instructor hasn't given you detailed information about the test (i.e., number and types of questions, weighting, etc.), one of you should be delegated to ask for it. Plan to meet once more closer to the test date to discuss answers to the questions you've come up with, share any new insights, and quiz each other on the material.

After you've taken the test and gotten your results, meet again. Find out if members felt the group was effective. Did the members feel more confident about the test? Do they think they did better than they would have without the group? What worked? What didn't? What could you do differently next time?

To Try It online, go to **www.mhhe.com/power**.

test is over because long-term retention is nearly impossible without thoughtful study. But . . .

> . . . it's been one of those weeks where everything went wrong.
>
> . . . the instructor sprang the test on you at the last minute.
>
> . . . you forgot about the test until the night before it was scheduled.

Whatever the reason, there may be times when you can't study properly. What do you do if you have to cram for an exam?

Don't spend a lot of time on what you're unable to do. Beating yourself up about your failings as a student will only hinder your efforts. Instead, admit you're human and imperfect like everyone else. Then spend a few minutes developing a plan about what you can accomplish in the limited time you've got.

The first thing to do is choose what you really need to study. You won't be able to learn everything, so you have to make choices. Figure out the main focus of the course, and concentrate on it.

Teaching Tip: A student's ability to focus and work productively in a study group has a lot to do with their learning style. Refer to the work you did in Chapter 3. Encourage students who want to use a study group to complete the Try It! 3 activity.

Once you have a strategy, prepare a one-page summary sheet with hard-to-remember information. Just writing the material down will help you remember it, and you can refer to the summary sheet frequently over the limited time you do have to study.

Next, read through your class notes, concentrating on the material you've underlined and the key concepts and ideas that you've already noted. Forget about reading all the material in the books and articles you're being tested on. Instead, only read the passages that you've underlined and the notes you've taken on the readings. Finally, maximize your study time. Using your notes, index cards, and concept maps, go over the information. Read it. Say it aloud. Think about it and the way it relates to other information. In short, use all the techniques we've talked about for learning and recalling information.

Just remember: When the exam is over, material that you have crammed into your head is destined to leave your mind as quickly as it entered. If you've crammed for a midterm, don't assume that the information will still be there when you study for the final. In the end, cramming often ends up taking more time for worse results than does studying with appropriate techniques.

Have you ever crammed for a test? If so, you know how exhausting it can be, and how easy it is to overlook crucial material. On the other hand, time pressures sometimes make cramming your only option. When that happens, there are strategies you can use to help you make the best use of limited time.

O RGANIZE: Facing the Day of the Test

You've studied a lot, and you're happy with your level of mastery. Or perhaps you have the nagging feeling that there's something you haven't quite gotten to. Or maybe you know you haven't had enough time to study as much as you'd like, and you're expecting a disaster.

Whatever your frame of mind, it will help to organize your plan of attack on the day of the test. What's included on the test is out of your hands, but you can control what you bring to it.

For starters, bring the right tools to the test. Have at least two pens and two pencils with you. It's usually best to write in pen because, in general, writing tends to be easier to read in pen than pencil. But you also might want to have pencils on hand. Sometimes instructors will use machine-scored tests, which require the use of pencil. Or there may be test questions that involve computations, and solving them may entail frequent reworking of calculations.

You should also be sure to bring a watch to the test, even if there will be a clock on the wall of the classroom. You will want to be able to pace yourself properly during the test. Just having your own watch will help you feel more in control of your time during the test.

Sometimes instructors permit you to use notes and books during the test. If you haven't brought them with you, they're not going to be of much help. So make sure you bring them if they're permitted. Even for closed-book tests, having such material available before the test actually starts may allow you a few minutes of review after you arrive in the classroom.

On the day of a test, avoid the temptation to compare notes with your friends about how much they've studied. Yes, you might end up feeling good because many of your fellow classmates studied less than you did. But chances

Student Alert: Ask your students to share their thoughts about cramming. If they are firmly convinced that cramming is effective, you will have a harder job teaching this chapter.

Teaching Tip: This is a good time to mention the physical aspects of test preparation, from sleep and nutrition to techniques for dealing with sweaty palms and fluttering stomachs, to the actual location where the test is given and how your students may need to adapt to that setting to be successful.

TABLE 5.3   Action Words for Essays

These words are commonly used in essay questions. Learning the distinctions among them will help you answer them effectively.

Analyze: Examine and break into component parts.

Clarify: Explain with significant detail.

Compare: Describe and explain similarities.

Compare and contrast: Describe and explain similarities and differences.

Contrast: Describe and explain differences.

Critique: Judge and analyze, explaining what is wrong—and right—about a concept.

Define: Provide the meaning.

Discuss: Explain, review, and consider.

Enumerate: Provide a listing of ideas, concepts, reasons, items, etc.

Evaluate: Provide pros and cons of something; provide an opinion and justify it.

Explain: Give reasons why or how; clarify, justify, and illustrate.

Illustrate: Provide examples; show instances.

Interpret: Explain the meaning of something.

Justify: Explain why a concept can be supported, typically by using examples and other types of support.

Outline: Provide an overarching framework or explanation—usually in narrative form—of a concept, idea, event, or phenomenon.

Prove: Using evidence and arguments, convince the reader of a particular point.

Relate: Show how things fit together; provide analogies.

Review: Describe or summarize, often with an evaluation.

State: Assert or explain.

Summarize: Provide a condensed, precise list or narrative.

Trace: Track or sketch out how events or circumstances have evolved; provide a history or timeline.

IRM Link: Use the Jigsaw Activity to assist students in learning these words. See Teaching the Text, Chapter 5, Sections IV and VIII.

First, read the instructions carefully to determine whether only one response will be correct, or whether more than one of the choices may be correct. In most cases, only one choice will be right, but in some cases instructors may want you to check off more than one answer.

Turn to the first question and read it carefully. *Before you look at the possible answers, try to answer the question in your head.* This can help you avoid confusion over inappropriate choices.

Next, *carefully read through every possible answer.* Even if you come to one that you think is right, read them all—there may be a subsequent answer that is better.

Look for absolutes like "every," "always," "only," "none," and "never." Choices that contain such absolute words are rarely correct. For example, an answer choice that says, "A U.S. president has never been elected without having received the majority of the popular vote" is incorrect due to the presence of the word "never." On the other hand, less-absolute words, such as "generally," "usually," "often," "rarely," "seldom," and "typically" may indicate a correct response.

Understand Action Verbs in Essay Questions

Answer the following questions about the Second Amendment to the United States Constitution by outlining your responses to them, paying attention to the different action verbs that introduce questions.

The Second Amendment states:

> A well-regulated militia, being necessary to the security of a free State, the right of the people to keep and bear arms, shall not be infringed.

1. Summarize the Second Amendment to the Constitution.

2. Analyze the Second Amendment to the Constitution.

3. Discuss the Second Amendment to the Constitution.

How do your answers differ for the each of the questions? Which of the questions provoked the lengthiest response? Which of the questions could you answer best?

To Try It online, go to **www.mhhe.com/power.**

Be especially on guard for the word "not," which negates the sentence ("The one key concept that is not embodied in the U.S. Constitution is . . . "). It's easy to gloss over "not," and if you have the misfortune of doing so, it will be nearly impossible to answer the item correctly.

If you're having trouble understanding a question, underline key words or phrases, or try to break the question into different short sections. Sometimes it is helpful to work backwards, *Jeopardy* style, and look at the possible answers first to see if you can find one that is clearly accurate or clearly inaccurate.

*Use an **educated guessing** strategy*—which is very different from wild or random guessing. Unless you are penalized for wrong answers (a scoring rule by which wrong answers are deducted from the points you have earned on other questions, rather than merely not counting at all toward your score), it always pays to guess.

The first step in educated guessing is to eliminate any obviously false answers. The next step is to examine the remaining choices closely. Does one response choice include a qualifier that makes it unlikely ("the probability

Discussion Prompt: Ask students to share when they have used educated guessing and the lessons learned from this practice.

Educated guessing
The practice of eliminating obviously false multiple-choice answers and selecting the most likely answer from the remaining choices

Discussion Prompt: The cartoon (above) poses an interesting question. Do your students agree? Encourage your students to place the specific techniques presented in this chapter in the context of a bigger picture; namely, what is higher education all about?

of war always increases when a U.S. president is facing political difficulties")? Does one choice include a subtle factual error ("when Columbus began his journey to the New World in 1492, he went with the support of the French monarchy")? In such cases, you may be able to figure out the correct response by eliminating the others.

- **True–False Questions.** Although most of the principles we've already discussed apply equally well to true–false questions, a few additional tricks of the trade may help you with this type of question.

  Begin a set of true–false questions by answering the ones you're sure you know. But don't rush; it's important to read every part of a true–false question, because key words such as "never," "always," and "sometimes" often determine the appropriate response.

  If you don't have a clue about whether a statement is true or false, here's a last-resort principle: Choose "true." In general, more statements on a true–false test are likely to be true than false.

- **Matching Questions.** Matching questions typically present you with two columns of related information, which you must link, item by item. For example, a list of terms or concepts may be presented in one column, along with a list of corresponding definitions or explanations in the second column. The best strategy is to reduce the size of both columns by matching the items you're most confident about first; this will leave a short list in each column, and the final matching may become apparent.

- **Short-Answer and Fill-In Questions.** Short-answer and fill-in questions basically require you to *generate and supply* specific information in your own words. Unlike essays, which are more free-form and may have several possible answers, short-answer and fill-in questions are usually quite specific, requiring only one answer.

  Use both the instructions for the questions and the questions themselves to determine the level of specificity that is needed in an answer. Try not to provide too much or too little information. Usually, brevity is best.

IRM Link: See Teaching the Text, Chapter 5, Section I, Chapter Summary and Section VII, refer to Connect to Practices and Programs in the Broader Academic Community; spend some time discussing the issue of integrity.

Academic honesty
Completing and turning in only one's own work under one's own name

About Academic Honesty

It's tempting: A glance at a classmate's test may provide the one piece of information that you just can't remember. But you owe it to yourself not to do it. Copying from a classmate's paper is no different from reaching over and stealing that classmate's calculator or cell phone. It is a violation of **academic honesty,** one of the foundations of civility in the classroom, as well as in society. Unless the work you turn in under your own name is your work, you are guilty of academic dishonesty.

Violations of academic honesty can take many forms. It may involve *plagiarism,* copying another's work and passing it off as your own. (We'll talk more about plagiarism in Chapter 7). Academic dishonesty may also include using a calculator when it's not allowed, discussing the answer to a question, copying a computer file when it's unauthorized, taking an exam for another person, or stealing an exam. It can take the form of ripping a page out of a book in the library, or lying to an instructor about the reason for a late paper. It includes using your textbook or conferring with a friend when taking a closed-book exam in an online, distance-learning course.

Academic honesty is the bedrock of college life. The risks of cheating—getting caught and causing damage to your academic future and sense of self-worth—far outweigh any momentary benefits.

You may feel that "everyone does it," so cheating is not so bad. Wrong. Everyone doesn't do it, just as most people don't embezzle from their companies or steal from others. Although you may know of a few cases of exceptionally dishonest classmates, most of your classmates try to be honest—you just don't notice their honesty.

Whatever form it takes, academic dishonesty is just plain wrong. It lowers the level of civility in the classroom, it makes the grading system unfair, and it ultimately reduces the meaning of your grade. It certainly hinders academic and personal growth. It can't help but reduce one's self-esteem, and it robs the cheater of self-respect.

Finally, academic dishonesty violates the regulations of every college (rules that you should familiarize yourself with), and instructors feel it is their obligation to uphold standards of academic honesty. Violations of honesty policies will lead to any number of potentially devastating scenarios: failing the exam on which the cheating has taken place, failing the entire course, being brought before a disciplinary board, having a description of the incident permanently placed on your grade transcript, being placed on academic probation, or even being thrown out of school. A single instance of cheating can permanently prevent you from embarking on the career of your choice. Cheating is simply not worth it.

 VALUATE: Taking Your Own Final Examination

The last few minutes of a test may feel like the final moments of a marathon. You need to focus your energy and push yourself even harder. It can be make-or-break time.

Save some time at the end of a test so you can check your work. You should have been keeping track of your time all along, so plan on stopping a few minutes before the end of the test period to review what you've done. It's a critical step, and it can make the difference between a terrific grade and a mediocre one. It's a rare person who can work for an uninterrupted period of time on a test and commit absolutely no errors—even if he or she knows the material backwards and forwards. Consequently, checking what you've done is crucial.

Start evaluating your test by looking for obvious mistakes. Make sure you've answered every question and haven't skipped any parts of questions. If there is

IRM Link and Teaching Tip: Post exam surveys allow students to evaluate and rethink the way they prepared for a test. Make the post exam survey a part of your class throughout the semester. See Teaching the Text, Chapter 5, Section IV and VIII.

Tests for a Lifetime

If you think the last tests you'll ever have to take are the final exams just before you graduate from college, you're probably wrong.

For one thing, increasing numbers of professions require initial licensing exams and some even require periodic exams to remain in good standing within the profession. For example, in some states, people who wish to become teachers must pass an exam, as in the case of Imani Brown described at the beginning of the chapter. Even experienced teachers are required to take periodic tests throughout their careers to remain in the teaching field.

In addition, you may have to take tests to continue your course of study for some professions. For example, if you are thinking about a career in medicine, law, or business, you'll need to take a national, standardized test (such as the MCAT or LSAT) to enroll in a postundergraduate program. How well you do on the test will determine whether you can go to graduate school and which graduate schools will accept you.

In short, good test-taking skills won't just bring you success in college. They're something that may benefit you for a lifetime as you pursue your career.

a separate answer sheet, check to see that all your answers have been recorded on the answer sheet and in the right spot.

If the test has included essay and short-answer questions, proofread your responses. Check for obvious errors—misspellings, missing words, and repetitions. Make sure you've responded to every part of each question and that each essay, as a whole, makes sense.

Check over your responses to multiple-choice, true–false, and matching questions. If there are some items that you haven't yet answered because you couldn't remember the necessary information, now is the time to take a stab at them. As we discussed earlier, it usually pays to guess, even randomly if you must. On most tests, no answer and a wrong answer are worth the same amount—nothing!

What about items that you initially guessed at? Unless you have a good reason to change your original answer—such as a new insight or a sudden recollection of some key information—your first guess is likely your best guess.

Know When to Stop

After evaluating and checking your answers, you may reach a point when there is still some time left. What to do? If you're satisfied with your responses, it's simply time to tell yourself, "Let it go."

Permit yourself the luxury of knowing that you've done your best, and hand the test in to your instructor. You don't have to review your work over and over just because there is time remaining and some of your classmates are still working on their tests. In fact, such behavior is often counterproductive, because you might start overinterpreting and reading things into questions that really aren't there.

Disaster! I've run out of time! It's a nightmarish feeling: The clock is ticking relentlessly, and it's clear that you don't have enough time to finish the test. What should you do?

Stop working! Although this advice may sound foolish, in fact the most important thing you can do is to take a minute to calm yourself. Take some deep breaths to replace the feelings of panic that are likely welling up inside you. Collect your thoughts, and plan a strategy for the last moments of the test.

If there are essays that remain undone, consider how you'd answer them if you had more time. Then write an outline of each answer. If you don't have time even for that, write a few keywords. Writing anything is better than handing in a blank page, and you may get at least some credit for your response. The key principle here: Something is better than nothing, and even one point is worth more than zero points.

The same principle holds for other types of questions. Even wild guesses are almost always better than not responding at all to an item. So rather than telling yourself you've certainly failed and giving up, do as much as you can in the remaining moments of the exam.

R ETHINK: The Real Test of Learning

Your instructor is about to hand the graded exams back. All sorts of thoughts run through your head: How did I do? Did I do as well as my classmates? Will I be happy with my results? Will the results show how much I studied? Will I be embarrassed by my grade?

Most of us focus on the evaluative aspects of tests. We look at the grade we've received on a test as an end in itself. It's a natural reaction.

But there's another way to look at test results: They can help guide us toward future success. By looking at what we've learned (and haven't learned) about a given subject, we'll be in a better position to know what to focus on when we take future exams. Furthermore, by examining the kinds of mistakes we make, we can learn to do better in the future.

When you get your test back, you have the opportunity to reflect on what you've learned and to consider your performance. Begin by actively listening to what your instructor says as he or she hands back the test. You may learn about things that were generally misunderstood by the class, and you'll get a sense of how your performance compares to that of your classmates. You also may pick up some important clues about what questions will be on future exams.

Then examine your own mistakes. Chances are they'll jump out at you since they will be marked incorrect. Did you misunderstand or misapply some principle? Was there a certain aspect of the material covered on the test that you missed? Were there particular kinds of information that you didn't realize you needed to know? Or did you lose some points because of your test-taking skills? Did you make careless errors, such as forgetting to fill in a question or misreading the directions? Was your handwriting so sloppy that your instructor had trouble reading it?

> **"The test of any man lies in action."**
>
> Pindar, author, *Odes*

Once you have a good idea of what material you didn't fully understand or remember, get the correct answers to the items you missed—from your instructor, fellow classmates, or your book. If it's a math exam, rework problems you've missed. Finally, summarize—in writing—the material you had trouble with. This will help you study for future exams that cover the same material.

Finally, if you're dissatisfied with your performance, talk to your instructor—not to complain, but to seek help. Instructors don't like to give bad grades, and they may be able to point out problems in your test that you can address readily so you can do better in the future. Demonstrate to your instructor that you want to do better and are willing to put in the work to get there. The worst thing to do is crumple up the test and quickly leave the class in embarrassment. Remember, you're not the first person to get a bad grade, and the power to improve your test-taking performance lies within you. (Now, take a deep breath and complete Try It 5.)

Name: Theresa Winebrenner

Education: Austin Community College, Austin, Texas

There's nothing like a test to create anxiety in students—we've all felt it. Theresa Winebrenner, a student at Austin Community College, is no different, except that her techniques for coping with test anxiety are a bit specialized. Both blind and hearing-impaired, Winebrenner combines technological solutions with her own ingenuity to cope with the task of preparing for the approximately 16 tests she has to take each semester.

Winebrenner's preparation begins with careful notetaking. "In class, I have a notetaker, called a Type and Speak, which is like a laptop computer. When I get home, I can download the lecture into my other computer, which has a synthesized voice capability," she noted. "Then, as the computer speaks the lecture for me, I take notes in braille.

"I also have a machine called a Reading Edge that reads to me. If I place a book face down on its screen, it reads the page while I take braille notes.

"Because of my hearing impairment, I have to take notes in braille; the audible signal doesn't always stick in my memory. Reading my notes in braille is very helpful; it forces me to have a clear understanding of what I'm saying," Winebrenner said.

As for taking tests, "that's more a matter of motivation and human help than technological assistance," Winebrenner said.

"I usually start about a week early to study for a test," Winebrenner explained. "I prepare a schedule for myself so I have a set of clear deadlines that I need to meet. Then I collect my notes, take them home, and review them.

"For the actual tests, the college's Special Services Department provides students who read the tests for me and write down my answers," she said. "One of the problems I run into is that some students are not familiar with the academic background of the course I'm taking and don't read the test well or write the answers appropriately."

While she prefers multiple-choice tests, Winebrenner has been successful on many different kinds of tests, using different techniques to study for each type.

"If it's a test with multiple-choice questions, I focus more on the end-of-chapter reviews. I go through those and make notes on the questions in the text. If it's an essay test, I look more at the examples in the book or in my notes and use the essay-type questions and solutions at the end of the chapter as a guideline.

"Finally," she added, "it gets to the point where you have to stop memorizing the material and start understanding it. There's no substitute for understanding the content of what you learn and its applications."

What kinds of tests will I encounter in college?

- Although tests are an unpopular fact of college life, they can provide useful information about one's level of knowledge and understanding about a subject.

- There are several types of tests, including brief, informal quizzes; more substantial tests; and even more weighty exams, which tend to be administered at the midpoint and end of a course.

What are the best ways to prepare for and take various kinds of tests?

- Good test preparation begins with doing the course assignments, attending class regularly, and paying attention in class. It also helps to find out as much as possible about a test beforehand and to form a study group to review material.

- If cramming becomes necessary, focus on summarizing factual information broadly, identifying key concepts and ideas, and rehearsing information orally.

- When you first receive the test, skim it to see what kinds of questions are asked, figure out how the different questions and sections will be weighted, and jot down complex factual information that is likely to be needed for the test.

- Answer the easiest questions first, write legibly, use only one side of each sheet of paper, mark answer sheets carefully, and record answers in the test book as well as the answer sheet.

What are the best strategies for answering specific kinds of test questions?

- For essay questions, be sure to understand each question and each of its parts, interpret action words correctly, write concisely, organize the essay logically, and include examples.

- For multiple-choice questions, read the question very carefully and then read all response choices. Educated guessing based on eliminating incorrect response choices is usually a reasonable strategy.

- For true–false and matching questions, answer all the items that you are sure of quickly and then go back to the remaining items.

- The best strategy for short-answer and fill-in questions is to be very sure what is being asked. Keep answers complete but brief.

KEY TERMS AND CONCEPTS

Test anxiety (p. 127)
Study groups (p. 130)
Cramming (p. 131)

Educated guessing (p. 137)
Academic honesty (p. 138)

RESOURCES

On Campus

Colleges provide a variety of resources for students having difficulties with test-taking. Some offer general workshops for students, reviewing test-taking strategies. Furthermore, if you are planning to take a specific standardized test, such as the tests required for admission to business, law, or medical school, you may be able to sign up for a course offered through your college (or through such commercial organizations as Princeton Review or Kaplan).

  If you find that you are experiencing significant test anxiety when taking a test or in the days leading up to it, talk to someone at your campus counseling center or health

Too Many Questions, Too Little Time

There was no reason to panic, said Mia Varela to herself at the start of the test. The exam, a midterm in her Greek civilization class, contained 50 multiple-choice questions (each worth 1 point) and two short-answer essays (worth a total of 50 points). And she had 75 minutes to complete the test.

"Let's see," she said to herself. "At one and a half minutes per multiple-choice question, that would take 75 minutes. Hmm . . . that's no good. How about a minute for each one? Fifty minutes for the multiple-choice questions, leaving 25 minutes for the essays. That ought to work. I'll get the multiple-choice questions out of the way first."

But things didn't work out the way she planned. After an hour she had completed only 40 of the multiple-choice questions and hadn't even started on the essay questions. With only 15 minutes left, panic began to set in. She had trouble thinking. She began to be certain that she'd fail the test. She thought about how she hadn't studied enough. If only she'd worked harder. How could she explain this failure to her friends . . . to her parents . . . to herself? The thoughts kept coming, and time kept ticking away.

1. Is there evidence that Mia didn't study effectively for this type of test?

2. What was right about Mia's initial approach to the test?

3. What should Mia have done differently in calculating the amount of time to devote to each portion of the test? Why?

4. What should Mia have done to be aware of and address her timing problem sooner?

5. How should Mia have dealt with her panic? Were her thoughts productive or counter-productive? Why?

6. If you were in Mia's shoes, what would you do with only 15 minutes left in the test?

Building Your Reading Skills

"**R**ead the first two chapters in your text by next Thursday." "I've put three articles on reserve in the library. You'll need to have them read by our next class." "Take a look at the first three Shakespeare sonnets in your book, and see if you can derive the major themes."

For Chris O'Hara, these reading assignments—handed down by different instructors on the same day in early October—felt like nails in his coffin. How was he supposed to finish all this reading in the next two days, in addition to studying for a Spanish test, writing a paper for history, and putting in eight hours at his part-time job?

Although the papers and tests were hard enough to deal with, it was the constant reading that was proving the most difficult challenge for Chris during his first term of college. He was a conscientious student who attempted to get everything done, but no matter how hard he tried, he just couldn't get everything read on time. When he pushed himself to read quicker and absorb more, he actually read and retained less. Thoughts about falling behind crowded out the meaning of whatever he was reading, and he had to go through the material all over again, slowing him down even more.

LOOKING AHEAD >>>

For students like Chris, reading assignments are the biggest challenge in college. The amount of required reading is often enormous. Even skilled readers may find themselves wishing they could read more quickly and effectively.

Fortunately, there are ways to improve your reading skills. In this chapter, we'll go over a number of strategies for reading more effectively. You'll assess your reading style and your attention span, consider what you should do before you even start reading an assignment, discover some ways of getting the most out of your reading, and learn how to retain what you've read.

In short, after reading this chapter, you'll be able to answer the following questions:

- **How do my reading style and attention span affect my reading?**

- **How can I improve my concentration and read more effectively?**

- **How can I best retain what I have read?**

Sharpen Your Reading Skills

What kind of reader are you? Ask yourself first of all about your reading *preferences:* what do you *like* to read, and why? What makes you pick up a book and start reading—and what makes you put one down?

Second, what's your reading *style?* Do you read at a comfortable pace and feel reasonably satisfied with how much you retain? Or do you plod through reading assignments, novels, and magazines and, like Chris, end up feeling that you're taking far too long? Perhaps you whip through chapters, devour books, and fly through the daily newspaper, but then find you can't recall the information as precisely as you'd like?

Before going any further, think about your own reading preferences by completing the *Journal Reflections,* and then consider your reading style—your characteristic way of approaching reading tasks—by completing Try It 1 on the next page.

Student Alert/IRM Link:
Teaching the Text, Chapter 6, Section I, Chapter Summary; be aware of how hard it is to convince students that these are skills they must conscientiously try to improve, particularly in light of the many different ways that students take in information.

Journal REFLECTIONS

My Reading Preferences

Think about what you like and don't like to read by answering these questions.

1. Do you read for pleasure? If so, what do you read (e.g., magazines, newspapers, novels, humor, short stories, non-fiction, illustrated books)?

2. What makes a book enjoyable? Have you ever read a book that you "couldn't put down"? If so, what made it so good?

3. What is the most difficult book you are reading this semester? Why is it difficult? Are you enjoying it?

4. Think about when you read for pleasure compared to when you read material for a class. How does the way you read differ between the two types of material?

5. Do you think there should be a difference between reading for pleasure and reading for a class? Why?

 PERSONAL STYLES

Discover Your Reading Style

Use the following questions to learn *how* you read—that is, your characteristic reading style. Rate how well each statement below describes you. Use this rating scale:

1 = Doesn't describe me at all

2 = Describes me only slightly

3 = Describes me fairly well

4 = Describes me very well

	1	2	3	4
1. I often reread passages in books that I particularly like.				
2. I often read good passages aloud to whomever is around.				
3. I often stop while reading to check that I understood what I just read.				
4. If I come across a long, unfamiliar name, I try to sound it out and pronounce it correctly.				
5. If there's a word I don't understand, I look it up in a dictionary right away or mark it so I can look it up later.				
6. Before I start reading a textbook or other serious book or article, I look for clues about how it is organized.				
7. I often question what I'm reading and "argue" with the author.				
8. I often try to guess what the chapter I'm about to read will cover.				
9. I often write comments or make notes in books that I own.				
10. I'm always finding typographical errors in books and articles I read.				

Reading styles range from a very holistic (i.e., broad-brushstroke, noncritical) style to a very analytic (i.e., detailed, critical) style. Add up the points you assigned yourself. Use this informal scale to find your reading style:

10–12 = Very holistic reading style

13–20 = Mostly holistic reading style

21–28 = Mostly analytic reading style

29–40 = Very analytic reading style

How do you think your reading style affects the way you learn material in textbooks? Is your style related to the kinds of subjects you prefer? Do you think your reading style affects your leisure reading?

To Try It online, go to **www.mhhe.com/power**.

Read for Retention, Not Speed

You may have seen advertisements promoting reading "systems" that promise to teach you to read so quickly that you'll be reading entire books in an hour or so and whizzing through assigned readings in a few minutes.

Forget it: It's not going to happen. For one thing, certain biological facts relating to the eye movements involved in reading simply prevent people from reading (and ultimately comprehending) so rapidly. Research has shown that claims of speed reading are simply groundless; it is unlikely that any system will overcome the built-in limitations of the human eye.

But even if it were physically possible to read a book in an hour, ultimately it probably doesn't matter very much. If we read too fast, comprehension and ultimately retention plunge. Reading is not a race, and faster readers are not necessarily better readers.

The act of reading is designed to increase our knowledge and open up new ways of thinking. It can help us achieve new levels of understanding and get us to think more broadly about the world and its inhabitants. Speed matters far less than what we take away from what we've read. The key to good reading is understanding—not speed.

In describing how you can use the principles of P.O.W.E.R. Learning to become a better reader, we'll focus on the type of reading that is typically called for in academic pursuits—textbook chapters, articles, handouts, and the like. However, the same principles will help you get more benefit and enjoyment out of your recreational reading as well.

Teaching Tip: Ask students to connect their learning styles to their reading styles (see Chapter 3.)

P REPARE: Approaching the Written Word

Preparation to begin reading isn't hard, and it won't take very long, but it's a crucial first step in applying P.O.W.E.R. Learning (summarized in the P.O.W.E.R. Plan on the right). Your aim in preparation is to become familiar with **advance organizers**—outlines, overviews, section objectives, or other clues to the meaning and organization of new material—provided in the material you are reading. Most textbooks have them built in; for an example, look at the start of every chapter in this book, which includes a chapter outline, plus a set of questions at the end of the "Looking Ahead" section. You can also create your own advance organizers by skimming material to be read and sketching out the general outline of the material you'll be reading.

Advance organizers pave the way for subsequent learning. They help you tie information that you already know to new material you're about to encounter. Ultimately, they can help us recall material better after we've read it.

In short, the more we're able to make use of advance organizers and our own prior knowledge and experiences, the better we can understand and retain new material. (To prove the value of advance organizers, complete Try It 2 on page 154, "Discover How Advance Organizers Help.")

Advance organizers Broad, general ideas related to material that is to be read or heard, which pave the way for subsequent learning

P.O.W.E.R. Plan

What's the Point of the Reading Assignment?

Before you begin an assignment, think about what your goal is. Will you be reading a textbook on which you'll be thoroughly tested? Is your reading supposed to provide background information that will serve as a context for future learning but that won't itself be tested? Is the material going to be useful to you personally? Realistically, how much time can you devote to the reading assignment?

3

Read the Frontmatter

Have you read the frontmatter of *this* book? Go there now. If you've already read it, review it. If you haven't, read it now. Then answer the following questions:

What are the goals of this book?

Who is the author, and what qualifies him to write this book?

Do you think the author has an understanding of students?

Do you think the author has an understanding of what students should do to become successful in their studies?

Is there anything in the frontmatter that made you curious? Does anything seem particularly interesting?

After reading the frontmatter, do you feel confident that you can learn what the author wants to teach? Do you feel that you *want* to learn it?

To Try It online, go to **www.mhhe.com/power**.

Discussion Prompt:
With this chapter, you are almost half way through this text. Use Try It! 3 as a mid-term evaluation of this text. Are your students learning what the author (and you) want to teach? Are they learning what they want to learn?

- A dictionary. You never know what new words you'll encounter while you're reading. If a dictionary is not handy, you'll be tempted to skip over unfamiliar words—a decision that may come back to haunt you. Note that some word-processing software includes a dictionary; there are also many good dictionaries available online (e.g., Merriam-Webster's at **www.m-w.com**, where you will also find an online thesaurus). The point is to use what's available—but use something!

4

Create an Advance Organizer

Use any information you have available to create an advance organizer for this chapter (or a chapter in another text you are using). Feel free to return to the frontmatter, skim the section headings, read the chapter summary, or recall anything your instructor may have said about the chapter.

Complete the following statements to prepare your organizer:

The key topics that will be covered in the rest of this chapter are . . .

I think I will be most interested in . . .

I think I will be least interested in . . .

I hope the chapter covers this topic . . .

Words, phrases, and ideas that are unfamiliar to me include . . .

If the author were here, I would ask . . .

Note: You may want to use this Try It as a starting point for advance organizers for each chapter in this book.

To Try It online, go to **www.mhhe.com/power**.

If you are reading a long assignment, taking a break can be a reward and reinvigorate you.

your grumbling stomach. There are a million and one possible distractions that can invade your thoughts as you read. Your job is to keep distracting thoughts at bay and focus on the material you are supposed to be reading. It's not easy, but there are things you can do to help yourself stay focused:

- **Read in small bites.** If you think it is going to take you 4 hours to read an entire chapter, break up the 4 hours into more manageable time periods. Promise yourself that you'll read for 1 hour in the afternoon, another hour in the evening, and the next 2 hours spaced out during the following day. One hour of reading is far more manageable than a 4-hour block.

- **Take a break.** Actually, plan to take several short breaks to reward yourself while you're reading. During your break, do something enjoyable—eat a snack, watch a bit of a ball game on television, play a video game, or the like. Just try not to get drawn into your break activity to the point that it takes over your reading time.

- **Deal with mental distractions.** Sometimes problems have a way of popping into our minds and repeatedly distracting us. If a particular problem keeps interrupting your concentration—such as a difficulty you're having on the job—try to think of an action-oriented strategy to deal with it. You might even write your proposed solution down on a piece of paper. Putting it down in words can get the problem off your mind, potentially making it less intrusive.

- **Manage interruptions.** You can't stop your roommate from receiving a cell phone call or—if you are a student who is also a parent—you can't prevent your children from getting a cut and needing immediate attention. But there are some things you can do to reduce interruptions and their consequences. For instance, you can schedule reading to coincide with periods when you know you'll be alone. You can also plan to read less critical parts of assignments (such as the summaries or book frontmatter) when distractions are more likely, saving the heavier reading for later. Or, if you are a parent with small children, you can get your child involved in an activity that they can perform independently.

Discussion Prompt: For a humorous aside, allow a few minutes for the class to share some of their favorite excuses for not reading. What is your own best example of being distracted?

Write While You Read

Writing is one of the most important aspects of reading. If you haven't underlined, jotted notes to yourself, placed check marks on the page, drawn arrows, constructed diagrams, and otherwise defaced and disfigured your book while you're reading, you're not doing your job as a P.O.W.E.R. reader.

The idea of writing on a book page may go against everything you've been taught in the past. (And of course you should never write on a library book or one that you've borrowed.)

However, once you've bought your book, *you own it and you should make it your own.* Don't keep your textbooks spotless so they will fetch a higher price if you sell them later. Instead, think of textbooks as documents recording your active learning and engagement in a field of study. In addition, you should look at your textbooks as the foundation of your personal library, which will grow throughout your lifetime. In short, writing extensively in your book while you're reading is an important tactic for achieving success. (For more on using textbooks, see the *Course Connections* feature.)

The ability to add your own personal notes, underlining, and other annotations to a clean text while you're reading is one of the reasons it usually pays to buy new, rather than used, textbooks. Why would you want a stranger's comments on something you own? Can you really trust that person's judgment over your own regarding what's important to underline? New books allow you to mark them up in your own, personal style, without the distraction of competing voices.

> **"What is reading but silent conversation?"**
>
> Walter Savage Landor, "Aristoteles and Callisthenes," author, *Imaginary Conversations* (1824–53)

What should you be writing while you are reading? There are several things you should write down:

- **Rephrase key points.** Make notes to yourself, in your own words, about what the author is trying to get across. Don't just copy what's been said. Think about the material, and rewrite it in words that are your own.

    Writing notes to yourself in your own words has several consequences, all good. First, you make the material yours; it becomes something you now understand and part of your own knowledge base.

Student Alert: Remind students that we each have to decide which reading techniques work best for us. At the same time, encourage them to be open to trying new techniques.

COURSE CONNECTIONS

Textbook Tips: Starting Off on the Right Page

You've just come back from the college bookstore, weighted down with a bookbag filled with the textbooks and other materials you've purchased for the upcoming term. Although you may be suffering from sticker shock—no doubt about it, textbooks are expensive—now is the time to take some preliminary steps to make the most of your investment.

- Make sure you've bought the correct textbooks. Look at each syllabus from your classes to ensure you've bought the appropriate text. Sometimes there are multiple sections of a course, and each section uses a different text. Be sure the book you've bought matches the description in the syllabus.

- Make the book your own. Write your name, e-mail address, and/or telephone number in the front of the book. If you misplace your book during the term, you want the person who finds it to be able to return it to you.

- Orient yourself to each of your textbooks. Take a quick look at each of the books, examining the table of contents, introduction, and/or preface (as we discussed earlier). Get a sense of the content and the general reading level of the book.

- Get yourself online. Many textbooks contain a card or insert with a password that gives you access to online material. Follow the directions and enter the book's Web site, making sure the password allows you to register. If you have trouble making the site work, call the tech support number that should be included with the password.

TRY It!

 WORKING IN A GROUP

Mark Up a Book Page

First, working alone, read the excerpt in Figure 6.2 on the opposite page. Then use the techniques we've discussed for marking up a page to highlight its key points.

Next, working in a group, compare and contrast your annotations with those of some classmates, and answer the following questions:

1. How do others' annotations differ from yours?

2. Why did they use the annotations they did?

3. Which annotation techniques worked best for you? Which did others prefer? Why?

4. How might these annotations help you to remember what is important?

5. If there were different sorts of material presented on the page, such as mathematical formulas, would you use different kinds of annotations?

To Try It online, go to **www.mhhe.com/power**.

However, just because you are having trouble with reading assignments doesn't automatically mean that you have a learning disability. Not only is the kind of reading you do in college more difficult than what you did in high school, but there's also more of it. It's only when reading represents a persistent, long-term problem—one that won't go away no matter how much work you do—that a learning disability becomes a possible explanation.

EVALUATE: What Does It Mean? What Do I Know?

Evaluation is a crucial step in reading. You need to be able to answer the seemingly simple question: "What does all this mean?"

But there's another aspect to evaluation. You need to evaluate, truthfully and honestly, your own level of understanding. What do you know as a result of your reading? Evaluation, then, consists of the following steps:

- **Identify the main ideas and themes and their value *to you personally*.** Try to determine the take-home message of the material you've read. For example, the take-home message of a chapter of an American history text might be, "Although Abraham Lincoln eventually called for the end of slavery, initially he was hesitant because of political considerations."

  Sometimes the main ideas and themes are spelled out, and at other times you will have to deduce them for yourself. Evaluating the main ideas and themes in terms of how they relate to you personally will help you understand and remember them more easily.

- **Prioritize the ideas.** Of all the information that is presented, which is the most crucial to the main message and which is the least crucial? Make a list of the main topics covered and try to rank them in order of importance.

- **Think critically about the arguments presented in the reading.** Do they seem to make sense? Are the author's assertions reasonable? Are there any flaws in the arguments? Would authors with a different point of view dispute what is being said? How would they build their own arguments?

- **Pretend you are explaining the material (talking—out loud!—about the material) to a fellow classmate who missed the assignment.** This is one time when talking out loud when no one is around is not only normal, but beneficial. Summarize the material aloud, as if you were talking to another person.

  Talking out loud does two things. First, it helps you identify weak spots in your understanding. Talking to yourself will help you nail down concepts that are still not clear in your own mind. Second, and equally important, because you are transforming the written word into the spoken word, you are thinking about the information in another way, which will help you remember it better.

- **Be honest with yourself.** Most of us are able to read with our minds on cruise control. But the net result is not much different from not reading the passage at all. If you have drifted off while you've been reading, go back and reread the passage.

- **Pat yourself on the back.** Just as you've done during each of your reading breaks, reward yourself for completing the reading passage. But keep in mind that there's one more step before you can really relax, and it's a crucial one: rethinking what you've read.

Teaching Tip: Encourage students to think of evaluation in another way. How directly do their reading skills determine how they will be evaluated (graded) in their other classes?

The more parents speak to their children, the better their children's language skills.

Understanding Language Acquisition: Identifying the Roots of Language

Anyone who spends even a little time with children will notice the enormous strides that they make in language development throughout childhood. However, the reasons for this rapid growth are far from obvious. Two major explanations have been offered: one based on learning theory and the other on innate processes.

The **learning-theory approach** suggests that language acquisition follows the principles of reinforcement and conditioning discussed in Chapter 6. For example, a child who utters the word "mama" is hugged and praised by her mother, which reinforces the behavior and makes its repetition more likely. This view suggests that children first learn to speak by being rewarded for making sounds that approximate speech. Ultimately, through a process of shaping, language becomes more and more like adult speech (Skinner, 1957).

The learning theory approach is supported by research that shows that the more parents speak to their young children, the more proficient the children become in language usage (see Figure 8-11). In addition, higher levels of linguistic sophistication in parents' speech to their young children are related to a greater rate of vocabulary growth, vocabulary usage, and even general intellectual achievement by the time the children are 3 years of age (Hart & Risley, 1997).

On the other hand, the learning theory approach is less successful when it comes to explaining the acquisition of language rules. Children are reinforced not only when they use proper language, but also when they respond incorrectly. For example, parents answer the child's "Why the dog won't eat?" as readily as they do the correctly phrased question "Why won't the dog eat?" Both sentences are understood equally well. Learning theory, then, has difficulty in providing the full explanation for language acquisition.

Pointing to such problems with learning theory approaches to language acquisition, Noam Chomsky (1968, 1978, 1991), a linguist, provided a ground-breaking alternative. Chomsky argued that humans are born with an innate linguistic capability that emerges primarily as a function of maturation. According to his analysis, all the world's languages share a similar underlying structure called a **universal grammar.** Chomsky suggests that the human brain has a neural system, the **language-acquisition device,** that both permits the understanding of the structure of language and provides strategies and techniques for learning the unique characteristics of a given native language.

learning-theory approach: The theory suggesting that language acquisition follows the principles of reinforcement and conditioning

universal grammar: Noam Chomsky's theory that all the world's languages share a similar underlying structure

language-acquisition device: A neural system of the brain hypothesized to permit understanding of language

FIGURE 6.2
Sample page to annotate

Reading in a foreign language. Use of a dictionary may be a big help when reading in a foreign language. But don't rely on it too much: If you can't remember the meaning of a word, first try to figure out what is being said from the context, and only then look it up. Also keep in mind this fundamental rule of language study: The more you immerse yourself in a language, the easier it will become.

Teaching Tip: Spend a few minutes connecting this information to ideas in Chapter 8 on memory.

Reading in the sciences. Be aware that the *scientific method* is the basis for much writing about scientific topics. In particular, scientists conduct experiments to support *hypotheses*, specific predictions that are derived from a theory. When reading about scientific research, try to identify the hypothesis that is being tested, and what alternative hypotheses might be used.

■ **Use your own reading system.** If you've already learned a reading system in the past and it works for you, use it. Many students employ the *SQ3R* system, which stands for *Study-Question-Read-Recite-Review*. Or make up your own system. The truth is that it doesn't really matter what system you use. What does matter is that you're systematic in the work of reading.

■ Dealing with Learning Disabilities

If you, like millions of people in the United States, have a learning disability of one sort or another, reading may prove to be particularly challenging. **Learning disabilities** are defined as difficulties in processing information when listening, speaking, reading, or writing; in most cases, learning disabilities are diagnosed when there is a discrepancy between learning potential and actual academic achievement.

Learning disabilities
Difficulties in processing information when listening, speaking, reading, or writing, characterized by a discrepancy between learning potential and actual academic achievement

One of the most common kinds of learning disabilities is *dyslexia*, a reading disability that produces the misperception of letters during reading and writing, unusual difficulty in sounding out letters, spelling difficulties, and confusion between right and left. Although its causes are not yet completely understood, one likely explanation is a problem in the part of the brain responsible for breaking words into the sound elements that make up language.

Another common disability is *attention-deficit hyperactivity disorder* (or *ADHD*), which is marked by an inability to concentrate, inattention, and a low tolerance for frustration. For the one to three percent of college students who have ADHD, planning, staying on task, and maintaining interest present unusual challenges.

Discussion Prompt: Take a moment to discuss disabilities. Developing sensitivities to differences of all kinds should be a theme throughout this course.

People with learning disabilities are sometimes viewed as unintelligent. Nothing could be further from the truth: There is no relationship between learning disabilities and I.Q. For instance, dozens of well-known and highly accomplished individuals suffered from dyslexia, including physicist Albert Einstein, U.S. General George Patton, poet William Butler Yeats, and—as we discuss in the Speaking of Success feature—writer John Irving.

By the time they reach college, most people with learning disabilities have already been diagnosed. If you do have a diagnosed learning disability and you need special services, it is important to disclose your situation to your instructors and other college officials.

In some cases, students with learning disabilities have not been appropriately evaluated prior to college. If you have difficulties such as mixing up and reversing letters frequently and suspect that you have a learning disability, there is an office on campus that can provide you with guidance. One place to start is your college counseling or health center.

The Job of Reading

Memos. Annual reports. Instructions. Continuing education assignments. Professional journals.

Each of these items illustrates the importance of developing critical reading skills for on-the-job success. Virtually every job requires good reading expertise, and for some professions, reading is a central component. Polishing your reading skills now will pay big dividends when you enter the world of work. The better you are at absorbing written information, the better you'll be at carrying out your job.

For instance, in many corporations, vital information is transmitted through the written word, via e-mails, hard-copy memos, technical reports, or Web-based material. The person who repairs your broken washing machine or automobile has probably read numerous service manuals while attending continuing education classes required to master the complex computer diagnostic systems that are now standard equipment. The physician who gives you a physical may have taken an online distance learning class that required reading about the newest medical technologies. And every one of your college instructors probably spends hours each month reading about the newest developments in his or her field.

Furthermore, because not all supervisors are effective writers, you'll sometimes need to read between the lines and draw inferences and conclusions about what you need to do. You should also keep in mind that there are significant cultural differences in the way in which people write and the type of language they use. Being sensitive to the cultural background of colleagues will permit you to more accurately interpret and understand what you are reading.

In short, reading is a skill that's required in virtually every profession. Developing the habit of reading critically while you are in college will pave the road for future career success.

R ETHINK: Getting It the Second Time

You're human, so—like the rest of us—when you finish a reading assignment you'd probably like nothing more than to heave a sigh of relief and put the book away.

By now you know that there's a crucial step you should take that will assist you in cementing what you've learned into memory: rethinking what you've read. If you do it within 24 hours of first reading the assignment, it can save you hours of work later.

> **"Reading furnishes the mind only with materials of knowledge; it is thinking that makes what we read ours."**
>
> John Locke, author, *Of the Conduct of the Understanding,* 1706

The best way to rethink an assignment is to reread it, along with any notes you've taken. "Yeah, right," you're probably thinking. "Like I have time for that." The goal, though, is not a literal rereading. In fact, it isn't necessary to reread word for word. You already know what's important and what's not important, so you can skim some of the less important material. But it is wise to reread the more difficult and important material carefully, making sure that you fully understand what is being discussed and why.

What's most critical, though, is that you think deeply about the material, considering the take-home message of what you've read. You need to be sure that your understanding is complete and that you're able to answer any questions that you had earlier about the material. Rethinking should be the central activity as you reread the passage and your notes.

The benefits of rethinking the material can't be overstated. Rethinking transfers material from your short-term memory to your long-term memory. It solidifies information so that it will be remembered far better over the long haul.

The Concept Map As a Rethinking Tool

As we saw in Chapter 4, **concept mapping** is a method of structuring written material by graphically grouping and connecting key ideas and themes. Each key idea is placed in a different part of the map, and related ideas are placed near it—above, below, or beside it. A concept map looks similar to a graphic of the solar system, with the central idea (the sun) in the center, surrounded by related concepts (the planets).

Concept maps help you to rethink material you've read about, especially if you have used a more traditional outline earlier. Furthermore, once you have developed a concept map for a particular aspect of the material, you can create additional, expanded concept maps involving related information.

Concept maps are particularly useful for people with learning styles that depend on spatial relationships. Furthermore, students with certain kinds of learning disabilities—a topic we discussed earlier in this chapter—can also benefit from the use of concept maps.

An example of a concept map involving the material we've discussed so far is illustrated in Figure 6.3. Note how it summarizes the material and shows how it is related to the central topic of "Reading with Understanding."

Concept mapping
A method of structuring written material by graphically grouping and connecting key ideas and themes

Teaching Tip: Connect the Concept Map information to Chapter 4 on taking notes.

FIGURE 6.3
This concept map illustrates the key ideas of reading with understanding.

- The "Great Books Index: An Index to Online Great Books in English Translation" (**www.mirror.org/books/**): Check out this lengthy list of books. While it is one person's interpretation of what constitutes great books, it nevertheless contains a variety of 20th-century works, as well as older classics, written by a very diverse collection of writers.

- "Increasing Textbook Comprehension by Using SQ3R" is one of several Online Study Skills Workshops sponsored by the Cook Counseling Center of the Virginia Polytechnic Institute and State University (**www.ucc.vt.edu/**). This site introduces the SQ3R approach to reading, and retaining, textual material. A summary of the method can be found at **www.ucc.vt.edu/stdysk/sq3r.html**.

TAKING IT TO THE NET

1 Read a historical document. Choose a document that interests you by going to the Netscape search site (**www.netscape.com**) and conducting a search by entering the phrase "historical documents." After finding a document, read it, and summarize it in a short essay.

2 Go to a newspaper's Web site, such as that of *The New York Times* (**www.nyt.com**) or the *Atlanta Constitution* (**www.ajc.com**), and read one of the current editorials. Take notes on the editorial, concentrating on evaluating the strength of the argument(s). How persuasive was the editorial, and why?

One thousand four hundred eighty-four.

That's all Chenille Lawrence could think about when she got to the bookstore to purchase *War and Peace,* which her instructor said they'd be reading over the next four weeks. Sure, she thought to herself, it's great literature, as her instructor had said. It's undoubtedly a classic that every well-educated person should read some time in his or her life. Sure, maybe reading it would change her life in unimaginable ways, as her instructor had also argued (although she had strong doubts that its immediate effect would be anything but pain).

All she could think about, though, was its length—1,484 pages, not even counting the introduction. How would she ever get through such a giant book?

1. How would you advise Chenille to prepare for her reading of *War and Peace?* What sort of advance organizers would you suggest she create?

2. How would you suggest Chenille organize her time so that she could finish the book in the allotted four weeks?

3. How might Chenille stay focused on her reading? How might she most effectively use writing as a way to accomplish her task?

4. Why is evaluation important for effectively reading a long book such as *War and Peace?* How might Chenille evaluate the book and her understanding of it as she reads?

5. In what ways can Chenille use rethinking techniques to improve her understanding of the book?

taring at the blank computer screen, Maria Ramos felt another surge of anxiety wash over her. She was beginning to panic.

The paper she was trying to get started on was due in two days, and she had not yet put a word down on paper. The problem was . . . well, that was just it: she didn't know what the problem was. The topic was completely hazy; she had no idea what her instructor was looking for.

As the minutes turned into hours, Maria was becoming increasingly desperate. Finally, for lack of a better idea, she decided to start writing down whatever came to mind, producing a flurry of stream-of-consciousness thoughts, recollections, and ideas.

Although most of the things that found their way to her computer screen had nothing to do with the paper topic, she was surprised to come up with a few thoughts that were relevant. And suddenly, she had an idea about how she could approach the assigned topic. Things gradually began to fall into place.

Maria had found her writing voice.

P.O.W.E.R. UP and IRM Link: An activity for introducing this chapter with a lively discussion is described in the IRM – Teaching the Text, Chapter 7, Section IV; activity on creating a list of beliefs and fears about writing and speaking.

LOOKING AHEAD >>>

Few activities raise so many concerns and anxieties as writing and public speaking. Yet few skills are as important to your success, not only in college but also in the world outside the classroom. Taking time now to learn how to write well and speak well will not only increase your chances of success, but it will also improve your peace of mind!

This chapter focuses on writing and speaking. We begin by considering how to write, with a focus on composing college-level papers. We'll talk about how to get started and how you can move from a rough first draft to a final draft of which you can be proud.

The second part of the chapter looks at oral presentations. We'll discuss ways of getting over stage fright and how to engage listeners from the very start of your talk. We consider the importance of practicing neither too little nor too much.

After reading this material, you'll be able to answer these questions:

- **What are the best techniques for getting started and writing a first draft?**

- **How can I move from my first draft to my final draft?**

- **How can I conquer my fear of public speaking and make effective oral presentations?**

The Writing Process

What happens when you sit down to write? Does the sight of a blank page or blank screen leave your mind blank as well? Do your fingers, which move so quickly when you're playing a game on the computer, become sluggish when poised over a keyboard to write a paper?

Writing is not easy, and for many students, writing assignments raise more anxieties than any other academic task. There are many reasons for this anxiety. For one thing, papers often have a large impact on your final course grades. If you do all your writing at the last minute, with a deadline looming, writing is almost certainly a tense experience. Perhaps you've never really been taught how to write well. Or maybe you believe that there's some sort of special writing gene that you just weren't born with.

Stop! Delete from your memory any negative preconceptions you may have about writing. There is no mystery to writing; it's a skill that can be taught and a skill that, with practice, anybody can learn. Writing is not a product you read; it is a thinking and reasoning *process* that is the means of producing that product, a skill that can be learned like any other.

Using strategies based on P.O.W.E.R. Learning (summarized in the P.O.W.E.R. Plan), you will be able to achieve the goal of writing clearly and competently. These strategies will help you to build upon your strengths and maximize your abilities. They will permit you to translate what's inside your head into words that communicate your experience or thoughts directly.

PREPARE
Approach writing as a process

ORGANIZE
Construct a scaffold by creating an outline and thesis statement

WORK
Get it down in the first draft; refine it in the second draft

EVALUATE
Be your own best critic: fine-tune your work

RETHINK
Reflect on the writing process: what worked, what didn't

P.O.W.E.R. Plan

Journal REFLECTIONS

How I Feel about Writing

Reflect on the feelings you have about writing by answering the following questions:

1. When I receive a writing assignment, my initial reaction is . . .

2. Do you ever write for pleasure? When? Under what circumstances?

3. Which writing experiences are particularly pleasant for you? Which are unpleasant?

4. Are you particularly good at finding ways to put off writing tasks? Do you do anything to prevent this?

5. Writing experts believe that the very act of writing can help one think better. Why would be this be true about writing? Have you ever experienced this phenomenon?

1 TRY IT!

Set Yourself Free: Freewriting

Use this space (or a separate sheet of paper) to practice freewriting for a 5-minute period. Optional guidance is offered below, but if you want to go ahead and "just do it," simply start writing. Be sure to keep your hand moving; stop controlling yourself. Write only for yourself; forget about what others might think.

If you need a little more guidance, you are not alone; most people need help the first time they try to freewrite. There are actually two kinds of freewriting: plain vanilla freewriting (like that above) and *focused* freewriting. Focused freewriting gives you a starting point.

Here are some starting points for focused freewriting:

Today I feel . . .

I remember . . .

I don't like . . .

I really like . . .

I get sick when . . .

I know . . .

I am . . .

I am not . . .

Using one of these lead-in phrases as a starting point, return to the blank space and begin your freewriting.

What is the main point of what you wrote? Was freewriting effective in helping you get something down on paper? Was it easy or difficult for you? Can you think of how the process of freewriting might help you when it's time to write a paper?

To Try It online, go to **www.mhhe.com/power**.

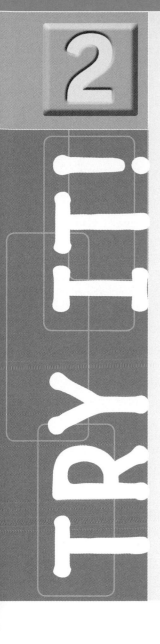

 WORKING IN A GROUP

Get Your Brain Storming:
Using Brainstorming to Generate Ideas

Your American history professor has asked you to come up with 10 ideas for a five-page paper on some aspect of the 1960s. Brainstorm in a group and come up with a list of possible topics, assigning one member of the group to record ideas below.

As you brainstorm, keep the length of the paper assigned and the sort of topic suited to American history generally in mind. Remember, the idea is to produce as many possibilities as you can, without evaluating how realistic or feasible they may be. Think quantity over quality.

After your group has concluded brainstorming, go back to your answers and circle each that you think is realistic for a paper topic. Did brainstorming work? Did you surprise yourself with the number of alternative possibilities you generated for each item?

To Try It online, go to **www.mhhe.com/power**.

information you find in a useable form, consider using a file-folder and note-card system, a proven technique that involves three steps:

1. **Assemble information folders.** Break down material you've found into subtopics by placing the raw information you've located (photocopies, computer printouts, and computer disks) into different multicolored file folders. Label each folder with a stick-on Post-It–type label, which will permit you to easily modify the topic of the folder if necessary in the future.

    This system can work on the computer, too: You can create a file-folder structure into which you put your notes and related material, assuming the information is in electronic form. For many of us this might not yet be completely practical—we still rely too heavily on handwritten notes and hard copies—but as more and more research material becomes available online, this will likely change.

Student Alert: Help your students distinguish between gathering information and processing it.

2. **Create note cards.** Taking notes on index cards is the best way of making information easy to use. *The key is to place no more than one major idea on each card.* If you stick to this rule, you will later find it easy to sort the cards and put them in logical order. It often helps to write the relevant subtopic (such as "Early Influences" or "Husband" or "Politics") at the top right-hand corner of the card for easy reference. (Once again, it is also possible to type notes directly into your computer and store them in a subfolder labeled "Early Influences," "Husband," "Politics," etc.)

Be sure to write the ideas on the note card in your own words, unless you are directly quoting from a source—in which case you must remember to use quotation marks. It's also a good idea to mark a note card with the word "paraphrase" when you put someone else's unique idea in your own words, as in the sample note cards in Figure 7.1. (A **paraphrase** is a restatement of a passage using different words.) Using your own words will prevent you from accidentally copying others' words and passing them off as your own—which, as we'll discuss, is the gravest of academic sins.

Keep in mind that even paraphrased material needs to be cited, unless it is what is called common knowledge. *Common knowledge* is information that is widely known, from multiple sources. For example, the September 11, 2001, terrorist attack on the United States is common knowledge and would not need to be cited. In contrast, one political scientist's explanation of *why* the terrorist attack occurred would need to be cited.

3. **Place source information on every note card.** Make sure every note card contains information that clearly identifies its source. It is extremely impor-

Discussion Prompt: Ask students to generate a list of all of the "10 minute tasks" associated with writing a 10 page paper.

Paraphrase
A restatement of a passage using different words

FIGURE 7.1
Sample Note Cards

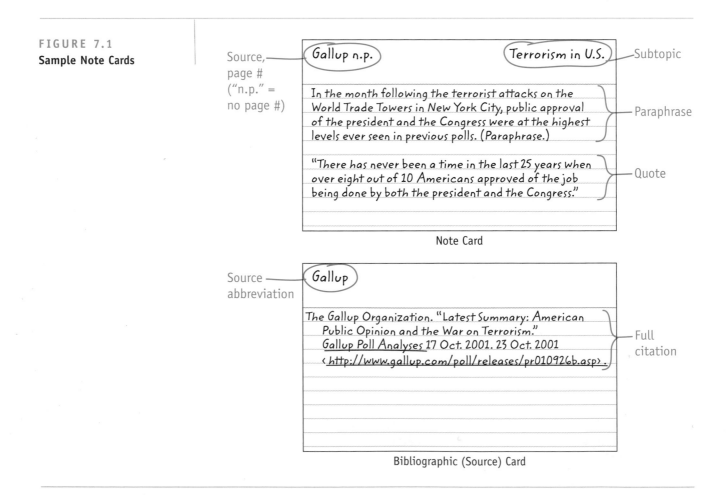

Source, page # ("n.p." = no page #)

Gallup n.p. · · · · · · · · · · · · · · Terrorism in U.S. —Subtopic

In the month following the terrorist attacks on the World Trade Towers in New York City, public approval of the president and the Congress were at the highest levels ever seen in previous polls. (Paraphrase.) —Paraphrase

"There has never been a time in the last 25 years when over eight out of 10 Americans approved of the job being done by both the president and the Congress." —Quote

Note Card

Source abbreviation — Gallup

The Gallup Organization. "Latest Summary: American Public Opinion and the War on Terrorism." *Gallup Poll Analyses* 17 Oct. 2001. 23 Oct. 2001 <http://www.gallup.com/poll/releases/pr010926b.asp>. —Full citation

Bibliographic (Source) Card

tant that you know where the idea on the note card came from so you can credit this source when you write your paper. You do not need to include complete bibliographical information on every note card, but you must keep a master list—either on a separate set of note cards or in a computer file—with the full citation. (Examples of citations for different kinds of sources are listed in Table 7.1. Your instructor will tell you which citation style he or she prefers.)

Teaching Tip: Primary sources are much easier to identify and reference when they are available in the library than on the Web. Take time to explain this as you discuss the importance of citations.

TABLE 7.1 Sample Citations for Different Types of Sources[2]

Book with One Author	Gladwell, M. *Blink: The Power of Thinking without Thinking.* Boston, MA: Little Brown, 2005.
Book with More than One Author	Kagan, Jerome, and Norbert Herschkowitz. *A Young Mind in a Growing Brain.* Mawah, NJ: Lawrence Erlbaum Associates, 2005.
Magazine or Newspaper Article	Allen, Scott. "Debate About Exposure to Sunlight Gets Nastier." *The Boston Globe* 18 Jan. 2005. Health Science, C2.
Scholarly Journal Article	Dayton, Carol. "Elder Abuse: The Social Worker's Perspective." *Clinical Gerontologist* 28 2005: 135–155.
Article with No Author Named	"Three for One; Space Exploration (The Latest from the Solar System)." *The Economist* 15 Jan. 2005: 74.
Article from CD-ROM Collection	Schrag, Peter. "The Near-Myth of Our Failing Schools." *Atlantic Monthly* Oct. 1997. SIRS CD-ROM database. Retrieved 4 Nov. 1997.
Article Reproduced on Internet	Golfen, Bob. "Barrett-Jackson Car Auction Revving Up." *Arizona Republic* 20 Jan 2005. Available on Internet (**www.azcentral.com/arizonarepublic**). Retrieved 20 Jan. 2005.
Internet Site with Author Listed	Gomez, Crystal. "Hot Spots to Visit." Ecotourism Explorer (Internet site at **www.ecotourism.org**). Retrieved 13 Nov. 2002.
Internet Site with No Author Listed	Cardiff University. "Cardiff: A Capital City." Guide to Cardiff, Wales (Internet site at **www.cardiff.ac.uk/about/cardiff/index.html**). Retrieved 20 Jan. 2005.
Newsgroup Posting	Dundjerovic, Nemanja. "Can Tennis Be Made More Interesting?" Online posting: **alt.rec.tennis.** (17 Oct. 1997). Retrieved 20 Nov. 1997.
E-mail	Graham, Heather, former editor, Purdue University student newspaper "Censorship of Student Newspapers." E-mail to Terry West. 13 Dec. 1997.
Interview	Harris, Jonathan, M.D., dermatologist. Personal interview. 15 Nov. 2002.
TV Program	Sawyer, Diane, narrator. "The Truth about Lying." *Primetime Thursday.* ABC News. 15 March 2001.
DVD Recording	*Tibet: Cry of the Snow Lion.* DVD. Artistic License Films, 2003.
For Items Lacking Full Identification—for example, pamphlets, charts, and handouts— put as much data as you can find	*Dangers of Chewing Tobacco.* New York: American Cancer Society. Undated booklet.

ORGANIZE: Constructing a Scaffold

Student Alert: Many students have written research papers. Have them share organizational methods they know. Are they willing to try out new strategies?

When builders begin construction on a building, they create a scaffold—a platform that is the framework allowing them to build the exterior of the building. In the same way, when we read and listen to information, the author or speaker has (hopefully!) already constructed an intellectual scaffold, or framework, for presenting the information to us. Our job as readers and listeners is to figure out what that organization is, like detectives following a trail of clues.

When we're writing, however, we're creating something new. Consequently, it's up to us to come up with the scaffolding for our written product.

Construct an Outline (and Be Ready to Change It!)

The key to organizing an extended piece of writing is the outline. Outlines provide a roadmap to follow when we're writing, a set of sequential steps that show us where we are heading and how we are going to get there.

The secret of successful outlining is flexibility: It is essential to keep an open mind about sequencing and to avoid getting "locked in" too early to a pattern that might later prove unworkable. The best approach is to write possible subtopics, based on your research, on index cards—or simply to type all of them into your computer. Then try to place them in a logical order. (If you use the computer, the program's outlining feature will even renumber the outline as you make changes.) Ask yourself how the subtopics build into a complete and convincing presentation. In doing so, always remember your audience: Consider what a reader would have to know already to understand a given fact or argument. Then try out several sequences and determine which order works best.

Teaching Tip: There are many organizational structures for preparing papers other than ABBCC. Ask your students which ones they know about.

Develop the Paper's Structure

Although instructors sometimes provide a structure for a paper, you will ordinarily have to construct one yourself. One way to do this is to follow the **ABBCC structure.** "ABBCC" stands for the five parts of a typical research paper: *a*rgument, *b*ackground, *b*ody, *c*ounterarguments, and *c*onclusion. Each of these plays a specific role:

ABBCC structure
The structure of the typical research paper, consisting of *a*rgument, *b*ackground, *b*ody, *c*ounterarguments, and *c*onclusion

Thesis
The main point of a paper, typically stating the writer's opinion about the topic of the paper

IRM Link: Teaching the Text, Chapter 7, Section V; have students identify the thesis statement in the two papers referred to in this section.

- **Argument.** Just as we introduce ourselves when we meet someone for the first time, a writer needs to introduce a reader to the main argument being put forward in the paper. Every paper should have a main argument or **thesis,** a one- or two-sentence description of the main point of the paper. For instance, your thesis might make the argument that "Personal character does not matter in leaders; what matters is their effectiveness in accomplishing the goals for which they were elected."

  A thesis should be stated as an assertion ("People are their own worst enemies."). An effective thesis statement takes a position on some issue; many times this is signaled by use of an action verb ("The current technological revolution *requires* that people receive computer training") or the use of such keywords as "should" or "ought." For instance, "Smoking should be banned from restaurants and bars" presents a thesis statement.

"This paper will discuss smoking in restaurants and bars," on the other hand, simply states the topic: we have no idea what stand the writer takes on smoking in restaurants and bars. Try It 3 on page 186 will help you to turn ideas into thesis statements.

Try It 3 on page 186

The thesis or argument need not be the first sentence of the paper. In fact, it is usually wise to start off with something that grabs readers' attention. Begin with a controversial quote, an illustrative story, or a personal encounter—anything that is likely to make a reader sit up and take notice.

In addition to presenting the main thesis of the paper, the first section should lay out the areas that you will cover and the general scope of the paper. You should use this section to present the paper's overall perspective and point of view. For example, "Taxpayers have every right to expect . . . " signals the writer's perspective on campaign finance reform— he or she is thinking about it as a taxpayer, as opposed to a legislator or political candidate.

- **Background.** You'll need to provide readers with a context in which to place your paper's arguments, and the background section is the place to do it. Provide a brief history of the topic, talking about different schools of thought on it. Introduce any unusual terms you might need to use. If the topic is highly controversial, discuss the reasons for the controversy. For example, if you are arguing that capital punishment should be abolished, you could briefly review the history of its use and of opposition to it

- **Body.** The body makes up the bulk of most papers. In the paper's body, you provide evidence as to why your thesis is correct.

  This evidence should be presented in a logical order. Exactly what this means depends upon your topic. You may need to work chronologically if you are discussing a historical event. In other cases, you will want to start with the least controversial arguments and gradually move into the ones that are most debatable.

  When deciding on the order, keep your audience firmly in mind. For instance, a paper on the dangers of electromagnetic radiation written for a community law class would be very different from one written for a physics class.

- **Counterarguments.** You will also need to touch on the counterarguments to your position: Acknowledge them and then go on to systematically refute each one. This section need not be long, but it is crucial. By doing this you help reinforce your own position and strengthen your argument, showing that you have arrived at your point of view fully aware of—and unconvinced by—opposing views.

- **Conclusion.** A good ending to a paper is as important as a good beginning. It's where you pull everything together. And it is your last chance to drive home your thesis.

  The conclusion should summarize the thesis and the arguments that you have made regarding it. Do not introduce new information: The conclusion is a recap. Do make an effort to close with a flourish. You might cite a quotation, present an anecdote that is linked to one you presented at the start of the paper, or pose a rhetorical question ("If the government turns its back on welfare recipients, how can we claim to have a just society?"). However you choose to conclude the paper, make sure that it ties the various pieces together.

If you've ever gone whitewater rafting, you know that following the water's rhythm permits you to remain afloat. In the same way, on those occasions when you achieve a steady rhythm while writing and the words are coming rapidly, stick with it and go with the flow. Revising can come later.

Voice
The unique style of a writer, expressing the writer's outlook on life and past writing experiences

> "I spend a great deal of my time thinking about the power of language—the way it can evoke an emotion, a visual image, a complex idea, or a simple truth."
>
> Amy Tan, author

Write whatever part of the paper you feel most comfortable writing, because just having something on paper will encourage you to write the rest.

- **Turn off your inner critic.** If you're anything like most people, with every word you write, there's probably a voice somewhere in your head that's whispering, "Terrible sentence. Dumb idea. Forget it, you idiot, you'll never finish this paper." Your job is to turn off the voice of that inner critic, at least for now. (You'll want to use it later, when the nagging may come in handy as you revise your work.) While you're working on your first draft, you want to give yourself permission to be creative. As long as you write things down, you'll be able to go back later and make your paper better. But you can't revise what isn't there.

- **Go with the flow.** When you're writing your first draft, try to write quickly. Writing often takes on a rhythm, and you should try to write in sync with that rhythm. If you're on a roll, go with it: Don't stop (yet) to edit your work.

   On the other hand, if you're having trouble getting into a rhythm, and each word is like pulling teeth, take a break. Do something entirely different for a few minutes and then return with a fresh mind.

   If you're really having trouble, try rearranging your note cards (or scrambling your outline). Placing them in a new or even a random order may provide a fresh way of looking at your topic, and this may in turn free you enough to get your writing started.

- **Don't be afraid to modify your outline.** When you start writing, it's easy to fall into the trap of viewing an outline as a rigid, unbending framework. Your outline is a living document, and you should feel free to rearrange headings and to deviate from it as you're creating your first draft.

Many writers find that their outlines need to be revised, and so might you. That's fine; that's why you're writing a first draft and not pretending to start with a final one.

- **Use your own voice.** Just as you have a distinctive speaking voice, each of us has a distinct *writing* **voice.** That voice represents our own unique style, a reflection of our outlook on life and of our past writing experiences.

   Novice writers sometimes get hung up trying to use a voice that isn't their own. For example, they may use words they would never normally use when speaking.

   Avoid the temptation to write as if you were someone else. Instead, use your own natural voice and vocabulary, and don't use big words in an effort to impress your audience. If you'd feel foolish saying "heretofore" in a conversation, you shouldn't use it when you're writing a paper. Don't scan the thesaurus in search of unusual words to use in place of simple ones. (Just because you can do something doesn't mean you should.)

- **Forget about it.** The last step in creating a first draft is the easiest: When you have finished your sketch of the entire paper, from introduction through conclusion, put it aside.

  You need to let your mind idle in neutral for a while so that it will be at full strength when you move on to the next phase of writing: revision.

Revising Your Draft

Remember that inner critic—that voice in your head—that you tuned out while you were writing the first draft? It's time to tune it back in.

The fact is that most of writing is *re*writing. Sure, it's possible to hand in a first draft, and sometimes you'll even get a passable grade. But if you want to reach your own potential as a writer, you *must* revise.

Don't feel that revising is something that only students have to do. Professional writers may go through dozens of drafts—and still not be completely satisfied. Virtually no one has the ability to write a first-draft paper that is so lucid and compelling that it stands on its own.

Following several basic rules can make the revision process work smoothly for you:

- **Read the first draft out loud.** Read your paper out loud—to yourself, a friend, a pet, or your computer. It doesn't matter who's listening.

  Reading out loud does several things. You'll more easily discover missing words, verbs that don't match the subject of the sentence, shifts in tense, missing transitions, and other things that you might have to fix. This is partly because speaking takes longer than silent reading; the slowed pace of reading out loud can help you identify problems that you'd otherwise miss.

IRM Link: Teaching the Text, Chapter 7, Section IV and VIII; activity on "Reading a Paper Out Loud."

- **Take the long view.** Start off by taking the broadest perspective possible and asking yourself a series of questions:

  What is the purpose of my paper? Has that purpose been fulfilled?

  Have I addressed every aspect of the assignment?

  Does the paper tell its readers everything they need to know?

  Will readers be able to follow its logic?

  Does the paper make its points clearly?

  Are the transitions between sections clear?

- **Be ruthless.** Words that we've put on paper tend to take on a life of their own—a life that we have created and so are often reluctant to change or part with.

  It is natural to feel a bit parental toward our first draft, but it is important to fight this instinct. You need to be merciless and unforgiving with passages, paragraphs, phrases, and words that don't sound right or that do not ultimately add to your argument. Don't tear *yourself* down, but, like a coach demanding the best from his or her players, be demanding of your performance.

  Start pruning at the paragraph level. Assess each paragraph to make sure that it adds to the final message, that it

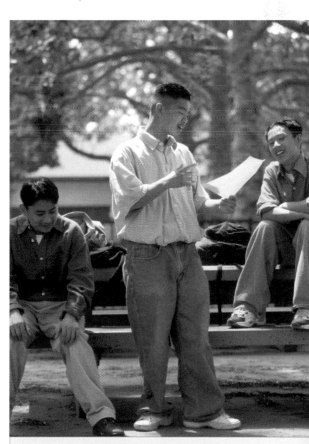

Reading the first draft of a paper aloud can help you identify problems that need to be addressed in a revised draft.

flows from the previous paragraph logically, and that it is consistent with what you are trying to accomplish.

Then move to the level of sentences and words. Evaluate each sentence, and then each word, to make sure that it adds to the clarity of your message.

By paring down your writing, you let your ideas shine through. If you are extremely fond of a phrase or a group of words that you suspect are unnecessary, write down or print out the sections and phrases, put them into an envelope, and toss the envelope into the top drawer of your dresser. You never know when you might need them. More important, knowing that you can save the cut material may make it easier to do the necessary cutting.

> "Wrestling with words gave me my moments of greatest meaning."
>
> Richard Wright, author

Teaching Tip: Ask students to read each other's papers and to provide feedback.

Discussion Prompt: Rather than you spending time trying to convince students about the importance of good spelling, ask them to tell you why correct spelling matters.

Teaching Tip: Bring in examples of appropriate "final" products.

■ **Check sequence and logic.** It's now time to reverse course. Whereas before the focus was on cutting extraneous material, you now need to check for what's *missing*.

For example, earlier cuts might have made it necessary to add or modify transitions between sections and paragraphs. You might also need to improve logic by reordering your ideas, by reordering sentences within paragraphs, and reordering paragraphs within sections.

■ **Check punctuation and spelling.** Check for the obvious stuff: Sentences should start with capital letters and end with the appropriate punctuation, commas should set off dependent clauses, and the like. Use a handbook or style manual if you're unsure.

Check your spelling carefully. This is one of the areas in which word processors earn their keep best. The spell-check feature will not only identify every misspelled word (that is, every word not in its dictionary), but it will also prompt you with alternative spellings.

Be careful not to rely completely on the spell-checker, however. Such programs can find only misspellings that do not form recognized words; if what you typed is a word, the spell-checker will ignore it, even if it is not the word you wanted to use. *Foe instants, know spelt-cheek pogrom wood fined eras inn thus sent-tense.* And yet every word in the preceding "sent-tense" is spelled incorrectly in this context.

■ **Check that all quotes are cited and referenced correctly.** As we'll discuss in detail later, it is critical that you give proper credit to others' ideas and words. Make sure that you haven't directly quoted or paraphrased a source without acknowledging it.

■ **Make it pleasing to the eye.** Instructors are human. They can't help but react differently to a paper that is neatly typed compared with one that is handwritten in a difficult-to-read scrawl.

A neat paper conveys a message: I'm proud of this paper. I've put time and effort into it. This is my best work.

A sloppy paper says something different.

Take the time, then, to make sure your paper looks good. This doesn't mean that you need to invest in a fancy plastic cover, or worry about the alignment of the staples, or spend a lot of time deciding which font to use on your word processor. But it does mean that the quality of the paper's appearance should match the quality of the writing.

Writing in Class: Strategies for Getting It Right

Your instructor pauses halfway through her lecture and says for the next 5 minutes you are to complete a short written assignment. Whether she calls it an in-class essay, a reaction paper, or a "pop paper," it calls for somewhat different strategies than an out-of-class writing assignment. Unlike traditional paper assignments—in which you have the luxury of time—an in-class writing assignment requires that you react immediately.

Here are some tips for completing in-class writing assignments:

- *Be prepared.* You should always come to class with pen and pencil, as well knowing your student ID number (at least in big classes). Just as important, make sure you're up-to-date in the reading assignments.

- *Think first.* Before you start writing, spend a minute thinking about the assignment. What is its goal? How can you best approach it? What is it that you want to get across?

- *Make a quick outline.* Creating an outline—even a short one—will help you collect your thoughts and prepare for what you're going to say.

- *Timing is everything.* Assuming your instructor lets you know how much time you'll have (and ask how much if he or she doesn't mention it), plan ahead appropriately. You don't want to run out of time before completing your assignment.

- *Be sure to answer every part of the question.* If your instructor asks for your opinion, be sure to give it; but if he or she also wants to know *why* you feel the way you do, don't forget that part.

- *Neatness counts.* Be sure your answer is legible. If your handwriting is terrible, then print. The most brilliant of responses does you no good if your instructor can't read it.

E VALUATE: Acting as Your Own Best Critic

Because you've already put so much work into your paper, you might be tempted to rush through the final stages of the P.O.W.E.R. process. Avoid the temptation. If you've carefully revised your paper, the last stages will not be time-consuming, and they may have a significant impact on your paper's ultimate quality—and your success.

Take these steps to *evaluate* what you've written:

- **Ask yourself if your paper accomplishes what you set out to do.** The beginning of your paper contains a thesis statement and the argument that you intended to make. Does your paper support the thesis? Is your argument upheld by the evidence you've reported? Would an impartial reader be convinced by what you've written?

- **Put yourself in your instructor's shoes.** Does the paper precisely fit the assignment requirements? Does it meet the instructor's underlying goals in giving the assignment?

Student Alert: Students may resist the idea that they can predict an instructor's evaluation. Help them see why it's important to make the effort to do so.

- **Check the mechanical aspects of the paper.** The grammar and spelling must be correct; the paper should also look good. If your instructor requires that citations or references be reported in a certain style, make sure you've followed it. For example, your instructor might specify Modern Language Association style (used in the humanities), American Psychological Association style (used in the social sciences) or Council of Science Editors style (used in the sciences).

- **Have an objective reader take a look.** Many colleges have writing labs or centers that will help you with your writing. In many cases, their staff will take a look at a paper and provide feedback. You can also have a friend or family member read the paper, giving you comments.

If you've revised the paper with care, it will likely pass muster. If it doesn't, though, go back and work on it once again. By this point, it should require only minor tinkering to get it into shape.

R ETHINK: Reflecting on Your Accomplishment

Discussion Prompt: Pair up students and have them talk about rethinking the message and the mechanics.

Rethinking is the homestretch of the writing process. It's a moment to savor, because it permits you take a long view of what you've accomplished. You've gone from a blank page to words on paper that tell a story. You've turned nothing into something—an achievement in and of itself.

Rethinking occurs on several levels: rethinking the message, mechanics, and method. But don't address them until a little time has passed: Wait a day or so to reread the paper. Then, bringing your critical thinking skills to bear, reflect on the following:

- **Rethink the message.** Be sure that the overall message your paper conveys is appropriate. A paper can be like an advertisement. In most papers, you are seeking to communicate information to convince someone of a particular opinion. Make sure that the message is what you wish to communicate, and that ultimately the paper is successful in making the case.

- **Rethink the mechanics.** A television commercial filled with fuzzy images and annoyingly unsteady camera shots would not be very compelling, no matter how good the underlying product. In the same way, a paper with mechanical errors will not impress your readers or persuade them. Take another look at your writing style; look at grammar, punctuation, and word usage to make sure the choices you've made are appropriate.

Teaching Tip: Ask students to attach a page to the end of every paper they turn in for you with responses to these "rethink" prompts.

- **Rethink the method.** Every time you finish a paper, you learn something—something about the topic of your writing and something about yourself. Ask yourself what you have learned to help you become a better writer in the future. What might you have done to improve the writing process? What could have gone better? What will you do differently the next time you write? Above all, remember what you've accomplished: You've transformed what's inside your head—your thoughts, your ideas, your values—into something that can potentially influence other people. You have exercised the ability to move others and get them to think in new ways. You've made a difference. That's the real power of writing.

Write Away

The first step in getting a job is putting pen to paper (or, probably more accurately, finger to keyboard). Whether you receive a lead for a job from a college career center, read an ad in the paper, or see a job listing on the Internet, you'll need to communicate in writing to the potential employer.

You are selling yourself in a letter of application. To be effective, keep these guidelines in mind:

■ **Brief is better.** Employers are likely to get many letters, and long ones are least likely to be read.

■ **State what you can do for the employer, not what the employer can do for you.** Don't tell a potential employer you really, really need a job to pay off your credit card bills. Instead, explain how your skills can help further an organization's goals.

■ **Summarize your qualifications.** Respond specifically to the skills required for the job. List specific experiences you've had that are relevant to what the employer is looking for.

■ **Enclose a résumé.** Your résumé should contain a detailed summary of your educational background and work experience, as well as other relevant qualifications.

■ **Ask for an interview.** Close your letter with a request to meet and discuss the job. Provide your telephone number and e-mail address.

■ **Proofread!** You must have zero tolerance for errors. Any mistake is likely to put you at the bottom of the pile of applications.

Acknowledging Others' Ideas: Academic Honesty and Plagiarism

As you move through the process of writing a paper, there are many temptations to cut corners. A friend may have written a paper the previous year on the same topic and offer to "lend" it to you . . . you may find a paper on the Web that addresses just what you intended to write . . . you and a friend may be enrolled in a very large class, and he may suggest that you each write part of the paper and "share" sections.

Don't yield to temptations such as these. Not only is honesty the best policy, but it's also the *only* policy in the world of academics. There's no greater academic sin than **plagiarism,** taking credit for someone else's words, thoughts, or ideas. In the academic world, plagiarism is about the same as stealing a stranger's car. Even if you just mean to "borrow" a passage, passing another person's work off as your own is totally wrong.

Furthermore, penalties for plagiarism are severe. In many colleges, plagiarism results in a comment on your transcript or can result in expulsion. You even could face legal charges, because almost all published material is copyrighted, which means that it is someone's *intellectual property.* If an author learns that you have used his or her writing as your own, the author has the right to take you to court and sue for damages.

Discussion Prompt: Plagiarism is but one form of cheating. Many sources tell us that cheating of all kinds is on the rise in colleges today. Have students discuss this topic using examples from their personal experience.

Plagiarism
Taking credit for someone else's words, thoughts, or ideas

"Now that we've considered the solutions, we need to take a look at their costs . . . "

"Let's go back for a moment to an earlier point I made . . . "

"To sum up, the situation offers some unexpected advantages . . . "

Discussion Prompt: Ask students to discuss advantages and disadvantages of giving a presentation using a paper (8 ½ by 11 sheets), note cards (3 x 5), overhead transparencies, slides, computers, videos, etc.

■ **Make your notes work for you, not against you.** A speaker is giving a talk, and suddenly she loses her place in her notes. She fumbles around, desperately trying to find her place and figure out what comes next.

It's a painful situation to watch—and even worse for the person experiencing the problem. How do you avoid finding yourself in such a predicament?

One way is by thoroughly acquainting yourself both with what you are going to say *and* with your notes. Once again, practice is your best friend. But the type of notes you have also makes a big difference.

Some speakers write out their entire talk in advance; others use no notes at all, counting on memorizing their talk. Avoid either extreme. If you write out your complete speech in advance, you'll experience an overwhelming urge to read it to your audience. Nothing could be more deadly. On the other hand, if you memorize your talk and have no notes at all, you'll be susceptible to a memory lapse that can make you feel completely foolish. Even if you can remember your talk successfully, you may end up sounding mechanical, like an amusement park guide who has given the same speech about the "jungle cruise" a thousand times.

Choose a middle ground. Develop an outline that includes the major points you wish to cover and have this outline in front of you when you speak. It might be written or typed on a sheet of paper, or you might use index cards (number them!). In addition, write out and memorize your opening and closing statements.

By memorizing the opening and closing statements, you'll have the opportunity to look your audience in the eye and engage them nonverbally at two of the most crucial junctures in your talk—the beginning and the end. Using an outline for most of your talk permits you to sound natural as you speak. You'll probably use slightly different words every time you give your talk, which is fine.

When used in a talk, maps like these and other audiovisual aids help to keep an audience interested in what you are saying. They also take the focus away from you, making public speaking less nerve-wracking.

IRM Link: Teaching the Text, Chapter 7, Section IV; suggested activity regarding visual aids.

■ **A picture can save you a thousand words.** Maps, charts, photos, drawings, figures, and other illustrations add another dimension to a presentation, helping to engage listeners. Computer programs, such as PowerPoint, permit you to create graphics relatively painlessly (as we'll discuss further in Chapter 10). Just be sure to give full credit to the source of anything you use that someone else created—the rules of plagiarism hold for talks you give, as much as for your writing.

You can even use props. For example, if you are talking about a series of Supreme Court rulings, you might incorporate a gavel into your talk. Effective visual aids make abstract concepts more concrete and immediate.

- **Use the right amount and kind of practice.** After you've written your opening and closing statements, constructed an outline, and decided what visual aids to use, it's time to practice. It's not just the amount of practice that is critical: How you practice is as important as how much you practice.

    Running through your speech mentally will help you to familiarize yourself with your presentation, but you really need to give the speech out loud. Only by hearing yourself speak can you actually get a sense of how the presentation works as an oral presentation.

    Practice in front of a friend or classmate. It is only by actually trying your talk out in front of a warm body that you'll be able to approximate the experience of actually speaking in public, and your audience can provide you with feedback regarding what is working and what is not.

    How much practice is enough practice? You've probably done enough when you do a good job giving a talk twice in a row. If you practice your talk too many times, you'll become so bored with it that the actual talk will sound canned and unconvincing.

- **Fight stage fright.** As you know, for many people, the mere thought of speaking in front of others causes a knot of fear to form deep in their gut. Even those who routinely speak in front of others experience some degree of anxiety. (Ask one or two of your course instructors if they ever feel nervous when teaching a class. Their answers may surprise you.)

    Although you won't be able to alleviate your stage fright completely, several techniques can reduce the anxiety that public speaking produces. First, make sure you're wearing clothes that are comfortable and that make you feel pleased with your appearance. If you feel good about your appearance, you'll be more relaxed.

    Five minutes before you get up to speak, take three slow, deep breaths. Concentrate on the feeling of the air going in and out of your body. If a particular part of your body feels tense, tighten it up even more and then relax it. Do it several times. Finally, visualize yourself giving the speech successfully and the relief that you'll feel afterward.

- **Monitor your nonverbal behavior.** Anxiety about public speaking can do strange things to people's bodies. Their hands may shake or feel icy cold. They may pace back and forth like a caged lion. They may sweat profusely. They may stand rigidly while speaking, looking like stiff toy soldiers. Or they may slump over a podium as if they wished they could dissolve into thin air.

    To avoid appearing as if you were scared to death—even if you are—stand up straight and tall. Look directly at different members of your audience, shifting your gaze from one person to the next. Eye contact engages audience members, making them feel that your words are directed straight toward them.

Teaching Tip: Videotape your students and allow them to take the video home to watch in private. Ask them to provide you with a written critique of their performance.

"I could have been a big celebrity but for my fear of public speaking."

It's not easy. We're all victims of information overload. We're exposed to more information in a year than our grandparents were exposed to in their entire lifetimes.

To determine what is important, look at the big picture. Don't get lost in minute details. Instead, prepare yourself by taking a broad overview of the material, and decide what your goal is going to be. (To begin testing your memory, complete Try It 1.)

O RGANIZE: Relating New Material to What You Already Know

Don't think of memorization as pumping gasoline (new information) into an almost-empty gas tank (your brain). You're not filling something that is empty. On the contrary, you are filling a container that already has a lot of things in it, that is infinitely expandable, and that never empties out.

> **"Human memory works its own wheel, and stops where it will."**
>
> William Saroyan, author, *Chance Meetings*, 1978

If you approach each new memorization task as something entirely new and unrelated to your previous knowledge, you'll have enormous difficulty recalling it. On the other hand, if you connect it to what you already know, you'll be able to recall it far better. The way to get your brain to do this organizational work for you is by thinking about the associations the new material has with the old.

- **Personalize information.** Suppose you need to remember information about the consequences of global warming, such as the fact that the level of the oceans is predicted to rise. You might think about the rising level of the ocean as it relates to your personal memories of visits to the beach. You might think what a visit to the beach would be like with dramatically higher water levels, visualizing a shrunken shoreline with no room for sunbathing. Then whenever you think about global warming in the future, your mind is likely to associate this fairly abstract concept with its concrete consequences for beaches. The association you made while rehearsing the information makes it personal, long-lasting, and useful. (You can see this for yourself in Try It 2 on page 214.)

- **Organize information by place.** *Where* you learn something makes a difference in how well you can recall it. Memory researchers have found that people actually remember things better in the place where they first studied and learned them. Consequently, one of the ways to jog your memory is to try to re-create the situation in which you first learned what you're trying to remember. If you

What would help you remember a person's name after you were introduced to him for the first time?

1

TRY IT!

Remember This

Read the following story. Pay attention to the details, but don't take notes or make lists.

Demain entered the marketplace slowly, feeling his way. He had never seen such confusion.

Hundreds of wagons, caravans, booths, and carts were drawn up in a broad U, occupying three sides of the enormous town square, their awnings and curtains open and inviting. The colors and odors were a sensual assault; he perceived them not just through his eyes and nose, but as if they were pressing forcibly against his skin. And the sounds! He could scarcely keep himself from bolting back the way he had come, to the safety of the countryside.

A sense of wonder pushed him forward. He walked past gold merchants, with their gray cloaks and watchful eyes, and a potter, her shop filled three shelves high with vases, bottles, and jars of deep blues, reds, and yellows that Demain—accustomed to the brown clay that adorned his mother's kitchen—had never even imagined possible. Cloths were on sale in the booth next to the potter's—shamelessly long bolts of impossibly patterned prints, depicting herons, bulls, schools of fish, a field of wheat, great bowls of fruit, and men and women engaged in the pursuits he knew from stories: They danced in bold colors and graceful postures, harvested vast fields of bounty, fought battles of intricate strategy, and drank and courted in riotous taverns.

Past the dealers in rugs, chairs, hats, shoes, and wagons; past the blacksmith's huge muddy arms beating out rugged tools and fine weapons; past the fortune tellers and musicians, Demain at last came to the vendors of food and drink. Never had he felt so hungry. He was lifted off his feet—he swore he was floating—by the aroma of long lines of sausages, sides of beef, whole lambs, chickens on spits the length of spears, bacon and hams, fried potatoes, great vats of boiling vegetables, stewing tomatoes, and breads—all shapes and sizes of loaves, twisted into braids, curled into circles, flattened, puffed, elongated, pocketed, and glazed.

Demain felt the two coppers in his pocket—his holiday bounty—and hoped they would be enough.

Note: We'll return to the story of Demain later. For now, read on.

To Try It online, go to **www.mhhe.com/power**.

---

memorized the colors that litmus paper turns when it is placed in acids and bases while you were in your campus science library, it might be helpful during a test to recall the correct colors by imagining yourself in the science library thinking about the colors.

Another effective place-related strategy is to introduce new data into your mind in the place that you know you're going to need to recall it at some future moment. For instance, suppose you know that you're going to be tested on certain material in the room in which your class is held. Try to do at least some of your studying in that same room.

Organize Your Memory

As critical thinking expert Diane Halpern points out, having an organized memory is like having a neat bedroom: Its value is that you know you'll be able to find something when you need it. To prove the point, try this exercise she devised.[1]

Read the following 15 words at a rate of approximately one per second:

girl

heart

robin

purple

finger

flute

blue

organ

man

hawk

green

lung

eagle

child

piano

Now, cover the list, and write down as many of the words as you can on a separate sheet of paper. How many words are there on your list? _____

WORK: Using Proven Strategies to Memorize New Material

One of the good things about the work of memorization is that you have your choice of literally dozens of techniques. Depending on the kind of material you need to recall and how much you already know about the subject, you can turn to any number of methods.

As we sort through the various options, keep in mind that no one strategy works by itself. (And some strategies don't seem to work: for example, forget about drugs like ginko biloba—there's no clear scientific evidence that they are effective.[2]) Instead, try the following proven strategies and find those that work best for you. Feel free to devise your own strategies or add those that have worked for you in the past.

After you've done this, read the following list:

> green
>
> blue
>
> purple
>
> man
>
> girl
>
> child
>
> piano
>
> flute
>
> organ
>
> heart
>
> lung
>
> finger
>
> eagle
>
> hawk
>
> robin

Now cover this second list and write down as many of the words as you can on the other side of the separate sheet of paper.

How many words did you remember this time? Did you notice that the words on both lists are identical? Did you remember more the second time? (Most people do.) Why do you think most people remember more when the words are organized as they are in the second list?

Working in a Group:

Discuss with your classmates ways in which you can organize material from this book to make it easier to remember.

To Try It online, go to **www.mhhe.com/power**.

Rehearsal

Think it again: rehearsal. Say it aloud: rehearsal. Think of it in terms of the three syllables that make up the word: re—hear—sal. OK, one more time—say the word "rehearsal."

If you're scratching your head over the last paragraph, it's to illustrate the point of **rehearsal:** to transfer material that you encounter into memory. If you don't rehearse information in some way, it will end up like most of the information to which we're exposed: on the garbage heap of lost memory.

To test if you've succeeded in transferring the word "rehearsal" into your memory, put down this book and go off for a few minutes. Do something entirely unrelated to reading this book. Have a snack, catch up on the latest sports scores on ESPN, or read the front page of the newspaper.

Rehearsal

The process of practicing and learning material to transfer it into memory

What Sort of Memory Do I Have—and Want?

1. What kinds of information do you remember best: faces, shapes, colors, smells, names, dates, or facts? Why do you think this is?

2. What kinds of information do you have the greatest difficulty remembering? Why do you think this type of information is hard for you to remember?

3. Is there any particular source of information about which you can remember exceptional amounts, such as baseball records or movie trivia? Why do you think you remember this information so effortlessly?

4. Do you use any memorization techniques now? Have you ever tried any in the past?

5. Suppose scientists devised a "memory drug" that would allow you to remember *everything* to which you were exposed. What would be the advantages and disadvantages of such a drug? Would you be likely to use it?

Are you back? If the word "rehearsal" popped into your head when you picked up this book again, you've passed your first memory test. You can be assured that the word "rehearsal" has been transferred into your memory.

Rehearsal is the key strategy in remembering information. If you don't rehearse material, it will never make it into memory. Repeating the information, summarizing it, associating it with other memories, and above all thinking about it when you first come across it will ensure that rehearsal will be effective in pushing the material into memory.

Mnemonics

This odd word (pronounced in an equally odd fashion, with the "m" silent—"neh MON ix") describes formal techniques used to make material more readily remembered. **Mnemonics** are the tricks of the trade that professional memory experts use, and you too can use them to nail down the sort of information you will often need to recall for tests.

Among the most common mnemonics are the following:

- **Acronyms.** You're already well acquainted with **acronyms,** words or phrases formed by the first letters of a series of terms. For instance, although you may not have known it, the word "laser" is actually an acronym for "light

Mnemonics
Formal techniques used to make material more readily remembered

Acronym
A word or phrase formed by the first letters of a series of terms

amplification by stimulated emissions of radiation," and "radar" is an acronym for "radio detection and ranging."

Acronyms can be a big help in remembering things. If you took music lessons, you may know that FACE spells out the names of the notes that appear in the spaces on the treble clef music staff ("F," "A," "C," and "E," starting at the bottom of the staff). Roy G. Biv is a favorite of physics students who must remember the colors of the spectrum (red, orange, yellow, green, blue, indigo, and violet). And P.O.W.E.R. stands for—well, by this point in the book, you probably remember.

The benefit of acronyms is that they help us to recall a complete list of steps or items. The drawback, though, is that the acronym itself has to be remembered, and sometimes we may not recall it when we need it. For instance, Roy G. Biv is not exactly the sort of name that readily comes to mind. And even if we do remember Roy G. Biv, we might get stuck trying to recall what a particular letter stands for. (For example, we'd probably prefer not to spend a lot of time during a test trying to remember if the "B" stands for brown or beige or blue.)

- **Acrostics.** After learning to use the acronym "FACE" to remember the notes on the spaces of the music staff, many beginning musicians learn that the names of the lines on the staff form the acrostic, "Every Good Boy Deserves Fudge." **Acrostics** are sentences in which the first letters spell out something that needs to be recalled. The benefits—as well as the drawbacks—of acrostics are similar to those of acronyms. (You can explore acronyms and acrostics in Try It 3).

- **Rhymes and jingles**. "Thirty days hath September, April, June, and November. . . ." If you know the rest of the rhyme, you're familiar with one of the most commonly used mnemonic jingles in the English language. Similarly, some of us learned the main theme of Schubert's Unfinished Symphony by singing the words "This is the symphony that Schubert wrote and never finished" when the theme first appears. For those who learned to recognize the symphony by using this mnemonic, it is virtually impossible to hear the symphony without recalling the words.

Although mnemonics are helpful, keep in mind that they have a number of significant shortcomings. First, they don't focus on the meaning of the items being remembered. Because information that is learned in terms of its surface characteristics—such as first letters that form a word—is less likely to be retained than information that is learned in terms of its meaning, mnemonic devices are an imperfect route to memorization.

There's another problem with mnemonics: Sometimes it takes as much effort to create a mnemonic device as it would to memorize the material in the first place. And because the mnemonic itself has no meaning, it can be forgotten.

Despite their drawbacks, mnemonics can be useful. They are particularly helpful when the material being memorized includes a list of items or a series of steps.

The Method of Loci and the Peg Method: Special Help for Recalling Sequences and Lists

The ancient Greeks had a way with words. Their orators could deliver speeches that went on for hours, without notes. How did they remember what they wanted to say?

They used a procedure called the **method of loci.** *Loci* (pronounced "low sigh") is the Latin word for "places," and it helps describe a procedure in

WORKING IN A GROUP

Do-It-Yourself Acronyms and Acrostics

In the first part of this Try It, work individually to create an acronym and an acrostic.

1. Figure out an acronym to remind you of the names of the five Great Lakes, using the first letters of their names (which are Erie, Huron, Michigan, Ontario, Superior).

2. Devise an acrostic for the nine planets in order of their average distance from the sun. Their names, in order, are Mercury, Venus, Earth, Mars, Jupiter, Saturn, Uranus, Neptune, Pluto.

After you've tried to create the acronym and acrostic, meet in a group and discuss these questions: How successful were you in devising effective acronyms and acrostics? Do some of the group members' creations seem more effective than others? Why? Is the act of creating them an important component of helping to remember what they represent, or would having them created by someone else be as helpful in recalling them? For your information, a common acronym for the Great Lakes is HOMES (**H**uron, **O**ntario, **M**ichigan, **E**rie, **S**uperior), and a popular acrostic for the order of the planets is **M**y **V**ery **E**ducated **M**other **J**ust **S**erved **U**s **N**ine **P**izzas.

To Try It online, go to **www.mhhe.com/power**.

Student Alert: The method of loci is complex and some students will reject working with it because of the level of thinking involved. Remind them that finding meaningful ways to put information together can help them to improve their memory. The complexity of this approach requires that they spend more time on it.

which items in a sequence you wish to remember—such as the sections of a speech or a series of events—are thought of as "located" in a different place in a building.

Consider, for example, a speech that has three major sections: an introduction, a main body, and a conclusion. Each of the three sections has various points that you need to recall also.

To use the method of loci, you'd first visualize the living room, kitchen, and bedroom of a house with which you were familiar. Next, you'd mentally "place" the introduction of the speech into the living room of the house. You would mentally place each of the *parts* of the introduction on a different piece of furniture, following the way in which the furniture was laid out in the room (for example, you might proceed clockwise from the door). The easy chair might contain the first point of the introduction, the sofa the next point, and an end table the last point. Then you'd move into the kitchen and do the same thing with the body of the paper, laying out your arguments on different pieces of kitchen furniture or appliances. Finally, you'd end up in the bedroom, where you'd "place" the conclusion.

You can use the method of loci not only for public speaking, but for any situation in which you are trying to remember a series of steps. For example, if you wanted to recall the steps in the scientific method (e.g., develop a theory, form a hypothesis, conduct an experiment, etc.), you could think of each step as taking place in a different part of your apartment.

A close cousin of the method of loci is the **peg method.** The peg method uses a series of keywords tied to the digits one to ten to help you recall an important sequence of numbers. For instance, a set of "pegs" that you could use would link numbers with these words:

One is a sun.

Two is a zoo.

Three is me.

Four is a store.

Five is a dive.

Six are sticks.

Seven is heaven.

Eight is a gate.

Nine is a pine.

Ten is a den.

By thinking of exotic images using the peg words tied to the numbers, it becomes easier to recall a specific group of numbers that you need to memorize. For instance, suppose you had trouble remembering the value of *pi*, used to calculate the circumference of a circle (3.14, in case you don't remember). Take the three relevant digits—3, 1, and 4—and translate them into the relevant peg words—me (3), sun (1), and store (4)—and think of an image linking the three.

For example, one possibility is to memorize the image of yourself wearing sunglasses, heading out to a store on a sunny day. Then, when you need to remember the value of *pi*, this image will pop into your head, and you'll be able to use the peg word system to figure out the number associated with each part of the image.

The peg method can also be used to memorize ordered lists of items, when the sequence in which they appear is important. For instance, you could use the peg system if you needed to recall the specific order in which bones of the foot and leg were connected to one another for your anatomy class. To use the peg system in this way, you link images of the ordered set of items to the 10 "numbers." The first item is linked with the sun, the second with a zoo, and so on.

Involve Multiple Senses

The more senses you can involve when you're trying to learn new material, the better you'll be able to remember. Here's why: Every time

Have you ever wondered how some waiters can remember what their customers have ordered without writing anything down? They use the same simple memory strategies that you can use to recall information you'll need to remember for tests.

TRY IT!

PERSONAL STYLES

Determine Your Memory Style

What's your dominant memory style? Do you most easily remember sounds, sights, or the way things feel? Read the statements below and circle the response choice that most closely describes your habits.

To help recall lectures, I . . .

V. Read the notes I took during class.

A. Close my eyes and try to hear what the instructor said.

K. Try to place myself back in the lecture room and feel what was going on at the time.

To remember a complex procedure, I . . .

V. Write down the steps I have to follow.

A. Listen carefully and repeatedly to the instructions.

K. Do it over and over again.

To learn sentences in a foreign language, I do best if I . . .

V. Read them on paper to see how they're written.

A. Hear them in my head until I can say them aloud.

K. See someone speaking them and then practice moving my mouth and hands the way the speaker did.

If I have to learn a dance move, I like . . .

V. To see a diagram of the steps before trying it.

A. Someone to coach me through it while I try it.

K. To watch it once and then give it a try.

Discussion prompt: Can your students attach powerful emotions to information they can remember?

we encounter new information, all of our senses are potentially at work. For instance, if we witness a car crash, we receive sensory input from the sight of the two cars hitting each other, the sound of the impact, and perhaps the smell of burning rubber. Each piece of sensory information is stored in a separate location in the brain, and yet all the pieces are linked together in extraordinarily intricate ways.

What this means is that when we seek to remember the details of the crash, recalling a memory of one of the sensory experiences—such as what we heard—can trigger recall of the other types of memories. For example, thinking about the *sound* the two cars made when they hit can bring back memories of the way the scene looked.

In fact, many of us have a favorite memory style—one that we use most often when trying to recall information. Take a moment to learn about your own memory style by completing Try It 4.

When I recall a very happy moment, I tend to . . .

> **V.** Visualize it in my head.
>
> **A.** Hear the sounds that I heard when experiencing it.
>
> **K.** Feel with my hands and body what I felt at the time.

When I have to remember driving directions, I usually . . .

> **V.** See a map of the route in my mind.
>
> **A.** Repeat the directions aloud to myself.
>
> **K.** Feel my hands steering and the car driving along the correct route.

Answer key:

If you chose mostly **V**s, your main memory style is visual; your preference is to remember things in terms of the way they appear.

If you chose mostly **A**s, your main memory style is auditory; your preference is to recall material in terms of sound.

If you chose mostly **K**s, your main memory style is kinesthetic; your preference is to remember using your sense of touch.

Keep in mind that this questionnaire only gives a rough idea of how we usually use our memories. Remember: All of us use all of the memory styles during the course of each day.

Consider these questions: How do you think your memory style affects the way you recall academic information? How does your memory style relate to your learning style? How does it affect the way you learn things initially? How could you make greater use of your less-preferred styles?

To Try It online, go to **www.mhhe.com/power**.

You can make use of the fact that memories are stored in multiple ways by applying the following techniques:

- **When you learn something, use your body.** Don't sit passively at your desk. Instead, move around. Stand up; sit down. Touch the page. Trace figures with your fingers. Talk to yourself. Think out loud. It may seem strange, but doing this increases the number of ways in which the information is stored. By involving every part of your body, you've increased the number of potential ways to trigger a relevant memory later, when you need to recall it. And when one memory is triggered, other related memories may come tumbling back.

- **Draw and diagram the material.** We've already considered (in Chapter 4) the power of concept maps, the method of structuring written material by graphically grouping and connecting key ideas and themes. When we create

Discussion Prompt: What influence can reading and writing about mathematical problems and graphing results have on the ability to understand and thus, remember and learn math?

Think Positively

Emotions matter. If you're in a negative frame of mind when you try to memorize something, your negative feelings can become attached to the memory, making you less likely to recall it because you'll automatically tend to avoid those bad feelings. The opposite is also true: If you think positively about the process of memorization, those more-positive feelings will end up being etched into your memory.

Of course, feelings can't be turned off in the same way we're able to turn off a light. If you feel nervous and scared about memorizing all the formulas you need to for your chemistry midterm, you can't just tell yourself it's great fun. But if you recognize your feelings, they lose much of their power to influence you and to block memories.

Overlearning

Think back to when you were learning your basic multiplication facts ($1 \times 1 = 1$; $2 \times 2 = 4$; and so forth). Let's suppose you had put each multiplication problem on a flash card, and you decided to go through your entire set of cards, trying to get every problem right.

The first time you went through the set of cards and answered all the problems correctly, would you feel as if you'd memorized them perfectly and that you'd never again make an error? You shouldn't. You would need several instances of perfect performance to be sure you had learned the multiplication facts completely.

Lasting learning doesn't come until you have overlearned the material. **Overlearning** consists of studying and rehearsing material past the point of initial mastery. Through overlearning, recall becomes automatic. Rather than searching for a fact, going through mental contortions until perhaps the information surfaces, overlearning permits us to recall the information without even thinking about it.

> **"Don't let those few Einsteins who can ace a test by never attending class and by sleeping on the textbook the night before trick you into using their study methods. My roommate tried to convince me that studying by osmosis was a proven method. Trust me, it isn't."**
>
> Keith Vernon, student,
> University of Puget Sound[3]

Overlearning
Studying and rehearsing material past the point of initial mastery to the point at which recall becomes automatic

To put the principle of overlearning to work, don't stop studying at the point when you can say to yourself, "Well, I'll probably pass this test." You may be right, but that's all you'll do—pass. Instead, spend extra time learning the material until it becomes as familiar as an old pair of jeans.

E VALUATE: Testing Your Recall of New Information

IRM Link: Teaching the Text, Chapter 8, Section I, Chapter Summary; read the information in the *Message to the Instructor* about deep learning.

The memory strategies just described can bring you to a point where you probably feel comfortable in your ability to remember the material you've been learning. Once you've used one or more of them to help you, it's time to test yourself—to evaluate whether you'll be able to recall the material when you need it. There are several ways to evaluate your memory:

■ **Use in-text review questions and tests.** Many textbook chapters end with a quiz or a set of review questions about the material. Some have questions scattered throughout the chapter. Don't ignore them! Not only do such questions indicate what the writer of the book thought was important for you to learn and memorize, but they can also provide an excellent opportunity for evaluating your memory.

Special Memorization Strategies for Special Courses

Foreign language courses, as well as those in math and science, often pose particular memorization challenges. Here are some special strategies you can use to attack these subject areas:

For foreign language courses:

- When memorizing vocabulary, don't just read words silently—say them aloud and write them out.

- Using Post-It notes, write the name of objects around your living space in the foreign language.

- Practice speaking in the language lab.

- When others are called on in class, give answers silently to every question.

- Don't be afraid to make mistakes—you probably occasionally mispronounce words in your native language, without dire consequences.

For math and science courses:

- Memorize formulas by learning how to derive them.

- Practice formulating problems, not just solving them.

- Don't memorize problems—memorize concepts. Once you fully understand a concept and know how to apply it, there's often little left to memorize.

- Memorize in an organized way, starting with the most simple concepts and moving to more complex ones. Think about how the concepts build on one another.

Even if you've answered the review questions earlier, while you were first reading the material (which is always a good idea), answer them again later as you study for the test and then the final.

- **Test yourself.** Temporarily transform yourself into your instructor, and prioritize what you're most likely to be tested on. Then create your own test, writing out some questions.

    Later, after as little as a few hours, take the test, and then grade it. How have you done? If you've achieved a grade that you're satisfied with, then fine. If, on the other hand, you've missed some key pieces of information, then you'll want to return to work and spend more time on memorization.

- **Team up with a friend.** When it comes to evaluating your memory, two heads are often better than one. Working with a classmate—especially one who may have a different preferred learning style from your own—can help you test the limits of your memory and assess areas in which you need work.

    For instance, you and a friend can take turns testing yourselves, switching back and forth between asking and answering questions. Turn it into a contest: One of you can be Alex Trebek of *Jeopardy,* and the other, a contestant. You can even work with several people, forming a study group. The important thing is to switch who's asking and who's answering the questions. Even when you're directing questions to others—officially evaluating their memory—you're giving your own memory a workout. (Put your memory to the test in Try It 6.)

Teaching Tip: Ask students to report which of their class texts have review questions.

Discussion Prompt: Ask students if they can remember a time they were totally immersed in an activity. Did they worry about their memory during those intensely focused times? Why or why not?

Name: Lamar Heckstall

School: Virginia Commonwealth University, Richmond, Virginia

For college sophomore Lamar Heckstall, an art major, developing memory skills has required proceeding along two fronts simultaneously. It has been important for him to remember not only the written word, but also the many images and visuals that are the stock-in-trade of an art major.

"For me visual memorization is actually easier," said Heckstall. "When it comes to remembering verbal information, like artists' names or titles of paintings, I try to create associations with the images. If the name of the artist is hard to pronounce, I try to put it into a rhyme or think of something I like that I can associate with the name. When we're viewing slides of artwork, I sometimes redraw the figure and then write the title underneath, and that helps. Most of the time I get them all right, or maybe miss only one or two."

Heckstall says he started developing his memory skills toward the end of high school, but the larger intellectual demands of college forced him to intensify his approach.

VCU
Virginia Commonwealth University

"Basically what I do when I'm studying is to take a word or definition and say it to myself five times," he explained. "I then write it down five times and actively try to recall it later on.

"I do have problems with memorizing long definitions or long descriptions of people. In the past I found myself trying to memorize too much and not learning anything, so what I've been doing is concentrating on one or two main things about the definition or individual," he says.

In conjunction with memorization techniques, Heckstall said that his study habits have changed dramatically since high school, and now he finds that getting an early start on studying reaps rewards.

"In high school the work was easier, and while I took it seriously, I didn't put in as much time as I should have," he admitted. "Now that I'm in college, I have to use my time wisely every day. As soon as I find out a test is scheduled, I start studying for it and generally put in about two or three hours a day until the day of the test."

What is memory and how does it function?

- Information we actively process is permanently etched into the brain, but it is not always readily available for retrieval.
- The challenge is to recall information when we need it, and the key to effective recall is learning material in a way that makes recall easy.

Why might I have problems with memory, and how can I deal with those problems?

- The problems we have with memory are mostly related to the inability to recall or retrieve information when it is needed. However, if information is rehearsed carefully, you can usually recall it more easily.
- Memory can be improved through careful preparation, by selecting in advance the pieces of information that are worthy of memorization and rehearsal.
- Another key to effective memorization is linking new information to information that is already in memory.

What are some techniques I can use for memorizing information?

- Many memory techniques are available to improve memorization. Rehearsal is a primary one, as is the use of mnemonics such as acronyms, acrostics, and rhymes.
- Other memory techniques are the method of loci, the peg method, visualization, and the use of multiple senses while learning new material.
- Overlearning is a basic principle of memorization.
- Memory takes some time—days or even longer—to reach the point of consolidation, when the physical links between brain cells that represent memory become stable. The need for consolidation explains why cramming is ineffective for long-term recall.

KEY TERMS AND CONCEPTS

Retrieval (p. 211)
Rehearsal (p. 215)
Mnemonics (p. 216)
Acronym (p. 216)
Acrostic (p. 217)

Method of loci (p. 217)
Peg method (p. 219)
Visualization (p. 222)
Overlearning (p. 224)
Memory consolidation (p. 227)

RESOURCES

On Campus

If you have considerable difficulty in memorizing material compared with your classmates, it's possible that you might have a learning disability. If you suspect this, visit the college learning disabilities office or counseling center.

In Print

In *Improving Your Memory* (Johns Hopkins, 2005), Janet Fogler and Lynn Stern provide an overview of practical tips on maximizing your memory. Barry Gordon and Lisa Berger provide insight into the functioning of memory and how to improve it in *Intelligent Memory* (Penguin, 2004). Finally, *The Memory Doctor* by Douglas Mason and Spencer Smith (New Harbinger Publications, 2005) offers simple techniques for improving memory.

Choosing Your Courses and Major

Major
A specialization in a particular subject area, requiring a set course of study

Teaching Tip: A critical part of academic planning is teaching your students about academic policy. Be sure to include information about calculating GPA, understanding academic "good standing", repeat policies, and every institutional rule that pertains to academic progress and retention.

Student Alert: If you have first generation college students or international students in your class, be particularly mindful of the vocabulary of higher education. As faculty, we are immersed in this language and may take for granted that our students know what we are talking about.

Prerequisites
Requirements that must be fulfilled before a student may enroll in a course or discipline

College advisor
An individual who provides students with advice about their academic careers

2. **Academic programs.** Most of the college catalog is a description of the school's academic departments and its **majors**—specializations in a particular subject area, each requiring a set course of study.

   Requirements for majors generally fall into two or three categories. First, typically, are collegewide requirements that every student enrolled in the college must fulfill. Second are specific requirements for each particular major; to major in an area, you must take a specified number of courses or credits in that area. Finally, if the major falls within a broader academic unit (such as a school of education), that broader entity may have its own requirements for a degree.

   For instance, a psychology major might be required to fulfill collegewide requirements that apply to all students enrolled in the college, such as a specified number of English, writing, math, and science courses. The Department of Psychology will have its own separate requirements for its majors to complete, such as taking no fewer than six psychology courses. Finally, because the Department of Psychology may be housed in a more general Division of Social Sciences, there may be divisional requirements to fulfill (perhaps a course in social science methodology or a foreign language requirement).

   The college catalog also provides information for students who have transferred from another college. For instance, transfer students may receive credit for only a certain number of courses or credits earned at their first institution. Or they may be required to take particular courses even if they already took them at their previous school.

   If you attend a two-year community college, your college catalog also may provide information on transferring to a four-year school. For instance, two-year colleges often have formal agreements (known as *articulation agreements*) with particular four-year colleges that will automatically accept certain courses or credits taken at your current institution. Articulation agreements may even spell out what groups or blocks of courses will be accepted, as a set, by a four-year college. Knowing what courses will automatically be counted at other colleges is crucial if you are thinking about transferring later. (To learn more about transferring, go to the P.O.W.E.R. Learning Web site at **www.mhhe.com/power**.)

3. **Course listings.** The college catalog usually lists all the courses the school offers, even though not all of them may be offered every term. Courses are listed by department, and the descriptions typically include the course name, the number of credits the course provides, and a short description.

   Some courses have **prerequisites**—requirements that must be fulfilled before one can enroll. If the course has a prerequisite, this will be stated. Take these prerequisites seriously, because you will not be permitted to enroll in a course if you haven't completed the prerequisite for it. In addition, the prerequisite course may not be offered every term, so you may have to wait a year (or more!) before getting into the course you want.

   Sometimes course descriptions also name the instructors who teach the course and the time and place the class meets. However, this information may also be published separately.

Make an Appointment with Your College Advisor

Your **college advisor**'s job is to give you good, clear-headed advice. Your advisor will be someone who knows the ins and outs of the college's regulations, and whose experience in working with other students provides a good deal of knowledge in other areas as well. Advisors can help you figure out what classes to take, how to overcome academic bureaucracies, whom to go to about a problem, and generally how to prepare yourself for graduation and beyond. They can even provide information on extracurricular activities, volunteer opportunities, and part-time jobs.

Advisors are particularly busy at the beginning of each term (as well as when the course schedule comes out). Consequently, find out their office hours, schedule an appointment early, and be sure to keep your scheduled appointment. Don't go unprepared when you do go. Figure 9.1 provides a checklist you should go through before your appointment.

Advisors can be tremendously valuable resources. Take some time to get to know your advisor as a person—and to let him or her get to know you. To get a better sense of who your own advisor is, complete Try It 1, "Get to Know Your College Advisor" on page 238.

College advisors can play an important role in your academic career, providing valuable advice, helping you to overcome problems, and making sure that you meet all the requirements needed to graduate.

Teaching Tip: TRY IT 1 is a good way for students to get to know their advisor. You may also want to invite an advisor to your class, or schedule a tour of your institution's advising center.

——— Check the college catalog for information about the advisor, noting any potential links or conversational topics that might be used to open the meeting.

——— Be on time, be aware of how much time is scheduled for your appointment, and check the time frequently during the appointment.

——— Summarize who you are (e.g., hometown, high school, grades in high school, interests, high school or community activities, etc.) to begin the more formal part of the meeting.

——— List some or all of the courses you plan to take in the next term.

——— Prepare some questions about your course choices (e.g., difficulty of the courses, whether they match your interests, whether they will fulfill your requirements, what future courses or career choices they might lead to, personality of the instructors, etc.).

——— List the extracurricular activities you're considering.

——— Prepare some questions about these activities (e.g., how time-consuming, how interesting, what sorts of students participate in them, etc.).

——— Be prepared to ask about the advisor's impressions of the college.

——— Be prepared to ask the advisor to recommend activities, events, and the like on campus or off, and which to avoid.

——— List any other issues you would like to raise (e.g., impressions of the college so far, roommate issues, personal issues, etc.).

——— Be prepared to ask about the availability of the advisor in the future (e.g., office hours, policy on calling outside office hours, etc.).

——— Remember to thank the advisor before leaving.

FIGURE 9.1
Advisor Visit Checklist
(You can also also complete this checklist online at **www. mhhe.com/power.**)

Create a List of Course Requirements

Use the form below to list all of your course requirements. The form covers both prerequisite courses (i.e., courses you must take before you can take other courses) and requirements imposed by your college, the division of which your department is a part, and your department. In addition, the form allows you to indicate both credit requirements and grade requirements.

List of Course Requirements					Whose Requirement?		
Type of Course	Credits Required	Credits Completed	Grade Required	Grade Achieved	College	Division	Department
I. Prerequisite Courses							
Total Prerequisite Courses							
II. Required Courses							
Total Required Courses							

What does the information in the chart tell you? How can you use it to plan your future course selections? What courses do you wish to take that are not requirements? How much leeway do you have to take nonrequired courses?

To Try It online, go to **www.mhhe.com/power**.

relevant information together on your computer, in a file folder, or even in a shoebox.) There's no worse surprise than finding out a month before you thought you'd be graduating that you lack some critical requirement. Don't count on others to keep track of this information for you. No one knows more about what you've done than you do.

Where Are You Going?

You should also use the information you have recorded to help determine which courses you should take in the upcoming term. Once you have declared a major, you can add those requirements to your record.

Now that you know where you are and where you are going, you are ready to start selecting courses to take you there.

W ORK: Choosing the Next Term's Courses

The course listings for the next term are published in a *course schedule*. It is organized by department, with each course in the department having a number, such as "History 204: The French Revolution." Generally, the higher the number, the more advanced the course. The course catalog will tell you when and where the class meets and whether there are any prerequisites for the course.

IRM Link: Teaching the Text, Chapter 9, Section V; this P.O.W.E.R. process includes good activities for teaching this part of the chapter.

Go with What You Know

Chances are, you already know of at least one or two courses you need to take in a given term. Perhaps this is the term you plan to fulfill your natural science or your foreign language requirement. There may be some courses you have been waiting to take, since some courses are only taught once a year. A good place to begin is to find out when these courses are given and where.

Draft a Personal Schedule for the Term

First, write down when the courses you absolutely have to take are scheduled. If, as is the case for many introductory courses in large colleges, you have a choice of times, choose one you prefer. In choosing times, take into consideration whether you are a "morning person," at your best first thing in the morning, or whether you usually drag yourself out of bed in the morning and don't fully function until noon. This will be the beginning of your time management for the upcoming term.

Student Alert: Remind students to consider their learning styles when planning their schedule. Have they scheduled their hardest classes when they learn best?

Next, choose **electives**—courses that are not required. Keep in mind broad considerations about the kinds of courses you need to take for your major and for graduation. But also explore courses that simply sound interesting to you. College offers the opportunity to discover who you are and what you like and do best, but the only way that can happen is by taking intellectual risks.

Electives
Courses that are not required

Try to balance easier and more difficult courses for a particular term. You don't want to load up on all highly challenging courses. In addition, signing up for too many courses in a single term—beyond the norm for you—can be self-defeating. (For more on choosing courses, see the *Course Connections* feature.)

COURSE | CONNECTIONS

What Are Courses *Really* Like? The Covert College Catalog

Although the official college catalog is the place to start to identify courses that you need to take, there's a wealth of other sorts of unofficial information about courses that you can make use of. Tapping into this often-hidden body of knowledge can help you make informed judgments about which courses are best for you.

Among the sources of information about courses you're considering:

- **Current instructors.** Your current instructors know their colleagues and their reputations and may be willing to provide you with off-the-record suggestions.

- **Your classmates.** Ask your classmates for advice and experiences in particular classes, knowing it is colored by their own performance in the class. In addition, students have their own biases, and they are not always objective in their evaluations of instructors. For some, "easy course" equals "good course."

- **Instructor evaluations.** Sometimes schools permit access to instructor evaluations from previous terms. If these are available, they can be used to get an idea of how other students have reacted to a class you're considering taking.

- **Previous course syllabus.** An instructor may post a class syllabus online or may keep it on file in a departmental office. By examining the syllabus, you'll see exactly what a course covers (and how it compares to the official course description in the catalog).

- **Course instructors themselves.** Sit in on a class that you're thinking about taking, or talk with instructors during their office hours. There's nothing more direct than what you'll learn from the person who will be teaching the course in the upcoming term.

To get started in deciding which courses to take for the upcoming term, complete Try It 3, "Choose Your Courses."

Register for Courses

Register
To enroll formally in courses

The rest of the work of choosing courses consists of **registering,** or completing the college's paperwork to become formally enrolled in your chosen classes.

Meeting with your advisor is an essential step. Sometimes, in fact, it's mandatory, and you won't be allowed to register without your advisor's signature. But even if it's not required, it's a good idea to go over your proposed course of studies. You may have overlooked something, or your advisor may be able to suggest some alternative courses that will work better for you.

Remember, though, that the ultimate responsibility for taking the right courses rests with you. Advisors sometimes make mistakes and overlook a requirement; ultimately, you know best what's right for you.

After meeting with your advisor, your next step will be to register. Course registration varies significantly from one school to another. In some cases, it's a matter of listing course numbers on a form, along with some alternatives.

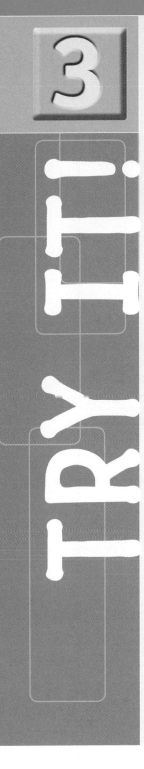

Choose Your Courses

Use the form below to make your course selections for the coming term. The form will allow you to verify that you are meeting course requirements, avoiding schedule conflicts, and signing up for instructors you want.

Course Selections

Term: _____

Course Name and Number	Credits	Required Course or Just for Fun?	Pre-requisites Met?	Meeting Grade Required	Days and Time	Schedule Conflicts	Instructor Name	Instructor Permission Required?

After completing the chart, answer these questions: How does the next semester seem to be shaping up? Will you be able to take courses you *want* to take, as opposed to those you *need* to take? Have you made any choices that open you to new intellectual possibilities?

To Try It online, go to **www.mhhe.com/power**.

In an increasing number of schools, you will be expected to register for your courses using an automated system over the telephone or online. If your college uses a telephone registration system, you will probably be given a specific time period in which to call. When you do call, you'll receive voice prompts to enter your course choices using your telephone's touch-tone key pad (see Figure 9.2).

If your college uses online registration, you will be prompted to enter course information on a Web form, and your registration will be accomplished completely online.

Before you begin your telephone call, fill in this entire worksheet, listing all courses you wish to add, drop, or change including laboratory and discussion sections, and the appropriate "action codes" you will enter. Be sure to fill in all boxed areas properly and to enter '##' at the end of your call.

1. *Call the system at (555) 444-3214 (From On-Campus, call 4-3214)*

2. *Enter your student ID number* `1` `2` `6` - `0` `4` - `9` `8` `1` `1`

3. *Enter your branch code* `1` *(Undergraduate ¡ 1, Graduate ¡ 2)*

4. *Enter your personal ID number (PIN)* `6` `7` `7` `5`

5. *If the Schedule Confirmation you receive in the mail instructs you to get from your advisor a Registration Approval Code before add/drop, enter that code* `☐` `☐` `☐` `☐`

6. *For each add, drop, or change you want to make, enter the appropriate action code from the list below and the schedule number for the course you want affected by that action.*

Action Code*	Schedule Number of Course Requested	Dept	Course #	Section #	Crd	Day/Time
`1` `0`	`7` `8` `2` `8` `4` `0`	Psych	102	1	3	T–T 11:15–12:30
`1` `0`	`6` `7` `2` `9` `9` `7`	Engl	231	1	3	M–W–F 9:05–9:55
`1` `0`	`2` `6` `0` `4` `6` `3`	Phed	102	2	1	M 4:00–4:50
`1` `0`	`1` `2` `0` `3` `0` `9`	Latn	124	1	3	T–T 9:00–10:15
`1` `0`	`8` `8` `0` `1` `8` `1`	Hist	102	1	3	M–W–F 10:10–11:05
`1` `0`	`7` `2` `4` `9` `6` `2`	Phys	101	3	3	T–T 2:30–3:45
`☐☐`	`☐☐☐☐☐☐`					
`☐☐`	`☐☐☐☐☐☐`					
`☐☐`	`☐☐☐☐☐☐`					
`☐☐`	`☐☐☐☐☐☐`					

7. *After entering your course requests, enter # # instead of an action code to terminate your call.*

*Action Code	Action
10	**ADD** a course or Swap between sections of a course (To **SWAP**, simply add the new section; the old section will automatically be dropped from your schedule.)
30	**ADD** a course with **Pass/Fail** option or **CHANGE** existing course to **Pass/Fail**
90	**DROP** a course
80	**REMOVE Pass/Fail** or **Audit** option from existing course
50	**CHANGE** variable credit for an existing variable credit course
40	**ADD** a course with **AUDIT** grading option or **CHANGE** existing course to **AUDIT** grading
60	**LIST** your course schedule (press any key to end listing)
*	**ERASE** an entry error before completion
	Note: Action Codes 30 and 80 are not available to graduate students. 40 is not available to undergraduates.

FIGURE 9.2

A Sample Telephone/Web Course Registration Worksheet

E VALUATE: Deciding Whether You Are in the Classes You Need

Picture this horror story:

You receive your grade report from the previous term. You're excited because you know you've done well. You're especially looking forward to seeing your Spanish grade because you know you were on the borderline between an A– and a B+. Instead you're astounded to see that there is no grade listed for the Spanish class, but you've received an F in a French class that you didn't even take. That F pulls down your grade point average, and at the bottom of your grade report is an announcement that you are on academic probation.

Here's the explanation: Because of an error during registration, you were never formally enrolled in the Spanish course, even though you actually spent the entire term attending classes in the course. To compound the mistake, your instructor never noticed that you weren't on her class roster. At the end of the term, when she was filling out her grade report, she didn't notice that your name wasn't listed. So no grade was reported for Spanish.

At the same time, the instructor of the French class in which you were erroneously enrolled had to give you a grade at the end of the semester. Because you never completed any assignments or took any tests, your average for the semester was 0—warranting an F for the term. That F is what appeared on your grade report.

The situation—which is far more likely to occur at a large university than a small college—might be seen as a comedy of errors if it weren't so painful. Fortunately, if this were actually your story, it would most likely have a happy ending—eventually. You would go to your college registrar, who would be able to tell you what to do to get the F erased and the appropriate grade added. Still, undoing the cascade of errors would take time and a considerable amount of effort.

Difficulties such as these are encountered by a surprising number of students every term. Many problems, however, can be avoided with a bit of "due diligence" on the part of the student. One key is to evaluate your success in registering.

Before the term starts, your school will provide you with a list of courses in which you are enrolled for the upcoming term. Immediately look it over. Use the following checklist to determine how successful your efforts to register have been:

- Are the courses to which you are assigned the ones you wanted?
- Are the times accurate? Are there any conflicts?
- Have any substitutions been made?
- Are you registered for the number of credits that you wanted to be registered for?

If there are any problems, try to correct the situation immediately. If there has been a clerical error, you should pay a visit to the registrar's office. Sometimes, though, you'll find that there was no mistake. Class sizes are almost always limited, and not every student who wants to enroll can do so, either because of physical limitations (the room can hold only a certain number of students) or because of educational considerations (learning may be maximized when only a small number of students are in the class).

Discussion Prompt: On-line faculty rating sources are common, and students are likely to consider these when registering for classes. Discuss the pros and cons of using this information.

IRM Link: Teaching the Text, Chapter 9, Section IV and VIII. Have students complete the four-year plan activity. Even if they do not stay with that specific major, the planning process will give them a sense of how essential it is to plan ahead.

Teaching Tip: While academic planning usually focuses on what students need to take for graduation, we need to encourage students to consider taking a few courses just for fun that may enrich their lives but doesn't fall into any required category.

When a course is overbooked, you have several alternatives. One is to sign up for another section of the course that is not overbooked. Another is to attempt to register for an entirely different course.

Finally, you may appeal directly to the course instructor. Instructors sometimes will permit particularly interested or motivated students to enroll in the class, even if the official capacity has been reached. You may find that approaching an instructor with a polite request may yield you a slot in the course after all.

If none of these alternatives works, you will have to add a course to the ones you have already registered for. How do you add courses after the registration period has ended? Typically, you'll need to complete a special form. Depending on the timing of your request, the form may require the signature of the instructor whose course you are adding.

Also keep in mind that if you drop a class during a term, you must do it officially, through the registrar. Simply ceasing to attend doesn't mean you'll be dropped from the class list. Instead, you'll probably end up with a failing grade in the course unless you complete the necessary paperwork to officially drop the course.

"Help—I Can't Get into the Courses That I Need to Graduate!"

Student Alert: Course availability is an issue on most college campuses. Encourage students to plan ahead and to meet with an advisor early. Students should get answers to all of their questions well in advance of registration time and, always have a back-up plan!

For some students, their efforts to register result in utter disaster. Sometimes most or all of their first choices are unavailable, and they end up enrolled in only a few of the courses they had requested. Or perhaps they cannot get into the one crucial course required for graduation.

Whatever the problem, there are several steps you can take to improve the situation:

- **Don't despair—act!** There is virtually no academic problem that can't be solved in some way. Focus your energies on finding a creative solution to the problem.

- **Identify classes that are still available and enroll in them.** There are probably many classes offered at your college that are still available. Registrars or departments often maintain lists of classes that have many openings.

- **Talk with your advisor.** Perhaps what you think of as an absolute requirement can be waived or appealed. Or maybe some other course can substitute for a particular required course.

- **Speak with individual course instructors.** It may be that the instructor of the course you need will make an exception and permit you to enroll; it can't hurt to ask.

- **Consider taking a must-have, required course at another college.** If you live in an area where there are other schools in the vicinity, it may be possible to enroll in a course that you simply must take at another school. It also may be possible to take the course using distance learning. As we'll discuss further in Chapter 10, **distance learning** courses are taught at some other institution, and students participate via either video technology or the World Wide Web.

Distance learning
The teaching of courses at another institution, with student participation via video technology or the World Wide Web

Before you take a course offered by a college other than your own, make sure that you'll receive credit for the course at your school. Also keep in mind that you'll probably have to pay for courses offered by other schools over and above what you've already spent for your own school's tuition.

RETHINK: Learning What You Love and Loving What You Learn

Take one step back. No, make that two steps back.

Stepping back and taking stock of where you are in your course of studies and where you're headed are absolutely essential tasks. In fact, they are among the most important things you can do during your college career. They can spell the difference between plodding through your courses, focused only on day-to-day deadlines and tribulations, and, alternatively, gaining a sense of satisfaction as you progress toward your own goals and see yourself growing as a person.

Taking stock of your course of studies is not something you need to do every day, or once a week, or even once a month. But you should do it, without fail, at least once every term. Circle a date on your calendar so you'll be sure to do it, and treat it no differently than any other deadline you simply can't miss.

When you do take stock, answer the questions in Try It 4 on page 248. If you're satisfied with your answers, feel affirmed in the choices you've made. You're on the right track, and you should feel secure in the knowledge that you're getting from college what you want to.

On the other hand, if you're less than satisfied with the answers you come up with, take action. Choose courses in the future that better match your goals. Consider changing your major to one that more closely reflects what you want to get out of college. And, if you're truly unhappy with the way your college career is proceeding, consider changing colleges.

Whichever option you choose, don't simply accept dissatisfaction with your college career. There are few times in our lives when we have the opportunity to partake of an experience that has the potential to raise us to new intellectual and emotional heights. College should be intellectually enlightening and exciting. We should be able to see how our education is preparing us for the rest of our lives. The worst thing we can do is let the time slip away without being confident that our college experience is the best experience possible.

Discussion Prompt: So much emphasis is placed on academic planning and career choice – moving through life expeditiously, making a good living, etc.—that we lose sight of the value of loving what we do. Have your students share their dreams for the future with the classmates.

Teaching Tip: Service learning is an excellent way to help students focus on potential majors. You may want to do a service project as a class activity. Remember that it is important to assign and evaluate students' written reflections of the experience.

Service-Learning: Helping Yourself by Helping Others

As you make decisions about what courses to take, you should be sure to consider those that involve service-learning. In courses with **service-learning,** you engage in community service activities—while getting course credit for the experience.

Service-learning is a win-win activity. As a student, you are able to gain valuable experience and knowledge that can give you significant insight into a subject area. In addition, you can learn useful skills that can be helpful in your future career. You also can learn more about yourself.

Your community is a winner, too. It receives critical support that immediately can improve the quality of life for its citizens. In fact, your efforts can have an impact that echoes for years.

Community service activities span a vast range. For instance, you might tutor an elementary school child in an after-school program as part of a course in elementary education. You'll learn firsthand about the reading process, while the skills (and perhaps motivation) of the child being tutored improve.

Service-learning
Courses that allow a student to engage in community service activities while getting course credit for the experience

 WORKING IN A GROUP

Reflect on Your College Experience

As you proceed in college, take a few moments at regular intervals (e.g., once a semester, once a year) to rethink your entire college experience. With a small group of classmates, discuss your reactions to the following topics and questions:

Course Work
- Are my courses moving me toward my educational, career, and personal goals?
- Are the classes I'm taking helping me to meet my short- and long-term goals?
- Are the classes I'm taking meeting my expectations?

Personal Commitment
- Am I working hard to get the most out of the classes I'm taking?
- Am I doing my best in every class?
- Am I keeping the goal of learning—apart from doing well in classes—in mind as I progress through my classes?

Personal Growth
- What personal growth am I experiencing?
- Am I becoming closer to the person I want to be?
- Are my critical thinking abilities growing?

College
- Is my school providing me with the best educational experience possible?
- Am I learning not only in the classroom but outside the classroom?
- Am I learning from my fellow students as well as my instructors?

Changes
- Is there anything (my course selections, my major, or my college) that I should consider changing?
- Have I made the best choices in the past? How can I remedy mistakes that I have made?

To Try It online, go to **www.mhhe.com/power.**

Or you might enroll in an abnormal psychology class and volunteer at a halfway house for patients with severe psychological disorders. You'll gain a firsthand understanding of disorders that would be impossible to gain simply from reading a textbook, while the patient may benefit from the social interaction you provide. Other examples of service-learning activities are shown in Table 9.1.

Whatever service-learning activity you do, there are several basic principles to keep in mind:

- **Ask questions.** Don't feel shy about asking for clarification of your responsibilities. It's the best way to maximize your learning. Remember, though, that the staff may be overworked and may not have time to immediately respond.

- **Maintain a positive outlook.** You may face challenges unlike those you've encountered before. You may see things that are upsetting and depressing.

TABLE 9.1	Service-Learning Possibilities

Here are just a few possibilities for service-learning activities:

- Develop a Web site for a social service agency.
- Participate in a "Big Brother" or "Big Sister" program.
- Raise funds for a local food bank.
- Register voters for the next election.
- Volunteer at a local government office.
- Help organize a Special Olympics for people with mental retardation.
- Participate in an educational program to protect the environment.
- Help staff a shelter for battered women.
- Volunteer to feed the homeless.
- Organize a blood drive.

To learn of more service-learning opportunities, go to the Web site of the National Clearinghouse for Service-Learning Organizations, Networks, and Resources at **www.service learning.org.**

Keep your own good fortunes in mind, and be grateful for the opportunity for growth that the experience is providing you.

- **Go with the flow.** You may not agree with everything that is being done at your placement site, but don't think that your ideas are necessarily better than the professionals who work there. Voice your concerns, but remember that you're at the site to help, not to make the rules.

- **Keep your commitments.** The staff depends on you. If you don't complete a task or show up, you are leaving someone in a lurch and shirking your responsibilities.

- **If you have concerns, discuss them with your supervisor and faculty sponsor.** Don't let your concerns fester. If you're asked to do things that you believe are inappropriate, discuss them with the appropriate person.

- **Keep a journal.** You'll probably be required to keep a journal of your experiences for the academic class attached to your service-learning experience. Even if you're not, keep a journal anyway. Writing in a journal offers a way of reflecting on the meaning of your experiences, as well as providing an enduring record of what you've accomplished.

Many students point to service-learning as the high point of their college career. And for most, it's not because of what they have gained personally—even though that's a significant part of it—but because of the difference they made in improving the lives of others. To consider service-learning further, complete Try It 5 on page 250.

Choosing Your Major

You attend a family gathering and encounter relatives you haven't seen for a while. What's the first question they ask when you say you're attending

Explore Service-Learning Opportunities

To find out about the service-learning opportunities available to you, complete the following activities:

A. Examine the courses offered at your college and identify three that contain service-learning components.

1. Course number and name _____

   What is the service-learning activity?

2. Course number and name _____

   What is the service-learning activity?

3. Course number and name _____

   What is the service-learning activity?

B. Identify three potential service-learning activities in your community by contacting social service agencies, food banks, the Red Cross, or religious organizations. You can also do research on the Web.

1. Organization name _____

   What is the service-learning activity you might conduct?

2. Organization name _____

   What is the service-learning activity you might conduct?

3. Organization name _____

   What is the service-learning activity you might conduct?

Working in a Group:

Compare your findings with other students in your class. What opportunities did you find? What service-learning opportunities might you seek out in the future? Discuss what you see as the advantages and disadvantages of service learning.

To Try It! online, go to **www.mhhe.com/power**.

college? You can bet on it: "What's your major?"

Although one could argue that there are lots of other important questions that you could be asked—"What interesting things have you learned?" comes to mind—having a major focus of study is an important part of college. A major is important because it focuses what we study, leading us to become experts in a specific area.

Some students know what they want to major in when they begin college; some don't have a clue. That's fine. No one says you should know right away.

In fact, using your first year in college to explore a range of possibilities is a very good idea. You might find after taking a civics course that you have a passion for legal studies. Or a physics class may lead you to consider a major in engineering. College is meant to be a time of exploration, and leaving yourself open to the future—and the unknown—is a completely reasonable

If you're having trouble choosing a major, one strategy is to consider the kinds of activities you most like doing outside the academic arena. For example, if you've enjoyed doing community service work as a volunteer, you might want to consider a major such as education, psychology, or social work.

thing to do. (To begin your own exploration of majors, complete Try It 6, "Identify Major Attractions" on page 252.)

But what if you don't have any idea which major you wish to pursue? If you are still in your first year of college, you have plenty of time to make up your mind. But here are some approaches that should help. You may also want to look ahead to the discussion of decision making in Chapter 11 as the time to declare a major (usually by the end of your second year) draws nearer.

1. **Celebrate your indecision.** If you don't have to make a decision for some time, take advantage of the situation. Enjoy the fact that you're uncommitted and that you have an uncommon degree of freedom.

2. **Focus on your interests.** Take a long look inward, paying attention to what your interests are. What do you most like to do in life? What are your strengths and weaknesses? What do you want to get out of life? The more you know about yourself, the easier it will become to narrow down the choices for a major. Completing the Journal Reflections, "Focusing on Your Interests," is a good place to start.

3. **Seek the help of others.** College campuses provide many resources to help their students choose a major (and also to help narrow the choices for potential careers). Talk to other students majoring in areas that interest you. Find out what they like and don't like about the field and its requirements. You will probably find your interest in the major grows or diminishes depending on how you feel about the issues they mention.

    Speak with your advisor. If you've gotten to know your advisor, he or she can often provide

> "I sat back thinking that the right major would just pop into my head. It didn't."
>
> Senior, University of Connecticut[2]

> "He who hesitates is sometimes saved."
>
> James Thurber, author

PERSONAL STYLES

Identify Major Attractions

To complete this assessment, check off each of the characteristics that applies to you. Then use the pattern of results to determine how closely your interests and personality style match with the characteristics of others who are already in a particular field of study.

Characteristic	Is This Me?	Possible Field of Study
• High interest in creative expression. • Appreciation of nonverbal communication. • Understanding of aesthetics. • Commitment to perfection. • Ability to manipulate form and shape.	_____ _____ _____ _____ _____	Arts (e.g., dance, drama, music, art, creative writing)
• Interest in organization and order. • Ability to lead and manage people. • Interest in practical problem solving. • Ambition and interest in financial incentives. • Can-do attitude. • Ability to simplify complexity.	_____ _____ _____ _____ _____ _____	Business
• Intense interest in solving real problems. • "Tinkerer" mentality a plus. • Extreme ability to focus on minute details. • Commitment to exactness and perfection. • Strong logical ability. • Ability to work alone for long stretches.	_____ _____ _____ _____ _____ _____	Engineering sciences (e.g., engineering, computer science)
• Interest in people. • Desire to solve real human problems. • Commitment to people more than money. • Tolerance of "messy" situations with multiple, partial solutions. • Insight and creativity. • Ability to work with people.	_____ _____ _____ _____ _____ _____	Helping professions (e.g., nursing, counseling, teaching, many areas of medicine)
• Interest in human emotions and motivations. • Interest in cultural phenomena. • Ability to integrate broad areas of study and inquiry. • Good skills of human observation. • Interest in the panorama of human life.	_____ _____ _____ _____ _____	Humanities (e.g., English literature, history, theater, film)

Characteristic	Is This Me?	Possible Field of Study
• Interest in words, word origins, and speech. • View of language as a science. • View of literature as human expression. • Appreciation of cultural differences as scientific phenomena.	_____ _____ _____ _____	Languages and linguistics
• Interest in physical performance. • Enjoyment of sports and athletics. • Commitment to helping others appreciate physicality. • Patience and perseverance. • Commitment to perfection through practice.	_____ _____ _____ _____ _____	Physical education
• Enjoyment of research questions; high level of curiosity about natural phenomena. • Quantitative thinking a requirement; high comfort level with mathematics and statistics. • Minute problem-solving skills; attention at great level of detail. • Strong logical ability. • Ability to work with others.	_____ _____ _____ _____ _____	Physical, biological, and natural sciences (e.g., physics, astronomy, chemistry, biology, some areas of medicine)
• Interest in people as individuals or groups. • Ability to think quantitatively and qualitatively. • High comfort level with mathematics and statistics. • High level of creativity and curiosity. • Ability to work with others. • Interest in theory as much as problem solving.	_____ _____ _____ _____ _____ _____	Social sciences (e.g., psychology, communication, sociology, education, political science, economics)
• Interest in the inner life. • Interest in highly theoretical questions. • Ability to think rigorously about abstract matters. • Appreciation of the human search for meaning.	_____ _____ _____ _____	Spiritual and philosophical studies

Use the results to focus on the kinds of courses and educational experiences that are involved in potential fields of study. Examining your responses may lead you toward some unexplored territory.

After you complete the chart, consider how you can use the information. Did you learn anything new about yourself or about various courses of study? Do your responses direct you toward a particular major? Do they direct you away from any major?

To Try It online, go to **www.mhhe.com/power**.

Focusing on Your Interests

The following questions are intended to lead you to explore areas of personal preference and interest that should inform your choice of a major. These questions are informal and designed to be answered briefly; more extended and formal "interest inventories" are available in your college's counseling office.

1. Do you think you would enjoy being told precisely what to do and how to do it, or would you rather work things out by yourself, without extensive instructions or supervision? What implications might your answer have for a choice of majors?

2. Are you ambitious and success-oriented and not ashamed to admit that you'd like to earn a lot of money, or are success and money of secondary importance to you? What implications might your answer have for a choice of majors?

3. Are you the artistic type and do you enjoy performing, creating, and viewing/listening to artistic works, or is art of relatively little interest to you? What implications might your answer have for a choice of majors?

4. Do you enjoy working with others, or do you prefer to work on your own? What implications might your answer have for a choice of majors?

Discussion Prompt: Ask your students to create a list of skills that they would like to have when they graduate. Have them look for courses that teach those skills. Does this lead to a major?

Double major
A course of study that fulfills all the requirements for two majors

Unique major
Specialization in a particular subject area that is geared to the student's own needs. Not offered by all colleges, and generally requires the support of faculty to oversee the process

reasonable, helpful information. For instance, you may be able to find out about the strengths and weaknesses of various departments.

You can also turn to your college counseling or career center. Most colleges have offices that can provide information about the different majors, including information about career opportunities typically available to graduates with the various majors. Sometimes it's possible to take tests that will help focus your choices, pinpointing how your interests, values, and personality type fit with particular careers.

4. **Consider double-majoring—or inventing your own major.** Although it's not easy, there are paths you can take if you know clearly what you want to do, but find it doesn't fit a single existing major.

A **double major** is a course of study that fulfills all the requirements for each of two majors. If you can't decide between two majors, or if you are interested in a career that overlaps two majors, this is a reasonable solution. The downside: It can be an awful lot of work. Because both majors usually carry a number of their own requirements, you may have very little freedom to pick courses other than those directly relating to one of the two majors.

Another option that some, although not all, colleges permit is the creation of a **unique major** geared to your own needs. Again, this is not an

Choosing a Job That's Right for You

It's a question no family member can resist asking, and one that you've probably asked yourself: What kind of work are you going to do when you graduate?

Happily, it's a question you don't have to answer, at least not yet. Although some students know from their first day in college what they want to do (and actually choose their college on that basis), many—perhaps most—don't decide on a career path until late in their academic career.

And that's fine. After all, one of the reasons you are in college is to expose yourself to the universe of knowledge. In one sense, keeping your options open is a wise course. You don't want to prematurely narrow your options and discard possibilities too early. And even if you're quite sure in your choice of careers, it doesn't hurt to explore new possibilities.

In the Career Connections features in previous chapters, we've discussed various strategies for exploring future professions. Here, in summary, are some steps to take to identify a career:

1. **Clarify the goal of your search.** There's no single perfect career choice. Some people search for the ideal career, assuming that they need to identify the one, and only one, career for which they have been destined. The reality is, though, that there are many careers that they could choose that would make them equally happy and satisfied.

   Start with what you already know about yourself. You've already done a lot of mental work toward narrowing down a profession. Do you hate the sight of blood? Then you're probably well aware you're not cut out to be a surgeon or a veterinarian. Does the sight of a column of numbers bring an immediate yawn? Count out accounting and statistics.

Awareness of your likes and dislikes already puts you on the road to identifying a future career. Knowing what you don't want to do helps to identify what you do want to do and to narrow down the kinds of occupations for which you're more suited.

2. **Gather information.** The more you know about potential careers, the better. Examine career-planning materials, read industry profiles, and visit relevant Web sites (such as the excellent Department of Labor site at **www.bls.gov/oco/**). Talk with career counselors. Discuss your options with people who work in professions in which you're interested. Find out how they chose their career, how they got their current job, and what advice they have for you. In addition, consider participating in an internship in a profession that you think might be attractive. As an intern, you'll gain firsthand experience—possibly college credit as well—for the work that you do.

3. **Narrow down your choices.** Once you've gathered enough information to give yourself a reasonable comfort level, narrow down the choices. If it's early in your college career, you don't need to make up your mind. If it's late and you feel the pressure to choose, then make the decision. Just do it. Remember, there's no single, absolutely correct decision; there are many right decisions.

   Whatever it is you ultimately choose as a career, think of it only as a first step. As the average life span continues to lengthen due to advances in medical technology, most people will pass through several careers during the course of their life. By periodically taking stock of where you are and considering your goals, you'll be in a position to make career changes that bring you closer to your ideal.

   (You can learn much more about career choices at the P.O.W.E.R. Learning Web site at **www.mhhe.com/power**.)

---

easy road to take because you must put together a cohesive set of courses that centers upon a discipline not normally offered through a major. Furthermore, you must also get the support of a faculty member or a committee of faculty members to oversee the process.

If double-majoring or inventing a major seems too daunting, there's another option that may resolve the difficulty of choosing between two majors: majoring in one field and minoring in another. A **minor** is a secondary specialization in a discipline different from one's major. Typically students must take at least four courses in a discipline for their study to qualify as a minor.

Teaching Tip: Visit the career center or check out your institution's career services Web site.

Minor
A secondary specialization in a discipline different from one's major

Teaching Tip: This is an excellent place to discuss international study. Invite a speaker to class or visit the international program office on your campus.

College counseling and career centers are excellent sources of information on potential majors and occupations.

"Far and away the best prize that life offers is the chance to work hard at work worth doing."

President Theodore Roosevelt

Teaching Tip: Visit the alumni office on your campus. Connect the "life-long learning" experiences and support that your campus offers its students and alums.

5. **Be career-oriented, but not too career-oriented.** If you have a good idea about what career you wish to embark upon once you graduate, you can easily find out which skills are required to be successful in that field. Knowing what you'll need to gain entry into a field can help you determine a good major that will set you on the road toward your desired profession.

Don't narrow your options too much, however. Students sometimes fear signing up for classes that don't seem to lead directly toward a career. Or they may avoid courses that seem to point them in the direction of a career that would be "unacceptable" to their parents or friends. One of the greatest sources of indecision in choosing a major stems from the mistaken notion that when you choose your major, you're also choosing a career.

Don't fall into that trap. Follow your heart—not always your head—and pursue courses without regard to how they may broaden or narrow your future job opportunities. You may discover a passion, and an aptitude, that you never knew you had. Even if you oriented toward a specific profession, remember that employers often prefer well-rounded employees over ones who are narrowly focused on a particular subject area.

6. **Always keep in mind that education is a life-long enterprise.** Educational opportunities will continue to present themselves not just through the undergraduate years, but for the rest of your life.

Consequently, no matter what your choice of major, you're not precluding the possibility of taking courses in other areas in the future. You may eventually end up in a graduate school pursuing a masters degree, a doctorate, or an MD. You also may take courses periodically at local colleges even after you graduate, enrolling in them because they will help you advance in your career or simply because they interest you.

In short, choosing a major is not a decision that places your life on a set, unchangeable course. Instead, it's one step in what can be a lifetime of learning.

As Chen Lee began his junior year, he still was unsure which major to choose. He had come to college as an "undeclared major" and that was still his official designation—although he thought "clueless major" would be a more accurate label.

Chen had thought seriously about several possibilities, including communications and marketing, but none seemed to offer just what he was looking for. Part of the trouble was, of course, that he really didn't know what he was looking for. In fact, he was a lot clearer about what he didn't want to major in than what he did want to major in.

The clock was ticking away, and he felt lost. His parents offered many suggestions, but that just seemed to increase the pressure. And now he was getting warnings from the school that he had to make a decision.

1. What seems to be Chen's main problem in coming to grips with the choice of a major?

2. How can Chen's prior consideration of majors such as communications and marketing help him move closer to a decision?

3. How would you advise Chen to make use of his understanding of what he doesn't want to major in?

4. How can Chen find out more about himself? Why is this important in choosing a major?

5. Do you think Chen is taking this decision too seriously or not seriously enough? What advice would you give him about the importance of the choice of a major?

10

Technology and Information Competency

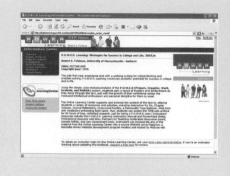

Brian Sullivan had never really gotten into computers. Coming to college from a small rural community, where the only high-speed Internet access available to him was at the public library, he'd never found much to like about the Web. Unlike a lot of his new college friends, he rarely used e-mail, preferring to keep in touch by phone.

So when his psychology instructor announced on the first day of class that her course required extensive use of the Web, Brian was not very enthusiastic. He was even less enthusiastic when the instructor said the class was going to be paperless. Assignments would be provided on the class Web site, and papers had to be "handed in" electronically.

For the first month, Brian had a hard time seeing the point to the system. Then, in the middle of the term, his best friend from high school was in a serious car accident. Brian rushed home to see him; his friend was in pretty bad shape. Brian wanted to stick around for a while, but he worried that if he did, he would fall behind in his classes.

Then he found out that the hospital had just installed high-speed Internet service that visitors could use. Though he was hundreds of miles away, Brian could get his psychology and other assignments and e-mail his responses back to his instructors.

The Internet probably saved his academic career that semester.

LOOKING AHEAD >>>

The technology that permitted Brian to keep up with his classes didn't even exist 15 years ago. Education is changing, as it takes increasing advantage of "virtual" resources—e-mail, the Web, and other evolving technologies. In fact, you might already be taking a course entirely on the Web, never setting foot in the same room as your instructor or your classmates.

Technology is making a profound difference in how we are taught, the ways we study and carry out our work, and how we communicate with our professors and other students. It is changing the way you can access the vast quantities of information published each year—tens of thousands of books, journals, and other print materials, and literally millions of Web pages. But successfully wading through all that information requires significant new skills in information competence that weren't necessary in the past.

In this chapter we discuss how technological advances increase your opportunities to achieve success in college.

We'll consider the basics of computers and the ways in which they can be used to manipulate data and present it. We'll also talk about distance learning, an approach to education that involves studying with an instructor who may be thousands of miles away. Finally, we'll consider how you can use technology to develop information competency—locating and using both the information traditionally held in libraries *and* information created for and in the virtual world of cyberspace.

In short, after reading this chapter, you'll be able to answer these questions:

- **What are the basic uses of computers?**
- **What is available on the Internet?**
- **What is distance learning?**
- **How can I develop information competency?**
- **What do I need to keep in mind as I use the Web to gather information?**

▪ You and Computers

They are an amazing time-saver. They're a great tool that can help you achieve success in your classes. They're the remarkable equivalent of a typewriter, archive, printing press, calculator, and proofreader, all rolled into one.

They can also, at times, be extremely frustrating, annoying, and maddening.

"They," of course, are computers. And you'll need to be able to use them to maximize your success in college. These days it's as much a necessity to learn to use a computer as it was for you to learn to use a calculator earlier in your schooling. No one facing the job market in the 21st century will want to leave college without basic computer skills.

If you are not yet at ease with computers, relax. No one is born with computer skills. With sufficient practice, however, using a computer will become second nature.

And if using computers already is second nature to you, be patient with those who are less familiar with them. A "digital divide"—often reflecting socioeconomic disparities—separates students who have had considerable and easy access to computers prior to college from those for whom access to computers was difficult. Many students grow up in homes without computers, and even those who had computers at home may not have had access to high-speed Internet connections. (To explore your feelings about computers, complete the *Journal Reflections* on page 266.)

P.O.W.E.R. UP and IRM Link: Find out what your students know before you proceed with teaching this chapter. They may be able to teach it for you. See Teaching the Text, Chapter 10, Sections IV and VIII, the Technology Survey.

Computer Basics

Even if you don't feel proficient with computers, they already play a big role in your life. Computers run your car's engine, make your digital camera work, allow you to rip or download tunes for your iPod, and make sure the bus you're waiting for runs on time.

Computers have revolutionized academic life as well. You're probably at least somewhat familiar with the three main types of programs that you'll likely encounter in your classes: word-processing programs, presentation programs, and spreadsheets. Here's a quick review.

Student Alert: How have your students used technology and computers? Has it been for fun only or for academic purposes? They may want to share their experiences. What are similarities and differences between using technology for entertainment or education?

Word-Processing Programs: Spreading the Word

A **word-processing program** turns your computer into a smart typewriter— a very smart typewriter. With a word-processing program, everything you write can be stored in a computer's memory, and you can check the spelling of the words you type, automatically keep track of your footnotes, and "cut and paste" material with incredible ease. Most important, word processors take much of the drudgery out of revision. You can quickly delete words and sentences that you don't want, substitute new material in place of what you deleted, and rearrange words, sentences, and entire paragraphs.

Word-processing program Computer application software that turns a computer into a very smart typewriter

How I Feel about Computers

1. If you had to characterize your general reactions when you hear the words "computer" and "the Web," what would you say?

2. Do you use e-mail? Do you use the Web much? Do you use a computer for other things? If so, what have your experiences been like?

3. How satisfied do you feel with your level of expertise in using computers/the Web? Do you intend to take any steps to increase it?

4. How do you feel about people who are expert in using computers? Do you ever use the term "computer geek" to describe them? If so, what do you mean by it? What do you think others mean by it?

5. Do you think it is harder for older adults to learn about computers? Why or why not?

Some of the most important things you can do with a word-processing program include:

- *Inserting and deleting text.* After you have created a document, you can easily add material—simply move the cursor to the appropriate spot and type. It's equally easy to delete text, even large blocks of it, simply by selecting (highlighting) the text and hitting "delete."

- *Moving and copying text.* Want to change the order of two paragraphs? It can be done simply by highlighting one of the paragraphs and dragging it with the mouse. Alternately, you can use a cut-and-paste function, highlighting the paragraph, "cutting" it so that it's temporarily stored on a virtual "clipboard," and then "pasting" the paragraph into the appropriate spot.

- *Changing the appearance of text.* You can easily type **bold**, *italic*, or <u>underlined text</u>, as well as change the style of the type (known as the *font*) to any look you prefer. Common fonts include Helvetica, Century Expanded, Optima, Times New Roman, and *Handwriting*, and each comes in different

Teaching Tip: Try to schedule this class in a computer lab or smart classroom. It makes teaching and learning this material more powerful.

sizes, measured in *points*. For instance, type can be 16 point, 12 point, or 10 point.

Obviously, before you use an exotic-looking font or extra-large or extra-small font size for a paper, consider your instructor's requirements. (And don't expect font size to rescue a paper that's too short: instructors are likely to notice if you use an oversized font to extend the page count of a paper!) Probably the most common font—primarily because it is so easy to read—is Times New Roman at 12 point.

- *Adding footnotes or endnotes.* Word processors are extremely helpful if you are writing a paper that requires footnotes (citations at the bottom of the page) or endnotes (citations listed on a single page at the end of a paper). You can insert a footnote or endnote anywhere in a document, and the program will automatically number it correctly—and renumber it if you add or delete a footnote before it.

- *Verifying the spelling of every word.* At the press of a button, a word-processing program will check the spelling of every word you have typed. If it finds a misspelling, it will alert you and provide alternatives with correct spellings. But spell-checking is not foolproof: all the program can do is check to see whether your spelling matches that of any word in its dictionary. For example, if you type "hear" when you meant "here," or "gong" when you mean "going," the word-processing program will not flag it. (To see this for yourself, complete Try It 1 on page 268.)

- *Checking for basic grammatical errors.* If you wish, your word processor will check the grammar of passages in a document. It may be able to catch simple problems such as errors in subject-verb agreement (for instance, you may have mistakenly written "Recent studies has found" instead of "Recent studies have found"). As with spell checks, grammar checks don't work perfectly: They sometimes miss errors that exceed their grammatical "knowledge," and they will sometimes tell you that something is wrong when it isn't. Consequently, you must always carefully edit and proofread your work yourself.

- *Saving what you write.* As you use a word-processing program, the computer stores your document in a temporary memory. If you turn off the computer, however, or if the power goes off, or if the computer freezes up, the material you've worked on can disappear, possibly forever.

That's why it's crucial to actively save your work. You can save a document to a computer's hard drive, a flash drive, or a network drive (if you have space on one). However you do it, *make sure you save material frequently and make backup copies.* Nothing is more frustrating than laboring over a document for hours and having it disappear into cyberspace.

Presentation Programs: Looking Good

Sometimes *how* you present material is as important as *what* you're presenting. **Presentation programs** such as Microsoft PowerPoint help you put your best foot forward by allowing you to create impressive, professional-looking visual materials, including charts, maps, animations, and other graphical elements

Presentation program
Computer application software that helps you create impressive, professional-looking visual materials that include words, charts, maps, and other graphical elements

1

TRY It!

Missing the Misspellings

Although word-processing programs can be a boon to those with poor spelling skills, they also can overlook many problems—sometimes very obvious ones. To test this, carefully type the following paragraph into your word-processing program, exactly as it appears below:

When they returned to there home, Jack and Devon found a bare lurking on there back porch. Scared to death, they searched for an acts, hoping to sleigh it, or at least frighten it. But the bare was sew frightening that Jack and Devon returned to there car and road away. "Weal never here the end of this," said Devon to Jack.

Now run a spelling check on the paragraph, and answer the following questions about the results you obtain:

1. How many words were indicated as misspelled by the word-processing program?

2. What words are actually misspelled, given the meaning of the paragraph?

3. Is there any way you could have made the word-processing program work more effectively?

After you've completed this exercise, share your results with others in your class or with your study group. Discuss any word-processing "failures" that you might have had, and consider ways that you might use word processors more effectively.

To Try It online, go to: **www.mhhe.com/power**.

(as in Figure 10.1). The resulting output can be printed onto paper, made into overhead transparencies or slides, run as a "slide show" from your computer, or projected directly from your computer onto a screen through a projector.
There are several keys to developing an effective presentation:

- **Include graphics.** Most presentation programs have an array of graphics (often called clip art) that can be added to a slide. A globe, a cap and gown, a shooting star, or other objects can add visual spice to your presentation. In addition, you can download material from the Web, such as photos, into your presentation.

- **Integrate audio and video.** Presentation programs also allow you to include sound and video clips. For instance, you could use a brief clip of a news event that you download from the Web.

- **Remember: Less is more.** Don't try to cram too much information on a particular slide. Avoid putting too many words on a line or using too many

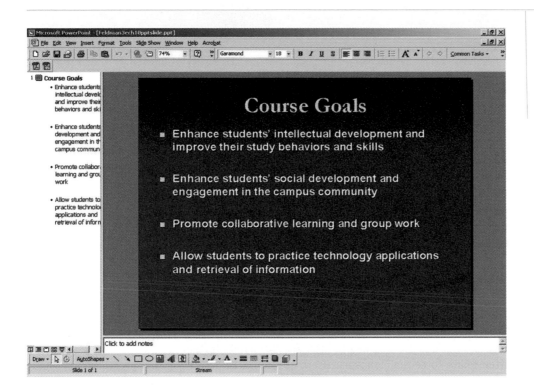

FIGURE 10.1
PowerPoint Presentation
PowerPoint slide background graphics add visual interest; large font and bullets direct attention to key points.

colors. Just because you can do all sorts of cool things with graphics doesn't mean that you *should*—at least not all at the same time.

- **Unify your presentation.** Individual slides or other presentation materials should have a similar look. Using similar fonts and font sizes unifies your presentation.

- **Check for spelling errors.** Most presentation programs have built-in spell checks. Use them! It's embarrassing to have a 1-foot-high spelling mistake projected onto a screen.

- **Use *animation* (sparingly).** Animation allows you to add movement to your presentation. Sentences, words, or even letters can be made to slide in from the left or right of the screen, or appear (or disappear) as you choose. But use animation sparingly; too much movement can be distracting and ultimately annoying to viewers.

For tips on making best use of instructors' presentation programs in class, see the *Course Connections* feature. And to test out a presentation program yourself, complete Try It 2 on page 271.

Teaching Tip: Incorporate this information with the speaking skills in Chapter 7. Combining technology and presentations will bring out the best in your students.

Spreadsheet Programs: Crunching the Numbers

Whether you love or hate math, you're going to like spreadsheet programs, for they take the drudgery out of crunching numbers. **Spreadsheet programs** like Microsoft Excel help you with budgeting and financial projections and are necessary for accounting and engineering courses. They allow you to perform calculations with complete accuracy.

Spreadsheet program
Computer application software that helps with budgeting and financial projections and is necessary for accounting and engineering courses

FIGURE 10.2
Excel Spreadsheet
Expense report generated by Excel spreadsheet software. Numerical calculations are embedded as formulas in the spreadsheet, simplifying the task of figuring totals.

	(1)Gas/Oil	Maint.	Plane, Train Limo, Taxi	Car Rental	Tolls Parking	Exhibit Fees	Office Supplies	Printing	Phone	Postage	Hotel & Lodging	Business Meals	Meals Alone	Entertain- ment	Misc.	Expens
9			356.29			250.00			12.35		375.29	85.37				$ 1,07
35				380.00	36.00						181.27	95.45				$ 69
40	0.00	0.00	356.29	380.00	36.00	250.00	0.00	0.00	12.35	0.00	556.56	180.82	0.00	0.00	0.00	$ 1,772

E-mail
Electronic mail, a system of communication that permits users to send and receive messages via the Internet

Instant messaging
A system that allows one to use a computer to communicate in real time with friends and instructors

World Wide Web
A highly graphical interface between users and the Internet that permits users to transmit and receive not only text but also pictorial, video, and audio information

Newsgroup
An electronic Internet area in which users may post and read messages relevant to a particular topic of the group's choosing

Listserv
A subscription service through which members can post and receive messages via e-mail on general topics of shared interest

via the Internet. The Internet is already the central storehouse for information in the 21st century.

The Internet provides the backbone of virtual communication. Among its specific features are the following:

- **E-mail.** The most widely used aspect of the Internet is **e-mail,** short for "electronic mail." E-mail offers a way for people to send and receive messages with incredible speed. On some college campuses, e-mail is the most common form of communication among students and faculty.

- **Instant messaging.** If you want to communicate in real time with friends and instructors, use instant messaging. With **instant messaging** (IM for short), you create a list of other users with whom you wish to communicate. If others on your list are online at the same time you are, you'll know instantly, and you'll be able to send messages back and forth. Instructors sometimes hold virtual office hours using instant messaging, and businesses increasingly use instant messaging in order to facilitate employee communication.

- **The World Wide Web.** Want to order flowers for your girlfriend in Dubuque? Find a long-lost friend? Hear the opening theme of Schubert's Unfinished Symphony? Read the latest health bulletin from the Centers for Disease Control?

  You can do all of these—and much, much more—on the **World Wide Web** (or, increasingly commonly, just **Web** for short) which provides a graphical means of locating and browsing through information on the Internet. Accessing the Web is rapidly becoming the standard way to find and use such information. The Web provides a way to transmit typewritten text, visual material, and auditory information—graphics, photos, music, soundbites, video clips, and much more.

- **Newsgroups.** The Internet contains thousands of electronic **newsgroups,** where people can read and post messages relevant to a particular topic. For example, there are newsgroups devoted to the stock market, snowmobiles, the *Real World,* the New York Yankees, Jennifer Lopez, and Shakespeare's sonnets.

- **Listservs.** A **listserv** is a subscription service that automatically e-mails messages on general topics of shared interest to people who have added their names to its mailing list. Members can respond to messages by replying to the listserv, and their responses will be distributed automatically to everyone on the mailing list. (In most cases it's also possible to respond directly to an individual who posts a message of interest, without sending that response to all members of the listserv.) Among the thousands of listservs online are those relating to jazz, tourism, privacy issues, and libertarianism.

Using E-Mail Effectively

What's the first thing you do when you turn on a computer? If you're like most people, you check first for new e-mail messages.

E-mail (illustrated in Figure 10.3) has become the preferred means of written communication for many of us. Quick, efficient, and (usually) reliable, e-mail is the most widely used feature of the Internet.

Every person using e-mail has at least one address, consisting of these elements:

Teaching Tip: Use the opportunity to share your institution's policies on electronic communication and use of university resources. Student honor codes may be relevant as well in explaining personal responsibility in the technological world.

- **Mailbox name.** The mailbox name—the name assigned to your account on an e-mail system—is often some variant of your own name (e.g., conan_obrien), though it may also be totally fictitious (e.g., hepcat9).

- **@.** The *at* sign.

- **Domain name.** The domain name is the name of the organization that hosts the e-mail "post office" to which the user subscribes—often an institution (e.g., umass.edu or mcgraw-hill.com), an Internet service provider (e.g., aol.com or earthlink.net), or a multifaceted system such as yahoo.com or hotmail.com. *Host computers* are connected directly to the Internet. You can usually tell what kind of an organization hosts an e-mail account by the last part of the address (the *extension*): for example, *.edu* is an educational organization, *.com* is a commercial organization, and *.gov* is a governmental organization (see Table 10.1 on page 274).

Many e-mail providers (e.g., Yahoo! Mail and America Online) have their own, unique e-mail systems on which e-mail can be retrieved anywhere you have access to the Web. Others use particular software programs such as Microsoft's Outlook to send and receive mail; you must have that software installed on your computer to retrieve your e-mail.

Discussion Prompt: In how many college classes has use of email been a course requirement? Has it enhanced or detracted from the learning process?

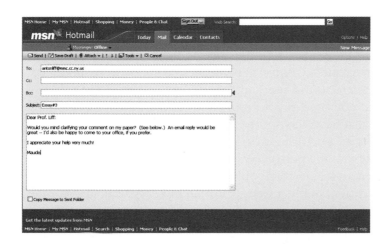

FIGURE 10.3
E-Mail
E-mail sent via Microsoft's Hotmail.

TABLE 10.1 Domain Extensions

E-Mail Address	Extension	Type of Organization
jasper.johns@asu.edu	.EDU	Arizona State University—Educational
dowd@nytimes.com	.COM	The New York Times—Commercial
send.help@redcross.org	.ORG	American Red Cross—Charitable or nonprofit
general@army.mil	.MIL	United States Army—Military
head.counter@census.gov	.GOV	U.S. Census Bureau—Government

In addition, colleges often require that you establish a college e-mail account to which they can send official communications. In such cases, even if you already have an e-mail account, you'll need to check mail coming to your official college address. One way to simplify matters is to have mail automatically forwarded from your college e-mail account to your personal account.

Writing and Responding to E-Mail

Writing e-mail messages is simple. First, type the address of the person to whom you are writing (or, if you've gotten that far already, select it from your e-mail address book). Next, type a brief description of the message in the subject line. Always use the subject line; it allows recipients to get a preview of what the message is about and to easily distinguish that message later from other messages that they may have received from you.

Finally, write the message itself. E-mail messages have several features that are not part of more traditional, formal 'snail-mail' letters. For instance, writers frequently include abbreviations. Some common ones are AFAIK ("as far as I know"), BTW ("by the way"), CYA ("see ya"), OIC ("oh, I see"), and WTG ("way to go"). They may also include **emoticons (or smileys),** which signal the emotion that the writer is trying to convey. Emoticons often look like faces on their side, with facial expressions related to the meaning of the emoticon. A list of the most common emoticons is shown in Table 10.2.

One of the ways that e-mail quickens the pace of communication is the ease with which you can respond to a message you've received. To respond you simply click an on-screen button marked "reply." A new message window appears on screen, and you type in your reply and send off the message to the original sender. (You also have the option of responding using the "reply all" function. With "reply all," everyone who received the original message will also get your reply, not just the person who sent it.)

You can also *forward* messages that you've received to another person who was not an original recipient of the message. E-mail messages can also contain *attachments,* files that do not appear in the body of the message but that can be opened separately. Attachments can take the form of word-processing documents, audio files, movies, and video clips.

Emoticons (or smileys)
Abbreviations used in e-mail messages that provide information on the emotion that the writer is trying to convey. Emoticons usually look like faces on their side, with facial expressions related to the intended emotion or tone

You can use attachments to submit a paper to an instructor. A paper sent as an attachment will be an exact copy of the original file that you produced using a word processor. (Of course, make sure that your instructor accepts assignments via e-mail before you send it.)

Spam Management

Not every message deserves a response. For example, you are likely to receive loads of *spam,* the virtual equivalent of junk mail. Spam may range from get-rich-quick schemes to advertisements for body enhancements or pornography. Spam is more than a nuisance; it takes up valuable transmission resources ("bandwidth"), disk space, and computer time.

Some e-mail systems apply a filter that uses a few simple rules to separate the wheat (e-mail you actually want to read) from the chaff (spam). Unfortunately, these systems are not perfect: they sometimes let junk through and can even at times dispose of messages you want. The only absolutely reliable way to deal with spam is to delete it yourself as quickly as possible.

Here are a few tips for dealing with spam:

- Consider using two e-mail addresses—one for personal messages and one you use when you visit newsgroups and chat rooms.

- Never respond to e-mails that ask for personal or financial information, even if it appears to be legitimate. For instance, in a practice called *phishing,* spam or pop-up messages are used to trick you into disclosing bank account or credit card numbers, passwords, or other personal information.

   In a phishing scam, the e-mail appears to be from a legitimate source and asks you to update or validate information by providing account information. In reality, such messages are from con artists seeking to steal your identity. If you think such a request may be legitimate, call the organization from which it appears to come. *Do not click* on any links in the e-mail message until you're sure it's real.

- Finally, *never* open an attachment from someone you don't know. Computer viruses, which can ruin everything on your hard drive, are often spread through e-mail attachments.

Netiquette: Showing Civility in E-Mail

Although e-mail communication is usually less formal than a letter, you still need to maintain civility. Here are some rules:

- **Don't write anything in an e-mail message that you'll regret seeing on the front page of the campus newspaper.** Yes, e-mail is usually private; but the private message you write can easily be forwarded by the recipient

TABLE 10.2	Emoticons
Meaning	**Symbol**
angry	(:-&
bored	:|
crying	:,(
exhausted	:-6
frown	:-(
funny	:-D
happy	:˜D
hug	[], ()
kiss	.
mad	>/<
sad	:(
sarcasm	:-]
sleepy	|:(
smile	:)
surprised	:-0
tear	:-(
wink	;)
yawn	:-0

IRM Link and Discussion Prompt: Connect this conversation to the broader topic of student civility. Why does electronic media allow us to feel an anonymity that we should not? Does this anonymity encourage uncivil behavior? See IRM, Chapter 10, Section III.

to another person or even scores of other people. Worse yet, it's fairly easy to hit "reply all" when you mean simply to "reply": In this case, you might think that you are responding to an individual, when in fact the e-mail will go to everyone who received the message along with you.

- **Be careful of the tone you convey.** It is harder on e-mail to convey the same kind of personality, and often the same degree of subtlety, that our voice, our handwriting, or even our stationery can add to other forms of communication. This means that attempts at humor and especially sarcasm can backfire. If you're using humor, consider adding an emoticon to clarify the intent of your message.

- **Don't use all capital letters.** Using all caps MAKES IT LOOK AS IF YOU'RE SHOUTING.

- **Never send an e-mail when you are angry.** No matter how annoyed you are about something someone has written in a message, don't respond in kind—or at least wait until you've cooled down. Take a deep breath, and wait for your anger to pass.

- **Be polite and professional when writing to instructors.** Instructors often get dozens, and sometimes hundreds, of e-mails from students each week, and they are especially sensitive to messages that are inappropriate. Instructors should be addressed politely (as in "Dear Professor xx," as opposed to, say, "Yo, Prof!"). You should identify what class you are in since instructors teach multiple classes at the same time. Avoid emoticons and nonstandard abbreviations; you're writing an instructor, not a friend. Finally, be sure to sign your complete name.

Distance Learning: Classes without Walls

Distance learning
The teaching of courses at another institution, with student participation via video technology or the World Wide Web

Do you find that your schedule changes so much from one day to the next that it's hard to fit in a course that meets at a regularly scheduled time? Interested in an unusual course topic that your own college doesn't offer? Want to take a class during the summer, but find yourself summering too far from a college campus?

The solution to your problem may be to enroll in a **distance learning** course. Distance learning is a form of education in which students participate via the Web or other kinds of technology. Although most distance learning courses are taught via the Web, some use teleconferencing, fax, and/or express mail.

The key feature of distance learning courses is the nature of interaction between instructor and students. Rather than meeting in a traditional classroom, where the instructor, you, and the other students are physically present, distance learning classes are most often virtual. Although some schools use "Webcasts" of lectures with virtual discussion rooms or employ lectures on videotape or CDs, many students in distance learning courses will never sit through a lecture or even participate in a real-time conversation with students in the class. They may never even know what their instructor or classmates look like or hear their voices.

Typically, if you take a distance learning course today, you may read lecture notes posted on the Web, search and browse Web sites, write papers, post replies to discussion topics on a *message board,* and take online quizzes and exams. You will see your instructor's and classmates' responses through comments they post on the Web. You may be expected to read a textbook entirely on your own.

Distance learning is not for everyone. Whether you're a good candidate for it or not depends on your preferred style of course-taking. Complete Try It 3 on page 278 to see whether you are suited to learn at a distance.

Distance learning classes have both advantages and disadvantages. On the plus side, distance learning courses offer the following:

- **You can take a Web-based distance learning course anywhere that you have access to the Web.** You can be at home, at the college library, or on vacation at the beach and still participate.

- **Distance learning classes are more flexible than traditional classes.** You can participate in a course any time of the day or night. You set your own schedule.

- **Distance learning classes are self-paced.** You may be able to spread out your work over the course of a week, or you may do the work in a concentrated manner on one day.

- **You may have more contact with your instructor than you do with a traditional class.** Even though you may not have face-to-face contact, you may have greater access to your instructor, via e-mail and the Web, than in traditional classes. You can leave messages for your instructor any time of the night or day; most instructors of distance learning classes respond in a timely way.

In distance learning, you can take classes at another institution without physically having to be on that campus. Although taking courses online can help you fulfill graduation requirements, make sure before you register that your own college will accept the course credits. What do you think the future of distance learning will be?

- **Shy students may find it easier to "speak up" in a distance learning class.** You can think through your responses to make sure you are communicating just what you wish to say. You don't have to worry about speaking in front of other people. For many people, distance learning is liberating.

- **You can become a better writer.** Because distance learning usually involves more writing than traditional courses, you receive more practice writing—and more feedback for it—than in traditional classes.

On the other hand, distance learning has disadvantages that you should keep in mind:

- **You are a prisoner of technology.** If you lose access to a computer and the Web, you won't be able to participate in the class until the problem is fixed.

- **You won't have direct, face-to-face contact with your instructor or other students.** Distance learning can be isolating, and students sometimes feel alone and lost in cyberspace.

- **You won't get immediate feedback.** In a distance learning class, it may be hours, or sometimes days, before you receive feedback on what you have

Student Alert: Can your students apply the information in TRY IT 3 to their learning style? How closely related are "course-taking styles" and "learning styles"?

3

 **PERSONAL STYLES**

Assess Your Course-Taking Style

Your preferred course-taking style—how you participate in classes, work with your classmates, interact with your teachers, and complete your assignments—may make you more or less suitable for distance learning. Read the following statements and indicate whether you agree or disagree with them to see whether you have what it takes to be a distance learner.

	Agree	Disagree
1. I need the stimulation of other students to learn well.		
2. I need to see my teacher's face, expressions, and body language to interpret what is being said.		
3. I participate a lot in class discussions.		
4. I prefer to hear information presented orally rather than reading it in a book or article.		
5. I'm not very good at keeping up with reading assignments.		
6. I'm basically pretty easily distracted.		
7. I'm not very well organized.		
8. Keeping track of time and holding to schedules is NOT a strength of mine.		
9. I need a lot of "hand-holding" while I work on long assignments.		
10. I need a close social network to share my feelings, ideas, and complaints with.		
11. I'm not very good at writing.		
12. Basically, I'm not very patient.		

The more you disagree with these statements, the more your course-taking style is suited to distance learning. Interpret your style according to this informal scale:

Disagreed with 10–12 statements = Excellent candidate for distance learning

Disagreed with 7–9 statements = Good candidate for distance learning

Agreed with 6–9 statements = Probably better taking classes on campus

Agreed with 10–12 statements = Avoid distance learning

To Try It online, go to **www.mhhe.com/power**.

posted to a message board, depending on how well the pace of other students matches your own.

- **Distance learning classes require significant discipline, personal responsibility, and time management skills.** You won't have a set time to attend class as you do in traditional courses. Instead, you must carve out the time yourself. Although instructors provide a schedule of when things are due, you have to work out the timing of getting them done.

Despite these potential drawbacks to distance learning courses, they are becoming increasingly popular. More and more colleges are offering them. Many companies encourage employees with crowded schedules to take distance learning as a way of providing continuing education.

If you are considering taking a distance learning course, follow these steps, which are summarized in the P.O.W.E.R. Plan on the right.

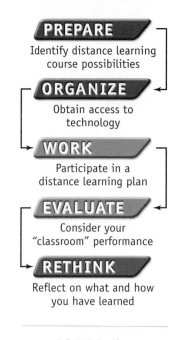

PREPARE
Identify distance learning course possibilities

ORGANIZE
Obtain access to technology

WORK
Participate in a distance learning plan

EVALUATE
Consider your "classroom" performance

RETHINK
Reflect on what and how you have learned

P.O.W.E.R. Plan

P REPARE: Identifying Distance Learning Course Possibilities

How do you find a distance learning course? In some cases, your own college may offer courses on the Web and list them in your course catalog. In other cases, you'll have to find courses on your own.

The best place to look is on the Web itself. By searching the Web, you can find distance learning courses ranging from agronomy to zoology. Don't be deterred by the physical location of the institution that offers the course. It doesn't matter where the college is located, because for most distance learning classes, you'll never have to go to the campus itself.

But before you sign up for a potential course that you would like to count toward your degree, *make sure that your own college will give you credit for it*. Check with your advisor and registrar's office to be certain.

You should also find out what the requirements of a course are before you actually sign up for it. Check the syllabus carefully and see how it meshes with your schedule. If it is a summer course and you are going to be away from your computer for a week, you may not be able to make up the work you miss.

Finally, try to talk with someone who has taken the course before. Was the instructor responsive, providing feedback rapidly? If necessary, could you speak with the instructor by phone? Was the course load reasonable? (Try It 4 on page 280 will help you to work through the process.)

Discussion Prompt: Have students brainstorm what courses and situations would encourage distance learning. Are they interested in exploring this option? Can they see where it would be expedient in their futures?

O RGANIZE: Obtaining Access to Technology

Although you don't need to be a computer expert, you will need some minimal e-mail and Web skills to take a distance learning course. If you don't have sufficient technological expertise, beef up your computer skills by taking a computer course or workshop *before* you actually sign up for the course.

You'll also need access to a computer connected to the Internet. It doesn't have to be your own computer, but you will certainly need regular and convenient access to one. Make sure that the computer you plan to use has sufficient internal resources to quickly connect to the Internet; a very slow connection is frustrating.

 WORKING IN A GROUP

Get Some Distance on the Problem

Working by yourself initially, see if you can find distance learning courses of interest to you: Start by checking your school's course catalog to see what might be offered there. If you're already comfortable online, you might also try the following:

■ *The Chronicle of Higher Education's* Distance Education: Daily Updates (**chronicle.com/distance/**).

■ The World Lecture Hall (**www.utexas.edu/world/lecture/index.html**), hosted by the University of Texas, which provides a list of distance learning courses offered worldwide.

Try to find five courses you would be interested in and list them below. After you have completed your list, share your list with others in a group.

1. How diverse were the courses you were able to find?

2. Were particular subject areas better represented than others?

3. Why?

To Try It online, go to **www.mhhe.com/power**.

Be sure to make all your arrangements for computer access prior to the start of a course. It can take several weeks to set up Internet service on a home computer if you don't have it already.

Student Alert and IRM Link: Ask students to explore distance learning and international education.

**ORK:** Participating in a Distance Learning Class

Successfully participating in a distance learning course involves several skills that are distinct from those needed for traditional classes. To get the most out of a distance learning course, you'll need to do the following:

■ **Manage your time carefully.** You won't have the luxury of a regular schedule of class lectures, so you'll have to manage your time carefully. No one is going to remind you that you need to sit down at a computer and work.

You will need every bit of self-discipline to be successful in a distance learning course.

- **Check in frequently.** Instructors may make crucial changes in the course requirements. Make sure to check for any changes in due dates or class expectations.

- **Find a cyberbuddy.** At the start of the semester, try to make personal contact with at least one other student in the class. You can do this by e-mailing, phoning, or actually meeting the student if he or she is geographically nearby. You can share study strategies, form a study group, and share notes. Connecting with another student can help you avoid feelings of isolation that may interfere with your success.

- **Make copies of everything.** Don't assume everything will go well in cyberspace. Make a printed copy of everything you submit, or alternatively have a backup stored on another computer.

- **Have a technology backup plan.** Computers crash, your connection to the Internet may go down, or an e-mailed assignment may be mysteriously delayed or sent back to you. Don't wait until the last minute to work on and submit assignments, and have a plan in place if your primary computer is unavailable.

Student Alert: This is a constant problem for students. A back-up plan is critical to academic success. Students need to be aware of the "time stamped" nature of many assignments which assures the instructor of submission deadlines.

E VALUATE: Considering Your "Classroom" Performance

As with any class, you'll be receiving feedback from your instructor. But unlike many courses, in which almost all the feedback comes from the instructor, much of the feedback in a distance learning course may come from your fellow students. What can you learn from their comments?

At the same time you'll be receiving feedback, you will likely be providing feedback to your classmates. Consider the nature of feedback you provide, and be sure that you use the basic principles of classroom civility.

R ETHINK: Reflecting on What and How You Have Learned

Distance learning is not for everyone. If your preferred learning style involves extensive, face-to-face interaction with others, you may find that your experience is less than satisfying. On the other hand, if you are at ease with computers and enjoy working on your own, you may find distance learning highly effective.

As you reflect on your distance learning experience, go beyond the technology and think about the learning outcomes. Ask yourself whether you learned as much as you would have in a traditional class. You should also consider ways that the experience could have been more effective for you. And think about whether you were so absorbed by the technology that you lost sight of the real goal of the course: learning new material.

Most educational experts believe that distance learning will play an increasingly important role in higher education. Furthermore, because it offers an efficient way of educating people in far-flung locales, it is a natural means of promoting lifelong learning experiences. In short, the first distance learning class you take is likely not to be your last.

Of course, you could also search on "Hemingway" as the subject, which would yield a list of books *about* him and his work; if you entered his name in a "keyword" search, the catalog would return a more comprehensive list of books both by *and* about him.

The key piece of information in a catalog entry is the book's **call number,** a code that tells you exactly where to find it. Most college libraries use the Library of Congress classification system, which assigns to each book a unique combination of letters and numbers.

Because the record illustrated on page 283 is from an electronic search, it contains further helpful information. The words "On Holdshelf" under "Status" tell you that the book has not been checked out by another patron and should be sitting on the shelf. You'll need to familiarize yourself with your library's particular system to know precisely how you can make most efficient use of the catalog. Chances are there's a handout or posted set of instructions nearby.

Once you have identified the material you need and where it is located, you'll need to go find it. In all but the biggest libraries, you can simply go into the **stacks,** the place containing shelves where the books and other materials are kept, and—using the call number—hunt for it. In libraries with closed stacks, you must fill out a form with the call numbers of the books you want. A library aide will find and deliver the material to a central location.

What if you go to the location in the stacks where the material is supposed to be and you can't find it? The material may be checked out, in use by someone else at that time, incorrectly shelved, or simply lost. Whatever the reason, *don't give up.* If the material is checked out to another user, ask a librarian if you can **recall** the material, a process by which the library contacts the person who has the book and asks him or her to return it.

If the librarian informs you that the material is not checked out, wait a few days and see if it appears on the shelf. Someone may have been using it while you were looking for it. If it was misshelved, the librarian may be able to find it. If the material is truly lost, you may be able to get it from another library through **interlibrary loan,** a system by which libraries share resources.

Finally, even if you do find exactly what you were looking for, take a moment to scan the shelves. Because books and other materials are generally grouped by topic, you may find other useful titles in the same place. One of the pleasures of libraries is the possibility of finding an unexpected treasure—material that your catalog search did not initially identify but that may provide you with exactly what you need.

Call number
A unique classification number assigned to every book (or other resource) in a library. Call numbers are used for ease of location

Stacks
The shelves on which books and other materials are stored in a library

Recall
A way to request library materials from another person who has them

Searching for materials in the library stacks can be frustrating if they are not on the shelves. However, you may unexpectedly find relevant and interesting material while browsing.

Interlibrary loan
A system by which libraries share resources, making them available to patrons of different libraries

The World Wide Web

As its name implies, the Web is vast—sometimes frustratingly so. In fact, no one knows how much material exists on the Web. Not only is more information added to the Web every day, but the information also resides on thousands of individual computers. Anyone with minimal Web savvy and access to a *server* (a computer with a permanent Internet connection) can set up a personal Web site.

The fact that anyone can put information on the Web is both the biggest asset and greatest disadvantage of using the Web as an information source. Because minimal computer skill is the only expertise a person needs to set up a Web page, there may be as much misinformation on the Web as there is information. Consequently, keep the usual consumer rule in mind: Buyer beware. Unless the Web site has been established and is maintained by a reliable organization, the information it contains may not be accurate.

It is becoming increasingly easy for anyone to put material on the World Wide Web, and many students are creating their own personal Web pages containing information and photos about their lives.

There are a number of key factors involved in each Web search. They include a browser, Web pages, links, and search engines.

■ **Browsers.** To use the Web, your computer has to have a browser. A **browser,** as its name implies, is a program that provides a way of looking at the information on the Web. Among the major browsers are Microsoft's Internet Explorer, Netscape's Navigator, and Firefox's Mozilla (see Figure 10.5).

Using a browser is a bit like taking a taxi: once you get in, you get to where you want to go by providing an address. The address, also known as a URL (Uniform Resource Locator), identifies a unique location on the Web, a *Web site* or a *Web page* (one of the parts of a site).

Web addresses are combinations of letters and symbols. They typically start off with "**www.[domain_name]**.[xxx]"—the address of the hosting Web

Browser
A program that provides a way of navigating around the information on the World Wide Web

Student Alert: Many first year students have done research in high school using the Internet, but that does not mean they have done good research. Check with your students about their experience in this area.

FIGURE 10.5
Internet Brower
Home page for Microsoft's Internet Explorer browser.

"Go ask your search engine."

site (e.g., **www.iastate.edu**, the home page for Iowa State University). If you're looking for a sub-site or a particular page on the site, the address becomes increasingly specific: **www.iastate.edu/visitors/** will take you to a "visitors" site—a collection of pages—hosted by **iastate.edu**. A *page* on that site—for example, **www.iastate.edu/visitors/directions.shtml**, which offers directions to campus—ends with a specific name, usually followed by ".htm," ".html," or ".shtml." Because most addresses begin with "http://," this part of the address is often dropped in references to a site.

You can often get a decent idea of what kind of site you're going to by taking a careful look at the Web address: you can tell that **www.mhhe.com/power**, for example, is a site that has something to do with "power" and is hosted by a commercial entity (which you might or might not recognize as McGraw-Hill Higher Education). (Hmm, might be worth checking out. . . .)

Web page
A location (or site) on the World Wide Web housing information from a single source and (typically) links to other pages

- **Web pages.** Web pages are the heart of the Web. A **Web page** is a document that presents you with information. The information may appear as text on the screen, to be read like a book (or more accurately, like an ancient scroll). It might include a video clip, an audio clip, a photo, a portrait, a graph, or a figure. It might offer a news service photo of the president of the United States or a backyard snapshot of someone's family reunion.

Link
A means of "jumping" automatically from one Web page to another

- **Links.** Web sites typically provide you with **links**—embedded addresses to other sites or documents that, at a click, cause your browser automatically to "jump" there. Just as an encyclopedia article on forests might say at the end, "See also Trees," Web pages often refer to other sites on the Web—only it's easier than with a book. You just have to click on the link with your mouse and—*poof!*—you're there.

Search engine
A computerized index to information on the World Wide Web

- **Search engines.** A **search engine** is simply a computerized index to information on the Web. When you know what information you want to find but don't have an address for it, a search engine can often steer you toward relevant sites.

The various parts of the Web are similar to the components of traditional libraries, as illustrated in Figure 10.6. A Web browser is equivalent to a library card; it gives you access to vast quantities of material. Web sites are like the books of a library; Web pages are the book pages, where the content resides. Links are analogous to "see also" portions of books that suggest related information. And search engines are like a library's card catalog, directing you to specific locations.

Locating Information on the Web

There is no central catalog of the contents of the Web: instead, there are a number of different search engines. Furthermore, depending on the search engine you use and the type of search you do, you'll identify different information.

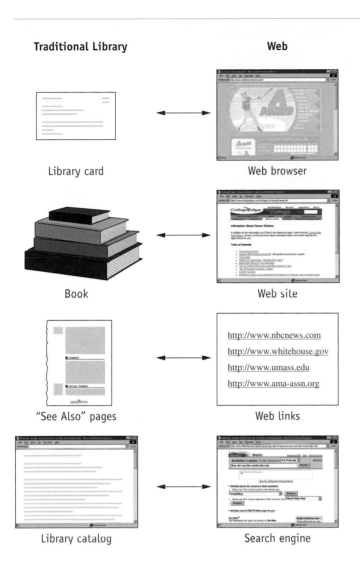

Traditional Library

Library card

Book

"See Also" pages

Library catalog

Web

Web browser

Web site

http://www.nbcnews.com
http://www.whitehouse.gov
http://www.umass.edu
http://www.ama-assn.org

Web links

Search engine

FIGURE 10.6
Comparison of Library and Web
The various parts of the Web are similar to the components of a traditional library.

Search engines themselves are located on the Web, so you have to know their addresses. After you reach the "home" address of a search engine, you enter your search terms. The search engine then provides a list of Web sites that may contain information relevant to your search.

Some search engines, such as Yahoo!, specialize in organizing information by subject, making it easy to search for information on, say, different dog breeds, the Islamic religion, or car repair. Using Yahoo! for its subject directories is like searching for information using the subject entries in a library catalog (see Figure 10.7 on page 288).

Other search engines, such as Google or AltaVista, catalog many more pages than Yahoo! but don't group them by subject: due to the breadth of their coverage, they might be more useful when you are looking for obscure pieces of information or for numerous sources for different perspectives on a topic. Using Google or AltaVista is like performing a keyword search in a library catalog.

Finally, a third type of search engine is exemplified by Ask Jeeves and Dogpile. Known as metasearch tools, these sites send your search commands to other search engines, compiling the results into a single, unified list.

Student Alert: This is a wonderful graphic to connect different generations and how we learned to seek information. Ask your students where they are most competent and comfortable.

FIGURE 10.7
Using a Search Engine
Yahoo! search page on animal rights.

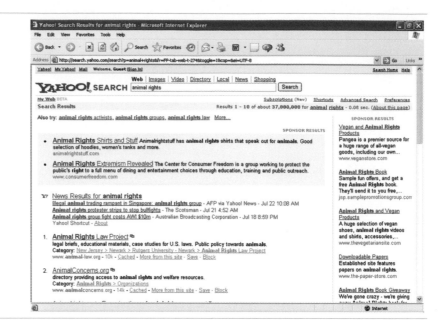

> **"Don't let that little glowing screen become an adversary. If you plan correctly, the computer can become your most useful tool at college—next to your brain."**
>
> Greg Gottesman, author

"First, they do an on-line search."

There's no single search engine that works best. Most people develop their own preferences based on their experience. The best advice: Try out several of them (some features are summarized in Table 10.3) and see which works best for you. To get started, work through Try It 5, "Work the Web: Information, Please!" on page 290.

Becoming a Savvy Surfer

The process you use to search the Web couldn't be easier—or more difficult. The vast amounts of material online and the relative ease of navigation afforded by the Web make finding information quite simple: What is hard is finding appropriate information.

Consider the search illustrated in Figure 10.8 on page 291. It is the result of entering "How do I use the Web?" into the home page of Google. The search identified over 930 *million* Web sites related to the topic.

Using the list of sites generated by the search is simple. With the mouse, click on the site address of the relevant document, and the home page of the site will (eventually) appear on your computer screen. You can then take notes on the material, in the same way you'd take notes on material in a book.

Many of the million sites Google returned, however, may well be of little use. It's easy in such a search to end up in a virtual dead end, in which the information you have found is only minimally related to the topic you're researching. If you do find yourself at a site that's of no use to you, simply hit the "back" button on your browser until you return to where you started.

How can you limit your search in the first place, so that you find sites more directly relevant? The following tips can help you to get the most from a search[1]:

TABLE 10.3   Major Search Sites on the Web[2]

Search Site	Comments
A9 www.a9.com	Amazon product that offers search results from Google along with a number of additional features, including search results from Amazon's "Search Inside the Book"; A9 also saves your search history and tracks the click history of sites you have viewed from your search results.
Open Directory www.dmoz.org	The **Open Directory Project** is the largest, most comprehensive human-edited directory of the Web. It is constructed and maintained by a vast, global community of volunteer editors.
Google www.google.com	Most popular search site. Ranks pages by tracking the links from pages ranked high by the service. Google offers a number of services and tools that are worth exploring.
Ask Jeeves www.askjeeves.com	Allows submission of questions in plain English and suggests relevant sites.
Alltheweb www.alltheweb.com	Returns results quickly from an extremely large database gathered by the Yahoo! crawler; offers multimedia and news searches; has a good advanced search interface.
Alta Vista www.altavista.com	Searches Web sites and Usenet newsgroups with advanced search options.
MSN Search www.search.msn.com	Microsoft's search engine that offers searches of the general Web as well as some deep Web sources; includes a Search Builder that includes an option to retrieve results based on recent updates, popularity, and exact or approximate match.
SearchEdu.com www.searchedu.com	Service that limits results to the .edu domain; also offers to search well-known dictionaries, encyclopedias, almanacs, etc.
IceRocket www.icerocket.com	Offers thumbnail images of retrieved sites; also saves a search history.
Lycos www.lycos.com	Emphasizes search results from the Open Directory and offers Web sites from the Fast Search index.
Teoma www.teoma.com	Returns results in three sections: popularity-ranked Web pages based on the number of same-subject pages that reference them; suggested terms to refine a search; and link collections created by topic experts.

1. **Before turning to your computer, phrase your search as a question.**
2. **Identify the important words in that question.** Then think of words that are related to the important words. Write all the words down.
3. **Go to your favorite search engine.** Google is probably the most popular today, but preferences vary.
4. **Type in two or three words from your list,** making sure they are spelled correctly, then search. Note: You can do a few things here to limit the number of results returned, thus making your search more efficient. Most search engines allow you to use the following:

   ■ *Quotation marks,* to denote a phrase—words that should appear together, in a specific order (e.g., "animal rights").

Discussion Prompt: How capable are you and your students in navigating this age of information? What are the associated benefits and concerns?

5

Work the Web: Information, Please!

Try to find the answer to the first question below on Yahoo! (**www.yahoo.com**), Google (**www.google.com**), *and* Dogpile (**www.dogpile.com**). Then use whichever search engine you prefer to find answers to the remaining questions.

1. What was the French Revolution and when did it occur?

2. Who is Keyser Soze?

3. What are the words of Dr. Martin Luther King Jr.'s, "I Have a Dream" speech?

4. Is the birthrate in the United States higher or lower than that in Brazil?

5. What is the ecu?

How easy was it for you to find the answers to the questions? Which search engine(s) did you prefer, and why?

To Try It online, go to **www.mhhe.com/power**.

- *Plus signs,* used before terms that must appear in all results returned (+ "animal rights" + experimentation).
- *Minus signs,* before terms you do not want to appear in results (+ "animal rights" + experimentation –fur).
- *Boolean operators*—words like AND, OR, AND NOT, and NEAR (e.g., "animal rights" AND experimentation NOT fur).

Check the "Help" section of your preferred search engine for more precise information on limiting your searches.

Teaching Tip: If you have access to a smart classroom, doing TRY IT 5 in class can be a fun, stimulating activity for your class.

5. **Open a new window,** type in a different arrangement of your terms, and search again.

6. **Identify the common links between the two searches.** Read the very brief summaries provided.

7. **When you choose a Web site, open the page in a new window** so that you can go back to your list of hits.

8. **Open a text editor window.** Copy and paste the site's address into that window and follow it with an annotation of your own. Do that for five sites.

9. **See if you have found the answer you were looking for.** If not, reformulate your question to come up with new key words.

10. **Resist the temptation to simply cut and paste the material into a new document,** once you've found the information you're looking for. It's too easy to succumb to plagiarizing what you've found if you copy material in an indiscriminate manner. Instead, take notes on the material using the critical thinking and notetaking skills you've developed for use with other, more traditional information sources.

Evaluating the Information You Find on the Web

In most instances, you'll find more information than you need, and you'll have to evaluate the information you have found. Some of the important

Discussion Prompt: How do you and your students determine what is important, credible and useful?

CAREER CONNECTIONS

Exploring Careers on the Web

The Web is one of the newest ways to explore careers that may interest you. You can begin to gather information by going to a Web site devoted to jobs, such as JobWeb (**www.jobweb.org**). The JobWeb site presents a variety of career-related sites. You can also find other sites using the various search engines we've been discussing.

In addition, you can find help wanted advertisements for many jobs on the Web. In fact, it is possible to apply directly for jobs using the Web. Some firms advertise their job needs on their company sites, and you can e-mail a cover letter and a résumé listing your education and experience. An increasing number of jobs are obtained in this way.

Keep this in mind, too: The computer expertise you develop during college will later help you in your professional life. Already, more and more jobs require at least minimal computer skills, and every projection of the future suggests that computers will become a central facet of the workplace.

---

questions you must address before you can feel confident about what you've found include the following:

Teaching Tip: Authenticity is much easier to determine with print media in a library with librarians everywhere than with electronic media at a computer, often by yourself. Who on your campus is an authority in this area and could be a good resource for your class?

- **How authoritative is the information?** It is absolutely essential to consider the source of the material. Approach every piece of information with a critical eye, trying to determine what the author's biases might be. The best approach is to use multiple sources of information. If one source diverges radically from the others, you may reasonably question the reliability of that source.

  Another approach is to consider the publisher of the material or sponsoring institution. For instance, sites established by well-known publishers and organizations are more likely to contain accurate information than those created by unknown (and sometimes anonymous) authors. Remember, the Web is completely unregulated: *anyone* can put *anything* on the Web.

  One way of evaluating Web information is to consider a site's host. Commercial Web pages (whose address includes the letters *.com,* short for commercial) often tend to include the least objective material. On the other hand, addresses including the letters *.gov* (government), *.org* (nonprofit organization), *.mil* (military), and *.edu* (educational and research institutions) generally include more objective information.

Teaching Tip: Refer to academic honesty issues in Chapter 7. Apply this discussion to the Internet. Students must understand their responsibility to practice academic integrity in all academic work.

  But not always. For example, some instructors place student papers on the Web, giving them an *.edu* address. Such papers vary considerably in their authoritativeness. Furthermore, *blogs,* which are personal Web sites that typically contain personal diaries or political views, are increasingly pervasive on the Web. Because they are not subject to any editorial scrutiny before they are published, they are of questionable authoritativeness. In short, any Web content must be evaluated on its merits.

- **How current is the information?** No matter what the discipline, information is changing at a rapid rate. Even a field like Chaucerian English, which concentrates on poetry written in the 14th century, advances significantly year by year as scholars make new discoveries, come to new insights, and reach new conclusions.

  Consequently, don't assume that, because you're researching a historical topic, old sources will suffice. Consider whether what you've found is the most recent and up-to-date approach. Compare older sources to newer ones to identify changes in the ways in which the topic is considered.

- **How well are claims documented?** Are there references and citations to support the information? Are specific studies identified?

- **Is anything missing?** One of the hardest questions to answer is whether your research is complete. Have you found all the relevant sources? Have you missed anything that is important?

  Although there is no way to answer these questions definitively, you can do a couple of things. One way to ensure that you haven't missed anything important is to check out the sources that you

"On the Internet, nobody knows you're a dog."

have found. Many will have bibliographies and lists of suggested additional readings. By carefully considering this information, you'll be able to get a good sense of the important work in your topic area and verify that you haven't overlooked some critical source.

You can also talk to your course instructor, describing generally what you've found. Probably the best person to turn to, however, is a reference librarian.

The stereotype of a librarian as someone whose main job is to stop people from talking in the library is dead. Librarians today are masters at information management and technology. They are people who can help you find your way through a huge range of data sources—both in the library and on the Web—and steer you to the right material.

Make use of librarians—but do it properly. If your library offers regular orientations, sign up for one. Then try looking for material yourself. If you're having trouble sorting through what you've found (or can't find material in the first place), ask for help.

The better the question, the better the answer. Don't ask vague, unfocused questions (e.g., "Where are the books about nuclear power?"). Instead, sharpen your question, being as precise as possible ("I'm writing a paper on the environmental effects of using nuclear power to generate electricity. I've found two books and several Web

Ultimately, most people master the use of computers, despite initial difficulties.

sites, but they're not quite right. I wonder if you have any ideas about where I might find additional material?").

Don't be afraid to ask. Think of librarians as highly trained guides who can save you hours of aimless wandering in an increasingly dense forest of information.

A Final Word

The Information Age presents us with great promise and opportunity. Through the use of media such as e-mail and the Internet, we have at our fingertips the ability to communicate with others around the world. We can break the bounds of our physical location and reach across geography to learn about others. The computer keyboard truly can be said to contain keys to the entire earth and its peoples.

SPEAKING OF Success

Name: Jerry Yang

School: Stanford University, San Francisco, California

If you've ever used Yahoo!, one of the most popular search engines on the World Wide Web, you've relied on the handiwork of Jerry Yang. Yang, along with his partner David Filo, developed the Yahoo! navigational guide in the mid-1990s.

Yang was born in Taiwan, and his father died 2 years later. Seeking a better life, his mother immigrated to the United States. Legend has it that "shoe" was the only English word Yang knew when he started school in San Jose, California, at the age of 10.

After graduating from high school, Yang enrolled in a college electrical engineering program. While still a student, Yang and his friend David Filo began, as a hobby, to catalog their favorite Web sites. The list of sites was initially called "Jerry's Guide to the World Wide Web." As the popularity of their list began to increase, Yang and Filo were forced to refine the listing into categories, and then subcategories. They also renamed their list "Yahoo!" standing for "Yet Another Hierarchical Officious Oracle."

In only a few years, what had started as a hobby had grown into a huge business. Today, with Yang and Filo as "Chief Yahoo!s," the search engine is used by 200 million people each month.

Despite his extraordinary success, Yang feels the future holds even more promise. "It'll probably be strange for me to say this, but I don't consider myself successful yet," Yang says. "So much that I want to do remains to be done. . . . It's important to continue to be modest and paranoid."[3]

But he adds, "It's not often that we get time to reflect on what we've done. But in the rare moments that I do, I look at the people that I work with at Yahoo! and feel pride and satisfaction."[4]

What are the uses of computers?

■ Word-processing, presentation, and spreadsheet applications are the basic kinds of programs.

What is available on the Internet?

■ The Internet is a vast network that connects millions of computers. It has numerous useful features, including e-mail, instant messaging, newsgroups, listservs, and the World Wide Web.

■ E-mail and the Web are the most frequently used features of the Internet.

■ E-mail permits instant communications across the world. Users can reply to messages, forward them, and include attachments.

What is distance learning?

■ Distance learning is a form of education that does not require the physical presence of a student in a classroom. It is usually conducted over the Web.

■ Distance learning requires some adjustments for students, but it is likely to increase in popularity in future years.

How can I develop information competency?

■ There are two main sources of information today: libraries and the Web.

■ Information in libraries is available in print form, electronic form, and microform.

■ Library resources can be found through the use of the library catalog, which may be print-based but is increasingly likely to be computerized.

■ The Web is another major source of information. Web users access Web pages (or sites) by using a browser, locate information by using search engines, and move from site to site by following links on each Web page.

What do I need to keep in mind as I use the Web to gather information?

■ Using the Web effectively to find information can be tricky. It has many dead ends, false trails, and distractions, and the accuracy of the information presented as fact can be difficult to assess.

■ Information on the Web must be carefully evaluated by considering how reliable the source is, how current the information is, how well the source's claims are documented, and how complete the information is.

KEY TERMS AND CONCEPTS

Word-processing program (p. 265)
Presentation program (p. 267)
Spreadsheet program (p. 269)
Internet (p. 271)
E-mail (p. 272)
Instant messaging (p. 272)
World Wide Web (p. 272)
Newsgroup (p. 272)
Listserv (p. 272)
Emoticons (or smileys) (p. 274)
Distance learning (p. 276)

Information competency (p. 282)
Online database (p. 282)
Call number (p. 284)
Stacks (p. 284)
Recall (p. 284)
Interlibrary loan (p. 284)
Browser (p. 285)
Web page (p. 286)
Link (p. 286)
Search engine (p. 286)

On Campus

If you are having difficulty connecting or surfing the Web, the first place to turn is your college's computer center. Most campuses have consultants who can help you with the technical aspects of computer usage.

The librarians at your college library are the people to whom you should turn first if you need help in locating information. In recent years, librarians—most of whom hold advanced degrees—have undergone a significant change in what they do, and most are equally at home using traditional print material and searching electronic information storehouses.

In Print

A good introductory guide to computer basics is Michael Miller's *Absolute Beginner's Guide to Computers* (Que, 2005). *Web Search Savvy: Strategies and Shortcuts for Online Research* by Barbara Friedman (Lawrence Erlbaum, 2004) provides a step-by-step guide to locating information of all sorts. Finally, *The Distance Learner's Guide* (Western Collaborative for Educational Telecommunications, Prentice Hall, 2004) offers clear instruction on becoming an effective online learner.

On the Web

Many sites on the World Wide Web provide the opportunity to extend your learning about the material in this chapter. (Although the Web addresses were accurate at the time the book was printed, check the P.O.W.E.R. Learning Web site [**www.mhhe.com/power**] for any changes that may have occurred.)

- Imperial College (London)'s Department of Computing offers FOLDOC (Free On-Line Dictionary of Computing) at **wombat.doc.ic.ac.uk/foldoc/index.html**. If you're having a hard time trying to figure out some computer jargon, this site—a dictionary of computer terminology—might help. Topics are listed alphabetically and a search engine helps locate specific information.

- The WWW Virtual Library (**vlib.org/**) is one of the oldest catalogs of the Web, providing useful links to thousands of subjects.

- Yahoo! (**www.yahoo.com**) is a very popular Internet search engine and subject directory; unlike Google and AltaVista, as a subject directory, Yahoo! allows browsing through prearranged categories (e.g., education, health, social science, and more). It also offers easy access to news, weather, maps, the yellow pages, and much more.

TAKING IT TO THE NET

1 Using the search engine of your choice, find the address for the Web site of the libraries of the University of California at Berkeley. Once there, try to find "Finding Information on the Internet: A Tutorial." Try the tutorial, which will help you understand many of the basic skills needed to use the Internet effectively. (Would taking the tutorial *first* have helped you to find it?)

2 To see for yourself how the Web can be a great resource for locating information on important issues, try to find the answer to this question: "What are the effects of media violence on children?" Go to a search engine (try **www.google.com**) and type in the phrase: "media violence and children" (being sure to include the quotation marks). Look over the first page of documents that the search engine turns up. Are they in fact about the effects of media violence on children? Do they answer the question you are asking? What is the answer to the question?

Katrisha was almost done with her paper. She'd been working in a marathon session, sitting in front of her computer screen with only a couple of breaks over the course of an afternoon.

She'd begun work just after noon, when the sky was bright and clear. By now, some 4 hours later, it was dark and gray and she heard thunder in the distance. But who cared about the weather? The main thing was that she was almost done.

She didn't usually put things off, but this time she'd gotten behind and was forced to do the work at the last minute. She was writing a report on software that blocks "adult" sites from home computers. Luckily she'd been able to find what she needed using various search engines and incorporating the information into her paper.

The assignment was due by 5:00 p.m., but the professor accepted papers submitted via e-mail. As long as the message was sent before 5:00, she would be OK. She still had an hour to put the final touches on the paper and send it off.

Suddenly, there was a bright flash of lightning, followed by a clap of thunder. At the same moment, her computer screen went black as the electricity was cut.

Much to Katrisha's relief, the outage lasted only a few seconds. Her computer began to reboot, and the screen powered up again. In a few moments, she figured, she could continue her work.

But when the computer had fully restarted, the file with the paper that she'd been working on all day was nowhere to be found. She searched frantically through the various files on the computer, but to no avail. Her heart sinking, she realized that everything she had done over the afternoon was lost.

1. How well did Katrisha use her time to work on her paper? What advice would you give her about the preparation stage of working on a paper?

2. Did Katrisha organize her work well? What would you tell her to do next time?

3. Clearly, Katrisha should have saved her work frequently while she was working. What else should she have done while working on her paper to help her recover from such a catastrophe?

4. What should Katrisha do first to start solving her immediate problem with her professor?

5. What should she do next to begin reconstructing her paper and recovering as much of her work as possible?

For Rich Rinkowski, the moment of truth was fast approaching. He had to make up his mind and decide what he was going to do when he graduated.

Throughout his college career he had intended to go to law school, and he had majored in criminal justice. He'd already been accepted to law school by the middle of his senior year and it seemed that his future was well in hand.

Except for one thing: He was no longer sure he wanted to be a lawyer.

The reason for his indecision was an internship he held working for a film director during the summer between his junior and senior years. Although Rich spent a good deal of his time photocopying and making coffee, he learned a lot about the film industry. In fact, after talking several times at length with the director, Rich began to wonder seriously if he might build a career in the movie industry.

Rich's girlfriend and family were dead set against it: They argued that law was a far safer choice.

As his final term went by, Rich knew he had to make up his mind. But how?

LOOKING AHEAD >>>

Like Rich, all of us face important decisions in our lives at one time or another. How can we make the right decisions? The best way is to employ some basic techniques that can help improve the quality of our decision making.

This chapter will give you a sense of what decision making is and is not, and it discusses a structured process that can help make your decisions the right ones. We'll also consider the related issue of problem solving. You'll confront a variety of problems as you proceed through college. We'll look at a number of proven techniques that will help you solve them.

Neither making decisions nor solving problems is easy. Sometimes the best decision or solution to a problem is one that we don't see at first; we all have mental blind spots. The best problem solvers and decision makers have learned how to use critical thinking to see around these blind spots. To help you improve your critical thinking skills, we'll examine some common problems that can affect our thinking and discuss several biases that can make us jump too quickly to conclusions.

In sum, after reading this chapter you'll be able to answer these questions:

- **How can I improve the quality of my decisions?**

- **What strategies can I use for problem solving?**

- **What are some problems that affect critical thinking and how can I avoid them?**

Making Good Decisions: A Framework

Decision making is the process of deciding among various alternatives. Whether you are trying to decide between a Ford or a Honda; between an apartment that is close to your job or one that is close to campus; or simply between a hamburger or pizza—every one of these choices requires a decision. Some decisions are easily made and have few consequences, but others, such as whether to major in music composition or follow a pre-med course of study, can involve the deepest examination of our beliefs and values.

Whatever the decision you face, it is possible to map out a strategy for making the choice that is best for you. Every decision can benefit from your systematically thinking through the options involved, based on the P.O.W.E.R. Plan illustrated below.

Decision making
The process of deciding among various alternatives

Teaching Tip: Remember to refer back to the information discussed in the first and third chapters. Incorporate information about values and goals.

P REPARE: Identifying Your Goals

Every decision starts with the end you have in mind: the goals you wish to accomplish by making the decision.

For example, suppose you are trying to decide between enrolling in one of two classes next term, neither of which is required: swimming or psychology. To decide, you need to consider both your short- and long-term goals. For instance, the swimming class may raise your level of fitness, and you'll end up with a certificate that will allow you to be a lifeguard during the summer. The psychology class may provide you with some useful information—perhaps information you can use in other classes, perhaps techniques that will help you learn and remember better—but this is by no means certain. In terms of short-term goals, then, the swimming class may be the better choice. On the other hand, while the psychology class may not provide as clear-cut an immediate payoff, it may help you meet your longer-term goal of graduating with honors and becoming a successful teacher.

In short, every decision should start with a consideration of what our short- and long-term goals are. Identifying the goals that underlie decisions ensures that we make decisions in the context of our entire lives and not just to provide short-term answers to immediate problems.

> **"Nothing is more difficult, and therefore more precious, than to be able to decide."**
>
> Napoleon I, *Maxims,* 1804–15

O RGANIZE: Considering and Assessing the Alternatives

Every decision is based on weighing various alternatives. Determining what those alternatives are, and their possible consequences, is often the most difficult part of decision making.

Develop a List of Flexible Alternatives

It's important not only to think thoroughly about the obvious alternatives, but also to consider those that are less obvious. For instance, if you are trying to obtain additional funds to support your college theater group, you might con-

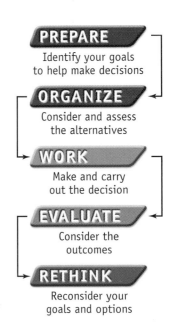

PREPARE
Identify your goals to help make decisions

ORGANIZE
Consider and assess the alternatives

WORK
Make and carry out the decision

EVALUATE
Consider the outcomes

RETHINK
Reconsider your goals and options

P.O.W.E.R. Plan

We've all been there: facing a mind-boggling array of similar choices. However, by systematically assessing the alternatives, we can make informed decisions that will satisfy us.

P.O.W.E.R. UP: The idea that there might be more than one right answer to a dilemma can be unsettling to freshmen. Convincing students to systematically analyze their decision-making process takes energy. What shared experience could you reference that would immediately focus the class on a decision-making moment?

sider raising ticket prices for productions, holding a raffle to raise funds, or asking for sponsorship from a local business. After additional thought, though, you might reframe the issue, considering how best to place pressure on the college administration to increase funding for your group.

In short, the way you develop and frame alternatives is critical to the solution that you ultimately reach. The more alternatives you have, the better able you will be to come to a good solution.

How can you be sure that you've considered all the alternatives? You can't. But using the freewriting technique described in Chapter 7 can help you maximize your efforts.

In *freewriting,* one writes continuously for a fixed period of time, perhaps 5 or 10 minutes. During this period, the idea is to write as many different ideas as possible, without stopping. It makes no difference whether the alternatives are good or bad or even whether they make sense. All that matters is that you let yourself brainstorm about the topic for a while and get it down on paper.

With freewriting, evaluating the worth of the ideas you've generated comes later. After you have produced as many possibilities as you can, then you go back and sift out the reasonable ones from those that are truly unlikely or just plain wacky. It's OK if you have to delete quite a few alternatives from your list; the process is likely to have liberated some truly reasonable alternatives that you might not otherwise have come up with. (Try the technique in the "Use Freewriting" exercise—see Try It 1.)

Assess Alternatives

Once you have generated as extensive a list of alternatives as possible, assess them. You need to follow three key steps when assessing each alternative:

1. *Determine the possible outcomes for each alternative.* Some outcomes are positive, some negative. Consider as many as you can think of. For example, if you are considering ways of solving transportation problems, one alternative might be to purchase a car. That alternative produces several potential outcomes. For example, you know that it will be easier to get wherever you want to go, and you might even have a better social life—clearly positive outcomes. But it is also true that buying and owning a car will be expensive, or it may be difficult to find convenient parking—both significant negative outcomes.

2. *Determine the probability that those outcomes will take place.* Some outcomes are far more likely than others. To take this into account, make a rough estimate of the likelihood that an outcome will come to pass, ranging from 100 percent (it is certain that it will occur) to 0 percent (it is certain that it

TRY IT! 1

Use Freewriting

Use freewriting to think of as many answers as you can to each of the following questions. The ground rules are that you should spend 3 minutes on each question, generating as many ideas as possible—regardless of whether they are feasible. To give yourself maximum freedom, write each answer on a separate page.

1. How can you make room in your schedule to take one more course next term than you're taking this term?

2. How can someone get from the 3rd floor to the 20th floor of a building?

3. What should you do if you suspect that one of your instructors is a space alien?

4. What would happen if the average life span were extended to 125 years?

After generating ideas, go back and evaluate them. How many were actually feasible or realistic? Do you think freewriting fed to the production of more or fewer ideas than you would have come up with if you hadn't used the process? Did the quality of ideas change?

Working in a Group:

After you have answered the questions above, form a group of classmates and compare your answers to those of others. As a group, try to identify the best answers to each question.

To Try It online, go to **www.mhhe.com/power**.

---

will never occur). For instance, consider the possible outcomes to buying a car illustrated in Figure 11.1 on page 304.

Obviously, the probabilities are just guesses, but going through the exercise of estimating them will make the outcomes more real and will permit you to compare the various alternatives against one another more easily.

3. *Compare the alternatives, taking into account the potential outcomes of each.* Systematically compare each of the alternatives as illustrated in Figure 11.1. Then ask yourself the key question: Which alternative, on balance, provides the most positive (and most likely) outcomes?

Obviously, not every decision requires such an elaborate process. In fact, most won't. But when it comes to major decisions, those that could have a large impact upon you and your life, it's worthwhile to follow a systematic process.

Teaching Tip: Point out that writing can serve to help students organize their ideas, which, in turn, can lead to better decision making.

FIGURE 11.1

Outcomes to Buying a Car

Making a rough estimate of the outcomes of buying a car can help in making comparisons of the alternatives as well as making a final decision.

Outcome	Probability
Easier transportation	100%
Greater expense	100%
Greater opportunities for part-time job	75%
Difficulty finding parking	40%
Improve social life	30%

Take a look at *Career Connections* for another process that you can follow to help you make a career decision.

W ORK: Making and Carrying Out the Decision

Working through the previous steps will lead you to the point of decision: choosing one of the alternatives you've identified. Having carried out the steps will make the actual decision easier, but not necessarily easy.

Choosing among Alternatives

The reason that important decisions are difficult is that the alternatives you have to choose from carry both benefits and costs. Choosing one alternative means that you have to accept the costs of that choice and give up the benefits of the other alternatives.

What if, after going through the steps of the process laid out here, you still can't make up your mind? Try these strategies:

- **Give the decision time.** Sometimes waiting helps. Time can give you a chance to think of additional alternatives. Sometimes the situation will change, or you'll have a change in viewpoint.

- **Make a mental movie, acting out the various alternatives.** Many of us have difficulty seeing ourselves in the future and envisioning how various options would play out. One way to get around this difficulty is to cast yourself into a series of "mental movies" that have different endings depending on the decision you make. Working through the different scripts in your head makes potential outcomes far more real and less abstract than they would be if you simply left them as items on a list of various options.

- **Toss a coin.** This isn't as crazy as it sounds. If each alternative seems equally positive or negative to you, pull out a coin—make option A "heads" and B "tails." Then flip it.

   The real power of the coin-toss strategy is that it might help you discover your true feelings. It may happen while the coin is in the air, or it may be that when you see the result of the coin toss, you won't like the outcome and will say to yourself, "No way." In such a case, you've just found out how you really feel.

If all else fails, toss a coin to decide what alternative to follow. Tossing a coin at least brings you to a decision. Then, if you find you're unhappy with the result, you'll have gained important information about how you really feel regarding a particular choice.

Weighing Career Possibilities

One of the most important decisions you'll ever make is choosing a career. Here's one method that can help you:

■ Generate a selection of choices to consider after graduation. Make a list of possibilities—including work (e.g., computer programming, banking, teaching, law, business, insurance, computer software development, etc.), further study (e.g., graduate school, business school, law school, etc.), and even some pie-in-the-sky possibilities (e.g., jazz musician, circus performer).

■ Determine life-satisfaction considerations that are important to you. Generate a list of criteria to use in weighing these postgraduation possibilities. For instance, you might want to consider the following:

Benefit to society

Income

Parents' opinions

Friends' opinions

Interest in the activity

Prestige

Job security/job openings

Benefits (vacation, health insurance, etc.)

Time off

Practicality/attainability

Everyday working conditions

■ Determine how well a particular option fulfills each of the life-satisfaction factors you consider important. By systematically considering how a potential postgraduation path fulfills each of the criteria you use, you'll be able to compare different options. One easy way to do this is to create a chart like the one in Table 11.1 (which shows an example of how computer programming might fulfill the various criteria).

■ Compare different choices. Using the chart, evaluate your possibilities. Keep in mind that this is just a rough guide and that it's only as accurate as (a) the effort you put into completing it and (b) your understanding of a given choice. Use the results in conjunction with other things you find out about careers—and yourself.

TABLE 11.1 Making Career Decisions

Life-Satisfaction Considerations	Possible Choice #1 *Computer programming*	Possible Choice #2	Possible Choice #3	Possible Choice #4
Benefit society	✓			
Income	✓			
Parents' opinions	✓			
Friends' opinions				
Interest in the activity	✓			
Prestige				
Job security/job openings	✓			
Benefits	✓			
Time off				
Practicality/attainability	✓			
Everyday working conditions				
Other				
Other				
Other				
Other				
Other				

My Decision Crossroads

Have you ever made a decision that proved to be of great importance in terms of the direction your life would take? For example, perhaps you broke off a romantic relationship, or decided to quit a sports team because practice took up so much time, or participated in an act of civil disobedience during a protest rally. Reflect on that decision by answering these questions.

1. What was an important decision that you made that had significant effects on your life?

2. What have been the main benefits and disadvantages that you derived from the decision?

3. Every decision to do something is also a decision not to do other things. What did your decision keep you from doing?

4. Considering both the benefits and disadvantages of the decision, would you say that you made a good decision?

5. Thinking critically about the approach you used to make the decision, what alternative approaches might you have used to make it? Could these alternatives produced a different decision? How?

■ **Ask for advice.** Although Western society teaches the virtues of rugged individualism, asking others for their advice is often an excellent strategy. A friend, instructor, parent, or counselor can provide helpful recommendations—sometimes because they've had to make similar decisions themselves. You don't have to take their advice, but it can help to listen to what they have to say.

■ **Learn to view indecision as a decision.** Sometimes we spend so much time making a decision that our indecision becomes a decision. It works like this: Suppose a friend asks you to help her work on a student government task force that is studying the use of alcohol on campus. You'd like to participate, but, because you'll have to commit to a term-long series of meetings, you're worried about the amount of time it will take up.

Because the first meeting isn't going to occur for a few weeks, you have some time to make up your mind. But you just can't seem to decide. Finally, it's the day of the meeting, and you still don't know what to do.

The truth is, you've made the decision: You don't really want to be on the committee. Your indecision is telling you that—bottom line—you don't have sufficient interest to make the commitment.

- **Go with your gut feeling.** Call it what you like—gut feeling, intuition, hunch, superstition—but sometimes we need to go with our hearts and not our minds. If you've thought rationally about a decision and have been unable to determine the best course of action but have a gut feeling that one choice is better than another, follow your feelings.

Following a gut feeling does not mean that you don't need to consider the pros and cons of a decision rationally and carefully. In fact, generally our "intuitions" are best when informed by the thoughtfulness of a more rational process.

> **"In any moment of decision, the best thing you can do is the right thing, the next best thing is the wrong thing, and the worst thing you can do is nothing."**
>
> President Theodore Roosevelt

Carrying Out the Decision

Ultimately, decisions must move from thought to action—they have to be carried out. Consequently, the final stage in making a decision is to act upon it. You need to turn your decision into behavior.

E VALUATE: Considering the Outcomes

Did you make the right decision?

Even if you've spent time and mental effort in thinking through a decision, you still need to consider the results. Even well-considered decisions can end up being wrong, either because you neglected to consider something or because something has changed: either you or the situation.

For instance, suppose you were trying to decide between a major in management or one in biology. If you decide to go into management, it means that you'll be taking more courses related to finance and economics. As you take these courses, you will find out whether you're enjoying them. If you find you are consistently unhappy with them, you should allow yourself to reevaluate your decision to major in management and reconsider the alternatives. It's not too late to change your mind.

In fact, even major life decisions are often reversible. That's why it's so important to evaluate your choices. If you chose the wrong alternative, reverse course and reconsider your options.

Remember: It's not a bad thing to change your mind. In fact, admitting that a decision was a mistake is often the wisest and most courageous course of action. You don't want to be so rigidly committed to a decision that you're unable to evaluate the consequences objectively. Give yourself permission to be wrong.

Teaching Tip: Refer back to information about learning styles in Chapter 3. How do individual learning styles and preferences influence decision-making styles?

R ETHINK: Reconsidering Your Goals and Options

We can get to most places by multiple routes. There's the fastest and most direct route, which will get us to our destination in the least amount of time. Then there's the longer, more scenic route, where the trip itself provides pleasure. You can "take the long way home," as the song goes.

Is one route better than the other? Often not. Both take us to our destination. However, the experience of reaching our goal will have been very different.

Decisions about how to achieve a goal are similar to traveling down different routes. There's often no single decision that is best, just as there's often no single road to a particular place. Consequently, it's important to periodically reconsider the major decisions that we've made about our lives.

Ask yourself these questions:

■ Are my decisions still producing the desired consequences?

■ Are my decisions still appropriate, given my circumstances and changes in my life?

■ Are my decisions consistent with what I want to get out of life?

■ Do my decisions fit with my mission statement (a written, guiding philosophy of life, discussed in Chapter 3)?

Periodically taking stock like this is the best way to make sure that your decisions are taking you where you want to go. Taking stock also helps you to be more effective in making future decisions.

Deciding to Change Colleges

One of the biggest decisions you'll potentially face involves changing colleges, or **transferring.** You may be changing from a 2-year to a 4-year school. Or you may find that your current school doesn't offer the course of study you want or meet some other important need. Whatever the reason, there are several questions to keep in mind when making such an important decision:

■ **Do I meet the minimum requirements for admission?** Every college has its own requirements for admission. For example, you'll probably be required to have a minimum grade point average for admission.

■ **What new requirements will I have to meet at another school?** Because every school has its own particular set of requirements, you'll want to know the courses you'll have to take to graduate.

■ **What courses have I taken that the other school will accept as meeting its requirements?** You'll need to determine the degree of *course equivalency*, in which courses you've already taken substitute for courses at another college.

■ **Is there an *articulation agreement* between my current school and the school I'm considering transferring to?** *Articulation agreements* are official pacts between schools that set out course equivalency.

Keep in mind that although your current school may smooth the way for a transfer, it's the school to which you are transferring that determines how successful the transfer process will be. (You'll find additional information on transferring to another college at the P.O.W.E.R. Learning Web site at **www.mhhe.com/power**.)

■ Problem Solving: Applying Critical Thinking to Find Solutions

Two trains are approaching one another, each moving at 60 miles an hour. If the trains continue moving at the same speed, how long will it be before . . .

If this is what comes to mind when you think of problem solving, think again. **Problem solving** encompasses more than the abstract, often unrealistic situations portrayed in math texts. It involves everyday, commonplace situa-

---

Discussion Prompt: Ask your students to answer these questions relating to their test preparation habits. If the results don't match intentions, then make a decision to change something.

Transferring
Changing colleges

Student Alert: First-year students come to your campus with a wide range of ideas about whether they will transfer to another institution. Be open to their questions and recognize that the time and connections on your campus will often be a deterrent to transferring.

Problem solving
The process of generating alternatives to work on

tions: How do we divide the grocery bill so that each person pays a fair share? How do I keep my 1-year-old from tumbling down the stairs when there seems to be no way to fasten a gate at the top? How can I stop a faucet from dripping? How do I manage to study for a test and complete a paper the same evening?

While decision making is most focused on choosing among various alternatives, the central issue in problem solving is *generating* alternatives. Since many problems require that decisions be made regarding alternatives, decision making and problem solving are often related.

What's the Problem?

The first step in solving any problem is to be as clear as you can about what the problem is. This may sound easy, but often it isn't. In fact, it may take some time to figure out just what is at stake. The reason is that some problems are big and hard to define, while others are quite precise, such as mathematical equations or the solution to a jigsaw puzzle. Determining how to stop terrorism or finding peace in the Middle East are big, ill-defined problems. Simply determining what information is required to solve such problems can be a major undertaking.

To determine what the problem is and set yourself on a course for finding a solution, ask yourself these questions:

Teaching Tip: Take any newspaper article about a world event and ask your students to "identify the problem." Ask them to practice this skill daily.

- What is the initial set of facts?
- What is it that you need to solve?
- Which parts of the problem appear to be most critical to finding a solution?
- Is there some information that can be ignored?

The more systematically you approach a problem, the better. For instance, you can apply the five P.O.W.E.R. steps to problems, similar to how it can be used to make decisions. By considering a problem systematically and thinking through your options, your choices will become clearer to you.

As you clarify what the problem is, you may find that you have encountered similar problems before. Your experience with them may suggest the means to the solution of the current problem. For example, consider the problem of the trains rushing toward one another. If you have worked on this kind of problem before, you might know a fairly simple equation you can write to determine how long it will take before they meet. If someone asks you about the problem they have keeping their toddler from tumbling down the stairs, you might offer your experience in keeping your puppy from visiting an off-limits area of your house.

On the other hand, to solve many of the problems we face in our daily lives, we have to do more than reach into our memories of prior situations. Instead, we need to devise novel approaches. How do you do this? There are several strategies you might use.

> **"Problems are only opportunities in work clothes."**
>
> Henry J. Kaiser (1882–1967), entrepeneur, *Maxim*

Strategies for Solving Life's Messier Problems

- **Break the problem down into smaller, more manageable pieces.** Break a problem down into a series of subgoals. As you reach each subgoal, you get closer to your overall goal of solving the problem. For example, if your goal is to spend your junior year in your school's program in St. Petersburg, a subgoal would probably be to learn some basic Russian. By reaching this subgoal, you move closer to reaching your ultimate goal—a year abroad in a country that interests you.

- **Work backward.** Sometimes you know the answer to the problem, but not how to get there. Then it's best to work backward. A **working backward** strategy starts at the desired solution or goal and works backward, moving away from the goal. For example, consider this problem:

    Water lilies on a certain lake double in area every 24 hours. From the time the first water lily appears until the lake is completely covered takes 60 days. On what day is the lake half covered?

    Most people solve this problem readily if they work backward. Here's how: If the pond is fully covered on day 60, how much is it covered the day before? Because the water lilies double each day, there had to be half as many the day before day 60. The answer, then, is that half the lake is covered on day 59. Only by moving backward could one see the solution clearly.

    Some kinds of academic problems can be solved using the same strategy. For example, if you know what courses you must have completed to gradu-ate, it's sometimes easiest to work backward from that point, determining the courses you need to take each year.

- **Use a graph, chart, or drawing to redefine the problem.** Transforming words into pictures often can help us to devise solutions that otherwise would elude us. One good example is this problem:

    A man climbs a mountain on Saturday, leaving at sunrise and arriv-ing at the top near sunset. He spends the night at the top. The next day, Sunday, he leaves at daybreak and heads down the mountain, fol-lowing the same path that he climbed the day before. The question is this: Will there be any time during the second day when he will be at exactly the same point on the mountain as he was at exactly that time on the first day?

    Trying to solve the problem through the use of algebra or words is quite difficult. However, there's a simpler way: drawing the two paths. As you can see from Figure 11.2, the drawing provides a clear solution.

- **Consider the opposite.** Problems can sometimes be solved by considering the opposite of the problem you're seeking to solve. For example, to define "good mental health" you might try to define "bad mental health."

- **Use analogies.** Some problems can be solved through the use of **analo-gies,** comparisons between concepts or objects that are alike in some respects, but dissimilar in most others. For instance, if you liken a disas-trous experience attending summer camp to a voyage on the *Titanic*, you're using an analogy.

    Analogies may help us gain additional insight into the problem at hand, and they may provide an alternative framework for interpreting the infor-mation that is provided. For instance, the manufacturers of Pringles potato chips found that they could cut packaging costs if they slightly moistened the chips before packaging them—an idea that came when researchers noticed that dry tree leaves, which normally crumble easily, could be packed together tightly when they were wet.

- **Take another's perspective.** By viewing a problem from another person's point of view, it is often possible to obtain a new perspective on the problem that will make the problem easier to solve.

- **Forget about it.** Just as with decision making, sometimes it's best simply to walk away from a problem for a while. Just a few hours or days away from a problem may give us enough of a break to jar some hidden solutions from the recesses of our minds. The idea of "sleeping on it" also sometimes works; we may wake up refreshed and filled with new ideas.

Test these problem-solving strategies in Try It 2 on page 312.

Assessing Your Potential Solutions

If a problem clearly has only one answer, such as a math problem, this step in problem solving is relatively easy. You should be able to work the problem and figure out whether you've been successful. In contrast, messier problems have several possible solutions, some of which may be more involved and costly than others. In these cases, it's necessary to compare alternative solutions and choose the best one. For example, suppose you want to surprise your best friend on her birthday. She is working in Omaha, about 90 miles from you, and you need to find a way to get there. Perhaps you could rent a car, take a bus, or find some other way. Money is an issue. You will want to figure out how much each alternative costs before choosing one as your solution to the problem. Since every penny you spend getting there is a penny less that you will have to celebrate, you will want to weigh the options carefully.

Finally, spend a bit of time seeing whether there is a way to refine the solution. Is the solution you've devised adequate? Does it address all aspects of the problem? Are there alternative approaches that might be superior? Answering these questions, and refining your solution to address them, can give you confidence that the solution you've come up with is the best. For example, if you're trying to get to Omaha, you might decide to use the ride board at your school to try to find a ride with someone going to Omaha that day. Maybe your friend's family is going to be driving in and could pick you up or could even lend you a car for the trip.

Remember that not every problem has a clear-cut solution. Sometimes we need to be satisfied with a degree of uncertainty and ambiguity. For some of us, such a lack of clarity is difficult, making us uneasy, and it may push us to choose solutions—any solution—that seems to solve the problem. Others of us feel more comfortable with ambiguity, but this may lead us to let problems ride, without resolving the situation.

Either way, it's important to consider what your own problem-solving style is when you seek to identify solutions. And keep in mind that often there is no perfect solution to a problem—only some solutions that are better than others. (To find out whether you have a high need for clarity in problem solving or whether you tolerate ambiguity more easily, complete Try It 3 on page 313.)

IRM Link: Refer to Teaching the Text, Chapter 7, Section IV; characters from a novel provide a way to practice thinking about an issue through another person's perspective.

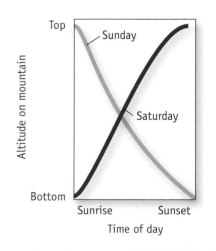

FIGURE 11.2
Up and Down the Mountain: The Paths to a Solution

2

TRY IT!

 WORKING IN A GROUP

Exercise Your Problem-Solving Skills

Working in a group, try to solve these problems.[1] To help you devise solutions, a hint regarding the best strategy to use is included after each problem.

1. One cold, dark, and rainy night, a college student has a flat tire on a deserted stretch of country road. He pulls onto the shoulder to change it. After removing the four lug nuts and placing them into the hub cap, he removes the flat tire and takes his spare out of the trunk. As he is moving the spare tire into position, his hand slips and he upsets the hub cap with the lug nuts, which tumble off into the night where he can't find them. What should he do? (*Hint:* Instead of asking how he might find the lug nuts, reframe the problem and ask where else he might find lug nuts.)

2. Cheryl, who is a construction worker, is paving a walk, and she needs to add water quickly to the concrete she has just poured. She reaches for her pail to get water from a spigot in the front of the house, but suddenly realizes the pail has a large rust hole in it and cannot be used. As the concrete dries prematurely, she fumbles through her toolbox for tools and materials with which to repair the pail. She finds many tools, but nothing that would serve to patch the pail. The house is locked and no one is home. What should she do? (*Hint:* When is a pail not a pail?)

3. What day follows the day before yesterday if 2 days from now will be Sunday? (*Hint:* Break it up or draw a diagram.)

4. A caterpillar has to climb up the muddy wall of a well that is 12 feet deep. Each day the caterpillar advances 4 feet, but each night as he sleeps, he slips back 2 feet. How many days will it take him to get out? (*Hint:* Draw it.)

5. Carrie has four chains, each three links long. She wants to join the four chains into a single, closed chain. Having a link opened costs 2 cents and having a link closed costs 3 cents. How can Carrie have the chains joined for 15 cents? (*Hint:* Can only end links be opened?)

6. What is two-thirds of one-half? (*Hint:* Reverse course.)

7. Juan has three separate large boxes. Inside each large box are two separate medium-sized boxes, and inside each of the medium boxes are four small boxes. How many boxes does Juan have altogether? (*Hint:* Draw it.)

After working to solve these problems, consider these questions: Which problems were the easiest to solve, and which were more difficult? Why? Were the hints helpful? Do you think there was more than one solution to any of the problems? Did your initial assumptions about the problem help or hinder your efforts to solve it? (*Note:* Answers to the problems are found on page 322.)

To Try It online, go to **www.mhhe.com/power**.

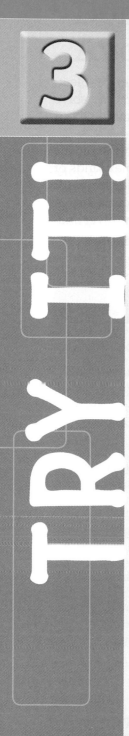

3

TRY IT!

PERSONAL STYLES

Find Your Problem-Solving Style

To get a sense of how much you prefer ambiguity versus clarity in the problems you face, rate how much you agree with each of the statements in the questionnaire[2] below. Use this rating scale:

1 = Strongly disagree   4 = Not sure, but probably agree

2 = Disagree   5 = Agree

3 = Not sure, but probably disagree   6 = Strongly agree

1. An expert who doesn't come up with a definite answer probably doesn't know too much. _____
2. There is really no such thing as a problem that can't be solved. _____
3. A good job is one where what is to be done and how it is to be done are always clear. _____
4. In the long run, it is possible to get more done by tackling small, simple problems than large and complicated ones. _____
5. What we are used to is always preferable to what is unfamiliar. _____
6. A person who leads a well-organized, routine life in which few surprises or unexpected happenings arise really has a lot to be grateful for. _____
7. I like parties where I know most of the people more than ones where all or most of the people are complete strangers. _____
8. The sooner we all acquire similar values and ideals, the better. _____
9. I would like to live in a foreign country for a while. _____
10. People who fit their lives to a schedule probably miss most of the joy of living. _____
11. It is more fun to tackle a complicated problem than to solve a simple one. _____
12. Often the most interesting and stimulating people are those who don't mind being different and original. _____
13. People who insist upon a yes or no answer just don't know how complicated things really are. _____
14. Many of our most important decisions are based upon insufficient information. _____
15. Teachers or supervisors who hand out vague assignments give opportunities for individuals to show initiative and originality. _____
16. A good teacher is one who makes you wonder about your way of looking at things. _____

To score this questionnaire, you'll first need to change the numbers you have in items 9 to 16 in this way: If you've put a 1, change it to a 6; change 2 to 5; change 3 to 4; change 4 to 3; change 5 to 2; and change 6 to 1. (Items 1 to 8 don't need to be changed.) Now add up your total score.

If you scored below 30, you have a low tolerance for ambiguity in problem solving. You prefer problems to be clear-cut and dislike uncertainty.

If you scored between 30 and 60, you have an average tolerance for ambiguity. Most of the time problems that are vague don't present you with any particular difficulty, although you generally prefer things to be fairly concrete.

If you scored above 60, you have a high tolerance for ambiguous problems. You don't mind—and in fact prefer—problems that are unclear.

To Try It online, go to **www.mhhe.com/power**.

If you believe that these statements provide an amazingly accurate description of your unique qualities, you're not alone: Most college students believe that the descriptions are tailored specifically to them.[4] But how is that possible? It isn't. The reality is that the statements are so vague that they are virtually meaningless. The acceptance of vague but seemingly useful and significant statements about oneself and others has been called the *Barnum Effect,* after showman and circus master P. T. Barnum, who coined the phrase "there's a sucker born every minute."

One impediment to critical thinking is difficulty in distinguishing fact from opinion. For example, although many people are of the opinion that older people have a hard time learning new material, age need not be a deterrent to learning.

■ **Don't confuse opinion with fact.** Opinions are not fact. Although we may be aware of this simple formula, almost all of us can be fooled into thinking that someone's opinion is the same as a fact.

A fact is information that is proven to be true. In contrast, an opinion represents judgments, reasoning, beliefs, inferences, or conclusions. If we accept some bit of information as a fact, we can use it to build our opinions. But if we are presented with an opinion, we need to determine the facts on which it is built to judge its reliability.

The difference between fact and opinion can sometimes be subtle. For instance, compare these two statements:

1. Every college student needs to take a writing course during the first term of college.

2. Many college students need to take a writing course during the first term of college.

The first statement is most likely an opinion, because it is so absolute and unqualified. Words such as "every," "all," and "always" are often evidence of opinion. On the other hand, the second statement is more likely a fact, since it contains the qualifier "many." In general, statements that are qualified in some way are more likely to be facts.

Complete Try It 4 to see the difficulties sometimes involved in distinguishing between fact and opinion.

■ **Avoid jumping to conclusions.** Read this riddle and try to answer it:

> *A father and his son were driving along the interstate highway when the father lost control of the car, swerved off the road, and crashed into a utility pole. The father died instantly, and his son was critically injured. An ambulance rushed the boy to a nearby hospital. A prominent surgeon was summoned to provide immediate treatment. When the surgeon arrived and entered the operating room to examine the boy, a loud gasp was heard. "I can't operate on this boy," the surgeon said. "He is my son."*

How can this be?

4

Distinguish Fact from Opinion

Read the following statements and try to determine which are facts and which are opinions.

1. College students should get at least 7 hours of sleep every night. _____

2. The average college student sleeps less than 7 hours a night. _____

3. Nikes offer better styling and comfort than any other brand of shoe. _____

4. Two out of five sports figures surveyed preferred Nikes over Converse shoes. _____

5. The U.S. government spends too much money on guns and missiles and not enough money on education. _____

6. Government figures show spending is much higher for guns and missiles than for education. _____

7. In general, U.S. high school students receive less classroom instruction in foreign languages than their counterparts in Europe and Asia. _____

8. No student in the United States should graduate without having studied a language other than English for at least 4 years. _____

9. Michael Jordan is the most outstanding, most exciting, and certainly most successful basketball player who ever stepped onto a court. _____

10. Items 1, 3, 5, 8, and 9 are opinions; the rest are facts. What are the main differences between opinion and fact?

To Try It online, go to **www.mhhe.com/power.**

If you find this puzzling, you've based your reasoning on an assumption: that the surgeon is a male. But suppose you had assumed that the surgeon was a female. Suddenly, the riddle becomes a lot easier. It's far easier to guess that the surgeon is the son's *mother* if we don't leap to embrace a faulty assumption.

Why is it so easy to jump to conclusions? One reason is that we sometimes aren't aware of the assumptions that underlie our thinking. Another is our reliance on "common sense."

■ **Be skeptical of "common sense."** Much of what we call common sense makes contradictory claims. For example, if you believe in the notion "Absence makes the heart grow fonder," you may assume that your high school girlfriend, now in college across the country from you, will arrive home at Christmas even more in love with you than before. But what about "Out of sight, out of mind," which suggests a less positive outcome? Common

Student Alert: Distinguishing an opinion from a fact can present difficulties. TRY IT 4 gives your students a chance to examine the power of language as well as the developmental nature of language.

What's the Real Explanation?

Even though two events are related to one another, it doesn't mean that one causes the other. Instead, there is often some other factor that is the actual cause of the relationship.

To see this for yourself, consider each of the following (actual!) findings. What might be a plausible explanation for each one?

1. Ice cream sales and the timing of shark attacks are highly related. Why?

2. The number of cavities children have and the size of their vocabulary are closely related. Why?

3. Skirt hemlines tend to rise as stock prices rise. Why?

4. Women with breast implants have a higher rate of suicide than those without breast implants. Why?

Discussion Prompt: Ask students to think alone for 2-3 minutes about a time when they jumped to a conclusion. Then, ask them to share with a classmate why they did so, and what the outcome was. What would they do differently in the future?

sense often presents us with contradictory advice, making it a less than useful guide to decision making and problem solving.

■ **Don't assume that just because two events occur together one causes the other.** Just because two events appear to be associated with one another—or, in the language of social science, are *correlated* with one another—we cannot conclude that one event has caused the other to occur. It's a basic rule: *Correlation does not prove causation.*

For example, suppose you read that a study showed that 89 percent of juvenile delinquents use marijuana. Does this mean that smoking marijuana *causes* juvenile delinquency?

5. People who own washing machines are more likely to die in car accidents than those who don't. Why?

6. Men who carry their cell phones in their front pants pockets have a lower sperm count than those who don't carry them in their front pants pockets. Why?

Once you've completed this Try It, look at the possible explanations listed below. Keep in mind that these are simply theories; we don't know for sure if they're correct:

6. Men with high stress jobs may be more likely to have cell phones, and it is the stress that produces the low sperm count—not the placement of a phone in their pocket.

5. People who own washing machines are more likely to own cars, and therefore they stand a higher risk of dying in a car crash.

4. Having breast implants and committing suicide both may be a result of unhappiness or a poor self-image.

3. Skirt hemlines go up, as does the stock market, when people are feeling less conservative and more optimistic.

2. Both the number of cavities children have and the size of their vocabularies are related to their age.

1. The actual cause is probably the temperature, which causes both sales of ice cream and ocean swimming to increase.

To Try It online, go to **www.mhhe.com/power.**

No, it doesn't. It is pretty safe to say that 100 percent of juvenile delinquents grew up drinking milk. Would you feel comfortable saying that milk causes delinquency? With correlations such as marijuana use and delinquent behavior, it is very likely that there's some third factor—such as influence of peers—that causes people both to (a) try drugs and (b) engage in delinquent behavior. The bottom line: We do not know the cause of the correlation.

In short, we need to be careful in assuming causality. Even if two events or other kinds of variables occur together, it does not mean that one causes the other. To see this for yourself, take a look at the statements in Try It 5, "What's the Real Explanation?"

Student Alert: False assumptions lead to many faulty conclusions. Ask your students why they have relied on similar faulty correlations.

SPEAKING OF
Success

Name: Dr. Ben Carson

School: Yale University, B.A.; University of Michigan Medical School, M.D.

Few who knew Ben Carson as a fifth grader would have guessed that he would become a surgeon whose skills would save the lives of hundreds of patients.

Dr. Carson grew up in a poor, single-parent household in Detroit. His mother, who had only a third-grade education, worked two jobs cleaning bathrooms.

To his classmates—and even to his teachers—he was thought of as "the dumbest kid in the class," according to his own not-so-fond memories. He had a terrible temper and once tried to stab another child.

Dr. Carson was headed down a path of self-destruction until a critical moment in his youth: His mother, convinced that she had to do something dramatic to prevent him from leading a life of failure, laid down some rules. He could not watch television except for two programs a week, could not play with his friends after school until he finished his homework, and had to read two books a week and write book reports about them.

His mother's strategy worked. As he wrote his weekly book reports for his mother, worlds opened to him.

"Of course, we didn't know she couldn't read, so there we were submitting these reports," he said. "She would put check marks on them like she had been reading them. As I began to read about scientists, economists, and philosophers, I started imagining myself in their shoes."[5]

As he got in the habit of hard work, his grades began to soar. Ultimately, he received a scholarship to attend Yale University, and later he was admitted to the University of Michigan Medical School. He is now head of pediatric neurosurgery at Johns Hopkins University, one of the most prestigious medical schools in the world; he is also the author of three books.

Dr. Carson tries to pass on to others the lessons he learned as a child. He has established a fund for students in grades 4 through 12 who maintain a 3.75 grade point average. Each month, 800 children come to his hospital, where he underscores the importance of education. As he says, "There is absolutely nothing in this world that you can't become simply through the acquisition of knowledge, because knowledge creates power and you make yourself into a more valuable person."[6]

How can I improve the quality of my decisions?

- A structured process of decision making can clarify the issues involved, expand our options, and improve the quality of our choices.

- Good decision making begins with understanding your short- and long-term goals.

- Decision making is improved if you have a large number of alternatives.

- For difficult decisions, strategies include giving the decision time, acting out alternatives, tossing a coin to test our feelings, understanding that indecision is often a decision itself, and acting on gut feelings.

What strategies can I use for problem solving?

- Problem solving entails the generation of alternatives to consider.

- We need to first understand and define the problem and to determine the important elements in coming to a solution to a problem.

- Approaches to generating solutions include breaking problems into pieces, working backward, using pictures, considering the opposite, using analogies, taking another's perspective, and "forgetting" the problem.

- Problem solving ultimately requires the evaluation and refinement of the solutions that have been generated.

What are some problems that affect critical thinking, and how can I avoid them?

- Labeling, using vague generalities, accepting opinion as fact, jumping to conclusions, mistaking common sense, and assuming correlation all pose threats to critical thinking.

- Awareness of the biases that may affect our thinking can help us avoid them.

KEY TERMS AND CONCEPTS

Decision making (p. 301)
Transferring (p. 308)
Problem solving (p. 308)

Working backward (p. 310)
Analogy (pp. 310–311)

RESOURCES

On Campus

Some colleges offer courses in critical thinking, and they are a good bet to help increase decision-making and problem-solving skills. In addition, courses in logic and philosophy will help improve critical thinking skills.

If you are having a personal problem that is difficult to solve, you can turn to staff at the campus counseling center, mental health center, or residential life office. Even if the person with whom you speak initially is not the right one, he or she can direct you to someone who can help.

In Print

If you have trouble making good decisions, John Hammond, Ralph Keeney, and Howard Raiffa's *Smart Choices: A Practical Guide to Making Better Decisions* (Broadway, 2002) is for you.

Another approach to decision making is found in Richard Mayer's book *Thinking, Problem Solving, and Cognition* (Freeman, 2005), which shows how we make good (and bad) decisions.

For a general overview of thinking critically, read Richard Paul and Linda Elder's *Critical Thinking Skills for College and Life* (Prentice Hall, 2005).

CHAPTER

Diversity and Your Relationships with Others

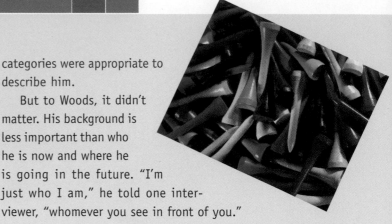

Cablinasian.

That's the word coined by star golfer Tiger Woods to describe his racial heritage. "Cablinasian" means a mix of Caucasian, Black, Indian, and Asian, and it was a label he didn't find on forms asking for his racial identity when he began college.

But Woods did not want to fit himself into some arbitrary racial category. His mother is from Thailand and his father is African-American, and none of the standard racial categories were appropriate to describe him.

But to Woods, it didn't matter. His background is less important than who he is now and where he is going in the future. "I'm just who I am," he told one interviewer, "whomever you see in front of you."

LOOKING AHEAD >>>

Whether you have skin that is black or white or brown, are Jewish or Muslim or Greek Orthodox, were born in Cuba or Vietnam or Boise, are able-bodied or physically challenged, college presents a world of new opportunities. Because almost every college draws students from a wider sphere than the average high school, college permits you to encounter people with very different backgrounds from your own. If you take the opportunity to form relationships with a variety of individuals, you will increase your understanding of the human experience and enrich your life.

In this chapter, we consider how social diversity and relationships affect your college experience. We examine the increasing diversity of college campuses, which reflects that of society at large, and consider the meanings and social effects of race, ethnicity, and culture. We look at practical strategies for acknowledging—and shedding—prejudice and stereotypes and being receptive to others on their own merits.

We next discuss relationships from a broader perspective, exploring ways that you can build lasting friendships with others. Finally, the chapter discusses the conflicts that can arise between people and what you can do to resolve them.

In short, after reading this chapter you'll know the answers to these questions:

- **Why is the increasing racial, ethnic, and cultural diversity of society important to me?**

- **How can I become more at ease with differences and diversity?**

- **How can I build lasting relationships and deal with conflict?**

Living in a World of Diversity

No matter where we live, our contacts with others who are racially, ethnically, and physically different from us are increasing. The Internet and Web are bringing people from across the globe into our homes, as close to us as the computer sitting on our desk. Businesses now operate globally, so co-workers are likely to come from many different countries and cultures. Being comfortable with people whose backgrounds and beliefs may differ from our own is not only a social necessity, but it is virtually a requirement for career success.

By the mid-21st century, the percentage of people in the United States of African, Latin American, Asian, and Arabic ancestry will be greater than the percentage of those of Western European ancestry—a profound statistical, and social, shift. College enrollments will mirror these changes, as populations that were minority become the majority.

Furthermore, it's not just racial and ethnic characteristics that comprise diversity. As you can see in the Diversity Wheel in Figure 12.1, diversity encompasses characteristics such as gender, sexual orientation, age, and mental and physical characteristics. Layer on top of that factors such as education, religion, and income level, and the complexity of others—and ourselves—becomes apparent. (You can examine the diversity of your own campus by completing Try It 1 on page 328.)

P.O.W.E.R. UP: What backgrounds do your students bring to the classroom? Ask them to describe their high school, families, and home communities. See the Journal Reflection on page 330. Compare this to the information you discover in TRY IT 1.

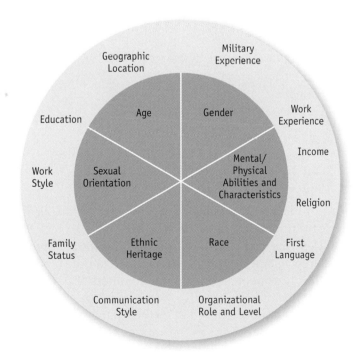

FIGURE 12.1
Diversity Wheel
Diversity is comprised of many different characteristics as exemplified by the Diversity Wheel.[1]

Determine the Diversity of Your Campus Community

Try to assess the degree of diversity that exists at your college, and the overall attitude toward diversity on your campus, by answering these questions. When thinking of diversity, remember to include the many different ways in which people can be different from one another, including race, ethnicity, culture, sexual orientation, physical challenges, and so on.

Overall, how diverse would you say your campus is?

What is the nature of your college's *student* diversity in terms of statistics regarding membership in different racial, ethnic, or cultural groups?

What is the nature of your college's *faculty* diversity in terms of statistics regarding membership in different racial, ethnic, or cultural groups?

Are many courses available that directly address diversity as an issue? (A good place to check is your college catalog listing of courses in the social sciences and humanities.)

Does your college have an explicit statement of policy and principles relating to diversity and/or the avoidance of discrimination?

Was diversity discussed during your orientation to the campus?

How does the diversity on your campus compare to the following statistics on diversity in the United States as of the 2000 census: white 75 percent; Hispanic or Latino 13 percent; black or African-American 12 percent; Asian 4 percent; two or more races 2.4 percent; American Indian and Alaska Native .9 percent; Native Hawaiian and other Pacific Islander .1 percent; other race 6 percent. (Note: Percentages add up to more than 100 percent because Hispanics may be of any race and are therefore counted under more than one category.)

Look back at your answer to the first question ("Overall, how diverse would you say your campus is?") and answer the question again. Did your response change?

To Try It online, go to **www.mhhe.com/power**.

Race, Ethnicity, and Culture

Discussion Prompt: Ask your students: What are the defining characteristics of your culture?

Are you African-American or black? Caucasian or white or Euro-American? Hispanic or Latino? American Indian or Native American?

The language we use to describe our ethnic and racial group membership, and those of other people, is in constant flux. And what we call people matters. The subtleties of language affect how people think about members of particular groups, and how they think about themselves.

One of the difficulties in understanding diversity is that many of the terms we use are ill-defined and often overlapping. The term **race** is generally used to refer to obvious physical differences that set one group apart from others. According to such a definition, whites, blacks, and Asian Americans are typically thought of as belonging to different races, determined largely by biological factors.

Race
Traditionally, biologically determined physical characteristics that set one group apart from others

Ethnicity refers to shared national origins or cultural patterns. In the United States, for example, Puerto Ricans, Irish, and Italian Americans are categorized as ethnic groups. However, ethnicity—like race—is very much in the eye of the beholder. For instance, a Cuban American who is a third-generation citizen of the United States may feel few ties or associations to Cuba. Yet whites may view her as "Hispanic," and blacks may view her as "white."

Finally, **culture** comprises the learned behaviors, beliefs, and attitudes that are characteristic of an individual society or population. But it's more than that: Culture also encompasses the products that people create, such as architecture, music, art, and literature. Culture is created and shaped by people, but at the same time it creates and shapes people's behavior.

Our cultural heritage plays an important role in shaping who we are.

Race, ethnicity, and culture shape each of us to an enormous degree. They profoundly influence our view of others, as well as who we are. They affect how others treat us, and how we treat them in turn. They determine whether we look people in the eye when we meet them, how early we arrive when we're invited to dinner at a friend's house, and even, sometimes, how well we do in school.

Because many of us grow up in neighborhoods that are not ethnically diverse, we may have little or even no experience interacting with people who are different from us. In fact, some college campuses don't have much diversity, and consequently even in college your exposure to people who have different backgrounds may be limited.

At some time, though, that will change. As the United States becomes increasingly diverse, it's not a matter of "if" but "when" you will be exposed to people who have profoundly different backgrounds from your own. Whether in the workplace or the neighborhood in which you reside, living in a diverse environment will be part of your life.

Building Cultural Competence

We're not born knowing how to drive a car or cook. We have to learn how to do these things. The same is true of developing a basic understanding of other races, ethnic groups, and cultures. Called **cultural competence,** this knowledge of others' customs, perspectives, background, and history can teach us a great deal about others, as well as ourselves. Cultural competence also provides a basis for civic engagement, permitting us to act with civility toward others and to make the most of our contributions to society.

Building cultural competence proceeds in several steps, outlined in the P.O.W.E.R. Plan on page 330.

Ethnicity
Shared national origins or cultural patterns

Culture
The learned behaviors, beliefs, and attitudes that are characteristic of an individual society or population, and the products that people create

Teaching Tip: This Journal Reflection and TRY IT 2 are worth doing in class. Although difficult to talk about, your students need to find a way to articulate their thoughts about this issue.

Cultural competence
Knowledge and understanding about other races, ethnic groups, cultures, and minority groups

Thinking about Race, Ethnicity, and Culture

1. Were race and ethnicity discussed in your family as you were growing up? In what ways?

2. Do you demonstrate—through your behavior, attitudes, and/or beliefs—your own ethnic background? How?

3. Are there cultural differences between you and members of other races or ethnicities? What are they?

4. Are you proud of your ethnicity? Why?

5. Think what it would be like to be a member of a racial group or ethnicity other than your own. In what ways would your childhood and adolescence have been different? How would you view the world differently?

PREPARE
Accept diversity as a valued part of your life

ORGANIZE
Explore your own prejudices and stereotypes

WORK
Develop cultural competence

EVALUATE
Check your progress in attaining cultural competence

RETHINK
Understand how your own racial, ethnic, and cultural background affects others

P.O.W.E.R. Plan

P REPARE: Accepting Diversity as a Valued Part of Your Life

In the title of her book on social diversity, psychologist Beverly Tatum asks, "Why Are All the Black Kids Sitting Together in the Cafeteria?"[2] She might just as well have asked a similar question about the white kids, the Asian-American kids, and so forth. It often appears as if the world comes already divided into separate racial, ethnic, and cultural groups.

It's more than appearances: We form relationships more easily with others who are similar to us than with those who are different. It's easier to interact with others who look the same as we do, who come from similar backgrounds, and who share our race, ethnicity, and culture because we can take for granted certain shared cultural assumptions and views of the world.

But that doesn't mean that "easy" and "comfortable" translate into "good" or "right." We can learn a great deal more, and grow and be challenged, if we seek out people who are different from us. If you look beyond surface differences and find out what motivates other people, you can become aware of new ways of thinking about family, relationships, earning a living, and the value of education. It can be liberating to realize that others may hold very different perspectives from your own and that there are many ways to lead your life.

Letting diversity into your own life also has very practical implications: As we discuss in Career Connections, learning to accept and work with people who are different from you is a crucial skill that will help you in whatever job you hold.

Diversity in the Workplace

Diversity, and issues relating to it, are a part of today's workplace. For example, in one California computer assembly company with several thousand employees, 40 different languages and dialects are spoken among people representing 30 nationalities.[3] Furthermore, employers must deal with issues ranging from whether time off for religious holidays should count as vacation time to whether the partner of a gay or lesbian worker should be covered by the worker's medical insurance.

The gulf in the workplace between people with different cultural backgrounds may be wide. For instance, an immigrant from Japan might consider it the height of immodesty to outline his or her accomplishments in a job interview. The explanation? In Japan, the general cultural expectation is that people should stress their incompetence; to do otherwise would be considered highly immodest.

The increasing diversity of the workplace means that increasing your cultural competence will serve you well. It will help you perform on work teams that are composed of people of different races and ethnic backgrounds; it will help you supervise people whose native language and customs may be different from yours; and it will help you to work for a boss from another country and cultural background.

Equally important, gaining cultural competence will help you respond to the legal issues that surround diversity. It is illegal for employers to discriminate on the basis of race, ethnic background, age, gender, and physical disability. Cultural competence will help you not only to deal with the letter of the law but also to understand why embracing diversity is so important to getting along with others in the workplace.

O RGANIZE: Exploring Your Own Prejudices and Stereotypes

Arab. Gay. African-American. Hispanic. Female. Disabled. Overweight.

Quick: What comes into your mind when you think about each of these labels? If you're like most people, you don't draw a blank. Instead, a collection of images and feelings comes into your mind, based on what you know, have been told, or assume about the group.

The fact that we don't draw a blank when thinking about each of these terms means that we already have a set of attitudes and beliefs about them and the groups they represent. Acknowledging and then examining these preexisting assumptions is a first step toward developing cultural competence: We need to explore our own prejudices and stereotypes.

Prejudice refers to evaluations or judgments of members of a group that are based primarily on their membership in the group, rather than on their individual characteristics. For example, the auto mechanic who doesn't expect a woman to understand the repair he is undertaking or the supervisor who finds it unthinkable that a father might want to take leave for child care are engaging in *gender prejudice,* evaluating individuals on the basis of their being a male or female and not on their own specific characteristics or abilities. Similarly, prejudice can be directed toward individuals because of their race, ethnic origin, sexual orientation, age, physical disability, or even physical attractiveness.

Prejudice is maintained by **stereotypes,** beliefs and expectations about members of a group. For example, do you think that women don't drive as well as men? Do you agree that "white men can't jump"? Do you believe that people raised in the jungles of South America are less intelligent than those raised in a Western society? Do you think that people on welfare are lazy? If you answered yes to any of these questions, you hold stereotypes about the group being referred to. It is the degree of generalization involved that makes

Prejudice
Evaluations or judgments of members of a group that are based primarily on membership in the group and not on the particular characteristics of individuals

Stereotypes
Beliefs and expectations about members of a group that are held simply because of their membership in the group

stereotypes inaccurate. Some white men can't jump. But the fact is, many can—and do—and the stereotypes ignore this diversity.

To develop cultural competence, it's important to identify our prejudices and stereotypes and to fight them. Sometimes they are quite subtle and difficult to detect. For instance, a wealth of data taken from observation of elementary school classrooms shows that teachers are often more responsive to boys than to girls. The teachers don't know they're doing it; it's a subtle, but very real, bias.

Why does this happen? In part it's because we're exposed to stereotypes from a very young age. Parents and relatives teach them to us, sometimes unwittingly, sometimes deliberately. The media illustrate them constantly and often in very subtle ways. For instance, African-Americans and Latinos are often portrayed as unemployed or as criminals, women are less likely than men to be shown as employed, and gay men are frequently depicted as effeminate.

But it's not only stereotypes that lead us to view members of other groups differently from those of our own. For many people, their own membership in a cultural or racial or ethnic group is a source of pride and self-worth. There's nothing wrong with this. However, these feelings can lead to a less desirable outcome: the belief that their own group is superior to others. As a result, people inflate the positive aspects of their own group and belittle groups to which they do not belong. The bottom line is continuing prejudice.

> ## "Prejudice is the child of ignorance."
>
> William Hazlitt, essayist

To overcome stereotypes and to develop cultural competence, we must first explore and identify our prejudices. To begin that process, complete Try It 2, "Check Your Stereotype Quotient."

Teaching Tip: Remind your class how important respectful language is when discussing sensitive topics.

W ORK: Developing Cultural Competence

Although it's neither easy nor simple to increase your understanding of and sensitivity to other cultures, it can be done. Several strategies are effective:

- **Study other cultures and customs.** Take an anthropology course, study religion, or learn history. If you understand the purposes behind different cultural customs, attitudes, and beliefs, you will be able to understand the richness and meaning of other people's cultural heritage.

  Many colleges offer workshops on diversity and prejudice reduction. These can help too. The important point is that understanding comes from knowledge, and you won't be able to fully appreciate others without learning about their background.

- **Travel.** There is no better way to learn about people from other cultures than to see those cultures firsthand. College vacations offer you the time to travel, and relatively inexpensive charter flights can take you to Europe, Asia, and other places around the globe. Sometimes, in fact, it's cheaper to take a transoceanic flight than to travel to closer locations in the United States.

  If you can't afford airfare, take a car or bus ride to Mexico or Canada. In many parts of Canada, French is spoken and the culture is decidedly different from that in the United States (or the rest of Canada, for that matter).

  Travel needn't be international, however. If you are from the northern states, head south. If you are from California, consider heading east. If you live in a large metropolitan area, travel to a different area from ones you're familiar with. No matter where you go, simply finding yourself in a new context can aid your efforts to learn about other cultures.

2

Check Your Stereotype Quotient

Do you hold stereotypes about other people? How pervasive do you think they are? Respond to the following informal questionnaire to get a sense of your susceptibility to stereotyping.

1. When you see five African-American students sitting together in a cafeteria, do you think that they are exhibiting racism? Do you think the same thing when you see five white students sitting together in a cafeteria?

2. When you are speaking with a person who has a speech-related disorder such as stuttering, are you likely to conclude that the person is less intelligent than a fluent speaker?

3. When an elderly woman can't remember something, do you assume her forgetfulness is because she is old or perhaps has Alzheimer's disease?

4. When an attractive blonde female student states an opinion in class, are you surprised if the opinion is intelligent and well expressed?

5. If a person with a mobility disorder turns down your offer for assistance, would you be offended and resentful?

6. If you found out that a star professional football player is gay, would you be surprised?

What do you think your answers tell you about yourself and your views of others?

🙌 Working in a Group:

Compare your answers with those of your classmates. What do you think causes the similarities and differences in responses?

To Try It online, go to **www.mhhe.com/power**.

Travel provides us with an opportunity to become immersed in very different cultures and to see the world—and ourselves—through different eyes.

- **Participate in service-learning.** Sometimes you can learn about people who are different from you in your own backyard—or, more precisely, the backyard of your college. By becoming involved in community service, such as tutoring middle school students, volunteering to work with the homeless, or working on an environmental clean-up, you get the opportunity to interact with people who may be very different from those you're accustomed to.

- **Don't ignore people's backgrounds.** None of us is color blind. Or blind to ethnicity. Or to culture. It's impossible to be completely unaffected by people's racial, ethnic, and cultural backgrounds. So why pretend to be? Cultural heritage is an important part of other people's identity, and to pretend that their background doesn't exist and has no impact on them is unrealistic at best, and insulting at worst. It's important, though, to distinguish between accepting the fact that other people's backgrounds affect them and pigeonholing people and expecting them to behave in particular ways.

- **Don't make assumptions about who people are.** Don't assume that someone is heterosexual just because most people are heterosexual. Don't assume that someone with an Italian-sounding last name is Italian. Don't assume that a black person has two black parents. (To get a sense of how our assumptions color our thinking, think about the questions in Try It 3.)

- **Accept differences.** Different does not mean better. Different does not mean worse. Different just means not looking, acting, or believing exactly the same as you. We shouldn't attach any kind of value to being different; it's neither better nor worse than being similar.

In fact, even people who seem obviously different on the surface probably share many similarities with you. Like you, they are students; they have fears and anxieties like yours; and they have aspirations and dreams, just as you do.

The important point about differences is that we need to accept and embrace them. Think about some differences you may have with people who are similar to you. Perhaps you really can't stand classical music, yet one of your childhood friends has taken piano lessons since he was five and loves it. Chances are you both accept that you have different tastes and see this difference as part of who each of you is.

IRM Link: Refer to Teaching the Text, Chapter 11, Section VII, Goals 2 and 3; these offer suggestions for extending the discussion of difference beyond the classroom.

E VALUATE: Checking Your Progress in Attaining Cultural Competence

Because cultural groups are constantly changing, developing cultural competence is an ongoing process. To evaluate where you stand, ask yourself the following questions:

- Do I make judgments about others based on external features, such as skin color, ethnic background, cultural customs, gender, weight, or physical appearance?

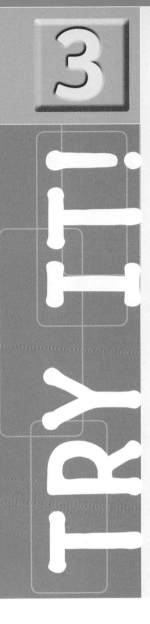

Contemplate a Questionnaire

Read and consider each of the following questions[4]:

1. What do you think caused your heterosexuality?
2. When and how did you decide you were heterosexual?
3. Is it possible that heterosexuality is just a phase you may grow out of?
4. Is it possible your heterosexuality stems from a neurotic fear of others of the same sex?
5. To whom have you disclosed your heterosexual tendencies?
6. Why do you insist on showing off your heterosexuality?
7. Why do heterosexuals place so much emphasis on sex?
8. There seem to be very few happy heterosexuals. Techniques have been developed that might enable you to change. Have you considered changing?
9. Considering the menace of hunger and overpopulation, can the human race survive if everyone were heterosexual like yourself?

What are your reactions to this questionnaire?

What do your reactions tell you about the assumptions you hold about what others are like?

How would your reactions differ if you substituted "homosexual" for each occurrence of "heterosexual" in the questionnaire?

To Try It online, go to **www.mhhe.com/power**.

- Who are my friends? Do they represent diversity or are they generally similar to me?
- Do I openly express positive values relating to diversity? Do I sit back passively when others express stereotypes and prejudices, or do I actively question their remarks?
- Am I educating myself about the history and varying experiences of different racial, ethnic, and cultural groups?
- Do I give special treatment to members of particular groups, or am I evenhanded in my relationships?
- Do I recognize that, despite surface differences, all people have the same basic needs?
- Do I feel so much pride in my own racial, ethnic, and cultural heritage that it leads me to look less favorably upon members of other groups?
- Do I seek to understand events and situations through the perspectives of others and not just my own?

IRM Link: Consider using one of the many activities listed in Teaching the Text in Chapter 12, Sections IV and VIII. Also, Section V suggests ways to use role playing to teach these concepts.

Dealing with Diversity in the Classroom

The increasing diversity of classrooms presents both opportunity and challenge. The opportunity comes from the possibility of learning on a firsthand basis about others and their experiences. The challenge comes when people who may be very different from us call into question some of our most fundamental beliefs and convictions.

Here are some ways that you can be better equipped to deal with the classroom challenges involved in diversity:

- **Present your opinions in a respectful manner.** Don't get annoyed or angry when others disagree with your point of view. Be tolerant of others' perspectives and their thinking.

- **Don't assume you can understand what it's like to be a member of another race, ethnicity, cultural group, or gender.** Talk about your own experiences, and don't assume you know what others have experienced.

- **Don't treat people as representatives of the groups to which they belong.** Don't ask someone how members of his or her racial, ethnic, or cultural group think, feel, or behave with respect to a particular issue. No single individual can speak for an entire group. Furthermore, group members are likely to display little uniformity on most issues and in most behaviors. Consequently, this type of question is ultimately impossible to answer.

- **Seek out students who are different from you.** If you are assigned a group project, volunteer to work with others who are different from you. You may learn more working with others who are dissimilar than those who are like you.

- **Don't be afraid to offer your opinion out of concerns for "political correctness."** If you offer an opinion in a respectful, thoughtful, and tolerant manner, you should feel free to voice your opinion. Even if your views are minority opinions, they deserve to be considered.

 ETHINK: Understanding How Your Own Racial, Ethnic, and Cultural Background Affects Others

Teaching Tip: Films, lectures, novels and other outside readings are valuable activities for helping your students evaluate their cultural competence.

If you are a member of a group that traditionally has been the target of prejudice and discrimination, you probably don't need to be told that your race, ethnicity, and cultural background affect the way that others treat you. But even if you are a member of a traditionally dominant group in society, the way in which others respond to you is, in part, a result of others' assumptions about the groups of which you are a part.

In short, both how we view others and how we ourselves are viewed are affected by the groups to which we—and others—belong. But keep this in mind: No matter how different other students are from you in terms of their race, ethnicity, and cultural background, they undoubtedly share many of the same concerns you do. Like all of us, they question themselves, wonder whether they will be successful, and fret about what they will do for the rest of their lives. Bridging the surface difference between you and others can result in the development of close, lasting social ties—a topic we consider next.

Building Lasting Relationships

Few of us lead our lives in isolation. There's a reason for this: Relationships with others are a critical aspect of our sense of well-being. The support of friends and relatives helps us feel good about ourselves. In fact, studies have found that our physical and psychological health may suffer without friendships. The social support of others acts as a guard against stress and illness. And if we do get sick, we recover more quickly if we have a supportive network of friends.

Our relationships with others also help us understand who we are. To understand our own abilities and achievements, we compare them with those of others who are similar to ourselves. Our attitudes, beliefs, and values are influenced—and shaped—by others. We are who we are largely because of the people with whom we come in contact.

Teaching Tip and IRM Link: Journaling is one of the most effective ways to teach this chapter and receive an honest appraisal from your students. If you have not used admit cards before now, this is an excellent place to do so.

Making Friends

Although some of us naturally make friends with ease, for others making friends is more difficult. But building relationships is not a mystery. Here are several ways to go about it:

- **Invest time in others.** There's no better way to demonstrate that you are interested in being friends than investing time. Relationships need to be nourished by the commitment of time. You can't expect friendships to flourish unless you spend time with people.

- **Reveal yourself.** Good friends understand each other. The best way to make that happen is to let others get to know you. Be open and honest about the things you like and dislike. Talk about where you come from, what your family is like. Find out about the other person. Having a deeper understanding of where someone comes from not only helps build bridges between people of different racial and ethnic backgrounds, but it also helps build friendships. By honestly communicating your beliefs and attitudes, you give others the chance to learn those things you have in common.

- **Let others know you like them.** It may seem scary, but don't be coy and try to pretend you are uninterested in the friendships of others. Take the risk of being rebuffed. You don't have to announce outright that you like someone. Instead, reveal your interest in a friendship by inviting the person to do something with you or simply by engaging in conversation, sharing something about your life. Your actions will speak louder than words.

- **Accept others as they are, not as you would like them to be.** One mark of friendship is acceptance of people the way they are, warts and all, and not the way you would like them to be. Do not impose conditions on accepting others. Keep in mind that no one is perfect and that everyone has both good and bad qualities.

- **Show concern and caring.** This is really the substance of friendship and the basis for the trust that develops between friends. Don't be afraid to show your interest in the fortunes of others and to share the sadness when they suffer some setback or loss.

TRY IT! 4

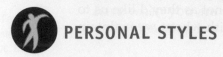

PERSONAL STYLES

Understand Your Relationship Style

Each of us has a general manner in which we approach close relationships with others. Read the three statements below, and determine which best describes you[6]:

1. I find it relatively easy to get close to others and am comfortable depending on them and having them depend on me. I don't often worry about being abandoned or about someone getting too close to me.

2. I am somewhat uncomfortable being close to others; I find it difficult to trust them completely and to allow myself to depend on them. I am nervous when anyone gets too close, and often love partners want me to be more intimate than I feel comfortable being.

3. I find that others are reluctant to get as close as I would like. I often worry that my partner doesn't really love me or won't want to stay with me. I want to merge completely with another person, and this desire sometimes scares people away.

The choice you make suggests the general style of emotional bonds that you develop with others.

If you thought the first statement described you best, it is probably easy for you to develop close ties with others. Around 55 percent of people describe themselves in this way.

If statement 2 describes you best, you probably have a more difficult time getting close to others, and you may have to work harder to develop close ties with other people. About 25 percent of people place themselves in this category.

Finally, if statement 3 describes you best, you, along with the 20 percent of people who describe themselves in this way, aggressively seek out close relationships. However, they probably present a source of concern to you.

Keep in mind that this is an inexact assessment and presents only a very rough estimate of your general approach to close relationships. But your response can be helpful in answering these questions: Are you generally satisfied with your relationships? Would you like to change them in some way?

To Try It online, go to **www.mhhe.com/power**.

what they are saying so that you can jump in with a response? Do you accidentally cut other people off or finish their sentences while they are speaking?

No one likes to be interrupted, even in casual conversation. In more personal relationships, it is a sign of not respecting what the other person has to say and is hurtful.

> "The reason why we have two ears and only one mouth is that we may listen the more and talk the less."
>
> Zeno of Citium, philosopher

2. **Demonstrate that you are listening.** Linguists call them "conversational markers"—those nonverbal indications that we're listening. They consist of head nods, uh-huhs, OKs, and other signs that we're keeping up with the conversation. Eye contact is important too. Listening this way shows that we're paying attention and are interested in what the other person is saying.

3. **Use reflective feedback.** Carl Rogers, a respected therapist, developed a very useful way to lend support to someone and draw him or her out. In **reflective feedback,** a listener rephrases what a speaker has said, trying to echo the speaker's meaning. For example, a listener might say, "as I understand what you're saying . . . ," or "you seem to feel that . . . ," or "in other words, you believe that . . ."

   In each case, the summary statement doesn't just "play back" the speaker's statements literally. Instead, it is a rephrasing that captures the essence of the message in different words.

   Reflective feedback has two big benefits. First, it provides speakers with a clear indication that you are listening and taking what they're saying seriously. Second, and equally important, it helps ensure that you have an accurate understanding of what the speaker is saying.

4. **Ask questions.** Asking questions shows that you are paying attention to a speaker's comments. Questions permit you to clarify what the speaker has said, and they can move the conversation forward. Further, people feel valued when others ask them about themselves.

5. **Admit when you're distracted.** We've all had those moments: Something is bothering you and you can't get it out of your mind, or you've simply got to finish something and don't really have time to chat. If at the same time someone wants to engage you in conversation, your distraction will undoubtedly show, making the other person feel you are not interested in her or him.

   The way to deal with this situation is to admit that you're distracted. Simply saying, "I'd love to talk, but I've got to finish reading a chapter," is enough to explain the situation to a classmate who wants to talk about his date.

Loneliness

Loneliness is a subjective state: We can be totally alone and not feel lonely, or we can be in the midst of a crowd and feel lonely. Loneliness occurs when we don't experience the level of connection with others that we desire. There are also different types of loneliness. Some of us feel lonely if we lack a deep emotional attachment to a single person, which can occur even if we have many friends. Others feel loneliness because they believe they don't have enough friends.

The reality is that there is no standard that indicates the "right" number of relationships. There's no standard against which to measure yourself and the number, and kind, of relationships that you have. It's something you need to decide. It is clear, though, that first-year college students almost always report higher degrees of loneliness than students in subsequent years of study.

On the other hand, loneliness is not inevitable. Several strategies for dealing with loneliness follow:

- **Become involved in campus activities.** Join a club. Volunteer to help some social organization. Try out for a play. You'll soon get to know others who have similar interests.

- **Find a study partner.** Ask one of your classmates to study with you. You can review your class notes, work together on a project, or study for tests together. Working together will not only help you to master the class material, but it

Reflective feedback
A technique of verbal listening in which a listener rephrases what a speaker has said, trying to echo the speaker's meaning

IRM Link: Refer to Teaching the Text, Chapter 12, Section V. The P.O.W.E.R. process can work here by turning students' ideas into an active learning process.

Loneliness
A subjective state in which people do not experience the level of connection with others that they desire

Participating in campus activities is a good way to meet people with similar interests and to avoid the loneliness that is sometimes a part of college life.

Teaching Tip: Throughout the term, you're talking about building community and about having your students become a part of this academic community. This is a good check point. If students in your class still feel lonely, more serious intervention may be warranted.

will also help you make what can become an important social connection.

- **Know that you're not alone in your loneliness.** If you're feeling lonely, you may find yourself looking at your classmates and noticing groups of people engaged in social activities. This can make you feel even more isolated. Don't be fooled by such social illusions into believing that you are the only one experiencing loneliness. Remember that for every person you notice who is socializing, there are others who are not doing so.

- **Take advantage of orientation and first-year student social events.** Even if you don't consider yourself particularly good at socializing, it's important to make the effort. If you're shy—and even if you're not—consider it a social success if you meet just one new person at such an event.

- **Take a job on campus.** Campus jobs provide not only income but social connections as well. Through work you can meet members of the college staff and make connections with other students.

- **Remember that loneliness is a subjective—and typically temporary—state.** If you interpret your feelings of isolation as due to your personal failings ("I'm alone because I'm not a very likable or interesting person"), you'll experience loneliness. On the other hand, if you view your isolation as a consequence of temporary, short-term factors ("Everyone has a lot of work this semester and there are few opportunities to socialize"), you're less likely to feel loneliness. In short, don't blame yourself for your sense of loneliness.

What if your feelings of loneliness are extreme and you experience a sense of complete isolation and alienation from your classmates? If the feeling persists, it's wise to talk to someone at your college counseling center, a health service provider, or your advisor. Although everyone feels isolated at times, such feelings shouldn't be extreme. Counselors can help you deal with them.

Lonely in a Crowd: Dealing with Too Many People

For some students, it's not a lack of social companionship that is difficult. Instead, juggling too many obligations leads to social overload and, in fact, a kind of loneliness. This is particularly true for nontraditional, older students who may be managing classes, jobs, and families.

For those who feel they never have a moment to themselves, it is important to carve out time for solitude. Write in breaks in your weekly schedule every once in while where you can get away from it all. Just taking a lunch break, eating by yourself on a park bench, can be rejuvenating if you're not interrupted. That means turning off your cell phone and not telling others where you'll be. Just 30 minutes of quality "alone time" can make a difference.

It's Not Just Talk: Avoiding and Handling Conflicts in Relationships

Listening communicates a great deal in personal relationships, but, as discussed previously, it is also important to put yourself forward. Generally, close relationships are built on good communication, so day to day there may be no problem in this regard. But when misunderstandings or conflicts occur—as they definitely will from time to time—communication can fall apart. In these situations your ability to communicate in words is tested, and more sensitive listening and more careful ways of saying what you think and feel are needed.

The Subject Is "I," and Not "You"

Suppose a close friend says something with which you disagree: "All you guys are the same—you expect to get everything your way!" You might respond by directing anger at the other person, directly or indirectly accusing the person of some imperfection. "You're always looking for something to complain about!" Such responses (and, as you will notice, the initial statement) typically include the word *you*. For instance, consider these possible responses to indicate disagreement: "*You* really don't understand"; "*You're* being stubborn"; and "How can *you* say that?"

These types of statements cast blame, make accusations, express criticism, and make assumptions about what's inside the other person's head. And they lead to defensive replies that will probably do little to move the conversation forward: "I am *not*!"; "I do so understand"; "I'm not being stubborn"; and "I can say that because that's the way I feel."

A far more reasonable tactic is to use "I" statements. **"I" statements** cast responses in terms of yourself and your individual interpretation. Instead of saying, for example, "You really don't understand," a more appropriate response would be, "I think we're misunderstanding each other." "You're being stubborn" could be rephrased as "I feel like you're not really listening." And "Why don't you call when you're going to be late?" becomes "I worry that something has happened to you when you don't call if you are going to be late." In each case, "I" statements permit you to state your reaction in terms of your perception or understanding, rather than as a critical judgment about the other person. (Practice using "I" statements in Try It 5 on page 344.)

Resolving Conflict: A Win–Win Proposition

Even with careful attention to putting our own feelings forward instead of making accusations, whenever two people share their thoughts, concerns, fears, and honest reactions with each other, the chances are that sooner or later some sort of conflict will arise.

Conflict is not necessarily bad.

Often, people are upset simply by the fact that they are having a conflict. It is as though they believe conflicts don't occur in "good" relationships. In fact, however, conflict is helpful in some very important ways. It can force us to say what is really on our minds. It can allow us to clear up misconceptions and miscommunications before they begin to undermine the relationship. It can even give us practice at resolving conflicts with others with whom we might not share such good relations.

Discussion Prompt: Ask your students how they deal with conflict. Before you teach new strategies for dealing with conflict, it's important to assess students' past experiences and attitudes towards conflict.

"I" statements
Statements that cast responses in terms of oneself and one's individual interpretation

WORKING IN A GROUP

Switch "You" to "I"

Working in a group or in pairs, turn the following "you" statements into less aggressive "I" statements. For example, a possible "I" statement alternative to "You just don't get it, do you?" would be "I don't feel I'm making my feelings clear."

1. You just don't get it, do you?

2. You never listen to what I say.

3. You don't see where I'm coming from.

4. You don't really believe that, do you?

5. You never try to see my point of view.

6. Please stop interrupting me and listen to what I'm saying for a change.

7. Stop changing the subject!

8. You're not making sense.

9. You keep distorting what I say until I don't even know what point I'm trying to make.

10. You use too many "you" statements. Use more "I" statements when you're talking to others.

To Try It online, go to **www.mhhe.com/power**.

Like anything else, though, there are good ways to resolve conflict, and there are bad ways. Good ways move people forward, defining the problem and promoting creative problem solving. Bad ways make the situation worse, driving people apart rather than bringing them together. The following are some fundamental principles of conflict resolution that you can use when conflict occurs in personal and professional relationships:

- **Stop, look, and listen.** In the heat of an argument, all sorts of things that otherwise would go unsaid get said. If you find yourself making rash or hurtful statements, stop, look at yourself, and listen to what you and the other person are saying.

  Stopping works like a circuit breaker that prevents a short circuit from causing a deadly fire. You've probably heard about counting to 10 to cool off when you're angry. Do it. Take a break and count to 10 . . . or 20 . . . or more. Whether you count to 10 or 100, stopping gives you time to think and not react rashly.

- **Defuse the argument.** Anger is not an emotion that encourages rational discourse. When you're angry and annoyed with someone, you're not in the best position to evaluate logically the merits of various arguments others may offer. It may feel exhilarating to get our fury off our chests in the heat of an argument, but you can bet it isn't taking anyone any closer to resolving the problem.

  Don't assume that you are 100 percent right and the other person is 100 percent wrong. Make your goal *solving the problem* rather than winning an argument.

- **Get personal.** Perhaps you've heard others suggest that you shouldn't get personal in an argument. In one sense that's true: Accusing people you're arguing with of having character flaws does nothing to resolve real issues.

  At the same time, you should be willing to admit personal *responsibility* for at least part of the conflict. The conflict would not exist without you, so you need to accept that the argument has two sides and that you are not automatically blameless. This creates some solid ground from which you and the other person can begin to work on the problem.

- **Listen to the real message.** When people argue, what they say is often not the real message. There's typically an underlying communication—a subtext—that is the source of the conflict.

  It's important, then, to dig beneath what you're hearing. If someone accuses you of being selfish, the real meaning hidden in the accusation may be that you don't give anyone else a chance to make decisions. Remember, arguments are usually about behavior, not underlying character and personality. What people *do* is not necessarily synonymous with what they *are.*

  If you rephrase the person's statement in your own mind, it moves from an insult ("You're a bad person") to a request for a change of behavior ("Let me participate in decision making"). You're much more likely to respond reasonably when you don't feel that the essence of your being is under attack.

- **Show that you're listening.** It's not enough only to listen to the underlying message that someone is conveying. You also need to acknowledge the *explicit* message. For example, saying something like "OK. I can tell you are concerned about sharing the burden on our group project, and I think we should talk about it" acknowledges that you see the issue and admit that

Teaching Tip: This is an excellent place to make career connections. Much of workplace success is based on an individual's ability to incorporate win-win attitudes and practices in everyday working situations.

it is worthy of discussion. This is a far more successful strategy than firing back a countercharge each time your partner makes a complaint.

■ **If you are angry, acknowledge it.** Don't pretend that everything is fine if it isn't. Ultimately, relationships in which the partners bottle up their anger may suffer more than those in which the partners express their true feelings. If you're angry, say so.

■ **Ask for clarification.** As you're listening to another person's arguments, check out your understanding of what is being said. Don't assume that you know what's intended. Saying something like "Are you saying . . . " or "Do you mean that . . . " is a way of verifying that what you *think* someone means is really what is meant.

■ **Make your requests explicit.** If you're upset that your roommate leaves clothes lying around your apartment or dorm room, remarking that he or she is a "pig" shows more than that you are angry. It also shows that your intent is to hurt rather than to solve the problem.

It's far better to be explicit in your concerns. Say something like "It would make me feel better if you would pick up your clothes from the floor." Couching your concern in this way changes the focus of the message from your roommate's personality to a specific behavior that can be changed.

■ **Always remember that life is not a zero-sum game.** Many of us act as if life were a **zero-sum game,** a situation in which when one person wins, the other person automatically loses. It's what happens when you make a bet: If one person wins the bet, the other person loses.

Life is not like that. If one person wins an argument, it doesn't mean that others automatically have to lose it. And if someone loses an argument, it doesn't mean that others have automatically won. In fact, all too often conflict escalates so much that the argument turns into a lose–lose situation, where everyone ends up a loser.

However, life can be a win–win situation. The best resolution of conflict occurs when both parties walk away with something they want. Each may not have achieved *every* goal but will at least have enough to feel satisfied.

Zero-sum game
A situation in which when one person wins, the other person automatically loses

IRM Link: Refer to Teaching the Text, Section VII, Goal 1. Look at the tools residence life professionals use to teach these skills by inviting a speaker to class.

Changing Relationships: Surviving Endings

Not all relationships last a lifetime. Sometimes they just wind down, as the two people involved slowly lose interest in maintaining their partnership. At other times, they break apart, as disagreements build and there is not a strong enough bond to hold the two parties together. Or there may be an abrupt rupture if some event occurs that destroys one partner's feeling of trust.

Caring for others is rewarding, but risky. When relationships don't work out, their endings can be painful, even devastating, for a time. Even when relationships evolve naturally and change is expected, the transformation in a relationship may not be easy. Parents die. Children grow up and move away from home. Siblings get new jobs on the other side of the country.

There is one sure cure for the heartache of a lost relationship: time. There are some other things you can do, however, as you wait for time to pass and for the pain to ease:

Teaching Tip: Making students aware of campus resources, such as a counseling center, is one of the most important functions of this class and this text.

1. **Do something—anything.** Mow the lawn, clean out the closets, go for a run, see a movie. It won't completely get your mind off your loss, but it beats languishing on your bed, thinking about what you might have done differently or what could have been.

2. **Accept that you feel bad.** If you're not experiencing unhappiness over the end of a relationship, it means that the relationship wasn't terribly meaningful in the first place. Understand that unhappiness normally accompanies the end of a relationship, and allow yourself some satisfaction over the fact that you'd been able to maintain a relationship that, at least at one point, was meaningful.

3. **Talk to a friend or relative.** Talking about your sadness will help you to deal with it better. Other people can help you feel better about yourself, offer different perspectives, and simply support you by listening. Make use of your network of existing relationships to get you through a difficult period.

4. **Write about the relationship.** If you have a journal, writing about the relationship and its aftermath can be therapeutic. You can say whatever you want without fear of being contradicted.

5. **Talk to a professional.** If your sadness over a relationship feels totally overwhelming or continues for what you perceive to be too long a time, talk to a counselor or other professional. He or she can help you gain a better understanding of the situation and perhaps help you understand why you are taking it so hard. And remember that, ultimately, the pain will disappear: Time does heal virtually all wounds.

Name: Sandra Marotta

School: Metropolitan State University, St. Paul, Minnesota

The first year of college creates a combination of excitement, uncertainty, and anxiety in almost every student. But when you are a nontraditional student, returning to college some 30 years after finishing high school, the experience can be nearly overwhelming.

It was not surprising, then, that when Sandra Marotta started her first year at Metropolitan State University, she found the experience remarkably challenging, despite her strong motivation to succeed. Many of the students were considerably younger than she was, and she wondered how she would fit into a college environment.

"I had no real direction when I was younger," said Marotta, who had started college just after high school but soon dropped out. However, after raising three children, she was determined to get a college degree.

"The biggest step I had to overcome was the self-doubt I had as to whether I could do it. Even taking that initial step of going to first-year orientation was hard," Marotta explained.

"But through programs at Metropolitan State, my advisors, faculty, and my relationships with other students, I found a lot of support. It's a place that is very adult-oriented with a student population that is very international and diverse," she added. "I received a great deal of guidance from teachers and especially my advisor. She knew the teachers and who would be accessible and helpful."

Marotta also had to learn to be a successful student.

"I recall going into the first-year experience program, and they were talking about critical thinking," she recalled. "When I heard that, I was concerned, since I have never had to think critically or analyze anything. So I went to my teachers to find how to do it. I had to learn a whole new way of approaching things."

Hard work, diligence, and support from her children and friends paid off. Although Marotta is carrying a heavy course load, she has maintained an A average—in addition to working a 40-hour week.

"I'm a very self-disciplined person, and I just make the time for school," she explained. "A lot of this motivation comes from the support of a good friend, who has encouraged me and made me believe in myself.

"I have more self-confidence, and am definitely much more comfortable with the whole idea of school and how to approach things," she said. "I have the feeling that the teachers and my fellow classmates respect me for what I'm doing at this point in my life."

Why is the increasing racial, ethnic, and cultural diversity of society important to me?

- The diversity of the United States—and of U.S. college campuses—is increasing rapidly, and the world is becoming smaller as television, radio, the Internet, the World Wide Web, and international commerce bring people and cultures closer together.

- Being aware of diversity can allow you to accept the challenge and opportunity of living and working with others who are very different.

How can I become more at ease with differences and diversity?

- Cultural competence begins with accepting diversity by seeking out others who are different, as well as exploring your own prejudices and stereotypes.

- You can learn about other cultures by traveling to other countries and geographic areas. It also helps to accept differences simply as differences.

How can I build lasting relationships and deal with conflict?

- Relationships not only provide social support and companionship, but they also help people understand themselves.

- The central components of good relationships are trust, honesty, mutual support, loyalty, acceptance, and a willingness to embrace change.

- Listening is an important skill for relationship building, demonstrating that the listener really cares about the other person.

- Conflict is inevitable in relationships, and sometimes it is useful because it permits us to clear up misconceptions and miscommunications before they escalate.

- Although the end of a relationship can be very painful, the pain does subside over time.

KEY TERMS AND CONCEPTS

Race (p. 328)
Ethnicity (p. 329)
Culture (p. 329)
Cultural competence (p. 329)
Prejudice (p. 331)

Stereotypes (p. 331)
Reflective feedback (p. 341)
Loneliness (p. 341)
"I" statements (p. 343)
Zero-sum game (p. 346)

RESOURCES

On Campus

For students who reside on campus, one of the most frequent sources of difficulties for first-year students involves roommate problems. If you and your roommate are having problems getting along, begin by speaking with your resident advisor or residence hall director. If the problem persists, talk with a member of the residential life office. You can also speak with a counselor at the college counseling office.

Anyone who feels he or she is facing discrimination based on race, gender, ethnic status, sexual orientation, or national origin should contact a university official *immediately*. Often there is a specific office that handles such complaints. If you don't know which campus official to contact, speak to your academic advisor or someone in the dean's office and you'll be directed to the appropriate person. The important thing is to act and not to suffer in silence. Discrimination is not only immoral, but it is against the law.

Money Matters

L eah Flores's college career depended on the contents of the envelope she held in her hands.

The letter inside from the financial aid office spelled out her school's offer of aid for the upcoming term. As she tore open the envelope, Leah wondered whether it would be enough. She knew that without a substantial amount of support, she would have to drop out. She couldn't stand the thought, particularly because she had been doing so well.

As she looked at the numbers on the form, Leah's heart soared. Not only had she been given a loan, but also most of her aid was in the form of a direct scholarship.

Things would still be tight, but she could manage. Her financial worries were over—at least for one more term.

Discussion Prompt: What history and experience do your students bring to this subject? Were they involved in financial discussions in their families? Do they have any idea about their family income? Have they ever lived on a budget? Held a job? Had a checking account? Finding out the answers to these questions will help you determine your approach to this chapter.

LOOKING AHEAD >>>

Money problems aren't always solved as happily as they were for Leah Flores. Even under the best of circumstances, our finances present us with many challenges. Money often plays a large role in where we go to college, where we live, and what jobs we take. It is the source of many of our problems and stress, forcing us to find a balance between what we need and what we want.

This chapter will show you how to manage your money. It begins by discussing the process of preparing a budget and identifying your financial goals—the basis for money management. The chapter goes on to examine ways you can keep track of your spending and estimate your financial needs and resources, and discusses ways to control your spending habits and save money.

Education is one of the largest financial expenditures anyone encounters in life. Knowing the best ways to meet the costs of a college education—finding loans, grants, and scholarships—can give your finances a big boost and help you avoid graduating with thousands of dollars of debt. You will also learn what to do if your personal finances get out of control and discover how to stop the downward spiral of unpaid bills, defaulted loans, and unfavorable credit ratings. The chapter ends by suggesting ways to develop a financial philosophy.

In sum, after reading this chapter you'll be able to answer these questions:

- **What purpose does a budget serve and how can I prepare and stick to one?**

- **What help is available to pay for my college education?**

- **What is the value of a college education?**

Managing Your Money

Do you know where your money goes? Do you spend more than you think you should? Do you never have quite enough cash to buy the things you want?

Answering these questions and understanding the role money plays in your life is the first step of wise money management. To begin getting a grip on your finances, answer the questions in the *Journal Reflections* exercise.

If you have money problems—and there's virtually no one who doesn't have some concerns about finances—the solution is to develop a budget. A **budget** is a formal plan that accounts and plans for expenditures and income. Taking your goals into account, a budget helps determine how much money you should be spending each month, based on your income and your other financial resources. Budgets also help prepare for the unexpected, such as the loss of a job or an illness that would reduce your income, or for sudden, unanticipated expenses, such as a major car repair.

Although all budgets are based on an uncomplicated premise—expenditures should not exceed income—budgeting is not simple, particularly when

Budget
A formal plan that accounts for expenditures and income

Journal REFLECTIONS

My Sense of Cents

Answer the following questions about your financial sense.

1. How much money do you now have in your pockets and wallet? (Guess first, then look.) How close did you come?

2. Do you know how much money you typically spend in a month, including money spent on food, lodging, and other items?

3. How good a sense of your finances do you think you have? How secure do you feel in your understanding of where your money goes?

4. How important is money to you? Why?

5. Research shows that although winning the lottery or other large sums of money brings an initial surge in happiness, a year later the winners' level of happiness returns to what it was before.[1] Why do you think this is true in general, and would it be true for you?

you are a student. There are several times during the year that require especially large expenditures, such as the start of a semester, when you must pay your tuition and purchase books. Furthermore, your income is usually erratic; it may be lower during the school year and higher during the summer. But a budget will help you deal with the ups and downs in your finances, smoothing the curves and extending your view toward the horizon. Learning budgeting skills also helps prepare you for the world of work, as discussed in this chapter's *Career Connections.*

Most of all, a budget provides security. It will let you take control of your money, permitting you to spend it as you need to without guilt, because you have planned for the expenditure. It also makes it easier to put money aside because you know that your current financial sacrifice will be rewarded later, when you can make a purchase that you've been planning for.

Budgeting is very personal: What is appropriate for one person doesn't work for another. For a few people, keeping track of their spending comes naturally; they enjoy accounting for every dollar that passes through their hands. For most people, though, developing a budget—and sticking to it—does not come easily.

However, if you follow several basic steps—illustrated in the P.O.W.E.R. Plan—the process of budgeting is straightforward.

> "There was a time when a fool and his money were soon parted, but now it happens to everybody."
>
> Adlai Stevenson, politician

PREPARE
Identify financial goals

ORGANIZE
Determine expenditures and income

WORK
Make a budget that adds up

EVALUATE
Review the budget

RETHINK
Rethink financial options

P.O.W.E.R. Plan

P REPARE: Identifying Your Financial Goals

Your first reaction when asked to identify your financial goals may be that the question is a no-brainer: You want to have more money to spend. But it's not that simple. You need to ask yourself *why* you want more money. What would you spend it on? What would bring you the most satisfaction? Purchasing a DVD player? Paying off your debt? Saving money for a vacation? Starting a business? Paying for college rather than taking out loans?

CAREER CONNECTIONS

Budgeting on the Job

If you've ever held a job, the salary you received was determined, in part, by your employer's budget.

Although they may not always be accessible to every employee, budgets are part of the world of work. Regardless of who the employer is—be it a small dry cleaning business or the massive federal government—there is a budget outlining anticipated income and expenditures. Managers are expected to keep to the budget, and if their expenditures exceed what is budgeted, they are held accountable.

For this reason, the ability to create and live within a budget is an important skill to acquire. Not only will it help keep your own finances under control, but it will also prepare you to be financially responsible and savvy on the job—qualities that are highly valued by employers.

You won't be able to develop a budget that will work for you until you determine your short- and long-term financial goals. To determine them, use Try It 1, "Identify Your Financial Goals" on page 358.

O RGANIZE: Determining Your Expenditures and Income

Student Alert: Can your students recall a situation when they had to sacrifice and save money for something really special? What was their financial goal? How did they make it happen?

Do you open your wallet for the $10 that was there yesterday and find only a dollar? Spending money without realizing it is a common affliction.

There's only one way to get a handle on where your money is going: Keep track of it. To get an overview of your expenditures, go through any records you've kept to identify where you've spent money for the last year—old checks, rent and utility receipts, and previous college bills can help you.

In addition, keep track of everything you spend for a week. *Everything.* When you spend 50 cents for a candy bar from a vending machine, write it down. When you buy lunch for $2.97 at a fast-food restaurant, write it down. When you buy a 23-cent postcard, write it down.

Record your expenditures in a small notebook that you carry with you all the time. It may be tedious, but you're doing it for only a week. And it will be eye-opening: People are usually surprised at how much they spend on little items without thinking about it.

Finally, make a list of everything you think you'll need to spend over the next year. Some items are easy to think of, such as rent and tuition payments, because they occur regularly and the amount you pay is fixed. Others are harder to budget for because they can vary substantially. For exam-

Keeping to a budget is a constant balancing act. For example, even though you know you'll need to purchase books at the start of each semester, you can't predict exactly how much they'll cost.

ple, the price of gasoline changes frequently. If you have a long commute, the changing price of gasoline can cause substantial variation in what you pay each month. Similarly, the cost of books varies considerably from one term to another. (Use Table 13.1 on page 360 to estimate your expenditures for the coming year.)

Determine Your Income Sources

You probably have a pretty good idea of how much money you have each month. But it's as important to list each source of income as it is to account for everything you spend.

IRM Link and Teaching Tip: Suggest that your students keep track of their expenditures on a time management chart. A good one to use is the Weekly 24-7 Planning Sheet located in the transparency masters of the IRM. This activity should reveal times during the day or week that your students are most likely to spend money.

 WORKING IN A GROUP

Identify Your Financial Goals

Step 1. Use the planning tool below to identify and organize your financial goals.

Short-Term Goals

What would you like to have money for in the short term (over the next 3 months)? Consider these categories:

Personal necessities (such as food, clothes, household supplies, shelter, transportation, loan payments, debts, medical expenses):

Educational necessities (such as tuition, fees, books, school supplies):

Social needs (e.g., getting together with family, friends, and others; charitable contributions; clubs; teams; entertainment):

Lifestyle improvements (optional but desirable personal or educational tools, such as computer hardware and software, living space improvements, transportation improvements, clothing "upgrades"):

Other:

Mid-Range Goals

What would you like to have money for soon (3 months from now to a year from now), but not immediately? Use the same categories:

Personal necessities:

Educational necessities:

Social needs:

Lifestyle improvements:

Other:

Long-Range Goals

What would you like to have money for 1 to 3 years from now? Use the same categories:

Personal necessities:

Educational necessities:

Social needs:

Lifestyle improvements:

Other:

Step 2. Now put each of your lists in **priority** order.

Short-Term Priorities:

Mid-Range Priorities:

Long-Range Priorities:

What does the list tell you about what is important to you? Did you find any surprises? Would you classify yourself as a financial risk-taker or someone who values financial security?

Working in a Group:

Consider these questions: Compare your priorities with those of your classmates. What similarities and differences do you find, and what can you learn from others' priorities?

To Try It online, go to **www.mhhe.com/power.**

TABLE 13.1 Estimated Expenditures, Next 12 Months

Category	Now to 3 Months from now	3–6 Months from now	6–9 Months from now	9–12 Months from now
Personal Necessities				
Food				
Clothing				
Shelter (rent, utilities, etc.)				
Household supplies				
Transportation (car payments, gas, repairs, bus tickets, etc.)				
Loan and debt payments				
Medical expenses				
Other				
Educational Necessities				
Tuition and fees				
Books				
Tools and hardware				
Computer costs				
Other				
Social Needs				
Relationships				
Clubs and teams				
Charitable contributions				
Other				
Entertainment				
Movies and shows				
Trips				
Recreation and sports				
Other				
Lifestyle Improvements				
Educational				
Living space				
Computer				
Transportation				
Clothing				
Other				
TOTAL				

TABLE 13.2	Estimated Income, Next 12 Months			
Category	**Now to 3 Months from now**	**3–6 Months from now**	**6–9 Months from now**	**9–12 Months from now**
Wages				
Family Support				
Financial Aid				
Tuition reductions				
Loan income				
Scholarship payments				
Other				
Interest and Dividends				
Gifts				
Other				
TOTAL				

Add up what you make from any jobs you hold. Also list any support you receive from family members, including occasional gifts you might get from relatives. Finally, include any financial aid (such as tuition reductions, loan payments, or scholarships) you receive from your college. Use Table 13.2 to record this information. When you do, be sure to list the amounts you receive in terms of after-tax income.

Student Alert: Caution students about hidden costs like phone bills and parking tickets. These are two areas that constantly cause financial woes for students.

WORK: Making a Budget That Adds Up

If you've prepared and organized your budget, actually constructing your budget is as easy as adding 2 + 2. Well, not exactly; the numbers will be larger. But all you need to do is add up your list of expenses, and then add up your sources of income. In a perfect world, the two numbers will be equal.

But most of the time, the world is not perfect: Most of us find that expenditures are larger than our income. After all, if we had plenty of excess cash, we probably wouldn't be bothering to make a budget in the first place.

If you find you spend more than you make, there are only two things to do: decrease your spending or increase your income. It's often easiest to decrease expenditures, because your expenses tend to be more under your control. For instance, there are many things you can do to save money, including the following:

- **Control impulse buying.** If you shop for your groceries, always take a list with you, and don't shop when you're hungry.
- **Make and take your own lunch.** Brown-bag lunches can save you a substantial amount of money over purchasing your lunches, even if you go to a fast-food restaurant or snack bar.

Bag it! One way to cut down on expenditures is to reduce everyday expenses, such as by making your own lunch, rather than grabbing a bite at a campus snack bar. Even small savings like this can add up fast.

- **Read the daily newspaper and magazines at the library or online.** Not only do college libraries subscribe to many daily newspapers and magazines, but major newspapers and magazines are also online.

- **Check bills for errors.** Computers make mistakes, and so do the people who enter the data into them. So make sure that your charges on any bill are accurate.

- **Cut up your credit cards and pay cash.** Using a credit card is seductive; when you take out your plastic, it's easy to feel as if you're not really spending money. If you use cash for purchases instead, you'll see the money going out.

- **Make major purchases only during sales.** Plan major purchases so they coincide with sales.

- **Share and trade.** Pool your resources with friends. Car pool, share resources such as computers, and trade CDs.

- **Live more simply.** Is cable TV an absolute necessity? Is it really necessary to eat out once a week? Do you buy clothes because you need them or because you want them? Do you really need to send so many text messages?

- **Do well in your classes.** One of the best ways to save money is to get good grades, because you avoid the hidden costs of poor performance. If you are forced to repeat a class because of a low grade, you'll have to take another course in the future as a substitute, and that may be an added expense. Doing well avoids the possibility of additional tuition costs.

There are as many ways to save money as there are people looking to save it. But keep in mind that saving money should not necessarily be an end in itself. Don't spend hours thinking of ways to save a dime, and don't get upset about situations where you are forced to spend money. The goal is to bring your budget into balance, not to become a tightwad who keeps track of every penny and feels that spending money is a personal failure. To help you get started, get a sense of your current style of saving money in Try It 2.

Finally, it's important to remember that budgets may be brought into balance not only by decreasing expenditures, but also by increasing income. The most direct way to increase income is to get a part-time job if you don't already have one.

Many students work during college. Although working adds to the time-management challenges you will face, it does not necessarily mean that your

Student Alert: Freshmen are often unaware of job opportunities on campus. The benefits are many – extra cash, a sense of belonging, a source of personal references, a broader sense of responsibility. Find out what resources are available on your campus, and share the information with the class, through guest speakers, student presentations or a campus tour.

2

PERSONAL STYLES

Determine Your Saving Style

Read each of the following statements and rate how well it describes you, using this scale:

1 = That's me

2 = Sometimes

3 = That's not me

	1	2	3
1. I count the change I'm given by cashiers in stores and restaurants.			
2. I always pick up all the change I receive from a transaction in a store, even if it's only a few cents.			
3. I don't buy something right away if I'm pretty sure it will go on sale soon.			
4. I feel a real sense of accomplishment if I buy something on sale.			
5. I always remember how much I paid for something.			
6. If something goes on sale soon after I've bought it, I feel cheated.			
7. I have money in at least one interest-bearing bank account.			
8. I rarely lend people money.			
9. If I lend money to someone repeatedly without getting it back, I stop lending it to that person.			
10. I share resources (e.g., CDs, books, magazines) with other people to save money.			
11. I'm good at putting money away for big items that I really want.			
12. I believe most generic or off-brand items are just as good as name brands.			

Add up your ratings. Interpret your total score according to this informal guide:

12–15: Very aggressive saving style

16–20: Careful saving style

21–27: Fairly loose saving style

28–32: Loose saving style

33–36: Nonexistent saving style

What are the advantages and disadvantages of your saving style? How do you think your saving style would affect your ability to keep to a budget? If you are dissatisfied with your saving style, how might you be able to change it?

To Try It online, go to **www.mhhe.com/power**.

grades will suffer. In fact, some students who work do better in school than those who don't work, because those with jobs need to be more disciplined and focused. In addition, a part-time job in an area related to your future career may prove to be helpful in getting a job after you graduate.

On the other hand, working too much can be harmful. Jobs not only take their toll in hours away from your studies, but in added stress. Consequently, it's sometimes better to take out a student loan to cover college costs than to work excessive amounts. Obviously you don't want to thoughtlessly get into debt, because you don't want to burden your future with loan payments. But the well thought-out use of loans, if they allow you to focus on your studies, may be a good investment in your future.

E VALUATE: Reviewing Your Budget

Budgets are not meant to be set in stone. You should review where you stand financially each month. Only by monitoring how closely actual expenditures and income match your budget projections will you be able to maintain control of your finances.

You don't need to continually keep track of every penny you spend to evaluate your success in budgeting. As you gain more experience with your budget, you'll begin to get a better sense of your finances. You'll know when it may be possible to consider splurging on a gift for a friend, and when you need to operate in penny-pinching mode.

The important thing is to keep your expenditures under control. Review, and if necessary revise, your budget to fit any changes in circumstances. Maybe you receive a raise in a part-time job. Maybe the financial aid office gives you more support than you expected. Or maybe you face a reduction in income. Whatever the change in circumstances, evaluate how it affects your budget, and revise the budget accordingly.

R ETHINK: Reconsidering Your Financial Options

If all goes well, the process of budgeting will put you in control of your financial life. Your expenditures will match your income, and you won't face major money worries.

In the real world, of course, events have a way of inflicting disaster on even the best-laid plans:

- You lose your job and can't afford to pay next semester's tuition.
- Your roommate moves out and leaves you with an $800 phone bill. You don't have $800.
- Your parents, who have promised to pay for your education, run into financial difficulties and say they can't afford to pay your college costs any longer.
- Your car breaks down, and repairing it will cost $1,500. If you don't have a car, you can't get to campus. But if you pay for repairs, you can't afford tuition.

All of us face financial difficulties at one time or another. Sometimes it happens suddenly and without warning. Other times people sink more gradually into financial problems, each month accumulating more debt until they reach a point at which they can't pay their bills.

However it happens, finding yourself with too little money to pay your bills requires action. You need to confront the situation and take steps to solve the problem. The worst thing to do is nothing. Hiding from those to whom you owe money makes the situation worse. Your creditors—the institutions and people to whom you owe money—will assume that you don't care, and they'll be spurred on to take harsher actions.

These are the steps to take if you do find yourself with financial difficulties (also see Table 13.3).

■ **Assess the problem.** Make a list of what you owe and to whom. Look at the bottom line and figure out a reasonable amount you can put toward each debt. Work out a specific plan that can lead you out of the situation.

■ **Contact each of your creditors.** Start with your bank, credit card companies, and landlord, and continue through each creditor. It's best to visit personally, but a phone call will do.

When you speak with them, explain the situation. If the problem is due to illness or unemployment, let them know. If it's due to overspending, let them know that. Tell them what you plan to do to pay off your debt, and show them your plan. The fact that you have a plan demonstrates not only what you intend to do, but also that you are serious about your situation and capable of financial planning.

If you've had a clean financial record in the past, your creditors may be willing to agree to your plan. Ultimately, it is cheaper for them to accept smaller payments over a longer time than to hire a collection agency.

■ **See a credit counselor.** If you can't work out a repayment plan on your own, visit a credit counseling service. These are nonprofit organizations that help people who find themselves in financial trouble. Your bank or a creditor can help you identify one, or you can call the National Foundation for Consumer Credit at 1-800-388-2227 or visit their Web site at **www.nfcc.org**.

Discussion Prompt: Why does our culture support the notion of living on borrowed funds? Why are we not better savers?

TABLE 13.3	Steps in Dealing with Financial Difficulties
Assess the Problem	Make a list of what you owe and to whom.
	Figure out a reasonable amount you can put toward each debt.
	Work out a specific plan.
Contact Each of Your Creditors	Start with your bank, credit card companies, and landlord.
	Explain the situation.
	Show them your plan to pay off debt.
See a Credit Counselor	If you cannot work out a repayment plan on your own, visit a credit counseling service.
Stick to the Plan	Once you have a plan, make a commitment to stick to it.
	Your bank or creditor can help you identify a credit counselor.

■ **Stick to the plan.** Once you have a plan to get yourself out of debt, follow it. Unless you diligently make the payments you commit to, you'll find your debt spiraling out of control once again. It's essential, then, to regard your plan as a firm commitment and stick to it.

Student Alert: How many students in your class carry credit cards? Are these issued in their name or their parents? What experiences can your students share with one another?

Credit Cards

"Congratulations! You've been preapproved for a Gold credit card! Just send us your signature on the enclosed authorization form, and we'll rush you your card."

> "It is difficult to learn the meaning of fiscal responsibility, especially when you've got a new VISA and there's a great-looking sweater in the shop window. It's even harder when the sweater is on sale."
>
> Lauren Pass, student,
> Grossmont Community College[2]

Teaching Tip: Consider bringing play money to class to demonstrate the point made in TRY IT 3. It will be more dramatic with dollars changing hands among class members.

Have you ever gotten such a letter in the mail? If so, you're far from the only one: Millions of people in the United States are regularly enticed to receive credit cards in just such a manner, and college students are especially attractive targets. In many cases, it doesn't even matter if you have income; the mere fact that you're a college student is sufficient to win you approval to receive a card.

Credit cards are not necessarily bad. In fact, used appropriately, they can help get you through brief periods when you must make a purchase—such as replacing a tire for your car—but temporarily don't have enough money to do so. But it's easy to fall into debt. That's why the average credit card debt owed by college students is close to $3,000. And about ten percent of college students owe more than $7,000.

You don't want to be years past your college graduation and still paying for a slice of pizza you purchased in your first month on campus. That's why it's important to consider the use of credit cards very carefully.

There are several questions you should ask when deciding whether to get and use a credit card:

1. **Is there an annual fee?** Many cards charge an annual fee, ranging from $20 a year to $100 a year. You need to determine whether the advantages of the card are worth the cost of an annual fee.

2. **What is the interest rate?** Interest rates—the percentage of the unpaid balance you are charged on credit cards—vary substantially. Some interest rates are as low as 12 percent per year, while some are as high as 25 percent per year. If the rate is 25 percent, you will be charged an additional $250 each year if you owe an average of $1,000. Furthermore, although some interest rates are *fixed*, meaning that they don't vary from month to month, others are *variable*, which means they change each month. How much they change is tied to various factors in the overall economy. To get a better sense of how interest rates add up, try "Maintain Your Interest" (Try It 3).

It's easy for most college students to get credit cards, and even easier to use them once they have them. The hard part comes later—paying the bills.

Maintain Your Interest

Suppose you saw a $275 television set on sale "for a limited time" for $240. The $35 discount tempts you. The trouble is you don't have $240 to spare. But you *do* have a credit card—and you decide to buy the TV with the card and pay it off over time.

The advantages of this strategy are that you get the discount and have immediate use of the television set. The main disadvantage is that you will end up paying more than the $240 figure that you have in mind as the bargain price for the TV. In fact, depending on how high your credit card's interest rate is, how long you take to pay your bill in full, and how large each monthly payment is, you may wipe out most or all of the $35 savings that caused you to make the purchase in the first place. The more slowly you pay off the loan, the more money you pay for the television set.

For example, suppose you use a card with an annual interest rate of 12 percent, compounded monthly, meaning that the interest charge is applied each month, rather than at the end of the year—making the true annual rate 12.68 percent. (Some cards even compound on a *daily* basis, resulting in a real interest rate that is even higher.) At the end of a year, assuming you pay $10 per month toward the $240 purchase, you will have paid $120 and still have $143.61 to pay. At the end of 2 years, you would end up paying $35 in interest on top of the $240 purchase price.

The 12-month calculation is illustrated in the first table below. To see how much of a factor the interest rate is, complete the second table, which shows the same purchase on a credit card with a 20 percent annual (approximately 1.67 percent monthly) interest rate, compounded monthly. (These calculations can also be figured automatically on several Web sites, including **www.bankrate.com** and **www.quicken.com**.)

Credit Card Payments: 12% Interest, Compounded Monthly (1% per month)

	Month 1	2	3	4	5	6	7	8	9	10	11	12
Unpaid Balance	$240.00	$232.40	$224.72	$216.97	$209.14	$201.23	$193.24	$185.18	$177.03	$168.80	$160.49	$152.09
Plus Interest of	2.40	2.32	2.25	2.17	2.09	2.01	1.93	1.85	1.77	1.69	1.60	1.52
Minus Payment of	10.00	10.00	10.00	10.00	10.00	10.00	10.00	10.00	10.00	10.00	10.00	10.00
Balance Due	$232.40	$224.72	$216.97	$209.14	$201.23	$193.24	$185.18	$177.03	$168.80	$160.49	$152.09	$143.61

Credit Card Payments: 20% Interest, Compounded Monthly (approx. 1.67% per month)

	Month 1	2	3	4	5	6	7	8	9	10	11	12
Unpaid Balance	$240.00	$234.01	$227.92	$221.72	$215.42							
Plus Interest of	4.01	3.91	3.81	3.70								
Minus Payment of	10.00	10.00	10.00	10.00	10.00	10.00	10.00	10.00	10.00	10.00	10.00	10.00
Balance Due	$234.01	$227.92	$221.72	$215.42								

How much would the $240 TV set cost if you bought it with this higher-rate card, paying $10 per month for 12 months and then paying the remaining balance by check? How does this compare with the nondiscounted purchase price of $275?

To Try It online, go to **www.mhhe.com/power**.

3. **Do I need a credit card?** There are good reasons for getting a credit card, and bad ones:

The pluses of credit cards:

- **Establishing a good credit history.** If you've ever owed money to a bank or your college, a computer file exists describing your payment history. If you have never missed a loan payment and always pay on time, you have a good credit history. If you haven't paid on time or have missed payments, your history will reflect this. Negative information can stay in a file for 7 years, and it can keep you from getting future loans, so it's important to establish and keep a clear credit history. (To get a copy of your credit report, complete Try It 4, "Learn What Your Credit History Shows.")

- **Emergency use.** Few of us carry around enough cash to deal with emergencies. A credit card can be a life saver if we're on a trip and the car breaks down and needs emergency repairs.

- **Convenience.** Sometimes it's just easier to make purchases using a credit card. For instance, we can make purchases over the telephone or online if we have a credit card. Furthermore, credit cards not only provide a record of purchases, but they also give us limited consumer protection should a product prove to be defective.

"Graduates, faculty, parents, creditors . . ."

The minuses of credit cards:

On the other hand, there can be significant drawbacks to the use of credit cards. Potential problems include the following:

- **Interest costs can be high.** As you saw in Try It 3, the interest rate on credit card purchases can be significant. Unless you pay off your entire balance each month, your account will be charged interest, which can add up rapidly.

- **It's too easy to spend money.** Credit cards are so convenient to use that you may not realize how much you're spending in a given period. Furthermore, spending can become addictive. Unless you're careful, you can end up exceeding your budget by a significant amount.

- **If you're late in making your payments or exceed your credit limit, your credit rating will be damaged.** Credit card companies have long memories, and any mistakes you make will be reflected in your credit record for close to a decade. That may prevent you from buying a car or house in the future and jeopardize your ability to take out student loans.

IRM Link: Refer to Teaching the Text, Chapter 13, Sections IV and VIII. The "Cost of Higher Education" activity in the IRM is a very effective way to make a point about the cost of college.

■ Paying for College

Tuition costs vary greatly from one school to another, but they are substantial everywhere. The average public community college costs $2,076 per year in tuition; the average 4-year public college costs $5,132; and the average private

4

Learn What Your Credit History Shows

Big Brother is alive and well, at least in terms of your credit history. If you've ever had a credit card in your own name, taken out a student loan, or sometimes just received an unsolicited offer for credit in the mail, there's probably a computer file describing who you are, where you live, and your financial history. It shows how high your credit lines are on every credit card you have, if you've ever been late on a payment, and a considerable amount of additional information.

Even worse: Many people's credit histories are riddled with errors. That's why it's important to periodically check the record. To get a complimentary copy of your credit report, contact one of the three major credit companies:

- Transunion: **www.tuc.com** or 1-800-888-4213.
- Experian: **www.experian.com** or 1-800 311-4769.
- Equifax: **www.equifax.com** or 1-800-685-1111

Be prepared: You will be asked for a variety of pieces of information, including your name, address, social security number, your birth date, your prior addresses for the past 5 years and other names (like a maiden name) you may have been known by.

Once you get your credit report, check it carefully. If you find any mistakes, contact the credit bureau and explain the error. They are legally responsible for investigating the report and correcting the file. It's a good idea to check your file at least once a year.

To try It online, go to **www.mhhe.com/power**.

---

college costs $20,082.[3] If you live on campus, count on another five or six thousand dollars for room and board.

Nothing about college is cheap. It takes enormous expenditures of three often scarce commodities: energy, time, and money. Perhaps surprisingly, many students find money the easiest of them to find. While it's not simple to get financial aid and no one is going to walk up to you and offer you an all-expenses-paid scholarship, you can find many sources of funding for your education if you are persistent.

To find this money, however, you will need to spend ample amounts of the other two scarce commodities: time and energy. The entire process of securing financial aid takes a considerable amount of preparation, because you need to identify potential sources of funds and then apply for them. You should assume the process will take somewhere between several weeks and several months, depending on the type of aid you're applying for.

Getting the Most Out of Your Classes: How Cutting Classes Costs

Think about how much college costs you each term. Go ahead and add it up: tuition, books, transportation, housing, food, supplies, etc., etc. It's a pretty hefty sum.

Now count the number of hours you're in class during the term. If you divide the number of hours into the amount you spend on college, you'll come up with a dollar value that shows how much every hour of the courses in which you're enrolled is worth.

What you'll immediately see is that every class is worth a great deal. For most students, missing a day's worth of classes is the equivalent of giving up $50 at the very minimum. Students attending expensive private colleges may be losing hundreds of dollars.

If all the other reasons for not missing a class aren't convincing enough, then think in these economic terms. Giving away something you've paid for is irrational. It's really no different than buying thousands of dollars worth of CDs and then throwing them away, one by one, over the course of the semester. Only in the case of your college courses, what you're giving is far more precious—your education.

Consequently, resolve to get your money's worth out of your courses by attending them faithfully. Not only will you benefit economically, but you'll maximize your chances for learning the material and ultimately being successful in your college career and beyond.

Identifying the Different Types of Funding Available

Funding for college comes in three basic categories: loans, grants, and scholarships. Although each supplies you with funds for college, they do so in very different ways.

Loan
Funds provided by a bank, credit union, or other agency that must be repaid after a specified period of time

■ **Loans.** When you receive a **loan,** a bank, credit union, or other agency provides funds that must be repaid after a specified period of time. A loan carries a particular interest rate, which is stated as an annual percentage rate. Think of a loan as renting money: As long as you have the use of someone else's money, you have to pay them "rent" for the privilege. Banks and other lending agencies make money through the interest they charge on loans, just as they do with credit cards.

For example, suppose a bank gives you a $5,000 loan that has an interest rate of 8 percent per year. Not only must you pay back the $5,000 over a specified period, but you must pay the bank interest of 8 percent on the balance that you owe on the loan. Obviously, the higher the interest rate, the more you are paying for the privilege of borrowing the bank's money.

Principal
The stated amount of a loan

Term
The length of time for which money is lent

Three factors must be considered when you receive a loan: the stated amount of the loan (called the **principal**), the interest rate (stated as a percentage), and the length of the loan (referred to as the **term** of the loan). All three factors are important, because they determine how much your payments will be when you pay the loan back.

Many loans for college have an enormous advantage over loans you'll take out for other purchases, such as a car or house, because payments on college loans are *deferred* until you graduate and (presumably!) begin to earn an income—that is, it is often not necessary to start paying back the loan until you graduate. Depending on the type of loan you take out, interest on the loan is either paid for by the government while you are enrolled in college or is deferred until you graduate.

There are several national loan programs, sponsored by the federal government, that lend money to students. The major ones include the following:

- **Stafford loans.** Stafford loans are available to any student who is registered at least half-time and is a U.S. citizen or permanent resident. They provide from just over $2,600 to $5,500 a year.

  Stafford loans come in two types: subsidized and unsubsidized. *Subsidized Stafford loans* are awarded through colleges on the basis of student financial need. For subsidized loans, the government pays interest until repayment begins, typically after the student graduates. *Unsubsidized Stafford loans* do not require demonstration of financial need. Interest is not paid by the government; instead it accumulates while the student is in college. However, the student doesn't have to make any payments until after graduation, when both principal and accumulated interest must be repaid over a specified period, which is up to 10 years.

- **PLUS loans.** If your parents support you and claim you as a deduction on their income tax return, they may take out a PLUS loan. PLUS loans can cover up to the full amount of a student's cost of college attendance and can be paid back over a 10-year period.

- **Perkins loans.** Perkins loans have a low interest rate. They are awarded on the basis of exceptional financial need, as determined by a student's college. The loans are made by a school's financial aid office.

Student Alert: Every college campus has its own financial aid packaging formula designed to conform to state and federal guidelines. Encourage students who are applying for aid to find out about your institution's policies.

Although college loans like these are relatively easy to get, it's important to remember that someday you'll need to pay them back. And many students are paying back a great deal. For instance, the average indebtedness is almost $9,000 for community college students and close to $20,000 for 4-year college students.[4]

Because college graduates often start off earning less than they thought they would after graduation, high levels of debt can lead to difficulties. More than half of graduates feel burdened by their debt, and a quarter report having significant problems paying back their loans. Consequently, think hard when taking out a loan and consider how much you'll have to pay back each month after you graduate.

- **Grants.** A **grant** is money that does not have to be repaid. Obviously, it's more advantageous to receive a grant than a loan. And not surprisingly, it's harder to qualify for grants than loans—harder, but not impossible. Several grant programs exist which can help reduce the amount you'll need to pay for college. They include the following:

Grant
An award of money that does not have to be repaid

  - **Pell grants.** Based on need, Pell grants are provided to undergraduate students who have earned no previous degrees. They are awarded by college financial aid offices, which follow a formula provided by the federal government. Every student who meets certain need criteria is eligible for a Pell grant, ensuring that the neediest students receive some support.

- **Federal Supplemental Educational Opportunity Grants (FSEOG).** The government supplies a limited number of FSEOGs to every college, which can provide these grants to needy students. Unlike Pell grants, which are guaranteed to every eligible student, FSEOGs are in limited supply. Once a college awards its allotment for a given year, no other awards are possible.

- **Work-study grants.** Work-study grants provide jobs for undergraduates with financial needs. The jobs are typically related to a student's course of study, and the salary is subsidized by the government. Because a work-study position is often part of a student's total package of financial aid, it is generally considered a grant, even though work is required.

■ **Scholarships. Scholarships** are support awarded by colleges, organizations, and companies. Like a grant, a scholarship is money that does not have to be repaid. Most scholarships are based primarily on a student's financial need, although some are based on merit. For instance, students with exceptional academic or athletic abilities may receive a scholarship even though they wouldn't necessarily qualify under typical need-based measures.

The most frequent source of scholarships is one's own college, which may give money to reduce tuition and fees. But there are literally thousands of organizations that provide scholarships, ranging from companies such as Microsoft to nonprofit groups, such as the Boy Scouts and Girl Scouts.

The federal government also provides some scholarships to students whose family income does not rise above certain levels. These include the following:

- **Hope scholarship.** The Hope scholarship is a tax credit that helps free up funds for college. Students receive a 100 percent tax credit for the first $1,000 of tuition and required fees, and a 50 percent credit on the second $1,000.

- **Lifetime learning tax credit.** This tax credit is targeted to older students who are going back to school, changing careers, or taking courses to upgrade their skills, as well as to juniors and seniors in 4-year colleges. Families can receive a 20 percent tax credit for the first $5,000 of tuition and fees, and the amount will increase in future years.

Researching Possible Sources of Financial Aid

As you can see, there are many sources of financial aid. The biggest problem often is finding them.

Your first stop on your search for sources of financial aid should be your college's financial aid office. Every college has one, and it tends to be one of the busiest places on campus.

Most student aid offices contain a great deal of information about possible sources of aid. But that's only a starting point. The library and World Wide Web also contain many types of information that can direct you to specific possibilities. One place to get started is the Federal Student Aid Information Center in Washington, which can be reached at 1-800-4-FED-AID (1-800-433-3243) or on the Web at **studentaid.ed.gov/students/publications/student_guide/index.html**. The center will send you "The Student Guide," which describes programs that account for almost three-fourths of all financial aid awarded to students.

Keep in mind, however, that where money is involved, there are scams. Do not pay money to someone who offers to identify obscure scholarships that will yield you thousands of dollars. It's unlikely that anyone could find sources that you couldn't find yourself through careful research. Be especially wary of Web sites that ask for a credit card number to provide you with online information. The results are likely to be disappointing. (The Web sites we provide at the end of the chapter are completely reputable.)

Whatever the potential source of financial aid, you'll be asked to bare your financial soul. There will also be forms galore. Before actually completing the forms, it will be important to gather the information you will need. If you are being supported by your parents, they will have to complete some of the forms.

Keep track of deadlines! If you miss a deadline for applying for financial aid, you'll be out of luck; no exceptions are made. You'll just have to wait for another aid cycle.

Finally, make sure you know what your needs are. The typical costs of college include not only tuition but also fees, books, and supplies, as well as associated costs, such as transportation, housing, food, and child care.

"Good day, Madam. I'm working my son's way through college."

Apply for Financial Aid

It may seem that for every dollar in aid you get, there is a different line to complete on a complicated form. Prepare yourself for a blizzard of paperwork.

Following are the steps in applying for financial aid:

- **Speak with a financial aid counselor at your school.** Because the best source of financial aid is your own college, make an appointment to discuss your needs with a campus financial aid counselor or officer. In addition to giving you the most up-to-date information about possible sources of aid, the college financial aid officer can provide you with the forms you need to fill out and a list of the deadlines you need to meet.

- **Decide how much aid you need.** It's important to ask for just the right amount of aid, neither too little nor too much. If you ask for too little aid, you may be strapped for funds during the school term. It's much more difficult to get aid in the middle of a term than during the normal application period.

  At the same time, don't apply for more financial aid than you actually need. First there is an issue of equity: What you get in aid may reduce the pool for others, and if you receive surplus aid you may be preventing other students from getting their fair share. Further, you don't want to load yourself up with unnecessary debt. Most graduates pay from $150 to $175 a month to pay off their student loans; you don't want to end up with so much debt that your loan payments are even higher than this.

- **Fill out your college's application for financial aid.** Colleges have their own forms to apply for financial aid. Carefully fill the form out, making sure you file it before the required deadline. In fact, the earlier you get the form in, the better: Most schools have a limited pool of funds, and the earlier you get your application in, the higher your chances of getting an appropriate share of the financial aid pie.

Student Alert: Deadlines are critical, particularly with federal aid. Many sources are available on a first come, first serve basis. Also, summer school is often considered separately from aid available for the academic year. Check out the policies on your campus.

- **Write a personal letter to accompany your application.** If you think there are factors that affect your ability to pay for college which are not adequately reflected in the application—such as a recent job loss—write a letter to the financial aid officer describing them.

- **Complete a Free Application for Federal Student Aid (FAFSA) and Financial Aid PROFILE.** The FAFSA and PROFILE are standard forms used to assess a student's financial capabilities and determine how much the student and family can be expected to contribute toward college expenses. One or both of the forms are used by almost every college. They require a great deal of information, including past, present, and expected income from all sources. Copies of several tax returns from prior years are also required.

  Be scrupulously honest when you complete the forms, which you can do on the Web at **www.fafsa.ed.gov** (for the FAFSA) and **profileonline.collegeboard.com** (for the PROFILE). If you fail to include a source of income that is later discovered by a financial aid provider, you may be required to repay immediately any aid that you have received. In addition, you may face disciplinary measures that put your education in jeopardy; in the worst case, you may even face legal charges.

- **Wait.** It takes time for loan applications to be processed and financial aid decisions to be made. Be prepared to wait, and consider contingency plans for various possibilities.

Evaluate Your Financial Aid Package

Sometime later, when the college has had time to consider your application for aid, you will receive an official response. This is most likely to be in the form of a "package"—a combination of loans, grants, scholarships, and, perhaps, an offer of an on-campus job. This is the time for a thorough evaluation of the offer. Consider the various elements of the package carefully to determine whether, taken together, they will fully meet your financial needs.

Keep in mind that you may not have to accept every element of the package that is offered to you. For instance, you may decide to accept a scholarship but turn down a loan. That decision may mean that you'll have less debt after you graduate, but that you'll have to work more hours at a part-time job—a trade-off that you may or may not wish to make.

Discussion Prompt: Direct the conversation to the discussion about the value of a college education in Chapter 1.

What if the package doesn't seem sufficient? The most important thing is not to give up. A polite visit or call to the financial aid office is in order.

When you speak to someone from financial aid, lay out your difficulty with the package. If the aid is so low that you won't be able to attend college, let the financial aid office know. If you had noted special circumstances in a letter, ask if they were taken into account. (Sometimes letters and other vital pieces of information get overlooked.) Ask if there is a formal appeal process and, if there is, ask how to begin it.

Your main goal is to get the financial aid office to take a second look at your application. By being polite and to-the-point in your dealings with the office staff, you stand a better chance of having them reevaluate your application.

Having good grades will help your chances of getting the financial aid office to take a second look, and poor grades will hurt: If you are not doing well in your classes, you have less bargaining power.

What if the school is unable to come up with a greater level of support? The first step is to ask the staff of the financial aid office for advice. They may be able to suggest an approach that you initially overlooked. The second step is to redouble your research efforts. You may be able to take out a loan to make up the deficit. Finally, consider alternatives to full-time college attendance. It may be preferable to attend school part-time while working than to give up college altogether or to get so much into debt that it will be hard to pay off your loans.

Above all, don't give up! If it's important enough to you, you will be able to find some way to afford an education.

Show Me the Money: Building a Financial Philosophy

It's hard to forget the famous line from *Jerry McGuire,* the movie in which Tom Cruise plays a sports agent: "Show me the money." That blunt statement might be used to illustrate one financial philosophy—that life revolves around money.

Many would disagree. For instance, authors Vicki Robin and Joe Dominguez argue in their book *Your Money or Your Life*[5] that most people find that money is a controlling force in their lives and, consequently, their major source of stress. Acquiring and spending money becomes an obsession, and the simple pleasures of life are lost. They outline an alternative approach in which we reprioritize our values, live frugally, and ultimately achieve financial independence.

Whether you choose to follow the path of Jerry McGuire or that of Vicki Robin and Joe Dominguez, the important thing is to develop your own personal financial philosophy. Consider the role that money plays in your life. How much does money motivate what you do? Are you interested in becoming rich, or do you tend to think more in terms of simply having enough to have a comfortable life, without lots of luxuries? What activities bring you the greatest satisfaction in life? Do those activities require a certain level of income? Explore these questions further in Try It 5 on page 376.

College is one of the biggest investments that you'll ever make. If you only think of it in terms of its eventual financial payoff—getting a better job and leading a more affluent life—you'll be missing some central aspects of the process of educating yourself.

Keeping in Mind the Value of a College Education

Our present focus on paying for college has led us, of necessity, to focus on the dollars-and-cents of education. Without a doubt, college is expensive. On the other side of the equation, there's no question that having a college education

Discover Your Personal Financial Philosophy

Begin to create a personal financial philosophy by completing this exercise. Start by completing this Attitudes Toward Money questionnaire.

	Strongly Disagree	Disagree	Neutral	Agree	Strongly Agree
1. Money is essential for happiness.					
2. Having money guarantees happiness.					
3. Money makes no difference to one's happiness.					
4. More money equals more happiness.					
5. Beyond having enough to live modestly on, money doesn't make much of a difference.					
6. I frequently worry about money.					
7. I frequently daydream about having a lot of money.					
8. If I suddenly had to live on very little money, I could adjust easily.					
9. If I suddenly won a lot of money, I would go on a spending spree.					
10. If I suddenly won a lot of money, I would share it with my relatives.					
11. If I suddenly won a lot of money, I would give a large percentage to charity.					
12. If I found a substantial amount of cash in a bag, I would try hard to find its rightful owner.					
13. If I could carry only a briefcase full of $100 bills out of a burning building or my pet dog, I would take the dog.					
14. I plan to make a lot of money in my career.					
15. I plan to make only enough money to live in reasonable comfort.					
16. It's great to have money.					
17. Money is a necessary evil.					
18. Money is the root of all evil.					

Teaching Tip: Try It 5 is a useful exercise. Consider using it as a "Forced Choice" activity (see IRM) that will have your students on their feet and moving around the classroom.

has vast financial value: People who are college graduates earn nearly twice as much money each year as those with only a high school degree.

But the money we spend on education buys us far more than a better salary. It gives us a better understanding of the world and its people, insight into who we are, better job opportunities, and a chance to befriend people who share the common goal of becoming well-educated citizens of a global society.

After completing the questionnaire, answer these questions about your sources of satisfaction.

1. Which activities that you engaged in over the last 5 years have given you the greatest satisfaction?

2. How much money did those activities cost?

3. How would you spend your time if you could do anything you chose?

4. How much money would this cost each year?

Personal Financial Philosophy

Based on the results of your Attitudes toward Money questionnaire and the sources of your satisfaction, sum up your personal financial philosophy here in a short paragraph:

To Try It online, go to **www.mhhe.com/power**.

It would be terribly shortsighted to put a price tag on education, deciding, in effect, that if you must pay a lot you won't bother with an education. You may need to choose your school according to the tuition it charges and the financial aid package it offers you, but that's not the same as choosing to skip college altogether because it is going to be financially stressful. An experience that will permit us to reach our potential is worth *everything*.

SPEAKING OF Success

Name: Edmund Fixico

School: Fort Berthold Community College, New Town, North Dakota

Although he always had thoughts about going to college, until recently circumstances and opportunities were not right for Edmund Fixico.

"I had always planned to go to college, but I dropped out of high school in the eleventh grade," said Fixico. Two years later, he completed high school work, but higher education remained a distant dream.

Fixico started work as a bricklayer at age 19 and continued for more than two decades before finally enrolling in college. His job and starting a family took much of his time and energy.

"I had to work, but also I knew I had to go back to school someday," he said. "My wife encouraged me, and finally—at the age of 42—I enrolled at Fort Berthold Community College."

Fixico, who is pursuing a degree in Human Services, had apprehensions about his return to school.

"I was concerned that everyone would be younger than me. But the average age at Fort Berthold is about 31, which made me feel more comfortable. I also wasn't sure I could still do many basic things, like math and writing. I felt I would have to learn everything over again in a short span of time," he added.

Fixico puts in long hours of studying, staying up late after the rest of his family has gone to bed. He also learned to ask for assistance from faculty and advisors.

"I'm pretty much a shy person, so it was hard for me to ask for help," he noted. "But the classes are small, and you have more time with the instructor. You can get to know them well, and they offered a lot of support."

One of the courses that proved to be a tremendous help was a class in study strategies. "One of my first classes had a writing assignment that asked us to describe what is going on in our lives, and so I wrote about starting college," said Fixico. "I also learned how to schedule my time because I work full-time."

Fixico is determined to succeed, and he is making good progress towards his degree. A member of the Cheyenne-Arapo tribe of Oklahoma, he is motivated by a desire to show future generations of American Indians the value of a college education.

What purpose does a budget serve and how can I prepare and stick to one?

- Concerns about money can be significantly reduced through the creation of a budget by which spending and income can be planned, accounted for, and aligned with your goals.

- Budgets provide security by helping you control your finances and avoid surprises.

- The process of budgeting involves identifying your financial goals, keeping track of current expenses and estimating future expenses, and making the necessary adjustments to keep income and spending in balance.

- If financial difficulties arise, contact your creditors and arrange a plan for paying off the debt. If you need help in designing a repayment plan, nonprofit credit counselors can help.

What help is available to pay for my college education?

- Loans for education are available with reasonable interest rates and conditions, especially the ability to defer paying the loans back until after graduation. Several federal programs offer loan guarantees, interest subsidies, and lower interest rates.

- Grants offer money without requiring repayment. They are harder to receive than loans because they are typically reserved for people with exceptional financial need.

- Scholarships are usually awarded by colleges and other institutions based on either financial need or academic, athletic, or other abilities.

What is the value of a college education?

- A college degree leads to a significantly higher salary (college graduates earn nearly twice as much as those with only a high school degree).

- In addition, a college education offers a better understanding of the world, insight into ourselves, better job opportunities, and a chance to befriend people in a global society.

KEY TERMS AND CONCEPTS

Budget (p. 355)   Term (p. 370)
Loan (p. 370)   Grant (p. 371)
Principal (p. 370)   Scholarship (p. 372)

RESOURCES

On Campus

The bursar's or treasurer's office handles money affairs. Not only does it collect money owed for tuition but may perform other services such as cashing checks.

If you are receiving financial aid, there is usually a particular office devoted to the complexities of scholarships, loan processing, and other forms of aid. The personnel in the office can be very helpful in maximizing your financial aid package as well as in solving financial problems related to your schooling. If you have a problem with your finances, see them sooner rather than later.

In Print

The Student Guide (U.S. Department of Education, 2005) is the most complete resource available on student financial aid, providing up-to-date and thorough explanations of financial aid programs. You can get a free copy by calling 1-800-4-FED-AID.

In addition, *Paying for College without Going Broke* by Kalman Chany and Geoff Martz (Princeton Review, 2005) includes many practical tips for finding ways to finance a college education.

Finally, Fred Rewey's *Winning the Cash Flow War* (Wiley, 2005) offers a clear path to getting all your finances under control.

On the Web

The following Web sites provide additional information about money matters. (Although the Web addresses were accurate at the time the book was printed, check the P.O.W.E.R. Learning Web site [**www.mhhe.com/power**] for any changes that may have occurred.)

- College Answer (**www.collegeanswer.com/index.jsp**) is a valuable, time-saving tool for students and their parents who are trying to identify sources of funds to pay for college. Through this service you can receive information about scholarships, fellowships, grants, work study, loan programs, tuition waivers, internships, competitions, and work co-operative programs.

- "FinAid: The SmartStudent Guide to College Financial Aid" (**www.finaid.org/finaid. html**) provides a free, comprehensive, independent, and objective guide to student financial aid. It was created by Mark Kantrowitz, author of *The Prentice Hall Guide to Scholarships and Fellowships for Math and Science Students*. The site's "calculators" page (**www.finaid.org/finaid/calculators/**) offers loads of online calculators including: College Cost Projector, Savings Plan Designer, Expected Family Contribution and Financial Aid Calculator, Loan Payment Calculator, and Student Loan Advisor (undergraduate).

- "Managing Your Money" (**www.nd.edu/%7Efinaid/managing_money/**), sponsored by the Office of Financial Aid at Notre Dame University, offers eight links covering everything from responsible borrowing to tips on developing credit card smarts.

TAKING IT TO THE NET

1 Find four sources of financial aid. One possible strategy: Go to Yahoo! (**dir.yahoo. com**) and choose "Education," "Financial aid," then "Grants" or "Scholarship programs." What is available? What are the differences between scholarships and grants?

2 Discover three new ways to save money. Possible strategy: Using the search engine of your choice, enter the phrase "saving money." Examine the sites for tips and tricks to help you hold on to what you earn.

Overdrawn, Overwrought, and Over Her Head

Her life was a house of cards, and someone had just pulled one out from the bottom.

At least that's what it felt like to Tara Kenko. The month had started out badly when Tara found that she had made a mistake in her checking account balance and had only $439, instead of the $939 she thought she had. After paying her share of the rent—$210—she didn't have enough money left to make her car payment. So she just put the bill aside, figuring that she'd take care of it later in the month when she got paid.

Things went from bad to worse 2 days later when her car refused to start. She had to have it towed to a mechanic, who told her that it would cost about $350 to get it fixed. She didn't have that, either, but she figured she could put it on her credit card. But later, when she went to pick up her car and pay for the repair, which turned out to be closer to $400 than $350, her card was rejected. She called the credit card company from the repair shop and was told that she had exceeded her authorized credit limit. The mechanic wouldn't let her take her car until she paid for the repairs, so she was forced to leave it and catch a bus to campus.

The final straw came in her chemistry class. The instructor announced that students in the class would have to buy yet another textbook to help them with a particular set of experiments. Having already spent $150 for books in that class alone, Tara was both angry and dismayed. She had no idea how she was going to find the money to pay for the book, let alone her regular car payment and the car repairs. She was in deep financial trouble, and she didn't know what to do.

1. What should Tara do now to start addressing her problem? What steps should she take immediately?

2. Can you suggest some approaches Tara can take to deal with the problem of the new book for her chemistry class?

3. How do you think the mistake may have occurred in Tara's checking account? What advice would you give her to avoid a similar mistake in the future?

4. Given that Tara does not have a lot of leeway in her finances for multiple disasters such as the ones that befell her this month, what general course would you advise her to take as a way to plan her expenditures more effectively?

5. What steps might Tara take to decrease her expenses? What might she do to increase her income?

Stress, Health, and Wellness

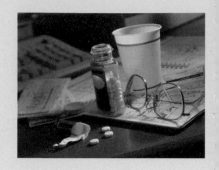

ouisa Denby's day began badly: She slept through her alarm and had to skip breakfast to catch the bus to campus. Then, when she went to the library to catch up on the reading she had to do before taking a test the next day, the one article she needed was missing. The librarian told her that replacing it would take 24 hours. Feeling frustrated, she walked to the computer lab to print out the paper she had completed at home the night before.

The computer wouldn't read her disk. She searched for someone to help her, but she was unable to find anyone who knew any more about computers than she did.

It was only 9:42 a.m., and Louisa had a wracking headache. Apart from that pain, she was conscious of only one feeling: stress.

LOOKING AHEAD >>>

Have you had days like Louisa's? Are most of your days like hers? Then you're no stranger to stress. It's something that all college students experience to varying degrees throughout their college careers. In fact, almost a third of first-year college students report feeling frequently overwhelmed with all they need to do.[1]

Coping with stress is one of the challenges that college students face. The many demands on your time can make you feel that you'll never finish what needs to get done. This pressure produces wear and tear on your body and mind, and it's easy to fall prey to ill health as a result.

However, stress and poor health are not inevitable outcomes of college. In fact, by following simple guidelines and deciding to make health a conscious priority, you can maintain good physical and mental health.

This chapter covers the ways you can keep fit and healthy during—and beyond—college. It offers suggestions on how you can cope with stress, improve your diet, get enough exercise, and sleep better. It also will help you consider particular threats to mental and physical health that you're likely to face while you are in college, including alcohol and drugs, pregnancy, sexually transmitted infections, and rape.

In sum, after reading this chapter you'll be able to answer these questions:

- **What is stress and how can I control it?**

- **What is involved in keeping fit and healthy, and why is it important for me to do so?**

- **What are the main threats to my health and well-being?**

- **What are the components of sexual health?**

▪ Living with Stress

Stressed out? Tests, papers, reading assignments, job demands, roommate problems, volunteer activities, committee work . . . It's no surprise that these can produce stress. But it may be a surprise to know that so can graduating from high school, starting your dream job, falling in love, getting married, and even winning the lottery.

Virtually *anything*—good or bad—is capable of producing stress if it presents us with a challenge. **Stress** is the physical and emotional response we have to events that threaten or challenge us. It is rooted in the primitive "fight or flight" response wired into all animals—human and nonhuman. You see it in cats, for instance, when confronted by a dog or other threat: Their backs go up, their fur stands on end, their eyes widen, and, ultimately, they either take off or attack. The challenge stimulating this revved-up response is called a *stressor*. For humans, stressors can range from a first date to losing our chemistry notes to facing a flash flood.

Because our everyday lives are filled with events that can be interpreted as threatening or challenging, stress is commonplace in most people's lives. There are three main types of stressors:

1. **Cataclysmic events** are events that occur suddenly and affect many people simultaneously. Tornadoes, hurricanes, and plane crashes are examples of cataclysmic events. Although they may produce powerful immediate consequences, ironically they produce less stress than other types of stressors. The reason? Cataclysmic events have a clear end point, which can make them more manageable. Furthermore, because they affect many people simultaneously, their consequences are shared with others, and no individual feels singled out.

2. **Personal stressors** are major life events that produce a negative physical and psychological reaction. Failing a course, losing a job, and ending a relationship are all examples of personal stressors. Sometimes positive events—such as getting married or starting a new job—can act as personal stressors. Although the short-term impact of a personal stressor can be difficult, the long-term consequences may decline as people learn to adapt to the situation.

3. **Daily hassles** are the minor irritants of life that, singly, produce relatively little stress. Waiting in a traffic jam, receiving a tuition bill riddled with mistakes, and being interrupted by noises of major construction while trying to study are examples of such minor irritants. However, daily hassles add up, and cumulatively they can produce even more stress than a single larger-scale event. (Figure 14.1 on page 386 indicates the most common daily hassles in people's lives.[2])

What Is Happening When We Are Stressed

Stress does more than make us feel anxious, upset, and fearful. Beneath those responses, we are experiencing many different physical reactions, each placing a high demand on our body's resources. Our hearts beat faster, our breathing becomes more rapid and shallow, and we produce more sweat. Our internal organs churn out a variety of hormones. In the long run, these physical responses wear down our immune system, our body's defense against disease. We become more susceptible to a variety of diseases, ranging from the common

Stress
The physical and emotional response to events that threaten or challenge us

Cataclysmic events
Sudden, powerful events that occur quickly and affect many people simultaneously

Personal stressors
Major life events that produce stress

Daily hassles
The minor irritants of life that, by themselves, produce little stress, but which can add up and produce more stress than a single larger-scale event

Teaching Tip: Connect the information regarding stress management to the information covered in Chapter 2 on time management.

FIGURE 14.1
Daily Hassles

Teaching Tip: Stress is one of the leading reasons college students visit an infirmary or a counseling center on college campuses. Spend time talking about the "daily hassles" identified in Figure 14.1 in an effort to determine ways to develop a healthy lifestyle.

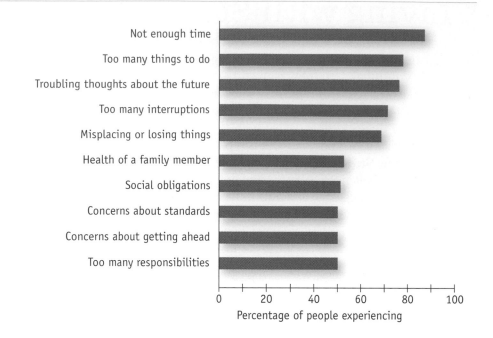

Percentage of people experiencing

Coping
The effort to control, reduce, or learn to tolerate the threats that lead to stress

PREPARE
Ready yourself physically

ORGANIZE
Identify what is causing you stress

WORK
Develop effective coping strategies

EVALUATE
Ask yourself if your strategies for dealing with stress are effective

RETHINK
Place stress in perspective

P.O.W.E.R. Plan

cold and headaches to strokes and heart disease. In fact, surveys have found that the greater the number of stressful events a person experiences over the course of a year, the more likely it is that he or she will have a major illness (see Try It 1 on page 388, "Assess Your Susceptibility to Stress-Related Illness").

Handling Stress

Stress is an inevitable part of life. In fact, a life with no stress at all would be so boring, so uneventful, that you'd quickly miss the stress that had been removed.

That doesn't mean, though, that we have to sit back and accept stress when it does arise. **Coping** is the effort to control, reduce, or tolerate the threats that lead to stress. Using the P.O.W.E.R. principles (illustrated in the P.O.W.E.R. Plan) can help you ward off stress and actively deal with it.

P REPARE: Readying Yourself Physically

Being in good physical condition is the primary way to prepare for future stress. Stress takes its toll on your body, so it makes sense that the stronger and fitter you are, the less negative impact stress will have on you. For example, a regular exercise program reduces heart rate, respiration rate, and blood pressure at times when the body is at rest—making us better able to withstand the negative consequences of stress. Furthermore, vigorous exercise produces endorphins, natural painkilling chemicals in the brain. Endorphins produce feelings of happiness—even euphoria—and may be responsible for the "runner's high," the positive feelings often reported by long-distance runners following long runs. Through the production of endorphins, then, exercise can help our bodies produce a natural coping response to stress.

If you now drink a lot of coffee or soda, a change in your diet may be enough to bring about a reduction in stress. Coffee, soda, chocolate, and a surprising number of other foods contain caffeine, which can make you feel jittery and anxious even without stress; add a stressor, and the reaction can be very intense and unpleasant.

Eating right can alleviate another problem: obesity. Around one-third of people in the United States are *obese,* defined as having body weight more than 20 percent above the average weight for a person of a given height. Obesity can bring on stress for several reasons. For one thing, being overweight drags down the functioning of the body, leading to fatigue and a reduced ability to bounce back when we encounter challenges to our well-being. In addition, feeling heavy in a society that acclaims the virtues of slimness can be stressful in and of itself.

Teaching Tip: Do not forget to give some attention to those college students who do not feel stress in their life. Sliding through life, always taking the easy way out, and never expecting the best of ourselves is certainly not the way to avoid stress.

O RGANIZE: Identifying What Is Causing You Stress

You can't cope effectively with stress until you know what's causing it. In some cases, it's obvious—a series of bad test grades in a course, a roommate problem that keeps getting worse, a job supervisor who seems to delight in making things difficult. In other cases, however, the causes of stress may be more subtle. Perhaps your relationship with your boyfriend or girlfriend is rocky, and you have a nagging feeling that something is wrong.

Whatever the source of stress, you can't deal with it unless you know what it is. To organize your assault on stress, then, take a piece of paper and list the major circumstances that are causing you stress. Just listing them will help put you in control, and you'll be better able to figure out strategies for coping with them.

Discussion Prompt: What makes us feel good? For a few minutes have your class write down as many healthy ideas as they can think of — then share them with the class.

Sources of Stress
1. Government professor talks so fast that notetaking is nearly impossible
2. Difficulty paying rent this month.
3. Not enough time to study for Tuesday's psych test

W ORK: Developing Effective Coping Strategies

A wide variety of tactics can help you deal with stress. Among the most effective approaches to coping are these:

■ **Take charge of the situation.** Stress is most apt to arise when we are faced with situations over which we have little or no control. If you take charge of the situation, you'll reduce the experience of stress. For example, if several assignments are all due on the same day, you might try negotiating with one of your instructors for a later due date.

Student Alert: Identifying the factors that cause stress is more difficult than it seems, and what is stressful to one person is not always stressful to someone else. Help your students (or let them help each other) find the real causes of their stress.

> **"A smooth sea never made a skillful mariner."**
>
> English proverb

Assess Your Susceptibility to Stress-Related Illness

Are you susceptible to a stress-related illness? The more stress in your life, the more likely it is that you will experience a major illness.

To determine the stress in your life, take the stressor value given beside each event you have experienced and multiply it by the number of occurrences over the past year (up to a maximum of four), and then add up these scores.[3]

87 Experienced the death of a spouse

77 Got married

77 Experienced the death of a close family member

76 Were divorced

74 Experienced a marital separation

68 Experienced the death of a close friend

68 Experienced pregnancy or fathered a pregnancy

65 Had a major personal injury or illness

62 Were fired from work

60 Ended a marital engagement or a steady relationship

58 Had sexual difficulties

58 Experienced a marital reconciliation

57 Had a major change in self-concept or self-awareness

56 Experienced a major change in the health or behavior of a family member

54 Became engaged to be married

53 Had a major change in financial status

52 Took on a mortgage or loan of more than $10,000

52 Had a major change in use of drugs

50 Had a major conflict or change in values

50 Had a major change in the number of arguments with your spouse

50 Gained a new family member

50 Entered college

50 Changed to a new school

■ **Don't waste energy trying to change the unchangeable.** There are some situations that you simply can't control. You can't change the fact that you have come down with a case of mono, and you can't change your performance on a test you took last week. Don't hit your head against a brick wall and try to modify things that can't be changed. Use your energy to improve the situation, not to rewrite history.

50 Changed to a different line of work

49 Had a major change in amount of independence and responsibility

47 Had a major change in responsibilities at work

46 Experienced a major change in use of alcohol

45 Revised personal habits

44 Had trouble with school administration

43 Held a job while attending school

43 Had a major change in social activities

42 Had trouble with in-laws

42 Had a major change in working hours or conditions

42 Changed residence or living conditions

41 Had your spouse begin or cease work outside the home

41 Changed your choice of major field of study

41 Changed dating habits

40 Had an outstanding personal achievement

38 Had trouble with your boss

38 Had a major change in amount of participation in school activities

37 Had a major change in type and/or amount of recreation

36 Had a major change in religious activities

34 Had a major change of sleeping habits

33 Took a trip or vacation

30 Had a major change in eating habits

26 Had a major change in the number of family get-togethers

22 Were found guilty of minor violations of the law

Scoring: If your total score is above 1,435, you are in a high-stress category and therefore more at risk for experiencing a stress-related illness. A high score does *not* mean that you are sure to get sick. Many other factors determine ill health, and high stress is only one cause. Other positive factors in your life, such as getting enough sleep and exercise, may prevent illness. Still, having an unusually high amount of stress in your life is a cause for concern, and you may want to take steps to reduce it.

To Try It online, go to **www.mhhe.com/power**.

- **Look for the silver lining.** Stress arises when we perceive a situation as threatening. If we can change how we perceive that situation, we can change our reactions to it. For instance, if your computer science instructor requires you to learn a difficult spreadsheet program in a very short time, the saving grace is that you may be able to use the skill to your advantage in getting a high-paying temporary job during school vacation. (You can practice finding the silver lining in Try It 2.)

2

TRY IT!

Look for the Silver Lining

Consider the following list of potentially stressful situations. Try to find something positive—a silver lining—in each of them. The first two are completed to get you started.

Situation	Silver Lining
1. Your car just broke down and repairing it is more than you can afford right now.	1. This is the perfect time to begin exercising by walking and using your bicycle.
2. Your boss just yelled at you and threatened to fire you.	2. Either this is a good time to open an honest discussion with your boss about your job situation, OR this is a good time to get a more interesting job.
3. You have two papers due on Monday and there's a great concert you wanted to go to on Saturday night.	3.
4. You just failed an important test.	4.
5. You're flat broke, you have a date on Saturday, and you wanted to buy some things beforehand.	5.
6. Your last date went poorly and you think your girlfriend/boyfriend was hinting that it was time to break up.	6.
7. Your parents just told you that they can't afford to pay your tuition next semester.	7.
8. You just got cut from a sports team or club activity you loved.	8.
9. Your best friend is starting to turn weird and seems not to enjoy being with you as much as before.	9.
10. You just realized you don't really like your academic major, and you're not even sure you like your college much anymore.	10.

⚎ Working in a Group:

After you have considered each of these situations individually, discuss each of them in a group. What similarities and differences in others' responses did you find? Evaluate the different responses, and consider whether—and why—some ways of reframing the situations were better than others.

To Try It online, go to **www.mhhe.com/power**.

- **Talk to friends and family. Social support,** assistance and comfort supplied by others, can help us through stressful periods. Turning to our friends and family and simply talking about the stress we're under can help us tolerate it more effectively. Even anonymous telephone hotlines can provide us with social support. (The U.S. Department of Health and Human Services maintains a master toll-free number that can provide telephone numbers and addresses of many national helplines and support groups. You can reach it by calling 1-800-336-4797.)

Social support
Assistance and comfort supplied by others in times of stress

- **Relax.** Because stress produces constant wear and tear on the body, it seems possible that practices that lead to the relaxation of the body might lead to a reduction in stress. And that's just what happens. Using any one of several techniques for producing physical relaxation can prevent stress. Among the best relaxation techniques:

    Meditation. Though often associated with its roots in the ancient Eastern religion of Zen Buddhism, meditation, a technique for refocusing attention and producing bodily relaxation, is practiced in some form by members of virtually every major religion. Meditation reduces blood pressure, slows respiration, and in general reduces bodily tension.

    How do you meditate? The process is actually rather simple. As summarized in Table 14.1, it includes sitting in a quiet room with eyes closed or focused on a point about 6 feet away from you and paying attention to your breathing. Though the specifics of what you do may vary, meditation works by helping you concentrate on breathing deeply and rhythmically, sometimes murmuring a word or sound repeatedly.

Teaching Tip: Do the meditation activity in class (Table 14.1) or invite a colleague from your counseling center to do this with your class. You may want to schedule this activity near the exam period at the end of the semester.

TABLE 14.1   Methods of Meditation

Step 1. Pick a focus word or short phrase that's firmly rooted in your personal belief system. For example, a nonreligious individual might choose a neutral word like *one* or *peace* or *love*. A Christian person desiring to use a prayer could pick the opening words of Psalm 23, *The Lord is my shepherd;* a Jewish person could choose *Shalom*.

Step 2. Sit quietly in a comfortable position.

Step 3. Close your eyes.

Step 4. Relax your muscles.

Step 5. Breathe slowly and naturally, repeating your focus word or phrase silently as you exhale.

Step 6. Throughout, assume a passive attitude. Don't worry about how well you're doing. When other thoughts come to mind, simply say to yourself. "Oh, well," and gently return to the repetition.

Step 7. Continue for 10 to 20 minutes. You may open your eyes to check the time, but do not use an alarm. When you finish, sit quietly for a minute or so, at first with your eyes closed and later with your eyes open. Then do not stand for 1 or 2 minutes.

Step 8. Practice the technique once or twice a day.

Try Progressive Relaxation

You can undertake progressive relaxation almost anywhere, including the library, a sports field, or a classroom, since tensing and relaxing muscles is quiet and unobtrusive. Although the following exercise suggests you lie down, you can use parts of it no matter where you are.

1. Lie flat on your back, get comfortable, and focus on your toes.
2. Become aware of your left toes. Bunch them up into a tight ball, then let them go. Then let them relax even further.
3. Now work on your left foot, from the toes to the heel. Without tensing your toes, tighten up the rest of your foot and then let it relax. Then relax it more.
4. Work your way up your left leg, first tensing and then relaxing each part. You may move up as slowly or as quickly as you wish, using big leaps (e.g., the entire lower leg) or small steps (e.g., the ankle, the calf, the front of the lower leg, the knee, etc.).
5. Repeat the process for the right leg.
6. Now tense and relax progressively your groin, buttocks, abdomen, lower back, ribs, upper back, and shoulders.
7. Work your way down each arm, one at a time, until you reach the fingers.
8. Return to the neck, then the jaw, cheeks, nose, eyes, ears, forehead, and skull.

By now you should be completely relaxed. In fact, you may even be asleep—this technique works well as a sleep-induction strategy.

To vary the routine, play with it. Try going from top to bottom, or from your extremities in and ending with your groin. Or target any other part of your body to end up at, and take the most circuitous route you can think of.

To Try It online, go to **www.mhhe.com/power**.

Progressive relaxation. Progressive relaxation does some of the same things that meditation does, but in a more direct way. To use progressive relaxation, you systematically tense and then relax different groups of muscles. For example, you might start with your lower arm, tensing it for 5 seconds and then relaxing it for a similar amount of time. By doing the same thing throughout the parts of your body, you'll be able to learn the "feel" of bodily relaxation. You can use the technique when you feel that stress is getting the better of you. (Use Try It 3 to experience progressive relaxation for yourself.)

■ **Remember that wimping out doesn't work—so keep your commitments.** Suppose you've promised a friend that you'll help him move, and you've promised yourself that you'll spend more time with your children. You've also been elected to the student body governing board, and you've made a commitment to bring more speakers to campus. Now you are facing all the demands connected to these commitments and feeling stressed.

Discussion Prompt: What does keeping your promises, keeping your commitments, really mean? This current generation of college students sometimes is accused of not knowing what it means to be committed to keeping a promise. Ask them to respond to this idea.

You may be tempted to cope with the feeling by breaking some or all of your commitments, thinking, "I just need to sit at home and relax in front of the television!" This is not coping. It is escaping, and it doesn't reduce stress. Ducking out of commitments, whether to yourself or to others, will make you feel guilty and anxious and will be another source of stress—one without the satisfaction of having accomplished what you set out to do. Keep your promises.

E VALUATE: Asking If Your Strategies for Dealing with Stress Are Effective

Just as the experience of stress depends on how we interpret circumstances, the strategies for dealing with stress also vary in effectiveness depending on who we are. So if your efforts at coping aren't working, it's time to reconsider your approach. If talking to friends hasn't helped ease your stress response, maybe you need a different approach. Maybe you need to see the silver lining or cut back on some of your commitments.

If one coping strategy doesn't work for you, try another. What's critical is that you not become paralyzed, unable to deal with a situation. Instead, try something different until you find the right combination of strategies to improve the situation.

R ETHINK: Placing Stress in Perspective

It's easy to think of stress as an enemy. In fact, the coping steps outlined in the P.O.W.E.R. Plan are geared to overcoming its negative consequences. But

---

CAREER CONNECTIONS

Anticipating Job Stress

Students are not the only ones who have to cope with stress. It's also one of the prime hazards of the world of work. Illnesses related to job stress result in costs of $150 billion each year.

Consequently, taking potential stress into account should be an important consideration when choosing a profession. Asking yourself the following questions can help you identify the factors that may induce stress on the job:

■ How much control over working conditions will I have? (The more control an employee has in day-to-day decision making, the lower the level of stress.)

■ What are the demands of the job? Will I face constant demands to do more work and to work

more quickly? (Higher work demands create a more stressful work environment.)

■ What is the tolerance for error? (Some occupations, such as air traffic controller, have no margin for error, while others, such as many white-collar professions, give workers a second chance if they make a mistake.)

■ How closely do my abilities and strengths match the requirements of the job? (A good match between one's abilities and the demands of a job is the best insurance against an unduly stressful work environment.)

■ How well do I cope with stress?

If your coping skills are good, you may be suited for entering a high-stress occupation. But if you have difficulty dealing with stress, choosing a career in a field that produces less stress makes more sense.

---

consider the following two principles, which in the end may help you more than any others in dealing with stress:

- **Don't sweat the small stuff . . . and it's all small stuff.** Stress expert Richard Carlson[4] emphasizes the importance of putting the circumstances we encounter into the proper perspective. He argues that we frequently let ourselves get upset about situations that are actually minor.

  So what if someone cuts us off in traffic, or does less than his or her share on a group project, or unfairly criticizes us? It's hardly the end of the world. If an unpleasant event has no long-term consequences, it's often best to let it go. One of the best ways to reduce stress, consequently, is to maintain an appropriate perspective on the events of your life.

- **Make peace with stress.** Think of what it would be like to have no stress—none at all—in your life. Would you really be happier, better adjusted, and more successful? The answer is "probably not." A life that presented no challenges would probably be, in a word, boring. So think about stress as an exciting, although admittedly sometimes difficult, friend. Welcome it, because its presence indicates that your life is stimulating, challenging, and exciting—and who would want it any other way?

▌ Keeping Well

Eat right. Exercise. Get plenty of sleep.

Pretty simple, isn't it? We learn the fundamentals of fitness and health in the first years of elementary school.

> **"The first wealth is health."**
> Ralph Waldo Emerson, author and poet

Yet for millions of us, wellness is an elusive goal. We eat on the fly, stopping for a bite at the drive-in window of a fast-food restaurant. Most of us don't exercise enough, either because we feel we don't have enough time or because it's not much fun for us. And as for sleep, we're a nation in which getting by with as little sleep as possible is seen as a badge of honor.

You can buck the trends, however; you can begin to eat more properly, exercise effectively, and sleep better by following several basic rules. They include the following:

Eating Right

- **Eat a variety of "whole" foods, including fruits, vegetables, and grain products.** Strive to eat a range of different foods. If you make variety your goal, you will end up eating the right foods. Also, the less processed the foods are, the better. Make an effort to choose "whole" foods, or foods in a state as close as possible to their natural state: brown rice is better than white rice, and both are better than a preservative-filled, packaged "rice casserole" mix.

- **Avoid foods that are high in sugar and salt content.** Read labels on product packages carefully and beware of hidden sugars and salts. Many ingredients that end in -ose (such as dextrose, sucrose, maltose, and fructose) are actually sugars; salt can lurk within any number of compounds beginning with the word *sodium.*

- **Seek a diet low in fat and cholesterol.** The fat that is to be especially avoided is saturated fat—the most difficult for your body to rid itself of.

- **Remember: Less is more.** You don't need to walk away stuffed from every meal. Moderation is the key. To be sure you don't eat more than your body is telling you to eat, pay attention to internal hunger cues.

- **Schedule three regular meals a day.** Eating should be a priority—a definite part of your daily schedule. Avoid skipping any meals. Breakfast is particularly important; get up early enough to eat a full meal.

- **Be sensitive to the hidden contents of various foods.** Soda and chocolate can contain substantial quantities of caffeine, which can disrupt your sleep and, along with coffee, become addictive. Many cereals—even those labeled "low fat"—contain a considerable amount of sugar or salt. Pay attention to labels. And watch out for fast foods: Research finds that eating fast foods just a few times a week leads to significant weight gains over the long run.[5]

The lure of fast food is difficult to resist, and eating a balanced, nutritious diet is a challenge for most college students.

- **Beware of eating disorders.** Between 1 and 4 percent of college-age women, and a smaller percentage of men, suffer from an eating disorder. Those with *anorexia nervosa* may refuse to eat, while denying that there is anything unusual in their behavior and appearance—which can become skeletal. Some 15 to 20 percent of those with anorexia literally starve themselves to death. *Bulimia* is a disorder in which individuals binge on incredibly large quantities of food, such as a gallon of ice cream and a whole pie, but later feel so much guilt and depression that they induce vomiting or take laxatives to rid themselves of the food. Eating disorders represent serious threats to health and require aggressive medical intervention.

Making Exercise a Part of Your Life

Exercise produces a variety of benefits. Your body will run more efficiently, you'll have more energy, your heart and circulatory system will run more smoothly, and you'll be able to bounce back from stress and illness more quickly.

- **Choose a type of exercise that you like.** Exercising will be a chore you end up avoiding if you don't enjoy what you're doing.

- **Incorporate exercise into your life.** Take the stairs instead of elevators. Leave your car at home and walk to campus or work. When you're on campus, take the longer way to reach your destination.

- **Make exercise a group activity.** Exercising with others brings you social support and turns exercise into a social activity. You'll be more likely to stick to a program if you have a regular "exercise date" with a friend.

- **Vary your routine.** You don't need to do the same kind of exercise day after day. Choose different sorts of activities that will involve different parts of your body and keep you from getting bored. For example, for cardiovascular fitness, you might alternate between running, swimming, biking, or using a cardio training machine.

One note of caution: Before you begin an exercise program, it is a good idea to have a physical checkup, even if you feel you're in the peak of health. This is especially true if you're starting an exercise program after years of inactivity. You also might consult a personal trainer at the gym to set up a program that gradually builds you up to more vigorous exercise.

Getting a Good Night's Sleep

Do you feel as if you don't get enough sleep? You probably don't. Most college students are sleep-deprived, a condition that causes them to feel fatigued, short-tempered, and tense. Sleep deprivation makes staying alert in class nearly impossible (see the *Course Connections* feature).

Ultimately, insufficient sleep leads to declines in academic and physical performance You can't do your best at anything if you're exhausted—or even tired.

Often the solution to the problem is simply to allow yourself more time to sleep. Most people need around 8 hours of sleep each night, although there are wide individual differences. In addition to sleeping more, there are also some relatively simple changes you can make in your behavior that will help you to sleep better. They include the following:

■ **Exercise more.** Regular exercise will help you sleep more soundly at night, as well as help you cope with stress that might otherwise keep you awake.

■ **Have a regular bedtime.** By going to bed at pretty much the same time each night, you give your body a regular rhythm and make sleep a habit.

■ **Use your bed for sleeping and not as an all-purpose area.** Don't use your bed as a place to study, read, eat, or watch TV. Let your bed be a trigger for sleep.

■ **Avoid caffeine after lunch.** The stimulant effects of caffeine (found in coffee, tea, and some soft drinks) may last as long as 8 to 12 hours after it's consumed.

■ **Drink a glass of milk at bedtime.** Your mom was right: Drinking a glass of milk before you go to bed will help you get to sleep. The reason: Milk contains a natural chemical that makes you drowsy.

■ **Avoid sleeping pills.** Steer clear of sleeping pills. Although they may be temporarily effective, in the long run they impair your ability to sleep because they disrupt your natural sleep cycles.

■ **Don't try to force sleep on yourself.** Although this advice sounds odd, it turns out that one of the reasons that we have trouble sleeping is that

To maintain the habit of exercising, you need to choose an activity you enjoy doing. In addition, working out with others, as these students at Appalachian State University's fitness center are doing, turns exercise into a social activity and gives you social support, increasing the chances you'll stick with an exercise regimen.

Staying Alert in Class

If you're having trouble staying alert and—even worse—staying awake in class, the best solution is to get more sleep. Short of that, there are several strategies you can try to help stay awake:

- Throw yourself into the class. Pay close attention, take notes, ask questions, and generally be fully engaged in the class. You should do this anyway, but making a special effort when you're exhausted can get you through a period of fatigue.

- Sit up straight. Pinch yourself. Stretch your muscles in different parts of your body. Fidget. Any activity will help you thwart fatigue and feel more alert.

- Eat or drink something cold in class. If your instructor permits it, the mere activity of eating a snack or drinking can help you stay awake.

- Avoid heavy meals before class. Your body's natural reaction to a full stomach is to call for a nap, the opposite of what you want to achieve.

- Stay cool. Take off your coat or jacket and sit by an open window. If it's warm, ask your instructor if there's a way to make the classroom cooler.

- Take off *one* shoe. This creates a temperature difference, which can be helpful in keeping you awake.

we try too hard. Consequently, when you go to bed, just relax, and don't even attempt to go to sleep. If you're awake after 10 minutes or so, get up and do something else. Only go back to bed when you feel tired. Do this as often as necessary. If you follow this regimen for several weeks—and don't take naps or rest during the day—eventually getting into your bed will trigger sleep.

Drug Abuse

For better or worse, drugs are part of all of our lives. It's virtually impossible to be unaware of the extent of the U.S. and international problem of illegal drug use, which involves millions of individuals who have used illegal substances at least once. Patterns of drug use or avoidance are often established in college. These patterns can have a big impact on your college career and your life, so it is a good idea to learn what you can now, before negative patterns of abuse, and in some cases, addiction, take hold.

Alcohol and Its Allure

The drug most likely to be found on college campuses is alcohol. It may surprise you to know that though it initially seems to raise your spirits, alcohol is actually a depressant. As the amount of alcohol one consumes increases, its depressive effects become more obvious. You've probably seen its other negative effects: Drinkers show poor judgment, their memory is impaired, and their speech becomes slurred and eventually incoherent. If you drink enough, you'll pass out. And as some well-publicized cases in the news illustrate, if you consume enough alcohol in a short period, you can die. It's that simple.

The potential negative consequences of drinking have done little to prevent the use of alcohol on college campuses. Although a not insignificant number of students drink little or no alcohol, more than 75 percent of college students say they've had a drink within the last 30 days. Some drink a great deal: 17 percent of female students and 31 percent of male students admitted drinking on 10 or more occasions during the past 30 days.[6]

Some students drink even more, and the extent of alcohol consumption can reach astonishing levels. Half of all male college students and 40 percent of all female college students have engaged in **binge drinking,** defined as having at least four (for females) or five (for males) drinks in a single sitting. Such heavy drinking doesn't just affect the drinker. Most college students report having had their studying or sleep disturbed by drunk students. Further, around a third of students have been insulted or humiliated by a drunk student, and 25 percent of women have been the target of an unwanted sexual advance by a drunk classmate.

Close to 20 million people in the United States are alcoholics, and college students make up their fair share of the total. **Alcoholics,** individuals with serious alcohol-abuse problems, become dependent on alcohol, experiencing a physical craving for it. They continue to drink despite serious consequences.

Binge drinking
Having at least four (for females) or five (for males) drinks in a single sitting

Alcoholics
Individuals with serious alcohol-abuse problems who become dependent on alcohol and continue to drink despite serious consequences

Journal REFLECTIONS ƧИOITƆƎ⅃ℲƎЯ

College Drinking Experiences

Examine your own feelings about alcohol use by answering these questions.

1. Why do you think people use alcohol?

2. What do you think the minimum age to legally drink alcohol should be, and why?

3. Do you know people who drink only to get drunk?

4. Have you ever suspected any of your friends or acquaintances of being alcoholics? Why? Did you do anything about it?

5. Efforts to alter one's states of consciousness through the use of alcohol or other drugs are found in almost every culture. Why do you think this is the case?

Furthermore, they develop a tolerance for alcohol and must drink increasing amounts to experience the initially positive effects that alcohol brings about.

The long-term consequences of high levels of alcohol consumption are severe. Heavy drinking damages the liver and digestive system, and can even affect brain cells. In fact, virtually every part of the body is eventually affected by heavy alcohol use.

To examine your own use of alcohol, complete Try It 4 on page 400.

Nicotine

Despite the recent multibillion-dollar tobacco settlements between all 50 state governments and the manufacturers of cigarettes, smoking remains a significant health problem. Smoking causes lung damage and increases the risks of developing cancer, emphysema, and a host of other diseases.

Why do people smoke, when the evidence is so clear about its risks? They start to smoke for a variety of reasons. Smoking is sometimes viewed as a kind of initiation into adulthood, a sign of growing up. In other cases, teenagers see smoking as "cool," a view promoted by movies and television.

> "I set some limits for myself, and my transcript thanked me for it from then on."
>
> Betty Baugh Harrison, student, University of North Carolina[7]

The problem is that, no matter what reason persuades a person to try out a few cigarettes, smoking can quickly become a habit, because a major ingredient of tobacco—nicotine—is an addictive drug. An *addictive drug* produces a biological or psychological dependence. The absence of the drug leads to a craving for it that may be nearly irresistible.

Smoking is one of the hardest addictions to break. Among the suggestions for quitting are the following:

- **Remain smoke-free one day at a time.** Don't think about not smoking tomorrow, or next week, or for the rest of your life. Instead, think of not smoking for the rest of the day. You can worry about tomorrow . . . tomorrow.

- **Visualize the consequences of smoking.** Visualize blackened, rotting lungs filled with smoke. Then think about the fresh, pink lungs that you'll have after you've stopped smoking.

- **Exercise.** The all-purpose antidote, exercise, will make you feel better physically and take your mind off smoking.

- **Use nicotine patches or nicotine gum.** "The Patch" and nicotine gum can provide enough nicotine to satisfy your craving for the drug, while permitting you to stop smoking. Physicians can also sometimes prescribe drugs that help reduce the craving for nicotine.

- **Avoid people when they're smoking.** It's nearly impossible to avoid the urge to smoke when others are lighting up. If you're trying to quit, stay away from people who are smoking.

- **Enlist the social support of family and friends.** Tell others that you're trying to quit, and accept their encouragement and praise.

- **Reward yourself.** Every few days, give yourself some kind of reinforcement for spending a period of time smoke-free. Go to a movie; buy a CD. Think about how you can afford these more easily since you aren't buying cigarettes anymore.

4

 PERSONAL STYLES

Consider Your Drinking Style

If you drink alcohol, do you have a style of use that is safe and responsible? Read the statements below and rate the extent to which you agree with them, using the following scale:

1 = Strongly disagree

2 = Disagree

3 = Neutral

4 = Agree

5 = Strongly agree

	1	2	3	4	5
1. I usually drink alcohol a few times a week.					
2. I sometimes go to class after I've been drinking alcohol.					
3. I frequently drink when I'm alone.					
4. I have driven while under the influence of alcohol.					
5. I've used a fake ID card to purchase alcohol.					
6. I'm a totally different person when I'm drinking alcohol.					
7. I often drink so much that I feel drunk.					
8. I wouldn't want to go to party where alcohol wasn't being served.					
9. I avoid people who don't like to drink alcohol.					
10. I sometimes urge others to drink more alcohol.					

The lower your score (i.e., the more 1s and 2s), the better able you are to control your alcohol consumption and the more likely it is that your alcohol use is responsible. The higher your score (i.e., the more 4s and 5s), the greater is your use and reliance on alcohol, and the more likely it is that your alcohol consumption may be reckless. If your score is over 40, you may have an alcohol problem and should seek professional help to control your alcohol usage.

To Try It online, go to **www.mhhe.com/power.**

- **Join a quit-smoking program.** Many college health services hold periodic programs to help students who want to stop smoking. By enrolling in one, you'll receive the support of others who are in the same boat as you are.

- **Keep trying.** If after quitting you start smoking again, just consider that lapse as part of the process of quitting. Many people quit several times before they manage to quit for good.

Illegal Drugs

"Just say 'no.'"

If it were only so easy. Decisions about drugs are quite a bit more complicated than simplistic antidrug slogans would have you believe. Using or not using drugs involves, at a minimum, peer pressure, your values, and the effects they have on your body, your behavior, and your self-image.

Several things are clear, however. Despite the prevalence of illicit drug use among college students—surveys show that around a third of college students report having used an illegal drug at least once in the previous year—the benefits of drug use are difficult to enumerate. Apart from a temporary high, the advantages of using drugs are nil, and the use of illegal drugs is among the riskiest activities in which people can engage. Not only does drug use make you vulnerable to arrest, but it also poses short- and long-term health risks. The escape from one's responsibilities that drugs provide is likely to make it even harder to later deal with those responsibilities—which aren't going to go away.

Not all illegal drugs are the same, and they produce widely varying effects and consequences (see Table 14.2 on page 402). But they all share a common result: a reduction in awareness of and engagement with what is happening around you.

People often fall into drug use without much thought. But doing so is still a choice. Preaching and slogans are not going to help you to make a sensible decision. You need to employ every critical thinking skill you can to determine exactly what you wish—and don't wish—to introduce into your body. Give some thought to why escape is attractive and consider seeking counseling instead. Allow yourself to consider the long- and short-term effects of drug use—both the physical effects as well as the potential effects on your own aspirations and dreams. Think about the legal consequences of drug use: A drug conviction can lead to expulsion from college and refusal by many employers to hire you. Furthermore, random drug tests are increasingly a part of corporate life, and your ability to qualify for and keep a job may be placed at risk if you use drugs—even only occasionally.

Drugs that produce addiction, such as cocaine and heroin, present a further set of problems. The lives of people with drug addictions become centered on the drug. They enter into a pattern of alternating highs—when on the drug—and lows. During their lows, much of their thinking is centered on obtaining the drug and looking forward to their next high.

Addiction's Warning Signs

Addictions to drugs—including alcohol—can begin subtly, and you may not be aware of the extent of the problem. Here are some signs that indicate when use becomes abuse:

- Feeling you need to be high to have a good time.

- Being high more often than not.

Student Alert: Who enforces the laws regarding illegal drug use on your campus - local or campus police? Have students research campus drug policies and bring this information to class.

Teaching Tip: Denial of behavior remains a big part of the problem in dealing with drug and alcohol abuse. Encourage students to keep a journal. They may find it easier to face their thoughts in private than in public.

TABLE 14.2　Illegal Drugs

Drug	Street Name	Effects	Withdrawal Symptoms/ Health Hazards
Stimulants			
Cocaine **Amphetamines**	Coke, blow, snow, lady, crack	Increased confidence, mood elevation, sense of energy and alertness, decreased appetite, anxiety, irritability, insomnia, transient drowsiness, delayed orgasm	Apathy, general fatigue, prolonged sleep, depression, disorientation, suicidal thoughts, agitated motor activity, irritability, bizarre dreams
Benzedrine	Speed		
Dexedrine	Speed		
Depressants			
Alcohol	Booze	Anxiety reduction, impulsiveness, dramatic mood swings, bizarre thoughts, suicidal behavior, slurred speech, disorientation, slowed mental and physical functioning, limited attention span	Weakness, restlessness, nausea and vomiting, headaches, nightmares, irritability, depression, acute anxiety, hallucinations, seizures, possible death
Barbiturates			
Nembutal	Yellowjackets, yellows		
Seconal	Reds		
Phenobarbital			
Rohypnol	Roofies, rope, "date-rape drug"	Muscle relaxation, amnesia, sleep	Seizures
Narcotics			
Heroin	H, hombre, junk, smack, dope, crap, horse	Anxiety and pain reduction, apathy, difficulty in concentration, slowed speech, decreased physical activity, drooling, itching, euphoria, nausea	Anxiety, vomiting, sneezing, diarrhea, lower back pain, watery eyes, runny nose, yawning, irritability, tremors, panic, chills and sweating, cramps
Morphine	Drugstore dope, cube, first line, mud		
Hallucinogens			
Cannabis	Bhang, kit, ganja, dope, grass, pot, smoke, hemp, joint, weed, bone, Mary Jane, herb, tea	Euphoria, relaxed inhibitions, increased appetite, disoriented behavior	Hyperactivity, insomnia, decreased appetite, anxiety
Marijuana			
Hashish			
Hash oil			
MDMA	Ecstasy	Heightened sense of oneself and insight, feelings of peace, empathy, energy	Depression, anxiety, panic attacks
LSD	Acid, quasey, microdot, white lightning	Heightened aesthetic responses, vision and depth distortion, heightened sensitivity to faces and gestures, magnified feelings, paranoia, panic, euphoria	Anxiety, depression, flashbacks

- Getting high to "get yourself going."
- Going to class or work high.
- Missing class or work because you are high.
- Being unprepared for class because you were high.
- Feeling regret over something you did while you were high.
- Driving while high.

- Having a legal problem due to being high.
- Behaving, while high, in a way you wouldn't otherwise.
- Being high in nonsocial, solitary situations.
- Thinking about drugs or alcohol much of the time.
- Avoiding family or friends while using liquor or drugs.
- Hiding drug or alcohol use from others.

Any one of these symptoms indicates that you have a drug or alcohol problem. If you do have a problem, seek professional help. Addictions to illegal drugs or alcohol are extremely difficult to deal with on your own. No matter how good your intentions, almost no one can overcome the cravings brought about by an addiction to a particular substance without help.

Here are some places to which you can turn:

1. **College health services, counseling centers, and mental health centers.** Most colleges provide services to help you overcome an addiction. They can evaluate the extent of the problem and refer you to the proper place for further help. (To learn about your own campus resources, complete Try It 5 on page 404.)

2. **Drug treatment centers and clinics.** Sometimes located in hospitals and sometimes independently run, drug treatment centers or clinics can provide help. You can also check your telephone book for a local listing of Alcoholics Anonymous or Narcotics Anonymous.

3. **Government hotlines.** The federal government provides extensive information about drug and alcohol use. For starters, call the National Clearinghouse on Alcohol and Drug Information at 1-800-729-6686. For alcohol difficulties in particular, call the National Council on Alcoholism and Drug Dependence at 1-800-622-2255. For drug problems, you can call the National Institute on Drug Abuse at 1-800-662-4357. Finally, you can visit the National Council on Alcoholism and Drug Dependence Web site at **www.ncadd.org**, for help with alcohol and drug problems.

Relationships and sexuality raise substantial issues, involving your attitudes, beliefs, values, and emotions, as well as your body, in a complex intermix. Making responsible decisions requires that you know who you are and what's important to you.

Sexual Health and Decision Making

Relationships. Contraception. AIDS. Rape.

Sexual health includes a host of issues, involving not just your body but your heart and mind as well. In fact, it is often said that our most important

5

TRY It!

Tap Into Campus Resources

Complete the following chart to identify the campus office locations and their services that deal with alcohol and drug problems.

Campus Resource	Where Is It?	What Service Does It Provide?	How Do You Get in Touch?
Health Center			
Mental Health Center			
Campus Chaplain			
Drug and Alcohol Education Center(s)			
Counseling Center			
Residential Life Office			
Ombudsman			
Campus Security Services			
(add other offices here)			
(add other offices here)			
(add other offices here)			
(add other offices here)			

To Try It online, go to **www.mhhe.com/power**.

Student Alert: After students complete Try It 5, they will have a better understanding of campus resources involved in health and wellness issues. Do they understand the commitment to confidentiality that most professionals bring to discussions involving sexual behavior? If students do not trust the system, they will not use it.

sexual organ is our brain. It determines what we view as sexually arousing, and it's what we use to make decisions and choices about our sexuality.

Although the focus of the brief discussion of sexual health here is on strategies for protecting yourself (from sexually transmitted infections, pregnancy, and rape), sexual decisions are also a reflection of your basic values. You can't make responsible decisions about sex without knowing what is important to you and how you view yourself. So you don't want to wait until a sexual encounter begins before thinking through your views of sexuality and what is and is not right for you. Deciding to have—or not to have—sex should be a conscious decision between two individuals which must be made with great responsibility and thoughtfulness.

Avoiding Sexually Transmitted Infections

Right now, one out of five people in the United States is infected with one of the many types of **sexually transmitted infections (STIs)**—infections acquired through sexual contact. At least one out of four will eventually contract an STI at some point in life.

There are many varieties of STIs, although all share a similar origin: sexual contact. Depending on the type of infection, symptoms may include warts in the genital area, pelvic infection, painful urination, infertility, blindness, and even death.

The STI that has had the greatest impact in the last decade is **acquired immune deficiency syndrome (AIDS)**. Although in the United States it initially most often affected homosexuals, AIDS quickly spread among heterosexuals. Some populations are particularly affected, such as intravenous drug users. Worldwide, more than 16 million people have already died from the disease. Some estimates suggest that 40 million people now carry the AIDS virus. Despite new treatments, AIDS remains incurable. In the United States, AIDS is the leading cause of death among men 25 to 44 years of age and the third leading cause of death among women in that age range.

Although AIDS is the best-known STI, the most common is chlamydia, an infection that if left untreated can cause sterility in some sufferers. Genital herpes is a virus that appears as small blisters or sores around the genitals. Although the sores heal after several weeks, the infection can remain dormant and reappear periodically. Other STIs, although somewhat less common, afflict millions of people. (See Table 14.3 on page 406 for a summary of the common STIs.)

The only completely effective way to avoid sexual transmission of these infections is through avoiding sexual activity. However, many people are unwilling to make such a choice. Several alternative approaches, called "smart sex" or "safe sex" practices, reduce the risk of contracting STIs. They include the following:

- **Know your sexual partner—well.** You should not have sexual contact with a person who is only a casual acquaintance. You want to know the person well enough to have a discussion with him or her in which you both talk about your sexual histories.

- **Prevent the exchange of bodily fluids during all sex acts.** Avoid unprotected intercourse (vaginal or anal) and oral sex.

- **Use condoms.** Condoms not only prevent the spread of AIDS and other STIs, but they also prevent pregnancy.

- **Be faithful to a single partner.** People in long-term relationships with only one other individual are less likely to contract AIDS and other STIs than those with multiple sexual partners.

Preventing Unwanted Pregnancy

There is one and only one totally effective means of preventing pregnancy: Not having sexual intercourse. **Abstinence,** refraining from intercourse, only works, however, if you practice it with absolute consistency—something that many people find difficult. But it certainly is possible. Despite the folklore that insists "everybody's doing it," they're not. In fact, if you think critically about what others say about their sexual activity, you'll probably conclude that what they say is more boasting (and outright lying) than straight talk.

Sexually transmitted infections (STIs)
Infections acquired through sexual contact

Acquired immune deficiency syndrome (AIDS)
A lethal, sexually transmitted disease that causes the destruction of the body's immune system

Teaching Tip: Invite a nurse or doctor who is comfortable talking to college students to address issues related to sexually transmitted diseases.

Abstinence
The avoidance of sexual contact

TABLE 14.3   Commonly Sexually Transmitted Infections

	Cause	Transmission	Symptoms
AIDS—HIV	Human immunodeficiency virus (HIV)	Coming in direct contact with infected blood, semen, or vaginal secretions. Anal or vaginal intercourse, being born to an infected female, receiving infected blood or blood products, or sharing needles and syringes with someone infected with the HIV virus.	In early stages of infection with HIV there typically are no symptoms. As the disease progresses the following are usual symptoms: Chronic or swollen glands. Weight loss of more than 10 pounds. Flu-like symptoms that persist. Purple spots on the skin and inside the mouth, nose, or rectum. Unusual susceptibility to parasitic, fungal, bacterial, and viral infections or certain cancers.
Chlamydia	Bacteria	Vaginal or anal intercourse or oral sex with someone who is infected.	Many infected people have no symptoms, but when present the most common are the following: Pain, burning or "itching" sensations with urination. Vaginal infections may be associated with abnormal discharge. Oral infections may be exhibited by a sore throat but usually have no symptoms. Penile infections may be associated with a yellowish discharge.
Gonorrhea	Bacteria	Vaginal or anal intercourse or oral sex with someone who is infected.	Many infected people have no symptoms but are still contagious. Most common symptoms are the following: Pain, burning or "itching" sensations with urination. Vaginal infections may be associated with abnormal discharge. Oral infections may be exhibited by a sore throat but usually have no symptoms. Penile infections may be associated with a yellowish discharge.
Hepatitis A	Virus	Spread through contaminated feces and anal–oral contact during sexual activity.	Symptoms for hepatitis A and B will be similar: nausea, vomiting, diarrhea, fatigue, lack of appetite, dark urine, light stools, and/or abdominal tenderness.
Hepatitis B	Virus	Spread via blood by sexual contact or via an injection with a contaminated needle.	Symptoms for hepatitis A and B will be similar: nausea, vomiting, diarrhea, fatigue, lack of appetite, dark urine, light stools, and/or abdominal tenderness.
Genital Herpes	Herpes simplex virus (HSV)	Contact with virus in infected blisters or virus being shed from the site of previous infections that may have no symptoms.	Cluster of tender, painful blisters, ulcers, or sores typically on or around the lips, mouth, genitals, or anus. Symptoms may be very mild or not present at all, but people are still infected and contagious. Blisters, ulcers, and sores last one to three weeks during initial outbreaks. Lesions heal, but person still has herpes. Lesions commonly recur without being re-exposed to the disease.
Genital Warts	Human papilloma virus (HPV)	Vaginal or anal intercourse or oral sex with someone who has the virus.	Small bumpy "cauliflower" looking warts that are usually painless and appear on or around the genitals or anus. Itching and burning around the lesions may occur, but such symptoms are rare. Infections without symptoms are common.

Those who do want to have a sexual relationship can still avoid pregnancy. Methods of contraception include the following:

- **Birth control pills.** Composed of artificial hormones, birth control pills are among the most effective ways of preventing pregnancy—as long as they are taken as prescribed. Except for women with certain medical conditions, the side effects are minimal.

- **Implants.** One of the newest forms of birth control, implants work through a simple surgical procedure in which a small capsule is inserted into a woman's arm. Implants last for 5 years, preventing pregnancy for the entire period. With few side effects, implants are highly effective, but they are only practical for women who wish to avoid pregnancy for extended periods.

- **Intrauterine device, or IUD.** IUDs are small pieces of plastic or copper inserted by a medical practitioner into a woman's uterus. Although highly effective, some have been found to produce unacceptable side effects, including infections and scarring that can make it impossible for a woman to get pregnant when she wants to.

- **Diaphragms and cervical caps.** Diaphragms and cervical caps are circular, dome-shaped pieces of thin rubber that a woman inserts into her vagina to cover the cervix. A sperm-killing (spermicidal) cream or jelly must be used simultaneously, and the diaphragm or cervical cap must be removed after sexual intercourse. Although side effects are few, the risk of pregnancy is somewhat higher than with the other forms of birth control we've discussed; some 18 percent of women using them become pregnant.

- **Condoms.** Condoms are thin sheaths that fit over the penis and prevent sperm from entering the vagina. When used with a contraceptive jelly that kills sperm and positioned properly, condoms are highly effective, with 2 pregnancies per 100 users per year. But with condoms used as they typically are, there are 15 pregnancies per 100 users per year.

- **Injections.** Progestin, administered as an injection every three months, provides excellent protection, but it cannot be used for more than two years.

- **Ring.** A polymer ring with hormones is worn in the vagina for three weeks, and then removed for one week. It provides excellent protection when used properly.

- **Contraceptive sponge.** The sponge, shaped like a large mushroom cap, is inserted into the vagina. It can be left in place for 24 hours, during which time it can be used for multiple acts of intercourse. Although it has few side effects, it has a failure rate of between 17 and 25 percent.

- **Periodic abstinence.** The only form of birth control that involves no chemical or mechanical intervention, periodic abstinence (also known as the rhythm method) consists of refraining from intercourse during times in a woman's menstrual cycle when pregnancy is possible. With a failure rate of 20 percent, periodic abstinence requires close scrutiny of calendars, body temperature, and cervical mucus—all of which can be indicators of the time of the month to avoid intercourse.

- **Sterilization.** Sterilization is a surgical procedure that causes a person (either a man or a woman) to become permanently incapable of having children.

- **Emergency contraception.** Several forms of birth control can prevent pregnancy after unprotected intercourse. These involve using increased doses of certain oral contraceptive pills within 72 hours or insertion of a copper intrauterine device (IUD) within 5 to 7 days following unprotected sex.

- **Withdrawal and douching (*ineffective* birth control).** Withdrawal, in which a man removes his penis from a woman's vagina before ejaculating, and douching, flushing the vagina with a liquid *after* the man has ejaculated, just don't work. *They should not be used for birth control* because they are so ineffective.

Date Rape

Date rape
Forced sex in which the rapist is a date or romantic acquaintance

We usually think of rape as a rare crime, committed by strangers. Unfortunately, rape is surprisingly common and rapists usually know their victims. In a national survey conducted on college campuses, one out of eight women reported having been raped. In about half the reported cases, the rapists were first dates, casual dates, or romantic acquaintances—situations categorized as **date rape.** Overall, women are far more likely to be raped by someone they know than by a stranger. There is a 14 to 25 percent chance that a woman will be the victim of rape during her lifetime.[8] Although date rape is the more common type on campus, it is only different from any other form of rape in that the victim is acquainted with the rapist.

What leads to rape? Most often, rape has less to do with sex than with power and anger. Rapists use forced sex to demonstrate their power and control over the victim. The rapist's pleasure comes not so much from sex as from forcing someone to submit. Sometimes sexual behavior is a demonstration of the rapist's rage at women in general.

In addition, rapes sometimes are brought about by the common—but untrue—belief that when women offer resistance to sex, they don't really mean it. If a man holds the view that when a woman says no to sex, she really means yes, he is likely to ignore a woman's protests, and the encounter may end in rape. Some men may even believe that it is unmasculine to accept no for an answer.

Discussion Prompt: The issue of violence in relationships of college-aged students is a difficult but important one. Open the floor to your students and encourage them to share their views.

Some rapists employ the illegal drug rohypnol, which has come to be known as the "date rape drug." When it is mixed with alcohol, it can prevent victims from resisting sexual assault. People who are unknowingly given the drug don't even remember the rape, so it's important to keep a careful eye on anything one drinks at a party.

Whatever the causes, rape is devastating to the victim. Victims experience extreme anxiety, disbelief, fear, and shock. These reactions may linger for years, and rape victims may experience a long-lasting fear of entering into relationships. (Victims of rape and other sexual assaults can call a 24-hour hotline at 1-800-656-HOPE or visit the Rape, Abuse, and Incest National Network Web site at **www.rainn.org**.)

Student Alert: Many states have specific laws that apply to sex and alcohol/drug use. Do your students know the facts?

Both men and women must be sensitive to the issue of date rape. Among the suggestions for reducing its incidence are the following:

- **Set limits.** You have the right to set firm limits, and these should be communicated clearly, firmly, and early on.
- **No means no.** When a partner says no, it means no—nothing else.
- **Be assertive.** You should never passively accept being pressured into an activity in which you don't want to engage. Remember that passivity may be interpreted as consent.

- **Communicate.** Women and men should talk about their views of sexual behavior and what is and is not permissible.

- **Be vigilant.** Women should keep close tabs on what they are given to drink in social situations; victims of date rape have sometimes been given mind-altering drugs.

- **Avoid assumptions.** Don't assume that certain kinds of dress or flirtatious behavior are an invitation to sex.

- **Keep in mind that alcohol and drugs cloud judgment.** Nothing hinders communication more than alcohol and drugs.

■ Responding to Death and Grief

One of the most stressful experiences that one can endure is the death of a loved one. Even if the death is not unexpected, as with an elderly grandparent, the finality and sense of loss can be immense. When it is a surprise—as when a friend commits suicide, a family member is killed in war, or a parent unexpectedly succumbs to a heart attack—the pain can be overwhelming.

Although everyone's grief is different, people's reactions usually follow a pattern. Initially, people feel shock, numbness, and may even deny the death. Reality soon sets in, however, and people experience the pain of the death. They typically feel enormous sadness, depression, and yearning for the dead individual.

In time, however, people accept the death and move on with their lives. Although intense feelings of grief may occur, people usually are able to pick up their lives, and their happiness returns to its previous level.

If you experience the death of a loved one, there are several things you can do to maintain your mental health and your academic standing:

- Expect that your grief will be intense and painful—but understand that it will not always be so painful. With time, feelings of sadness begin to subside.

- Talk to others about your feelings. Family and friends, some of whom may also be experiencing the grief, can help you sort out your reactions and bring you comfort.

- Don't hesitate to voice your recollections of the person who has died. Talking about the person who has died can be therapeutic.

- Be sure to let your college officials know about your situation. If you have to leave campus to attend a funeral, tell someone in your Dean's Office, and they can contact your instructors. When you return to campus, get in touch with each of your instructors to catch up on the work you missed.

SPEAKING OF
Success

Name: Justin McCarthy

School: Washington College, Chestertown, Maryland

Justin McCarthy was an all-around athlete in high school—he wrestled and played football, soccer, and lacrosse. He was a good student, too. But things changed when he became a freshman at Washington College.

"Sports always played a huge role in my life," McCarthy said. "In high school I could play sports and do my work, but in college I found both to be much more demanding. I had almost convinced myself that studying and sports were no different in college, but soon I was struggling at both."

McCarthy attributes his problems to his living situation in college. He shared a residence with an all-male, all-athlete group, and it proved to be the wrong setting for him.

"We all just hung out and procrastinated. Wasting time was our biggest problem," he said. "We were all so happy to be in college, but we didn't understand that to stay there we had to commit ourselves and discipline ourselves to the work."

At the end of his freshman year McCarthy had a dismal 1.75 grade point average, and it became clear that something had to give.

"My mother would tell me that if I put half the effort into my studies that I put into sports, I would be fine," McCarthy recalled. "I heard her, but I never listened. But that summer I realized I had to make some changes and reevaluate my priorities."

McCarthy made two major changes when he returned to campus as a sophomore. First, he changed his living situation, and second, he got organized.

"I went from living with all these guys who weren't sure what they wanted to do, to a more controlled environment. I moved in with some of my best friends who were organized and motivated," he said. "I started to take notes, to highlight reading assignments. I noted when tests and papers were due, established a rapport with my teachers, and, instead of sitting in the back of the class, I started to sit up front.

"I've completely evolved into this person who is constantly organized and dedicated to his goals. Now I'm willing to sacrifice and study that extra hour. I didn't know what success was like before."

At the end of his sophomore year McCarthy's grade point average jumped to 3.1. "My whole outlook and perspective have come full circle since my freshman year," he noted. "I know if I try a little harder I can attain the goals that I set for myself."

What is stress and how can I control it?

■ Stress is a common experience, appearing in three main forms: cataclysmic events, personal stressors, and daily hassles. Excessive stress is not only unpleasant and upsetting, but it also has negative effects on the body and mind.

■ Coping with stress involves becoming prepared for future stress through proper diet and exercise, identifying the causes of stress in one's life, taking control of stress, seeking social support, practicing relaxation techniques, training oneself to redefine and reinterpret stressful situations, and keeping one's promises.

What is involved in keeping fit and healthy, and why is it important for me to do so?

■ For all people, keeping fit and healthy is both essential and challenging. It is vital to learn to eat properly, especially by eating a variety of foods on a regular schedule and by restricting your intake of fat, cholesterol, and salt.

■ Exercise is valuable because it improves health and well-being. Choosing exercises that we like, making everyday activities a part of exercise, and exercising with others can help form the habit of exercise.

■ The third key element of good health is sleeping properly. Good exercise and eating habits can contribute to sound sleep, as can the development of regular sleeping habits and the use of sleep-assisting practices.

What are the main threats to my health and well-being?

■ One of the major threats that college students (and others) face is the improper use of drugs. The most commonly abused drug is alcohol, which is a depressant (despite an initial reduction of inhibitions and feeling of euphoria) and can lead to a physical or psychological dependence. Nicotine is the second most commonly abused drug.

■ The use of illegal drugs presents not only potential dangers related to law-breaking and prosecution, but short- and long-term health risks as well. Drugs cause a reduction in awareness and involvement in life, and some drugs can be dangerously addictive.

Teaching Tip: Make it a point to let your students know that you care about them and their lifestyle choices. You are a new and influential role model for them.

What are the components of sexual health?

■ Sexual health is as important as other forms of health. People must make their own individual decisions about their sexuality and how they will express it.

■ Many forms of contraception are available, ranging from abstinence to surgical implants. Each form has different procedures, risks, and effectiveness.

■ The incidence of sexually transmitted infections (STIs) is high in the United States, with about 25 percent of the population contracting an STI at some point in life.

■ Rape is a surprisingly common crime, with most victims knowing the rapist—often in a circumstance known as date rape.

KEY TERMS AND CONCEPTS

Stress (p. 385)
Cataclysmic events (p. 385)
Personal stressors (p. 385)
Daily hassles (p. 385)
Coping (p. 386)
Social support (p. 391)
Binge drinking (p. 398)

Alcoholics (p. 398)
Sexually transmitted infections (STIs) (p. 405)
Acquired immune deficiency syndrome (AIDS) (p. 405)
Abstinence (p. 405)
Date rape (p. 408)

On Campus

Your college health service/medical provider is the first line of defense if you become ill. The staff can provide you with advice and often medical care and can give help if you are the victim of rape or in other emergencies. Furthermore, colleges often have health education offices that help educate students on safer sex practices, on how to eat in healthier ways, and generally on how to increase wellness. Finally, colleges sometimes offer stress reduction workshops to help students cope more effectively.

In Print

The title says it all: *The Everything Stress Management Book: Practical Ways to Relax, Be Healthy, and Maintain Your Sanity* (Adams Media, 2002), by Eve Adamson, offers a guide to both the reasons we experience stress and ways of coping with it.

The New York Times Book of Health: How to Feel Fitter, Eat Better, and Live Longer (Times Books, 1998), by Jane Brody, provides an up-to-date, commonsense guide to living well.

Deborah Schoeberlein's *EveryBody: Preventing HIV and Other Sexually Transmitted Infections, Revised Edition* (RAD, 2001) offers clearheaded and accurate advice on decisions relating to sexual behavior.

On the Web

The following sites on the World Wide Web provide the opportunity to extend your learning about stress, health, and wellness. (Although the Web addresses were accurate at the time the book was printed, check the P.O.W.E.R. Learning Web site [**www.mhhe.com/power**] for any changes that may have occurred.)

■ The American Dietetic Association's Web site not only provides information for its professional members, but it also includes updated consumer tips and articles (**www.eatright.org/Public/**). Features include strategies for smart grocery shopping, discussion of the latest fad diets, and guidelines for healthy eating.

■ "Stress Management" (**stress.about.com/od/copingskills/**), on About.com, offers in-depth and comprehensive information on coping with stress. Dozens of links cover teens through the elderly, self-assessment, psychotherapy and relaxation techniques.

■ "Eating Disorders: Mirror, Mirror" (**www.mirror-mirror.org/eatdis.htm**) is a guide to eating disorders offering definitions, coping strategies, links to related organizations, and personal messages from survivors.

■ "Healthy Women" (**www.healthywomen.org/content.cfm?L1 = 3**), from the National Women's Health Resource Center, offers a number of good articles on health issues, including a concise presentation and discussion of various methods of contraception.

■ The Massachusetts Department of Public Health (**www.mass.gov/dph/cdc/bcdc.htm**) offers information on the prevention and control of sexually transmitted infections, including links to fact sheets and publications containing further information. Also discussed are tuberculosis and the West Nile virus.

TAKING IT TO THE NET

1 Find two stress reduction techniques. One possible strategy: Go to AltaVista (**www.altavista.com**) and enter the phrase "stress reduction techniques" into the search field. Examine the sites located until you find two stress reduction techniques. Try each of the techniques. Do you feel less stressed and more relaxed? Which of the techniques works best for you?

2 Locate the most-recent statistics on drug use by U.S. students. One possible approach: Go to Yahoo! (**www.yahoo.com**) and enter the phrase "drug statistics government." Examine the results and consider how they compare to your own perceptions of the extent of drug use.

The Opposing Perspectives

It started out innocently, as a date to study for an exam. And then it turned wrong.

Here's what Bob had to say:

Patty and I were in the same statistics class. She usually sat near me and was always very friendly. I liked her and thought maybe she liked me, too.

Last Thursday after class I suggested that she come to my place so we could study for midterms together. She agreed immediately.

That night everything seemed to go perfectly. We studied for a while and then took a break. I could tell that she liked me, and I was attracted to her. I started kissing her. I could tell that she really liked it.

We started touching each other and it felt really good. All of a sudden she pulled away and said "stop." I figured she didn't want me to think that she was "easy" or "loose." . . .

I just ignored her protests and eventually she stopped struggling. I think she liked it but afterwards she acted bummed out and cold.

Patty, on the other hand, had a very different view of their encounter:

I knew Bob from my statistics class. He's cute and we are both good at statistics, so when a tough midterm was scheduled, I was glad that he suggested we study together. It never occurred to me that it was anything except a study date.

That night everything went fine at first. We got a lot of studying done in a short amount of time, so when he suggested we take a break, I thought we deserved it.

Well, all of a sudden he started acting really romantic and started kissing me. I liked the kissing, but then he started touching me below the waist. I pulled away and tried to stop him but he didn't listen. After a while I stopped struggling; he was hurting me and I was scared. He was so much bigger and stronger than me. I couldn't believe it was happening to me. I didn't know what to do.

He actually forced me to have sex with him. I guess looking back on it I should have screamed or done something besides trying to reason with him, but it was so unexpected. I couldn't believe it was happening.[9]

1. Was Bob being dishonest in setting up the study date? Was he dishonest during the sexual encounter?

2. What could Patty have done when Bob began acting "romantic"?

3. Was Bob right to interpret Patty's initial responsiveness to his advances as acceptance of a sexual relationship? Was Patty "leading him on"?

4. Did Patty's initial responsiveness justify Bob's pursuing sex beyond the point at which she said "stop"?

▪ A Final Word

Throughout this book you've seen how the principles of P.O.W.E.R. Learning can be applied to a variety of situations, ranging from reading and writing to coping with stress. You can use the framework in any situation where you need to organize your thinking and behavior in a systematic way. It's a tool you can call on throughout your lifetime.

College is the beginning of a journey that leads to your future. This book has been designed to help you with the demands and challenges of college, but at the same time to prepare you for life after school. It has tried to show you that it is *you* who must make things happen to fulfill your goals and aspirations.

Ultimately, however, there are some key ingredients to success that no book can teach you and that only you can provide: integrity and honesty, intellectual curiosity, and love. I hope this book will help you as you consider what your contribution to the world will be and as you work to make that contribution.

ABBCC structure: The structure of the typical research paper, consisting of *argument*, *background*, *body*, *counterarguments*, and *conclusion*.

Abstinence: The avoidance of sexual contact.

Academic honesty: Completing and turning in only one's own work under one's own name.

Acquired immune deficiency syndrome (AIDS): A lethal, sexually transmitted disease that causes the destruction of the body's immune system.

Acronym: A word or phrase formed by the first letters of a series of terms.

Acrostic: A sentence in which the first letters of the words correspond to material that is to be remembered.

Active listening: The voluntary act of focusing on what is being said, making sense of it, and thinking about it in a way that permits it to be recalled accurately.

Advance organizers: Broad, general ideas related to material that is to be read or heard, which pave the way for subsequent learning.

Alcoholics: Individuals with serious alcohol-abuse problems who become dependent on alcohol and continue to drink despite serious consequences.

Analogy: A comparison between concepts or objects that are alike in some respects, but dissimilar in most others.

Analytic learning style: A style that starts with small pieces of information and uses them to build the big picture.

Attention span: The length of time that attention is typically sustained.

Auditory/verbal learning styles: A style that favors listening as the best approach to learning.

Binge drinking: Having at least four (for females) or five (for males) drinks in a single sitting.

Brainstorming: A technique for generating ideas by saying out loud as many ideas as can be thought of in a fixed period of time.

Browser: A program that provides a way of navigating around the information on the World Wide Web.

Budget: A formal plan that accounts for expenditures and income.

Call number: A unique classification number assigned to every book (or other resource) in a library. Call numbers are used for ease of location.

Cataclysmic events: Sudden, powerful events that occur quickly and affect many people simultaneously.

College advisor: An individual who provides students with advice about their academic careers.

Community service: Making contributions to the society and community in which you live.

Concept mapping: A method of structuring written material by graphically grouping and connecting key ideas and themes.

Coping: The effort to control, reduce, or learn to tolerate the threats that lead to stress.

Cramming: Hurried, last-minute studying.

Critical thinking: A process involving reanalysis, questioning, and challenge of underlying assumptions.

Cultural competence: Knowledge and understanding about other races, ethnic groups, cultures, and minority groups.

Culture: The learned behaviors, beliefs, and attitudes that are characteristic of an individual society or population, and the products that people create.

Daily hassles: The minor irritants of life that, by themselves, produce little stress, but which can add up and produce more stress than a single larger-scale event.

Daily to-do list: A schedule showing the tasks, activities, and appointments due to occur during the day.

Date rape: Forced sex in which the rapist is a date or romantic acquaintance.

Decision making: The process of deciding among various alternatives.

Distance learning: The teaching of courses at another institution, with student participation via video technology or the World Wide Web.

Double major: A course of study that fulfills all the requirements for two majors.

Educated guessing: The practice of eliminating obviously false multiple-choice answers and selecting the most likely answer from the remaining choices.

Electives: Courses that are not required.

E-mail: Electronic mail, a system of communication that permits users to send and receive messages via the Internet.

Emoticons (or smileys): Abbreviations used in e-mail messages that provide information on the emotion that the writer is trying to convey. Emoticons usually look like faces on their side, with facial expressions related to the intended emotion or tone.

Ethnicity: Shared national origins or cultural patterns.

Evaluation: An assessment of the match between a product or activity and the goals it was intended to meet.

Flash cards: Index cards that contain key pieces of information to be remembered.

Freewriting: A technique involving continuous, nonstop writing, without self-criticism, for a fixed period of time.

Frontmatter: The preface, introduction, and table of contents of a book.

Grade point average (GPA): Also known as *quality point average*. A numeric average in which letter grades are transformed into numbers.

Grant: An award of money that does not have to be repaid.

Hearing: The involuntary act of sensing sounds.

"I" statements: Statements that cast responses in terms of oneself and one's individual interpretation.

Impromptu talk: Unprepared presentations that require speaking on a moment's notice.

Information competency: The ability to determine what information is necessary, and then to locate, evaluate, and effectively use that information.

Instant messaging: A system that allows one to use a computer to communicate in real time with friends and instructors.

Interlibrary loan: A system by which libraries share resources, making them available to patrons of different libraries.

Internet: A vast network of interconnected computers that share information around the world.

Learning disabilities: Difficulties in processing information when listening, speaking, reading, or writing, characterized by a discrepancy between learning potential and actual academic achievement.

Learning style: One's preferred manner of acquiring, using, and thinking about knowledge.

Left-brain processing: Information processing primarily performed by the left hemisphere of the brain, focusing on tasks requiring verbal competence, such as speaking, reading, thinking, and reasoning; information is processed sequentially, one bit at a time.

Link: A means of "jumping" automatically from one Web page to another.

Listserv: A subscription service through which members can post and receive messages via e-mail on general topics of shared interest.

Loan: Funds provided by a bank, credit union, or other agency that must be repaid after a specified period of time.

Loneliness: A subjective state in which people do not experience the level of connection with others that they desire.

Long-term goals: Aims relating to major accomplishments that take some time to achieve.

Major: A specialization in a particular subject area, requiring a set course of study.

Master calendar: A schedule showing the weeks of a longer time period, such as a college term, with all assignments and important activities noted on it.

Memory consolidation: The process by which the physical links between brain cells that represent memory become fixed and stable over time.

Meta-message: The underlying main ideas that a speaker is seeking to convey; the meaning behind the overt message.

Method of loci: A memory technique by which the elements in a list are visualized as occupying the parts of a familiar place.

Minor: A secondary specialization in a discipline different from one's major.

Mnemonics: Formal techniques used to make material more readily remembered.

Motivation: The inner power and psychological energy that directs and fuels behavior.

Newsgroup: An electronic Internet area in which users may post and read messages relevant to a particular topic of the group's choosing.

Online database: An index in electronic form composed of a organized body of information on a related topic.

Overlearning: Studying and rehearsing material past the point of initial mastery to the point at which recall becomes automatic.

Paraphrase: A restatement of a passage using different words.

Peg method: A memory technique by which a series of memorized words is linked by images to a list of items to be remembered.

Personal Mission Statement: A formal statement regarding what a person hopes to achieve during his or her lifetime.

Personal stressors: Major life events that produce stress.

Plagiarism: Taking credit for someone else's words, thoughts, or ideas.

P.O.W.E.R. Learning: A system designed to help people achieve their goals, based on five steps: *Prepare, Organize, Work, Evaluate,* and *Rethink.*

Prejudice: Evaluations or judgments of members of a group that are based primarily on membership in the group and not on the particular characteristics of individuals.

Prerequisites: Requirements that must be fulfilled before a student may enroll in a course or discipline.

Presentation program: Computer application software that helps you create impressive, professional-looking visual materials that include words, charts, maps, and other graphical elements.

Principal: The stated amount of a loan.

Priorities: The tasks and activities that one needs and wants to do, rank-ordered from most important to least important.

Problem solving: The process of generating alternatives to work on.

Procrastination: The habit of putting off and delaying tasks that need to be accomplished.

Race: Traditionally, biologically determined physical characteristics that set one group apart from others.

Recall: A way to request library materials from another person who has them.

Receptive learning style: The way in which we initially receive information.

Reflective feedback: A technique of verbal listening in which a listener rephrases what a speaker has said, trying to echo the speaker's meaning.

Register: To enroll formally in courses.

Registrar: The college official designated to oversee the scheduling of courses, the maintenance of grades and transcripts, and the creation and retention of other official documents.

Rehearsal: The process of practicing and learning material to transfer it into memory.

Relational learning style: A style that starts with the big picture and breaks it down into its individual components.

Retrieval: The process of finding information stored in memory and returning it to consciousness for further use.

Right-brain processing: Information processing primarily performed by the right hemisphere of the brain, focusing on information in nonverbal domains, such as the understanding of spatial relationships and recognition of patterns and drawings, music, and emotional expression.

Scholarship: An award of money to a student based on need or merit.

Search engine: A computerized index to information on the World Wide Web.

Self-concept: People's view of themselves that forms over time, comprising three components: the physical self, the social self, and the personal self.

Self-actualization: A state of self-fulfillment in which people realize their highest potential in their own unique way.

Self-efficacy: The expectation that one is capable of achieving one's goals in many different kinds of situations.

Self-esteem: The overall evaluation we give ourselves as individuals.

Self-fulfilling prophecy: A phenomenon that occurs when we hold a belief or expectation that affects our behavior, thereby increasing the likelihood that our beliefs or expectations *will* come true.

Service learning: Courses that allow a student to engage in community service activities while getting course credit for the experience.

Sexually transmitted infections (STIs): Infections acquired through sexual contact.

Short-term goals: Relatively limited steps toward the accomplishment of long-term goals.

Social support: Assistance and comfort supplied by others in times of stress.

Spreadsheet program: Computer application software that helps with budgeting and financial projections and is necessary for accounting and engineering courses.

Stacks: The shelves on which books and other materials are stored in a library.

Stereotypes: Beliefs and expectations about members of a group that are held simply because of their membership in the group.

Stress: The response to events that threaten or challenge us.

Study groups: Small, informal groups of students whose purpose is to help members work together and study for a test.

Study notes: Notes taken for the purpose of reviewing material.

Tactile/kinesthetic learning style: A style that involves learning by touching, manipulating objects, and doing things.

Term: The length of time for which money is lent.

Test anxiety: A temporary condition characterized by fears and concerns about test-taking.

Thesis: The main point of a paper, typically stating the writer's opinion about the topic of the paper.

Time log: A record of how one spends one's time.

Transcript: A college's official record of courses taken and grades received by students.

Transferring: Changing colleges.

Unique major: Specialization in a particular subject area that is geared to the student's own needs. Not offered by all colleges, and generally requires the support of faculty to oversee the process.

Visual/nonverbal learning style: A style that favors material presented visually in a diagram or picture.

Visual/verbal learning style: A style that involves a preference for written material, favoring reading over hearing and touching.

Visualization: A memory technique by which images are formed to help recall material.

Voice: The unique style of a writer, expressing the writer's outlook on life and past writing experiences.

Web page: A location (or site) on the World Wide Web housing information from a single source and (typically) links to other pages.

Weekly timetable: A schedule showing all regular, prescheduled activities due to occur in the week, together with one-time events and commitments.

Word-processing program: Computer application software that turns a computer into a very smart typewriter.

Working backward: The strategy of starting at the desired solution or goal and working toward the starting point of the problem.

World Wide Web: A highly graphical interface between users and the Internet that permits users to transmit and receive not only text but also pictorial, video, and audio information.

Zero-sum game: A situation in which when one person wins, the other person automatically loses.

Endnotes

Chapter 1

1. "The American Freshman: National Norms for 2003," Published by American Council on Education and University of California at Los Angeles Higher Education Research Institute.
2. Gottesman, G. (1994). *College survival.* NY: Macmillan. p. 70.
3. Ibid.
4. Adapted from "How Is College Different from High School?" Web site at Southern Methodist University Altshuler Learning Enhancement Center, **www.smu.edu/alec/transition.html**.
5. Ibid.
6. Arenson, K.W. (2004, November 22). In a first, 2 CUNY students win Rhodes scholarships. *New York Times,* p. B1.

Chapter 2

1. Adapted from Ferner, J.D. (1980). *Successful time management.* NY: Wiley. P. 33.
2. National Survey of Student Engagement: 2004 Annual Report.
3. Adapted from Ferner, J.D. (1980). *Successful time management.* NY: Wiley. P. 33.
4. Gottesman, G. (1994). *College survival.* NY: MacMillan.

Chapter 3

1. Adapted from Lazear, D. (1999). *The intelligent curriculum: Using MI to develop your students' full potential.* Tucson, AZ: Zephyr Press.
2. Rosenberg, M. (1979). *Conceiving the self.* NY: Basic Books.
3. Maslow, A.H. (1987). *Motivation and personality* (3rd ed.). NY: Harper & Row.
4. **www.benjerry.com/our_company/our_mission/index.cfm**.
5. Bolles, R.N. (1999). *The 1999 what color is your parachute?* Berkeley, CA: Ten Speed Press.
6. Waldron, C. (1988, August 9). How college education enriched the lives of stars. *Jet,* pp. 16–18.
7. Herbert, S.J., & Hill, G.H. (1990). *Bill Cosby.* Danbury, CT: Grolier. P. 38.
8. Ibid., p. 40.

Chapter 4

1. Pauk, W. (2004). *How to study in college* (8th ed.). Boston: Houghton Mifflin.
2. Tyler, S. (1997). *Been there, should've done that.* Haslett, MI: Front Porch Press. P. 117.
3. Based on McPherson, J.M. (1988). *Battle cry of freedom: The Civil War era.* NY: Ballantine Books. Pp. 504–510.
4. Tyler, S. (1997). *Been there, should've done that.* Haslett, MI: Front Porch Press. P. 114.

Chapter 5

1. Tyler, S. (1997). *Been there, should've done that.* Haslett, MI: Front Porch Press. P. 126.
2. Tobias, S. (1995). *Overcoming math anxiety.* NY: W. W. Norton & Company.
3. Tyler, S. (1997). *Been there, should've done that.* Haslett, MI: Front Porch Press. P. 128.

Chapter 6

1. Bransford, J.D., & Johnson, M.K. (1972). Contextual prerequisites for understanding: Some investigations of comprehension and recall. *Journal of Verbal Learning and Verbal Behavior,* 11, p. 722.
2. Quotes from Irving, J. (December 11, 1995). Slipped away: At fifty-three, the novelist remembers his first love: wrestling. *The New Yorker,* pp. 70–77; and Gussow, M. (April 28, 1998). John Irving: A novelist builds out from fact to reach the truth. *The New York Times* on the Web. **www.nytimes.com/library/books/042898irving-novel.html**.

Chapter 7

1. Elbow, P. (2001). *A community of writers.* New York: McGraw-Hill.
2. Adapted from Gregory, H. (1999). *Public speaking for college and career.* New York: McGraw-Hill.
3. Davidson, J.W., Gienapp, W.E., Heyrman, C.L., Lytle, M.H., & Stoff, M.B. (1996). *Nation of nations: A concise narrative of the American republic.* New York: McGraw-Hill. P. 540.
4. Scale items are adapted from A. Fenigstein, A. Scheier, & A. Buss (1975). Public and private self-consciousness, assessment and theory. *Journal of Consulting and Clinical Psychology,* 43, Table 1, p. 324.
5. Wydro, K. (1985). *Thinking on your feet: The art of thinking and speaking under pressure.* Englewood Cliffs, NJ: Prentice Hall.

Chapter 8

1. Halpern, D.F. (1996). *Thought and knowledge: An introduction to critical thinking.* Mahwah, NJ: Erlbaum. P. 48.
2. Gold, P.E., Cahill, L., & Wenk, G.L. (2003, April) The lowdown on ginkgo biloba. *Scientific American,* pp. 86–91.
3. Gottesman, G. (1994). *College survival.* NY: Macmillan. P. 59.
4. Greenberg, J., & Baron, R.A. *Behavior in organizations* (6th ed.). Upper Saddle River, NJ: Prentice Hall.
5. Kandel, E.R. (1995). Steps toward a molecular definition of memory consolidation. In D.L. Schacter (Ed.), *Memory distortions: How minds, brains, and societies reconstruct the past.* Cambridge, MA: Harvard University Press.

Chapter 9

1. Tyler, S. (1997). *Been there, should've done that.* Haslett, MI: Front Porch Press.
2. Ibid.

Chapter 10

1. Liebovich, L. (2000, August 10). Choosing quick hits over the card catalog. *The New York Times,* pp. 1,6. Based on material from Eliot Soloway, University of Michigan, School of Education.
2. Adapted from Internet Search Engines. State University of New York, Albany, Libraries. February 1, 2005. **library. albany.edu/internet/engines.html**.
3. Schibsted, E. (June 1999). The legends: Jerry Yang and David Filo. *Business,* 20 June 1999.
4. Ibid.

Chapter 11

1. Adapted from Haplern, D.F. (1996). *Thought and knowledge: An introduction to critical thinking* (3rd ed.). Mahwah, NJ: Erlbaum; and Bransford, J.D. & Stein, B.S. (1993). *The ideal problem solver* (2nd ed.). New York: W. H. Freeman.
2. Table 1, "The scale of tolerance-intolerance of ambiguity," p. 34, in Budner, S. Intolerance of ambiguity as a personality variable. *Journal of Personality,* 30(7), pp. 29–50. Copyright © Duke University Press, 1962.
3. Forer, B. (1949). The fallacy of personal validation: A classroom demonstration of gullibility. *Journal of Abnormal and Social Psychology,* 44, pp. 118–123.
4. Byrne, D., & Kelley, L. (1981). *An introduction to personality* (3rd ed.). Englewood Cliffs, NJ: Prentice Hall. P. 304.
5. *21st century lives: Neurosurgeon Ben Carson.* (Accessed September 8, 2000). **www.abcnews.go.com/onair/ WorldNewsTonight/wnt000908_21st_carson_feature.html**. ABC News.
6. Ibid.

Chapter 12

1. Nolan, M.F. (1997, April 26). Tiger's racial multiplicity. *The Boston Globe,* p. A11.
2. Tatum, B.D. (1997). *"Why are all the black kids sitting together in the cafeteria?" And other conversations about race.* New York: Basic Books.
3. Malone, M.S. (1993, July 18). Translating diversity into high-tech gains. *New York Times,* p. B2.
4. Adapted from *Working it out: The newsletter for gay and lesbian employment issues,* 1992.

5. Sponholz, M., & Sponholz, J. (1996). *The Princeton Review college companion.* New York: Random House. P. 24.
6. Adapted from Hazan, C., & Shaver, P. (1987). Romantic love conceptualized as an attachment process. *Journal of Personality and Social Psychology,* 52, pp. 511–524.

Chapter 13

1. Diener, E., & Biswas-Diener, R. (2002). Will money increase subjective well-being? *Social Indicators Research,* 57, pp. 119–169.
2. Gottesman, G. (1994). *College survival.* New York: Macmillan. P. 206.
3. The College Board, "Annual Survey of Colleges, 2004."
4. *College on credit: How borrowers perceive their education debt: Results of the 2002 national student loan survey* by Dr. Sandy Baum and Marie O'Malley, Nellie Mae Corporation.
5. Dominguez, J., & Robin, V. (1993). *Your money or your life: Transforming your relationship with money and achieving financial independence.* New York: Penguin USA.

Chapter 14

1. Sax, L.J., Astin, A.W., Korn, W.S., & Mahoney, K. (1999). *The American freshman: National norms for fall 1999.* Los Angeles: Higher Education Research Institute, UCLA.
2. Chamberlain, K., & Zika, S. (1990). The minor events approach to stress: Support for use of daily hassles. *British Journal of Psychology,* 81, pp. 469–481.
3. Source of table: Marx, M.B., Garrity, T.F., & Bowers, F.R. (1975). The influence of recent life experience on the health of college freshman. *Journal of Psychosomatic Research,* 19, pp. 87–98.
4. Carlson, R. (1997). *Don't sweat the small stuff . . . and it's all small stuff.* New York: Hyperion.
5. Pereira, M., Kartashov, A.I., Ebbeling, C.B., Van Horn, L., Slattery, M.L., Jacobs, Jr., D.R., & Ludwig, D.S. (2005, January 1.) Fast-food habits, weight gain, and insulin resistance (The CARDIA Study): 15-year prospective analysis. *The Lancet,* 365, pp. 36–42.
6. Wechsler, H., Lee, J.E., Nelson, T.F., & Kuo, M. (2002). Underage college students' drinking behavior, access to alcohol, and the influence of deterrence policies. *Journal of American College Health,* 50, pp. 223–236.
7. Gottesman, G. (1994). *College survival.* New York: Macmillan. P. 160.
8. Koss, M.P. (1993). Rape: Scope, impact, interventions, and public policy responses. *American Psychologist,* 48, pp. 1062–1069.
9. Adapted from Hughes, J.O., & Sandler, B.R. (1987). *"Friends" raping friends: Could it happen to you?* Washington, DC: Association of American Colleges.

Credits

Index

Note: Page numbers followed by italicized letters *f* and *t* refer to figures and tables, respectively.

Indiana University, "Plagiarism: What It Is and How to Recognize and Avoid It" (Web site), 206
Information competency, 282–293
    definition of, 282
    libraries and, 282–284
    resources on, 296
    World Wide Web and, 284–293
Information processing
    individual styles of, 63–66, 68t
    left-brain, 68, 69t
    in notetaking, 97–108
    right-brain, 69, 69t
Injections, birth control, 407
Instant messaging (IM), 272
Instructors
    acceptance of, 93
    and course information, 242, 259–260
    distance learning and, 277
    e-mail communication with, 276
    evaluations from previous term, 242
    getting to know, 242
    goals of, identifying, 93
    instructions before test, 134
    learning styles of, connecting with, 72
    overbooked courses and, 246
    presentation programs of, making best use of, 270
    "problem," special techniques for, 106–108
    summary at end of lecture, listening for, 106
    talking with after class, 108
    teaching styles of, 70
    and tests, dislike for, 123
    virtual office hours of, 272
Intellectual property, 193
Intellectual risks, taking, 314
Intelligence, learning disabilities and, 166
Intelligent Memory (Gordon and Berger), 229
Interest rates, credit card, 366–367
Interests, exploration of
    and career choice, 85, 255
    and choice of major, 251, 254
Interlibrary loan, 284
Internal time clock, awareness of, 39
Internet
    definition of, 271
    features of, 272–273
    See also World Wide Web
Internet resources, 271–272
    for career choice, 255, 260, 291
    citing in writing assignments, 195
    for college success, 26
    for conflict resolution, 350
    for course selections, 260
    for cultural competence, 350
    for date rape, 408
    for distance learning, 280
    for drug and alcohol problems, 403
    for financial aid, 372–373
    for financial problems, 365
    for health and wellness, 412
    for learning styles, 88
    for memorization skills, 230
    for notetaking, 119
    for P.O.W.E.R. Learning, 26
    for public speaking, 206
    for reading skills, 171–172
    for service learning, 249t
    for stress management, 412
    for test-taking, 127, 146
    for time management, 57

for writing skills, 206
Internet service provider, 273
Internships, and career choice, 255
Interruptions, management of, 33, 47–48, 160
Intrauterine device (IUD), for birth control, 407
Introverts vs. extroverts, 66–67, 69t
Intuitors vs. sensors, 67, 69t
Iowa State University Web site, 286
Irving, John, 166, 170

J
Jigsaw puzzles, approaches to, 63
Job(s)
    balancing school and, 51–52
    campus, 342
    part-time, 362–364
    stress on, anticipating, 393
    See also Career(s)
Job applications, writing, 193
JobWeb (Web site), 291
Johnson, Samuel, 282
Journal, service-learning, 249
Judgers vs. perceivers, 67–68, 69t

K
Kaiser, Henry J., 309
Kantrowitz, Mark, 380
Kearsley, Greg, 88
Keeney, Ralph, 321
Keirsey, David, 88
Keller, Helen, 93
Kelly, Julia, 56
Kesselman-Turkel, Judy, 118
Key points
    highlighting or underlining, 162
    listening for, during lecture, 97–99
    in PowerPoint presentations, 270
    rephrasing during reading, 161–162
Keywords
    listening for, 98–99
    in Web searches, 289

L
Laertius, Diogenes, 54
Landor, Walter Savage, 161
Langan, John, 205
"Language and Culture" (Web site), 350
Lao Tzu, 7
Laptop(s)
    use for class notes, 97
    use for study notes, 115
LASSI (Learning and Assessment Strategies Inventory), 66
Learn More Resource Center (Web site), 26
Learning
    lasting (overlearning), 224
    as lifelong habit, 5, 256
    from mistakes, 257
    See also Learning disabilities; Learning styles
Learning and Assessment Strategies Inventory (LASSI), 66
Learning disabilities
    campus resources for, 118, 166, 171, 229
    definition of, 166
    and notetaking difficulties, 118
    overcoming, 170
    and reading problems, dealing with, 166–167
Learning styles
    analytic, 66, 68t

auditory/verbal, 63, 68t
    brain processing and, 68–69, 69t
    changes over time, 70
    definition of, 61
    and effective studying, 63, 68t
    evaluating, 62
    instructor's, connecting with, 72
    key facts about, 69–70
    left-brain processing and, 68, 69t
    personality and, 66–68, 69t
    receptive, 62–63, 68t
    relational, 66, 68t
    resources on, 88
    right-brain processing and, 69, 69t
    tactile/kinesthetic, 63, 68t
    visual/nonverbal, 62–63, 68t
    visual/verbal, 62, 68t
Lectures
    attendance of, as test preparation, 124
    notetaking during, 97–108
    See also Class(es)
Left-brain processing, 68, 69t
Lennard, Erica, 56
Librarians, 293, 296
Libraries, 282–284
    basic collections of, 282–283
    locating information in, 283–284
    World Wide Web compared with, 286, 287f
Library of Congress classification system, 284
Lifetime learning tax credit, 372
Lim, Phyllis, 118
Links, on Web sites, 286
Listening
    active, 97
    in class
        for key ideas, 97–99
        during PowerPoint presentations, 270
    in conflict resolution, 345
    in personal relationships, 339–341
    style of, determining, 98
Listservs, 272–273
Loans, 370–371
    definition of, 370
    vs. part-time job, 364
    types of, 371
Loci, method of, 217–219
Locke, John, 168
Lombardo, Allison, 26
Loneliness
    definition of, 341
    strategies for dealing with, 341–342
Long-term goals, 7
    in balancing school and work, 52
    short-term goals' fit with, 9
Long-term memory, rethinking and transfer of information into, 111
Longview Community College, "Critical Thinking Core Concepts" (Web site), 322
LSD, 402t
Lucas, Stephen, 205
Lycos (search engine), 289t

M
Machine-scored tests, 133, 135
Major(s)
    choice of, 249–256
        vs. career choice, 256
        Internet resources for, 260
        rethinking of, 247
    course requirements for, creating list of, 239, 240

Strategies for Success for Student Athletes

It was two days before the basketball game with Kansas State, and Lucas Givens had just found out that the coach had rescheduled practice. Usually this wouldn't have been a problem, but the time of the practice overlapped with an exam review session that his biology class instructor was offering.

Lucas hadn't done as well as he'd hoped on his last exam, and he really needed to do well on this test in order to get a decent grade in the course. He knew his biology instructor would notice if he missed the review session, because Lucas had been forced to take a makeup exam the last time because of another game. He understood that the instructor didn't like giving what she called "spe-

cial privileges" to athletes, and Lucas felt like his every move was being scrutinized. If he missed the review session, he knew the instructor would be unwilling to cut him any slack in the future.

To top it off, Lucas's arm wouldn't stop hurting. He'd hurt it a few weeks before, and despite hours of physical therapy, it didn't seem to be getting any better. The dull, aching pain was a constant reminder of the demands—both academic and athletic—that Lucas faced.

LOOKING AHEAD >>>

If you are a student athlete, you may find yourself in a situation similar to that of Lucas. Many student athletes at times feel overwhelmed by the day-to-day challenges that confront them as they navigate the demands of college life.

The good news is that your status as an athlete provides you with special strengths in meeting the challenges of college. You already know the importance of hard work and perseverance. You are aware of how to seek the best from yourself.

Most of all, as an athlete, you know the value of training. You realize that there are skills that you have learned that have made you a better athlete, regardless of your natural abilities. You know that the way you have developed these skills is by practicing them, over and over, until they have become a natural part of who you are.

Ultimately, you understand the equation that *hard work = success*. You recognize that good athletes are made, not born. Although certainly an athlete's natural talents are important, it is how he or she builds on those talents that determines the athlete's ultimate success.

In the same way, good students are made, not born. While academic success comes easier to some and is more

difficult for others, the way that we build on our natural talents shapes how successful we will be academically. Just as with athletics, we need to study, learn, and practice the strategies that lead to success.

In this chapter, we examine the special challenges that student athletes face. We will show you how to use the attributes and values you probably already have as an athlete to help maximize your academic success. In addition, we will discuss strategies for juggling the demands on your time and taking advantage of help that is available to you.

After reading this chapter, you'll be able to answer these questions:

- **What are the special advantages of being a student athlete that help meet the challenges of college?**

- **How can I deal most effectively with course instructors and time management issues?**

- **What are the best ways to seek and use help?**

- **How do I best deal with pain, injury, and the potential of burnout?**

Strategies for Success for Student Athletes

It was two days before the basketball game with Kansas State, and Lucas Givens had just found out that the coach had rescheduled practice. Usually this wouldn't have been a problem, but the time of the practice overlapped with an exam review session that his biology class instructor was offering.

Lucas hadn't done as well as he'd hoped on his last exam, and he really needed to do well on this test in order to get a decent grade in the course. He knew his biology instructor would notice if he missed the review session, because Lucas had been forced to take a makeup exam the last time because of another game. He understood that the instructor didn't like giving what she called "spe-cial privileges" to athletes, and Lucas felt like his every move was being scrutinized. If he missed the review session, he knew the instructor would be unwilling to cut him any slack in the future.

To top it off, Lucas's arm wouldn't stop hurting. He'd hurt it a few weeks before, and despite hours of physical therapy, it didn't seem to be getting any better. The dull, aching pain was a constant reminder of the demands—both academic and athletic—that Lucas faced.

LOOKING AHEAD >>>

If you are a student athlete, you may find yourself in a situation similar to that of Lucas. Many student athletes at times feel overwhelmed by the day-to-day challenges that confront them as they navigate the demands of college life.

The good news is that your status as an athlete provides you with special strengths in meeting the challenges of college. You already know the importance of hard work and perseverance. You are aware of how to seek the best from yourself.

Most of all, as an athlete, you know the value of training. You realize that there are skills that you have learned that have made you a better athlete, regardless of your natural abilities. You know that the way you have developed these skills is by practicing them, over and over, until they have become a natural part of who you are.

Ultimately, you understand the equation that *hard work = success*. You recognize that good athletes are made, not born. Although certainly an athlete's natural talents are important, it is how he or she builds on those talents that determines the athlete's ultimate success.

In the same way, good students are made, not born. While academic success comes easier to some and is more difficult for others, the way that we build on our natural talents shapes how successful we will be academically. Just as with athletics, we need to study, learn, and practice the strategies that lead to success.

In this chapter, we examine the special challenges that student athletes face. We will show you how to use the attributes and values you probably already have as an athlete to help maximize your academic success. In addition, we will discuss strategies for juggling the demands on your time and taking advantage of help that is available to you.

After reading this chapter, you'll be able to answer these questions:

- **What are the special advantages of being a student athlete that help meet the challenges of college?**

- **How can I deal most effectively with course instructors and time management issues?**

- **What are the best ways to seek and use help?**

- **How do I best deal with pain, injury, and the potential of burnout?**

Your Special Strengths in Meeting the Challenges of College

There is no doubt that your status as a student athlete brings with it certain advantages. For example, the strong work ethic and high expectations you need to succeed as an athlete also will help you succeed as a student.

However, at the same time each of those advantages has a downside. Specifically, consider these benefits—and their related drawbacks—to being a student athlete:

Your Work Ethic

- *The upside.* As an athlete, you know the value of hard work. You know that success in sports is unattainable unless you put in sufficient practice. This work ethic, when applied to academics, can help you maximize your own success.
- *The downside.* The long hours of work that you devote to athletics may prevent you from putting in as much time as you would like—and need—into academic endeavors. You may experience stress and unhappiness over this lack of time.

Expectations

- *The upside.* You are almost certainly the recipient of other people's high expectations for you, and you probably hold high expectations for yourself. High expectations help you maintain your motivation, and they put you in the proper frame of mind to succeed. Holding positive expectations can help you do your best.
- *The downside.* If your expectations are unrealistically high, you may be setting yourself up for disappointment. It's unlikely that you'll do equally well in every domain of your life, and you need to be realistic about what you can and cannot expect to do. Your expectations need to be realistic in order for them to be helpful. In addition, if you don't meet the expectations of others, you may feel that you have disappointed them. Such negative feelings may hinder your abilities to rebound from failure.

Availability of Student Services

- *The upside.* Colleges and universities often provide athletes with special student services to help them navigate college life. These services can range from help with registering for classes to keeping tabs on your academic progress.
- *The downside.* You may have so many demands on your time that making use of the special services may be difficult or impossible. Alternatively, you may become so dependent on student services that you lose valuable opportunities to solve problems on your own.

P.O.W.E.R. UP: Athletes are not a homogeneous group of students. Diversity is represented by different sports, different skills, different career choices, and different levels of academic preparedness. Perhaps the only thing they have in common is that they are all student athletes.

Student Alert: Student athletes are often lumped together. It is imperative for you to approach them as individuals if you are to be a trusted academic mentor.

Teaching Tip: Do not miss an opportunity to explore time management skills in this chapter. There are many student athletes who are outstanding time managers and who may have a great deal to teach your class.

Teaching Tip: Academic support services differ greatly from campus to campus. The placement of these services says much about the campus philosophy regarding academic support. Ask your students to list the resources available to support their academic success. Are these services available only to student athletes or are they available to all students? What advantages or disadvantages result from the manner in which these services are accessed?

Social Networks

- *The upside.* You have a built-in social network. One of the greatest challenges students face when they begin college is building a network of friends. Because you are playing a sport, your teammates provide a ready-made group of people who are probably similar to you in many ways.
- *The downside.* Although it is usually easy to make friends among your teammates, it may be more difficult to make friends who are not athletes. You may have limited time available to socialize and to expand your social network. Furthermore, because your teammates are having experiences similar to yours, they may not be able to provide the objective advice and support that you might be able to get from a friend who is not part of your athletic network.

Discussion Prompt:
Isolation and loneliness are often issues for student athletes because of team obligations and expectations. Balancing the demands of the sport and the rich world of co-curricular offerings on a college campus is extremely tough. Explore this topic with your students.

Physical Health

- *The upside.* As an athlete, you are probably at the peak of physical conditioning. The hours of practice you put in help keep your body in excellent shape.
- *The downside.* Your health may be compromised by the wear and tear on your body that you suffer during training. You may experience persistent pain, and you are subject to physical injuries. There may also be restrictions on what you can and cannot do, and if you are injured, it may take a long time to heal and regain your physical strength.

Journal REFLECTIONS

On Being a Student Athlete

1. What do you enjoy most about your participation in college athletics?

2. Have your course instructors treated you, as an athlete, differently from nonathletes? How?

3. What academic difficulties have you faced because of your participation in college athletics?

4. What academic advantages have you experienced because of your participation in college athletics?

Public Visibility

- *The upside.* If you play in a highly visible sport on campus, you may be a role model for others. Being a role model is a real responsibility, but it can provide significant benefits if you handle it wisely. Others may seek out your opinion and ask your advice. You may influence how campus issues are resolved, and you may have the opportunity to participate in fund-raising for causes you support. You may inspire disadvantaged children and adolescents to become more involved in academics and to attend college.

Discussion Prompt:
Ask student athletes to discuss their thoughts about the expectation to be role models.

- *The downside.* There's a downside to being highly visible: Your every move may be scrutinized. Each word you utter in class, every object that you pick up while browsing in a store, even what you order at a fast-food restaurant may be analyzed and dissected because of your notoriety. That means you must be on your best behavior—literally all of the time. Use this test: If you wouldn't want to have something you do on the front page of your college newspaper, then don't do it.

> **"There are a lot more gifted people that have surrounded me throughout my life. What separates me is my work ethic."**
>
> Anonymous baseball player[1]

Teaching Tip:
Ask your student athletes to report regularly their "points of pride" from their participation in sports. Cut out articles in local and student newspapers highlighting their successes and post them in the classroom or your office. Let them know that you know what is going on.

Financial Issues

- *The upside.* For many athletes, the only reason that they are able to attend college may be athletic scholarships. Scholarship aid offers a wonderful opportunity to attend a college or university that otherwise would be financially out of reach.

- *The downside.* Athletic scholarships come with many strings attached. It is not easy to supplement one's income, because NCAA rules allow athletes to work for only a limited number of hours each term. In addition, if you are

---

CAREER CONNECTIONS

Building Networks That Can Lead to a Job

As a college athlete, you will likely be invited to more than your share of dinners, lunches, banquets, and a range of events that mark a variety of occasions. Although you may look at your attendance at some of these events as an obligation that you would like to avoid, they are actually golden opportunities. The opportunity comes from the potential to network with people—people who just may be able to help you get your first job.

When you go to ceremonial events, take the time to talk with attendees other than your teammates and other students. The community members who are present are people who appreciate what you do. In fact, they may have been involved in athletics themselves when they were in college. This gives you a common bond that will make conversation flow more easily. In addition, attendees are often community leaders—the kind of people who are likely to have many connections that can help you get an internship or, eventually, a job.

If socializing doesn't come easily to you, push yourself. Give yourself the goal of meeting a certain number of strangers. At first, set your goal low, such as meeting only two new people. As you become more comfortable with networking, you can set your sights higher. The important thing is to make the connections.

Ultimately, *who* you know is less important than *what* you know. Still, the reality is that developing a network of people in the world outside of college can only help you get the job you want.

---

injured or you stop participating in athletics, there is the possibility that you may lose your scholarship. Finally, an athletic scholarship may require you to maintain a certain minimum grade point average, adding to the pressure and stress you face.

NCAA Oversight

- *The upside.* The NCAA (as well as the NAIA or NJCAA) offers a broad range of support services. For example, many schools make use of the CHAMPS/Life Skills program to help student athletes achieve academic, athletic, career, and general personal development success. (You can learn more about this program at the NCAA Web site at **www.ncaa.org** under "Education Programs.")
- *The downside.* The regulatory bodies are strict, and if you break the rules, the consequences could be severe. You must become acquainted with a variety of regulations (involving such topics as the total prohibition of gambling and maintaining eligibility).

■ Time Management for Student Athletes

Student athletes have no more than the 168 hours in a week that every other student has, but the demands on those hours are often greater for athletes. Perhaps the biggest difficulty is the lack of flexibility in scheduling activities. Games are scheduled months, and sometimes years, in advance, and practices are scheduled at the beginning of the season, sometimes even before classes begin. Still, there may be changes in practice times, rescheduled games, and—if you're lucky—playoff games at the end of the season that can't be anticipated in advance.

> **"You can practice shooting eight hours a day, but if your technique is wrong, then all you get is very good at shooting the wrong way. Get the fundamentals down and the level of everything you do will rise."**
>
> Michael Jordan, basketball star[2]

All these demands make effective time management particularly crucial for student athletes. Detailed time management strategies are laid out in the full chapter on time management, but there are some lines of attack that are especially relevant to athletes. Among the most important tips for effective time management that especially apply to student athletes are the following:

- **Be sure of your priorities.** Only you can know what is most important to you as you navigate your way through college. Take the time to determine what is most important to you by asking yourself several key questions:

1. What are the most important reasons I am in college?
2. What are my most important long-term goals?
3. How can I best achieve those goals?
4. How does managing my time bring me closer to my goals? (For help in determining your priorities, use Try It 1 on page A-8.)

Dealing with Course Instructors

Behind the faces of the course instructors that you see in class are human beings—human beings with particular beliefs, attitudes, values, and even prejudices about the students in their classes. Some instructors may hold student athletes in high esteem, particularly if they themselves participated in athletics when they were in college.

On the other hand, some instructors may harbor negative feelings about student athletes, believing that they receive special privileges from the college or that the athletics program receives too much emphasis or requires too big a budget. In some cases, instructors simply may be unaware of the particular challenges that student athletes face.

What should you do if you encounter an unsympathetic instructor? How can you avoid alienating an instructor in the first place? Consider using one of these strategies to win over instructors and make them more likely to be your ally:

- *Know the class policies and syllabus.* Before you ask an instructor for something special, be sure you already have studied the class syllabus and know the instructor's policies on makeup exams and paper extensions. The class policy may already provide for makeups and extensions, and you want to stay within the normal guidelines as much as possible. Instructors do not like to reexplain things that they've already talked about in class or have included on the course syllabus.

- *Ask for exceptions well in advance.* You have a much better chance of receiving an extension on a paper or rescheduling an exam if you ask in advance. In most cases, you will know your schedule months ahead. Check out the course schedule to see if there are any conflicts. Instructors tend to be more sympathetic if they see you actively planning in advance, rather than waiting until the last minute to make a special request.

- *Be flexible.* If you are asking to reschedule a test or get an extension on a paper, be as flexible as you possibly can when asking for the change. If an instructor agrees to give you a makeup test, for example, make a real and visible effort to schedule the makeup at a time convenient for the instructor, even if you are inconvenienced. Remember that it is the instructor who is doing you a favor, not the other way around.

- *Give 100 percent to the class.* You can't expect to receive special consideration if your instructor does not view you as a motivated, hard-working student. Do your best, and make it apparent that you are doing your best.

- *Never act as if you deserve special consideration because you are a student athlete.* You should never convey the impression that you think you warrant special privileges that are unavailable to other students. All students have their own unique, personal set of challenges and demands. Any request that you make is just one of many that an instructor receives during the course of the term, and you should not act as if yours are somehow more important than others'.

- *Seek the intervention of others in dealing with very difficult instructors.* What if you are unable to win the cooperation of an unsympathetic instructor, and your academic success in the course is jeopardized? If all else fails, you might consider asking for the intervention of someone in the athletic department.

  However, this is an extreme measure. Be aware that there is a chance that your situation may go from bad to worse if your instructor views the intervention as a personal attack. Instructors who are unsympathetic to student athletes in their classes may be just as unsympathetic to a call from a representative of the athletic department.

Determining Your Priorities

Use this Try It to consider your priorities and assess how well your current activities relate to your goals and reasons for being in college.

Reasons for Attending College:
What are the two main reasons that you are in college? Answer this question in terms of your future, not your past (i.e., avoid answers like "My parents made me attend").

R1:

R2:

Goals:
What are your two most important long-term goals in life?

G1:

G2:

Priorities:
Think about your main college-related activities during the current academic term, as listed in column 1. Indicate in the second column the reason for attending college and/or the goal to which each activity relates. Then, in the third column, set a priority for each activity, from a high of 1 to a low of 5. (Many activities will have the same priority level, but try to spread your priority assignments as much as possible.)

Activities	Related to Reason/Goal Number:	Priority
Academic Activities		
Attending classes		
Doing daily (short-term) homework assignments		
Doing long-term assignments (e.g., papers)		
Studying each day		
Studying for major examinations		
Other—specify:		
Athletic Activities		
Attending practices, strategy sessions, etc.		

Activities	Related to Reason/Goal Number:	Priority
Attending games		
Training/exercising outside of formal practices		
Attending athletic events for fund-raising, publicity, alumni relations, etc.		
Attending other athletics-related meetings		
Studying strategies, plays, defenses, etc.		
Other—specify:		
Social/Personal Activities		
Attending school events (including athletic and other events)		
Being with friends		
Dating, partying		
Television watching		
Video/computer game playing		
Reading		
Internet surfing		
Reading/writing e-mail, instant messaging, etc.		
Other—specify:		
Other		
Traveling, visiting family and friends		
Necessities: eating, sleeping		
Maintenance: laundry, shopping, hygiene		
Other—specify:		

Wrap-Up:

How well do your priorities match your reasons for being in college and your goals for when you finish college?

Should you make any adjustments?

- **Use your traveling time well.** Traveling to away games and meets can eat up big chunks of time. Make use of that time wisely. You can read, study, make and go through flash cards, or write outlines. The more you do while traveling, the less there is to do when you get back to campus.

- **Use a PDA (personal digital assistant) or a traditional calendar.** Think using a Palm, Handspring Treo, or some other type of hand-size personal digital assistant is too, well, geeky for you? Think again. PDAs are widely used in business, and many companies purchase them for their employees and require their use.

    PDAs are replacements for traditional schedule books and calendars. PDAs have all the features of a traditional book, but offer several significant advantages. For one, entering an event into the daily schedule makes it also appear in a weekly, monthly, and annual calendar. Recurring events, like classes, can be entered once and then repeated across the term. The information can also be synchronized with a computer, so your schedule is stored in more than one place.

    But if you don't want to go high tech and use a PDA, that's fine. Just be absolutely sure to use some kind of traditional calendar.

Discussion Prompt:
Ask students to generate a list of ways that technology can be utilized to enhance their academic performance. How is technology used to enhance athletic performance?

- **Be flexible.** Although the goal of time management is to schedule your time in advance, it's important to remain flexible. If you slip behind on a project that has a high priority, allocate more time to it. Think of schedules as living, breathing documents that can be revised.

- **Don't let short-term goals overshadow your long-term goals.** You should not let your short-term goals make you forget your long-term goals. It is tempting to place all your energies into activities that can bring about a clear-cut and immediate outcome, such as winning the next game you play.

    However, don't let your desire to win make you forget your long-term goals. For the vast majority of your life you will not be a student athlete but a wage earner, family member, and world citizen. Keep that in mind as you make choices about how to expend your time.

- **Make use of the off-season.** One thing you do know for sure: every sport has an off-season. Try to budget your time in a way that allows you to take advantage of terms in which the demands on your time are lower. Schedule more, and harder, classes during the off-season.

Teaching Tip:
Travel can be a time management "black hole" or it can provide substantial blocks of time for studying. Ask your students to share tips for maximizing this time.

- **Learn the art of saying "no."** A key to effective time management is knowing when to say "no"—no to that after-game party, that spur-of-the-moment movie, that trip to get a burger. There will be times when you can participate in those things, but there are other times when you will just have to postpone the fun. Knowing when to say no (and yes) is a key aspect of time management for student athletes. (To learn strategies for saying no, complete Try It 2.)

Getting Help

You're facing your nightmare scenario. You haven't had enough time to study for the first few tests in several of your classes, and you are falling further and further behind. Although things are going well on the field, you feel as if your academic life is heading for a giant collision with reality. If you don't

2

TRY IT!

Saying No to Temptation

You will often face difficult choices during your college career. Among the most difficult (and most frequent) are choices between fun and work. Use this Try It to plan ahead for making such choices wisely.

Consider each choice that does NOT relate to your goals in college and does NOT fit into your priorities as a "temptation." Write down below the most common temptations that you are likely to face during the next few months. Then consider the WORST reason to say Yes to that temptation and the BEST reason to say No. Fill in the table below to prepare yourself. (The table has been started for you to show you how to proceed.)

Temptation	Worst Reason to Say Yes	Best Reason to Say No
Let's go see that great new movie tonight.	I can probably finish studying for the big exam tomorrow morning, just before class.	Who am I kidding? I'll never study tomorrow morning, and there's no way I'm going to fail an exam for a movie I can see later.
What a bummer—a 2-point loss. Let's go out and drown our sorrows.	Why not? I'm too bummed to write this paper anyway.	I'm not going to make one loss the excuse for another. I'm going to knuckle down and finish my paper.
Wow! A 1-point win at the final buzzer! Party! Party!		I'll party a little later, after I finish reading this assignment. Go ahead without me, and I'll try to catch up with you.
Hey, this TV show is going to be great! We're all going to watch it at Joe's place. Come on.	If I don't show up people will think I'm a jerk.	
Your girlfriend/boyfriend called and would really like to see you tonight—but you've got a paper to do.		

PREPARE
Decide you
need help

ORGANIZE
Determine the kind
of help you need
and where to get it

WORK
Make effective use
of help

EVALUATE
Assess your
progress

RETHINK
Reconsider your views
of receiving help

P.O.W.E.R. Plan

Student Alert:
Student athletes are competitive and may find it difficult to ask for help. Reassure them that all students need help with different skills and that they are no different.

start doing better academically, you'll be ineligible to play. And if you don't play, you might lose your athletic scholarship.
You need help . . . and you need it fast.

If you ever find yourself in such a situation, you know the feeling of desperation that can come over you. But there are steps you can take to salvage the situation. The worse thing you can do is to do nothing. Act! Use the following steps (which are summarized in the P.O.W.E.R. Plan) to obtain and then make effective use of the resources that are available to you.

P REPARE: Deciding You Need Help

Coming to the realization that you are in trouble and need help is the first step in improving the situation. As an athlete, you've been trained to be self-reliant, so you may feel that even asking for help is a failure.

Quite the contrary: Seeking out help is an indication that you are aware of the situation. Realizing that the situation has moved beyond your own abilities to resolve it is a sign of maturity.

O RGANIZE: Determining the Kind of Help You Need, and Where to Get It

Realizing that you need help is just the first step. You also need to get straight in your own mind the kind of help that you need and to identify where you can find that help. In order to do that, ask yourself these questions:

■ *What are the specific courses in which I am having trouble?* You're probably not having the same level of difficulty in all of your courses. Choose the ones that are most troublesome and focus on those.

■ *What is the specific difficulty I am encountering?* Are you doing badly on the tests in one or more courses? Are you having trouble producing satisfactory papers? Is the problem class participation? First determine specifically what the problem is, and then you can figure out what you need to do to address it.

■ *What kind of help do I need?* If you don't perform well on the multiple-choice exams in a class, perhaps tutoring in the course content would be helpful. Or perhaps your problems stem from difficulties in taking multiple-choice tests in general, and you would benefit from learning effective strategies for taking such exams. Sometimes using publisher-generated material can help. For example, many textbooks are accompanied by a *Student Study Guide* or have an online Web site with practice tests.

■ *Can a study group help?* Sometimes the simplest route for receiving help is to organize a study group with other students in a class. It doesn't need to be a group. In fact, just meeting regularly with another student in the class to go over assignments and study for tests can be beneficial. Whether it

If you find yourself struggling in your academic work, don't wait until it's too late for help. There are a number of resources available to you to help you succeed in class, but you must make the first move.

consists of only you and another student, or is made up of a larger number of students, a study group can help you pinpoint difficult issues and make sure you are on the right track when studying. It can also give you extra motivation to tackle the more challenging aspects of a class.

■ *Have I discussed the problem with my course instructor?* The individuals who are in the best position to determine the help you need are the instructors of the courses in which you need help. They can provide guidance about the specific areas in which you need help. In addition, some instructors may be willing to go over material with you and provide personalized instruction. (Don't expect this to happen very often; most instructors simply don't have the time to provide extensive tutoring on class material to individual students.)

In some cases, individual classes will have a support system built into the course. For example, if the class is large, teaching assistants may be able to provide support and perhaps even individual tutoring for students who are having problems with the course content.

Discussing your difficulties with your course instructor serves another purpose beyond simply getting information: It shows that you are concerned about your class performance. Instructors will be more likely to go the extra mile for students who are genuinely concerned about how they are doing than for those who appear to ignore the problem.

Discussing your difficulties with your course instructor serves another purpose beyond simply getting information: It shows that you are concerned about your class performance. Instructors will be more likely to go the extra mile for students who are genuinely concerned about how they are doing than for those who appear to ignore the problem.

Teaching Tip: Trust and accessibility are essential elements for students seeking academic assistance. Teammates are a rich and ready resource to be considered.

■ *Where can I get help?* If you are lucky, finding help will not be difficult. Colleges want their students to be successful, and they try to provide the resources students need in order to make that success a reality. In some cases, though, you may have to dig through a college bureaucracy to find the appropriate person who can help you.

As a student athlete, your first point of contact should be your academic advisor. Many athletic departments offer academic support to athletes, and that's the person you should speak with first. If the athletic department doesn't provide an advisor, then you most likely will have been assigned an advisor in some other unit of the college. Make an appointment with your advisor to discuss the situation and get advice about where to go next.

If you don't have an advisor, there are sure to be other offices on campus where you can seek help. Try your campus Office of Student Services or Student Affairs or your campus Counseling Center. With persistence, you will eventually reach a person who can help you—or at least lead you in the right direction.

Complete Try It 3 to identify the resources on your own campus that are available to student athletes.

W O R K: Making Effective Use of Help

You've identified the kind of help you need and found someone to help you. Now the real work begins.

As a recipient of aid, it's easy to think of yourself as being in a passive role, assuming that the person who is helping you is responsible for making sure you make progress. However, that's just not true. *You* have the responsibility for ensuring that the help you receive is effective. It will take your effort and hard work to produce the desired outcome, in the same way that it is the effort and hard work of players that make a coach's guidance effective.

3

Identifying Campus Resources

As an athlete and a member of a college community, you have many resources you can turn to when things get tough. The key is to find them in time. Do some legwork in advance to identify good resources for a range of academic challenges you may face in the future. Be creative: Consider teachers, coaches, academic advisors, counselors, library staff, friends, classmates, academic support services—anyone who might help. List the best resources in the second column and information on how to contact them (phone number, office location, e-mail address, etc.) in the last column.

Use this Try It table to find and list the resources in advance of your need for them. Update it as you continue your college career.

If I Need Help with:	I Can Go to:	Contact Information
A specific course (list courses):		
Understanding a homework or paper assignment		
Coming up with a good paper topic		
Understanding how to write a paper		
Finding articles or books as background for a research paper		
Learning to take tests		
Writing more effectively		
Basic math concepts and skills		
Basic grammar skills		
Reading better		
Studying more effectively		
Managing my time better		
Overcoming my anxiety about getting everything done on time		
Other:		

How can you make best use of the help you are receiving? Here are some guidelines:

- **Treat tutoring sessions as a regular class.** Even though the help you are receiving is personalized, you shouldn't treat your tutor as an employee whose job description can change on a whim. Treat your tutor with respect. Arrive at tutoring sessions on time, and don't leave early. If you must miss a session, notify the tutor as far in advance as possible.

- **Coordinate your tutoring with your course instructor.** Let instructors of courses in which you are receiving help know about the assistance you are getting. They may be able to suggest particular areas on which you should concentrate. They also may be able to suggest specific study materials (such as a *Student Study Guide* that accompanies your textbook) that would be helpful. Finally, letting your instructor know that you are seeking help demonstrates your effort and motivation.

- **Don't expect your tutor to do your work.** You should not expect your tutor to write papers for you, to complete assignments, or to supply you with test questions. There are limits—both practical and ethical—that constrain just what a tutor can do, and you need to keep those limits in mind.

- **Learn the process of studying a subject area, as well as its content.** A good tutor will teach you not only course content but also ways of studying the material effectively. The study strategies you use for an English class are different from those you will use for a math class. The more you learn strategies for dealing with new material, the better the ultimate outcome.

- **If it's not working out, discuss the situation with your tutor.** Tutors are no more alike than college instructors. Some work hard and go the extra mile, while others may behave in a mechanical, unsympathetic manner. If you find the help you are receiving is inadequate or problematic, discuss the problem with your tutor. If you can't find an acceptable solution, try to identify another tutor.

E VALUATE: Assessing Your Progress

It's important to check out whether the help you are receiving is beneficial. Keep track of how you perform on tests, papers, and other assignments. Get feedback from your instructors after each graded assignment to check your progress. If you are still dissatisfied with your grade, consider how it might be improved. Ask yourself these questions:

- Is my tutor providing the help I most need?
- Am I making the most of each tutoring session?
- Have I focused on the right areas of study?
- Do I need more practice in certain areas?
- Am I putting in sufficient work outside of tutoring sessions?

Remember, ultimately it is you who is responsible for your success in school—not your tutor. Your successes and failures are due to the amount of hard work that you invest in your studies.

Teaching Tip:
Encourage student athletes to approach a tutoring session with the same level of preparation that they would approach a practice for their sport.

Teaching Tip:
Right or wrong, fair or unfair, athletes are judged far more publicly than others regarding academic integrity. Emphasize the importance of academic honesty beyond exams and tests.

R ETHINK: Reconsidering Your Views of Receiving Help

Teaching Tip:
Encourage freshmen to ask upperclassmen to serve as tutors or academic mentors.

One central value of North American society is self-reliance. While this independent streak motivates people to "make it on their own," it also makes many feel reluctant to seek out much-needed help. When help is provided, it may be accepted with hesitation.

Consequently, it is important to understand the dynamics of receiving help. It is important to be aware that those who provide help are doing so with your best interests in mind. There is nothing wrong with seeking out help—and there is a problem if you actively avoid making use of assistance that is available to you.

As a student athlete, you face challenges that nonathletes don't confront. Make use of the academic opportunities that are available to you as much as you make use of the athletic opportunities you find in college.

■ Pain and Injury: The Special Challenge to the Student Athlete

You hurt. You hurt a lot. Practices have been tough; the coach is pushing you hard; and your knee, which you injured in high school and has always been your weak point, is throbbing five minutes after you run onto the court. The pain doesn't even let up after practice. It's there all the time. You sometimes awake in the middle of the night in agony. Even just sitting at your desk and twisting your knee in a certain way can produce shooting pain.

Now you're supposed to be studying for two tests tomorrow. All you can think about is the pain.

The pain that comes from an injury can be overwhelming, focusing your attention on little else but the pain itself. How can you deal with such pain? There are several things you can do to respond effectively to pain and the sports injuries that cause it, including the following:

Student Alert:
Student athletes need to be their own best health advocates. They may hear conflicting information from the institution's infirmary and the athletic trainer. In the end, student athletes must live with decisions relating to their bodies.

■ **Understand what pain is.** Pain is a symptom of something else. It is your body's way of alerting you to an injury to some cells that make up the body.

However, pain is not only a direct physical reaction to something that is wrong. The way that we react to an injury influences how much pain we experience. Even a minor stimulus can produce the experience of strong pain if it is accompanied by anxiety. (That's why even minor dental procedures sometimes produce great pain.) Consequently, the amount of pain we experience reflects our emotions and thoughts.

In addition, pain is an important warning sign. If we never experienced pain, we wouldn't be aware of situations in our bodies that required attention.

■ **Deal with the source of the pain.** Under no circumstances should you ignore pain. Pain is a warning that something is wrong. Don't "suck it up" and pretend that everything is fine. Instead, use pain as the warning it is meant to be, and act on it. Consult your team trainer, a physician, or another health practitioner. Visit your student health center. Even if you have experienced similar pain in the past, you cannot make a self-diagnosis. Go to a professional, even if you are apprehensive about what you may find out.

[
"Success is a choice."

Rick Pitino,[3] basketball coach
]

- **Follow through on treatment for the pain.** Once you know what is causing your pain, follow through on the advice you receive about how to treat the pain. Don't decide that you know better and things will improve on their own. If it is recommended that you do physical therapy, follow through. Put as much effort into the therapy as you would into a team practice.

- **Use drug therapies to reduce pain with exceptional care.** Drugs work: They can reduce pain significantly. Furthermore, by reducing the pain, they can make the body relax, which in turn makes the natural healing process proceed more rapidly.

  However, there's a potential price to be paid for the habitual use of drugs: They can be addictive. Even superstar athletes like Brett Favre, quarterback for the Green Bay Packers, developed a dependency on the painkiller Vicodin. It took six weeks in rehab to overcome the drug habit.

  To avoid drug problems, follow prescriptions *precisely.* If a drug seems ineffective, go back to the person who prescribed it and ask for a change. There are many potentially effective drugs, and if one doesn't work, an alternative can be tried.

  Furthermore, avoid the use of steroids. Although they can increase muscle mass and strength and decrease body fat, they also can lead to heart attacks, strokes, cancer, depression, and even violent behavior. They are dangerous, and their side effects outweigh any possible benefits.

  In any case, **never** use illegal drugs or drugs that have been prescribed for someone else. Not only are you playing Russian roulette with your body, but such drugs may have side effects that produce depression, anxiety, and social withdrawal. If you are caught using illegal drugs, this can lead to expulsion from school or legal action.

- **Use stress-reduction techniques.** Because stress makes pain worse, use stress-reduction techniques. For example, you might try to reduce the things that are causing you stress. If a relationship is causing you stress, consider ending it. If you are overwhelmed with course work, seek out help from your instructors or a teaching assistant, or consider working with a tutor.

  You can also use relaxation techniques, such as progressive relaxation or meditation, that can help you deal with the physiological reactions that accompany stress. Finally, try *self-talk,* in which you either think or say to yourself affirmations that you have the ability to deal with a situation. Such self-talk can be in the form of action words ("You can do it!") or mood words ("Relax!").

- **Understand the side benefits of recovering from injury.** It seems obvious that recovering from an athletic injury is beneficial. But awareness of the side benefits of recovery can at the least be comforting and, at most, can actually be psychologically beneficial, thereby speeding recovery time.

  What are the side benefits of recovery? You may gain a broader perspective, be able to focus on other areas of your life while recovering, and learn better time management strategies. In addition, physical therapy for the injury may improve your overall fitness level. Finally, as with facing and overcoming any adversity, recovering from an injury may give you a kind of mental toughness that will help you deal with future challenges.

Student Alert:
Student athletes may be less willing than their classmates to use group therapy or individual counseling. They have learned to play with physical pain and the psychological implications of this attitude may have lasting repercussions.

Teaching Tip:
Bring an alternative health care provider to class who can provide additional options for your students to consider for health, such as a campus wellness coordinator, nutritionist, biofeedback specialist, etc.

Discussion Prompt:
What is the difference between a team-building initiation ritual and hazing? Don't make an assumption that hazing doesn't occur on your campus just because you don't hear about it. You may be "out of the loop."

Hazing
An activity that humiliates or degrades a person joining a team or other group

◼ Hazing

When Jean-François Caudron came to training camp on a hockey scholarship, he knew he had to prove himself to his coaches. But it wasn't only his coaches that he felt he had an obligation to, it was to his teammates as well. So he willingly participated in an initiation ritual called "Rookie Night." It involved shaving his body, painting his toenails, and tossing back enough warm beer to make him vomit.[4]

In some ways, Caudron was lucky. There are instances in which hazing has led to severe injury and even death.

Hazing is an activity designed to humiliate or degrade a person who is joining a team or other group. It encompasses a wide variety of abusive behaviors, including yelling, making people wear embarrassing clothing, forcing them to drink large quantities of liquor or foul-tasting liquids, tattooing and piercing, beatings, paddling, bondage, and confining someone in a small space.

Although it is universally banned on college campuses (and is illegal in most states), four out of five athletes say they have participated in some form of a hazing ritual.[5] In most cases, it is fairly benign, but in others it can lead to terrible consequences.

Hazing is a difficult practice from which to escape, because teammates may exert enormous peer pressure to go along with the ritual. However, keep these facts in mind:

- ◼ You don't need to accept hazing. It is your decision. You do have a choice.
- ◼ No one should be allowed to do something that harms you. Period.
- ◼ You don't owe it to anyone to allow yourself to be hazed. You can be accepted by your teammates and not be hazed.
- ◼ Your first allegiance is to your family and friends—not your team. Family members and real friends don't make you suffer indignity and pain.

It's important to keep in mind that your job as a team member is to do your best at your sport. That's where your responsibility as a teammate lies, and not as a participant in an illegal practice that can harm you.

◼ Burnout: When Athletics No Longer Matter

When I was sixteen, I was swimming worse than when I was thirteen, and I felt like I was never going to come out of it. I really wasn't enjoying the sport anymore because I was doing so poorly, and that time was really tough. . . . I'd done it for over ten years, and it's hard to give up something after that long. . . . I guess I realized that you have to make it fun. If you're so serious about it all the time and it starts going bad, then it's really going to destroy you.

Leslie Hoh, University of Missouri–Columbia, swimmer[6]

Burnout
A condition in which an athlete feels dissatisfaction, physical or emotional exhaustion, disillusionment, and frustration

Have you ever felt that you'd reached the end of your rope, that sports competition was bringing you no pleasure, and that you would welcome the opportunity to drop out of athletic activity altogether? If so, you may have been suffering from burnout. **Burnout** is a condition in which an athlete feels dissatisfaction, physical or emotional exhaustion, disillusionment, and frustration. In burnout, sports are devalued, and athletic accomplishment may decline.

There are many reasons why athletes experience burnout. One is feeling chronic stress. Student athletes may feel torn by the athletic, academic, and social demands of college. They may feel they have too much to do and not enough time to do it in.

Furthermore, the special demands of athletics may be particularly difficult to surmount. Athletes face constant pressure to win, and their successes and failures are extremely public. They may have to spend excessive amounts of time in practice, and then the payoff—in terms of actual playing time—may be relatively low. In addition, student athletes may feel that they have relatively little control over their lives. Each moment may seem scheduled, and in such situations it is hard to develop a sense of independence and self-sufficiency. (To see if you have the symptoms of burnout, complete Try It 4 on page A-20.)

Burnout may lead student athletes to be less effective physically. Your performance can suffer, and you may lose your motivation to succeed. If burnout is not addressed, it can ultimately cause you to drop out of athletics completely. In the worst case, it can have a negative impact on your academic success, too.

You can use several strategies to avoid burnout. They are:

Teaching Tip:
Does your campus have a sports psychologist? Consider inviting this person to class.

- **Be sensitive to the early warning signs of burnout, and take steps to prevent it.** Know the symptoms of burnout. If you begin to experience them, talk to someone about it—a family member or friend, an instructor, or a counselor at your college's counseling center. Think hard about changes you can make in your life to make burnout less likely.

- **Be clear in your own mind as to why you are playing.** Play for yourself, not for others. You should not be on a team only to make others feel proud of you or because others expect it of you. If it's not enjoyable in and of itself, then you shouldn't be doing it.

- **Hold realistic expectations.** You may not always play as well as you want; you may not always receive all the playing time you'd like; you may be asked to do more than you think you can do and may not always receive support from all your instructors. These are the facts of life for student athletes. Being aware that you may face tough times, and that things will not always proceed as you'd like them to, can help you confront the problems more effectively when they do occur.

- **Manage your time more effectively.** As we discussed, time management is one of the keys to avoiding burnout. If you use effective time management techniques, you'll be better prepared to face the multiple demands on your time.

- **Take time off.** If you're experiencing the symptoms of burnout, take some time off every once in a while. Relax and do something entirely different from what you usually do.

- **Give it up.** What if you are profoundly unhappy about your participation in athletics? If you are honest with yourself and you are truly unhappy, then it is not unreasonable to end your sports participation, at least for a while.

    Of course, leaving sports should be your last response to burnout, not your first. It is a momentous decision, and it will have implications that reverberate throughout every aspect of your college life. You certainly shouldn't end your team participation without talking it through with a coach, academic advisor, friend, or some other person who can provide you with good advice. Ultimately, though, you may come to the conclusion that the most reasonable course for you might be to end your participation on a team.

Athletes can be under so much pressure that they can succumb to burnout.

4

TRY IT!

Are You Burning Out?

Consider the symptoms below that may indicate burnout and note whether you have experienced each symptom often, sometimes, or never. If you have a pattern of four or more "sometimes" answers and three or more "often" answers, talk to a friend or go to your campus counseling center and ask for some help from a professional.

	Never	Sometimes	Often
1. I'm tired for days at a time without being able to figure out why.			
2. My friends and teammates tell me that I'm moody.			
3. I experience periods when my mood is bad and stays bad no matter what I do.			
4. I can't even get happy about winning.			
5. Nothing seems to give me pleasure.			
6. Others tell me to cheer up and quit acting so sad.			
7. I go through periods when I can hardly think.			
8. I have way too much to do and no time to do it in.			
9. I just can't seem to pay attention in class.			
10. I can't even pay attention to my coaches.			
11. I keep making stupid mental mistakes.			
12. I have times when it's hard even to get out of bed.			
13. I go through periods when I can't sleep well.			
14. I'm not getting enough playing time and respect from my coaches.			
15. I have serious doubts about my athletic abilities.			
16. I wonder what I'm even doing in college.			
17. I think I'm really a fake and that my incompetence will soon be found out.			
18. People tell me I'm no fun to be with.			
19. I get into arguments with people for no real reason.			
20. I think I'm letting everyone down—my team, my coaches, and my parents.			

SPEAKING OF
Success

Name: Dr. Rod Paige, former U.S. Secretary of Education

School: Jackson State University, Jackson, Mississippi

From his earliest years, Rod Paige had two loves: education and football. He excelled at both, ultimately becoming the U.S. teacher-in-chief as Secretary of Education via several coaching stints at a number of colleges.

Paige has come a long way from his poor roots in rural Mississippi. His father was a barber and high school principal, and his mother was a librarian. "My parents told us the solution to the world's problems was education," said Paige, and he took those words to heart.

Paige attended Jackson State University, a historically black college that was segregated at the time. There he played end on the football team and became an honor student. Said his college roommate, Walter Reed, "If there was a test and somebody had made a 98, we knew it had to be Rod." On the field, Paige was known as a hard-hitting, dogged player.

Sports were critical to Paige's success. He credits football coach Harrison Wilson for motivating him to look ahead and to be aggressive. "He was always looking forward, preparing and planning. He would say, 'I'm going to own a house like that one day,' or 'I'm going

to be a president of a university one day.' That kind of rubbed off on me. . . . He created the ambition in my life," said Paige.

After graduating from college, Paige became a teacher and college football coach. He also pursued his education, receiving a masters and a doctorate degree from Indiana University. It wasn't easy. Because he had attended a segregated, underfunded college as an undergraduate, his academic preparation did not equal that of many of his graduate school classmates. Nevertheless, through hard work and determination he succeeded. "I adopted a philosophy that if you can do this in an hour, I'll do it in three. When we come to class, I'm not going to take a backseat," he said.

Paige went on to become athletic director and then dean of Texas Southern University's education school. He eventually was hired as superintendent of the Houston school system, which led to his appointment as the U.S. Secretary of Education.

Athletics remains an important part of who Paige is, and the values he learned as a student athlete are a central part of his life. "The game of football has left an indelible mark on my heart and on my life," says Paige.[7]

What are the special advantages of being a student athlete that help meet the challenges of college?

- The special advantages include having a strong work ethic, holding high expectations, the availability of special services, a strong social network, good health, the possibility of acting as a role model, and financial support.

- At the same time, each of those advantages is accompanied by potential disadvantages of being a student athlete.

How can I deal most effectively with course instructors and time management issues?

- Among the strategies for dealing effectively with course instructors is knowing the class policies and syllabus well, asking for exceptions in advance, being flexible, giving 100 percent to a class, never demanding special consideration, and seeking the intervention of others.

- Effective time management depends on being certain of one's priorities, using a PDA (personal digital assistant), or calendar, being flexible, keeping long-term goals in mind, making use of the off-season, and just saying "no."

What are the best ways to seek and use help?

- Effective help-seeking involves determining the kind of help that is needed and identifying potential resources.

- To use help effectively, student athletes should be active recipients of the aid, taking responsibility for their own progress.

How do I best deal with pain, injury, and the potential of burnout?

- Pain and injury can be dealt with by seeking treatment and following medical advice carefully, following through with treatment, and not ignoring pain.

- Burnout, in which an athlete may be physically and psychologically exhausted, can be addressed by being sensitive to the early warning signs, understanding why one is playing, holding realistic expectations, managing time effectively, and taking time off.

KEY TERMS AND CONCEPTS

Hazing (p. A–18)   Burnout (p. A–18)

RESOURCES

On Campus

As a student athlete, your college's athletic department usually provides support ranging from physical therapy to tutoring. If you are unsure of the resources that are available to you, ask your coach.

In Print

Hilary Abramson's *Student Athlete's Guide to College* (Princeton Review, 1999) provides a wealth of information on the advantages of athletic participation, including a clear summary of NCAA, NAIA, and NJCAA eligibility rules. *The Student Athlete Survival Guide* by Marc Isenberg and Rick Rhoads (McGraw-Hill, 2001) provides a broad overview of the benefits and challenges facing college athletes. Finally, Becky Bell's *If I Knew Then What I Know Now* (Game of Life, 2003) offers advice and strategies from student athlete leaders.

On the Web

The following sites on the World Wide Web provide the opportunity to extend your learning about the material in this chapter. (Although the Web addresses were accurate at the time the book was printed, check the P.O.W.E.R. Learning Web site [**www.mhhe.com/power**] for any changes that may have occurred.)

■ This link (**www.marquette.edu/cof/SAA/athletes-report-final.htm**) provides an in-depth discussion of the issues confronting student athletes, and is an interesting look at how a university is attempting to deal with the issues of athletes and academics.

■ This interview with a Purdue University football player, at **www.purdueexponent.org/2001/12/03/features/**, will give you an inside look at the demands faced by a college athlete and the importance of time management.

■ Created by the National Collegiate Athletic Association (NCAA), this site (**www.ncaa.org/news/2001/20010924/active/3820n26.html**) provides a checklist of health issues for student athletes, coaches, trainers, and athletic administrators.

TAKING IT TO THE NET

1 Are athletes exceptionally healthy—or do they have more health problems than nonathletes? Locate one or more sites on the Web with information about the health issues that athletes face, including both advantages and risks of being a college athlete. Write down any information that appears helpful or interesting.

2 What stereotypes do athletes have to deal with in college? Use a search engine to locate on the Web five or more stereotypes about college athletes (e.g., "the dumb jock"). Try to find factual information about these stereotypes. Write down a summary of what you find.

NOTES

1. Quoted in Bell, B. (2003). *If I knew then what I know now.* Tucson, AZ: Game of Life.

2. Quoted in Isenberg, M., & Rhoads, R. (2001). *The student athlete survival guide.* Camden, Maine: Ragged Mountain Press/McGraw-Hill.

3. Pitino, R. (1997). *Success is a choice.* NY: Broadway Books.

4. O'Hara, J. (2000, March 6). "The hell of hazing." *Maclean's,* p. 50.

5. Hoover, N.C. (1999, August 30). National survey: Initiation rites and athletics for NCAA sports teams. Alfred University.

6. Quoted in Quitmeir, L. (2000, November 16). Olympic trial and error. *Columbia Missourian,* pp. B1, B3.

7. Paige quotes from Fields-Meyer, T., & Kramer, L. (2001, November 19). Class act. Pp. 151–155; Winters, R. (2001, February 5). Teacher in chief. **www.cnn.com/allpolitics/time/2001/02/12/teacher.html**; Chappell, K. (2001, October). Rod Paige: America's education chief; America's coach. USA Football site. **www.usafootball.com/features/rodPaige.html**.

PHOTO CREDITS

THE CASE OF...
The Icy Pressure

There was pressure on Gino Criswell. Although he hadn't been a starter on the hockey team at the beginning of the season, one of his teammates had been severely injured. He was out for the season, leaving a starting position open for Gino.

Although starting was a dream come true, it brought enormous pressures that Gino hadn't anticipated. The coach pushed him mercilessly during practice, trying to raise his level of play. Furthermore, the team was having a winning season, which brought even more pressure as the team edged nearer to a playoff berth. The coach was constantly extending practice and even adding some additional ones to the schedule. The hockey games, which usually drew small crowds, were playing to a full rink. He felt that his every move on the ice was being watched—and criticized—by the fans.

To add to the pressure, Gino was devoting so much time to the hockey team that he barely could keep up with his classes. Even when he found time to study, he was usually so exhausted that he couldn't concentrate effectively. The professor in his hardest class, macroeconomics, was no help. In fact, he acted downright hostile when Gino asked if he could postpone a paper that was due the following week. The professor said that he would grant no favors to any student, but particularly to athletes.

Gino didn't know what to do. His grades were slipping, and he wasn't even playing that well on the ice. He didn't think he could handle the pressure.

1. What advice might you give Gino?

2. Is there anything Gino could have done in advance to prevent getting into a situation like this one?

3. What specific strategies could Gino use to deal with his professors?

4. Is there anything Gino can do in terms of his participation on the hockey team that would help the situation?

5. What advice could you give Gino to prevent a situation like this from occurring again in the future?

Taking Charge of Your Career

Darla Ketcham thought she was ready for the job interview.

She'd spent quite a bit of time thinking about her upcoming interview for the product manager's position at a Pepperidge Farm frozen food processing subsidiary, readying answer after answer for the position. She'd carefully researched the company online, reviewed her own experience, and had even gone so far as to purchase and try a sampling of Pepperidge Farm products (which proved to be not much of a sacrifice, actually).

But when the interviewer, seemingly out of the blue, asked her, "Why are manhole covers round?" she was clueless. How should she know? What did that question have to do with frozen cheesecake?

P.O.W.E.R. UP and IM Link:
Broaden the context of career planning from the beginning. Students often connect careers with post graduation decisions and we want them to begin that process of self-discovery now! Teaching the Text, Career Module, Section VIII; the "What Job Am I?" activity is a quick way to start class.

LOOKING AHEAD >>>

Luckily for Darla, what she later called the "manhole incident" was a turning point. Once she got beyond her initial shock, she realized that the aim of the question was to test not her knowledge of manhole covers but her problem-solving skills. After first noting that not all manhole covers are round, she then came up with a few creative possibilities. The interviewer, clearly satisfied, moved on to other, more predictable questions.

Job interviews can be anxiety-producing events. But they are just one of a series of challenging activities that are part of the process of choosing a career and finding a job. In this chapter, we address strategies for identifying your career goals and planning to achieve them. We consider the things you need to know to find the right career path and examine ways to get the job you want.

After reading this chapter, you'll be able to answer these questions:

■ **How do I identify my ideal career and job?**

■ **What are the best strategies for finding and getting a job?**

■ **How can I maximize my job interviewing skills?**

Career Planning

PREPARE
Identify your ideal job, skills, and career goals

ORGANIZE
Find career opportunities

WORK
Create a career portfolio

EVALUATE
Get feedback on your résumé and cover letter

RETHINK
Reconsider your career choices

You're just beginning college. How are you supposed to know for sure what you want to do professionally for the rest of your life?

Happily, you're *not* supposed to know for sure. You're not even expected to have a clue about what you're going to do professionally. That's what college, and some thoughtful career planning, are all about. Your college years are a time to find out who you are, identify your strengths and weaknesses, and gain more understanding of your likes and dislikes.

Furthermore, career planning is not about preparing yourself for a rest-of-your-life job. Sure, there are people who know that they want to be an airline pilot from the fifth grade on, and they train for that career single-mindedly and stick with it for their entire working lives. Those people are the exception. For most of us, career planning is an ongoing process. You're planning for your *next* job, not the job that has to last a lifetime.

P REPARE: Identifying Your Ideal Job, Skills, and Career Goals

The first step in career planning is to forget about specific jobs and occupations. Instead, think about what it is you enjoy doing. Consider how you'd like to spend your time, even if you didn't get paid for it. Are you mechanically inclined, easily able to take things apart and put them back together? Do you like to spend time outdoors? Do you enjoy numbers, or crossword puzzles, or playing with computers, or surfing the Web? Do you like to organize others into activities?

Use your likes and dislikes as a start to making your ideal job description. Complete Try It 1 to get a sense of what your dream job would be like.

It's also important to consider the skills that you have. For example, you may dream of playing professional baseball, but unless you have certain physical skills, it's unlikely you'll be the next Derek Jeter. As you think about your skills, don't limit yourself to specific areas. For instance, you should consider not only your natural abilities, those skills you've inherited from your parents and other relatives, but also skills involving intellectual, academic, and social domains.

Once you've reflected on the activities involved in your ideal job and the skills that you have, use that information to help determine your specific career goals. Apart from what you might do during the day, do you want a job that helps others? A job that pays very well? One with flexible hours? Is having an impact on future generations important to you? Use Try It 2 on page C-6 to identify your long-term career goals.

P.O.W.E.R. Plan

IRM Link:
Teaching the Text, Career Module, Section VIII; the Ideal Job is another approach to Try It 1.

> "If a man is called to be a street sweeper, he should sweep streets even as Michelangelo painted, or Beethoven composed music, or Shakespeare wrote poetry. He should sweep streets so well that all the hosts of heaven and earth will pause to say, here lived a great street sweeper who did his job well."
>
> Martin Luther King, Jr.

IRM Link:
Teaching the Text, Career Module, Section V; the Career Planning Timeline provides a work plan for each year of college.

Discovering Your Ideal Job

Part I:

The first column of the table below contains questions about your personal preferences, focusing on *what* you like to do and *how* you like to do it. Briefly answer the questions, using the space in the second column.

Questions	Your Preferences
When you have some time on your hands, what do you find yourself doing?	
Have you ever gotten so engrossed in something that you completely lost track of time? What were you doing?	
At school, what classes have you enjoyed most?	
After or outside of school, what activities have you found most enjoyable?	
Have you ever watched someone doing something and thought you would really like to try it? What was it?	
What would you willingly get out of bed early to do?	
What sort of problem would you willingly stay up all night to solve?	
Have you ever seen or read about a job and wondered how a person learns to do it? What was the job?	
Have you ever thought, *"Now, that's a cool job. I wonder how you get to do that?"* What was that job?	
Do you like working alone or with others?	

 **ORGANIZE:** Finding Career Opportunities

Research, research, research.

That's the name of the game when it comes to identifying possible careers. There are literally thousands of different occupations, and the number—and variety—of jobs are constantly shifting.

Do you prefer indoor or outdoor work?	
Do you prefer sitting or moving around while working?	
Do you like a fairly formal setting or a completely informal one?	
When you are in a group, do you prefer to lead or to be led?	
Do you prefer continually doing tasks with which you are completely familiar, or learning new tasks all the time?	
Do you prefer to use your muscles, your brain, or your other talents?	
Are you good at explaining complex tasks so that others can perform them?	
Do you enjoy persuading people that your views or ways of doing things are right?	
Do you enjoy solving problems? If so, do you prefer to work alone or with others?	

Part II:

Now use your work preferences to write a description of your ideal job in the space below. Be as brief as you can, and in no case exceed four lines.

My ideal job would involve:

   There's no way anyone can keep track of every option. Fortunately, there are several classification systems that can help you organize information about career possibilities and make your research manageable.

   However you decide to carry out your search for information about careers, be sure to keep notes about what you find. Your notes don't have to be elaborately written or suitable for handing in to an instructor. Just keep them simple, legible, and organized, and make sure that they include the source of the information you're describing.

2

TRY IT!

Identifying Your Long-Term Career Goals

Consider each of these areas as you determine your long-term goals:

- Achievement
- Advancement opportunities
- Challenge
- Contribution to society
- Control, power
- Creativity

- Financial
- Friendships with co-workers
- Helping others
- Independence
- Leadership
- Learning new things

- Loyalty
- Prestige
- Recognition from others
- Security
- Variety
- Working with others

Using this list, create a set of your three most important occupational goals. For example, three primary goals might be to (1) be challenged to reach my potential, (2) work with others in a cooperative environment, and (3) make a lasting contribution to society. However, don't be influenced by these examples—choose goals that are your own.

My Primary Career Goals Are to:

1.

2.

3.

Stating your career goals up front, even before you know the range of careers that exists, is important. Identifying your goals helps you know what it is that *you* want out of work. Future employers are more interested in what you bring to your job, rather than how well a job fulfills your important goals. It's crucial that you consider what has significance to you before making career decisions. If an occupation doesn't fulfill your major goals, it will not be a good choice for you.

Books and Web Sites

A good first step in obtaining career information is the U.S. Department of Labor's *Occupational Outlook Handbook (OOH)*. The *OOH*, published every two years, categorizes occupations into 11 broad groupings. It provides information on kinds of work, working conditions, job outlook, earnings, education and training requirements, and expected job prospects.

You can also visit the Department of Labor Web site at **www.bls.gov/oco/**, which provides a wealth of additional information. Among the most interesting features of the Web site is a compilation of the most up-to-date information on the hottest professions, in terms of projected future growth. (This information, summarized in Table C.1, must be used with care: the mere fact that a job is expanding rapidly doesn't necessarily mean that there are huge numbers of openings. A quickly growing profession may have only a few openings, and even with rapid growth, the absolute number of jobs may still be relatively small in coming years.)

TABLE C.1   Fastest Growing Occupations, 2000–2010

Occupation	Year		Percent Increase from 2000 to 2010	Education and Training Category
	2000	2010		
Computer software engineers applications	380	760	100	Bachelor's degree
Computer support specialists	506	996	97	Associate's degree
Computer software engineers, systems software	317	601	90	Bachelor's degree
Network and computer systems administrators	229	416	82	Bachelor's degree
Network systems and data communications analysts	119	211	77	Bachelor's degree
Desktop publishers	38	63	67	Postsecondary vocational award
Database administrators	106	176	66	Bachelor's degree
Personal and home care aides	414	672	62	Short-term on-the-job training
Computer systems analysts	431	689	60	Bachelor's degree
Medical assistants	329	516	57	Moderate-term on-the-job training
Social and human service assistants	271	418	54	Moderate-term on-the-job training
Physician assistants	58	89	53	Bachelor's degree
Medical records and health information technicians	136	202	49	Associate's degree
Computer and information systems managers	313	463	48	Bachelor's or higher degree, plus work experience
Home health aides	615	907	47	Short-term on-the-job training
Physical therapist aides	36	53	46	Short-term on-the-job training
Occupational therapist aides	9	12	45	Short-term on-the-job training
Physical therapist assistants	44	64	45	Associate's degree
Audiologists	13	19	45	Masters degree
Fitness trainers and aerobics instructors	158	222	40	Postsecondary vocational award
Computer and information scientists, research	28	39	40	Doctoral degree
Veterinary assistants and laboratory animal caretakers	55	77	40	Short-term on-the-job training
Occupational therapist assistants	17	23	40	Associate's degree
Veterinary technologists and technicians	49	69	39	Associate's degree
Speech-language pathologists	88	122	39	Masters degree

(Numbers in thousands of jobs.)
Source: From Table 3, Fastest growing occupations, 2000–2010, in "Occupational employment projections to 2010," published in the November 2001 Monthly Labor Review.

You are likely to find the *OOH,* and a wealth of other information, either in the career center of your college or in its library. In addition, almost every public library has a reference section on careers, and state employment centers often have extensive materials to help identify careers.

In addition to books, you may find CD-ROMs, pamphlets, and other helpful material at career centers, libraries, and employment centers. These resources also may offer on-site computers with software that can help you gather job-related information. For example, the *Discover Career Guidance and Information System* and *SIGI PLUS (System of Interactive Guidance and Information)* are widely used computer programs that have proven helpful to college students engaged in career searches.

Interest and Personality Assessments

In many cases, college career centers can administer occupational assessments that will systematically assess your interests and personality. These standardized tests, for which there is sometimes a charge, take about an hour to complete. They provide detailed feedback on who you are and the kinds of professions for which you seem to be most suited. Among the most widely available assessment inventories are:

- **Campbell Interest and Skill Survey (CISS).** In this inventory, people are asked to identify their interests and skills. Based on their results, test takers receive suggestions regarding whether they should pursue—or avoid—particular professions.

- **Kuder Occupational Interest Survey.** The Kuder test assesses your interests and compares them to the interests of others already in the field. The test assumes that if you have similar interests to people in a profession, you are particularly well suited to that line of work. (It also provides advice on appropriate majors.)

- **Strong Interest Inventory (SII).** The SII measures your likes and dislikes to get a sense of your personality. It uses your personality type to match you with professions that are populated with people who have similar personality types.

Visit the career center at your school to learn of job opportunities and available resources. Schedule a meeting with one of the career counselors who can help you with choosing a career, creating a portfolio, and preparing for the job interview process.

Personal Interviews

To get a close-up-and-personal look at a profession, another strategy is to talk with people who are already in it. People love to talk about their jobs, whether they love them or hate them, so don't be afraid to ask for an interview. You don't need a lot of their time—just enough to get an inside view of what it's like to work in their profession. Some questions you might want to ask:

- What's your typical day like?
- How did you find your job?
- What are the best and worst aspects of being in your profession?
- What do you look for in someone who wants to enter your field?

Instructors as Career Guides

Each of your instructors has a job—that of college instructor. But despite the similarity in job title, each got that job in a different way, using different tactics and strategies. Each followed his or her own particular career path and has a distinct educational background. Furthermore, your instructors may have had a variety of positions, and possibly a number of previous careers, prior to becoming a college instructor.

You can learn a great deal about career opportunities and the process of getting a job by talking to your course instructors about their own careers. Set up an appointment with each of your course instructors, and ask questions such as these:

- What is your educational and professional background?

- How did you get your current job?

- What students have you had that have been particularly successful careerwise? What qualities did they have that set them apart from other students of yours?

- What general advice do you have for someone seeking to identify careers and looking for a job?

- Knowing me from your course, what skills would you encourage me to work on and develop in order to increase my chances of successfully getting a job?

You can gain valuable insights into careers and job searches from your course instructors. Furthermore, talking with your course instructors can help you get to know them better, and it may eventually pave the way for your course instructors to provide letters of recommendation. Instructors also sometimes get leads on jobs, and if they know your career plans, they may pass them on to you. Finally, if you build a relationship with your instructor, it may help you do better academically in your course—no small benefit!

Keep in mind, of course, that the answers you get will be the opinions of one individual, reflecting his or her unique, personal experience. That's why it is a good idea to talk to several practitioners of a particular occupation, and to consider what they say in the context of other research that you have conducted about the profession.

Be sure to write a thank-you note following an interview. Not only is it a common courtesy, but it serves the additional purpose of reinforcing who you are and your interest in their profession. You never know: One day, they might have a job opening, and you might want to ask them for a job!

Teaching Tip:
Discuss the concept of an informational interview. Instead of asking for a job, you are becoming informed about the work—which may increase or decrease your desire to pursue this type of work.

W ORK: Creating a Career Portfolio

The research you've done on careers forms the foundation for creating a Career Development Portfolio. A **Career Portfolio** is a dynamic record that documents your skills, capabilities, achievements, and goals, as well as provides a place to keep notes, ideas, and research findings related to careers. Such a portfolio will provide an easy-to-access history of your job-related activities, and it will include material that will be helpful for you and, later, for potential employers. You'll want to keep and update your Career Portfolio as long as you are pursuing a career.

A Career Portfolio consists of a number of key components, which will vary depending on your year in college and—later—the stage you have reached in

Career Portfolio
A dynamic record that documents your skills, capabilities, achievements, and goals, as well as provides a place to keep notes, ideas, and research findings relating to careers.

your career. No matter where you are in career planning, though, your Career Portfolio will consist of two main parts. The first part, background information, will hold information to help you keep track of your accomplishments and notes on your career research; the second part, which includes your résumé and cover letter, will be material that you share with potential employers. (You can build a Career Portfolio online by going to the P.O.W.E.R. Learning Web site at **www.mhhe.com/power**.)

Career Portfolio Part I: Background Information

The information in this section of your Portfolio is meant to help you make career-related decisions and record your thinking about careers. This part is for your eyes only. Although you will draw on the material for the "public" part of your Portfolio that potential employers will see, think of it as your own, private repository of information.

Thinking about Work

At some point in your life, you've almost surely had a job. Maybe it was a summer position delivering mail, working in a factory, painting houses, or entering data. Or maybe it was selling lemonade when you were a kid or raking leaves for the neighbor next door. Or maybe it was unpaid community service in which you volunteered your time.

Whatever your specific experiences, you no doubt have developed some ideas about what it's like to work. Here's a chance to explore your thinking about work.

1. What was most rewarding about the work you did: the ability to earn money, social aspects involving your fellow employees, or enjoyment of the work itself?

2. What would you see as the positive and negative aspects of supervising other people? Would you like to supervise others at some point in your career?

3. How important is the amount of money that you're paid for the work you do?

4. Do you see work as something you must do in order to earn a living, or something that is a central and important aspect of life in and of itself?

5. How important is variety in what you do? How important is stability in what you do?

- **Basic personal data.** Keep a record of data and identification numbers that you think you'll never forget—but, even with the best intentions, you probably will not remember at the least opportune moment. For example, include your social security number, addresses (home and college), college ID number, and telephone numbers. If you're a renter, keep a record of your landlord's name and address; you might need a credit reference one day.

- **Career research notes.** Whether you have notes collected from book- or Web-based research, results of personality and interest assessments, or interviews with people in a particular occupation, they belong in your Career Portfolio. They will provide a record of your career-related activities.

- **Syllabus and outline from courses you have taken.** Include a copy of the syllabus and course outline of every course you take, along with the grade you received in the course. The information contained in a course syllabus and outline will serve to jog your memory about the material the course covered. Without these materials, you're at the mercy of your memory when you're trying to recall the content of a course you may have taken several years earlier.

  For further documentation relating to your courses, you could include a copy of the course description from the college catalog and, if the class had a list of competencies that students were to attain, a copy of these as well.

- **Transcripts.** Include the most recent version of your transcript, listing the courses that you took, credits earned, and grades you received in your classes.

- **Your personal history.** If someone were to write your biography, what are the key events that you'd want him or her to know about?

  The events that would be included in your biography can form the core of a list that you should make of every significant experience you've had. Although the list should include every employment-related experience you've had, such as last summer's job with a landscape service, don't limit yourself only to job experiences. Also include other accomplishments, such as the community service you performed in a battered women's shelter. Personal events that have had a major impact on who you are should also earn a place in your personal history, such as the car accident you had and the six months of physical rehabilitation that followed. Use Try It 3 on page C-12 to help make this list, which you'll use later to create a résumé.

- **Description of your ideal job.** Include a copy of the ideal job description you created in Try It 1.

- **Long-term career goals.** Your Career Portfolio should have the statement of your long-term career goals that you developed in Try It 2.

- **Writing samples.** Add examples of your best writing. These can be papers that you've handed in for classes or other writing you have done on your own. The idea is to have a sample of your writing easily available should a potential employer ask for one.

- **Credentials.** Include copies of any credentials you have earned. For example, place in the Portfolio a copy of diplomas you have earned, certificates of workshop or training participation you have received, proof of noncredit continuing education courses you have taken, and the like. You never know when an employer might want to see documentation of your accomplishments.

3

TRY IT!

Cataloging Your Personal History

	Activity or Event	When Activity or Event Took Place	Where Event Occurred (e.g., company, hospital, social agency)	Responsibilities or Actions Performed	Skills or Talents Used	Achievements, Results, or Insights
Did you work for pay or not, during or before high school?						
Were you a member of any clubs or other organizations in high school?						
Have you held any paid jobs since high school?						
Have you performed any community service?						
Have you provided any services to a religious institution?						
Are you working, either on campus or off campus, while at college?						
Are you in any clubs or organizations at college?						
Have you had any personally significant life experiences?						
Have you ever been called upon to exercise skills or talents you didn't know you had?						
Have you ever solved a tough problem and felt great satisfaction?						
Have you ever worked in a group to solve a problem?						
Have you ever organized a complex task on your own?						
Have you ever led a group in the performance of a large task?						
What is the best thing you have ever done?						

🚶 Working in a Group:

Compare your responses to those of other students in the group. What are the unique capabilities that you have, the things that set you apart from others in the group? How could you take advantage of those unique capabilities when you are seeking a job?

Career Portfolio Part II: Résumé and Cover Letter

This section of your Career Portfolio encompasses information that you will share with potential employers. Whereas the material in the first part of your Portfolio provides the background for your career planning, this is the public face of your Portfolio.

Think of the components of the first part as the equivalent of the backstage of a play, with a director and crew working behind the scenes to pull things together. In contrast, this second part of the Portfolio is the play the audience sees, the part that should proceed flawlessly. You want the critics to offer nothing less than two thumbs up for your production.

You may wonder: If you're not going to use your résumé and cover letter until you're actually looking for a job, why should you prepare it now? The answer is that it's much easier to prepare job-search materials when you're not under time pressure to produce them than when you're in the middle of looking for a job. You'll be able to create several drafts, rewrite them, receive feedback from others, and incorporate their suggestions.

By taking the opportunity to write a résumé and cover letter under (relatively!) leisurely conditions, you'll be better able to perfect what you produce. When you actually do begin your job search, your task will be updating rather than starting from scratch. Consequently, the work you put in now will pay big dividends later.

The two primary elements that belong in the second part of your Career Portfolio are your résumé and your cover letter.

Résumé A résumé (pronounced res-oo-may) is a brief summary of your qualifications for a job. It is the first thing that potential employers see and should serve to arouse their interest. Actually, a human may not even initially see it: an increasing number of employers use computers to screen résumés. The computers look for key skills, and if they are lacking, they send an automatic rejection.

Consequently, the résumé must be crafted with great precision and care. If you've created a personal history statement earlier for Part I of your Career Portfolio, use it to get started.

The key elements of a résumé include the following and are illustrated in a sample résumé in Figure C.1 on page C-14.

- **Contact information.** Include your name, address (current and permanent if they're different), phone number(s), and e-mail address. *Don't* include your sex, age, race, or marital status. Not only are they irrelevant, but employers who take them into consideration are breaking antidiscrimination laws.

- **Job objective.** If you are targeting a specific job, include a specific objective (such as, "to obtain a position as a buyer for a major retail department store"). However, if you're willing to be flexible, provide a more

Teaching Tip:
Explore the idea of computer screening of résumés and job opportunities. What words are essential in this stage of the career search?

Catherine M. Diaz

Present Address	Permanent Address
5327 Meridian St.	47 Franklin Lane
Kansas City, MO 64110	Springfield, MA
816 555-1212	413 555-7711

JOB OBJECTIVE—To obtain a position as entry-level news reporter

WORK EXPERIENCE
The University News, University of Missouri–Kansas City campus newspaper
Campus News Editor/Reporter

- Shared position of Campus News Editor; was responsible for assigning, coordinating, and editing of news stories and features relating to UMKC campus two times a week.
- Occasionally reported on issues of student housing, tuition, and diversity.
- Member of editorial board responsible for editorials.
- Wrote musical reviews on everything from local rock bands to Kansas Symphony Orchestra.

Kansas City Star, Kansas City, Missouri
News Intern
- Contributed background and library research for both feature and human interest stories.
- Aided in putting together special insert on Kansas Symphony Orchestra 2003 season.

EDUCATION
University of Missouri–Kansas City
BA English, June 2005

HONORS AND AWARDS
Academic Dean's List
The University News 2003 Award for Best Feature News Story on shortage of student housing

CAMPUS AND COMMUNITY ACTIVITIES
Women International Student Organization
Association of Latin American Students, Secretary

PROFESSIONAL MEMBERSHIP
Associated Collegiate Press

PARTICULAR SKILLS
Play piano and flute in local band
Speak fluent Spanish

REFERENCES
Available upon request

FIGURE C.1
Sample Résumé

general job objective (for example, "to obtain an entry-level position in retail sales").

Teaching Tip:
Ask students to go online and find sample résumés for positions they would like to explore.

- **Education.** Include the colleges you've attended or are currently attending, with the actual or anticipated year of graduation and degree earned.

- **Awards and honors.** If you've won any awards or honors (such as membership in an honors program or inclusion on the Dean's List) mention them. If you have none that you want to include, leave this category off your résumé.

- **Campus and community activities.** Include activities in which you've participated, and indicate any in which you've had a leadership role. You want to demonstrate that you are an involved, contributing member of your community.

- **Professional memberships.** Do you belong to any professional organizations that are relevant to the job you'll be seeking? If so, include them.

- **Work experience.** List your experience, starting with your most recent job and working backward. Include the job title, dates, and your major on-the-job responsibilities.

  Don't feel you need to include every job you're ever held (for example, leave out the occasional pet sitting). Instead, focus on the key positions that illustrate your ability to hold a job and to carry out responsibilities. Furthermore, as you present your work experience, always remember that the focus should be on how your past work can get you a job in the profession you want in the future.

- **Particular skills.** Do you know how to program in Linux? Can you speak Spanish fluently? Are you a certified lifeguard? Can you use an Excel spreadsheet or PowerPoint?

  Include a brief list of the special skills you have. Once again, make sure that the skills you list are related to the job you're seeking. For example, if you're seeking a job as an emergency medical services technician, lifeguard training is relevant, but it may not be if you're looking for a programming job.

- **References.** A "reference" category is optional, but if you include it simply say "References available upon request." Don't list specific names, but have them available should you be asked for them. (We'll discuss who to ask and how to obtain references later in the chapter.)

As you create a résumé, keep in mind some general rules. First, keep it short. In a résumé, less is more. Generally, résumés should be no longer than one page.

Second, make it look good. Your résumé should appear professional. Use plenty of white space, with one-inch margins on every side. Use strong action words, such as those in Table C.2 on page C-16. Avoid articles (such as "the," "a," and "an") and pronouns (such as "I" or "we"); don't write in full sentences.

Finally, proofread, proofread, proofread. You want to be sure that no typographical errors or misspellings find their way into your résumé.

TABLE C.2   Action Words

Using strong action words and making sentences short will help you prepare a professional and eye-catching résumé. Here is a list of action words to get you started. Use words that best describe what you do and who you are.

Achieved	Directed	Investigated
Administered	Discovered	Launched
Advised	Drafted	Led
Aided	Edited	Managed
Approved	Educated	Moderated
Arranged	Enabled	Monitored
Archived	Established	Negotiated
Assigned	Evaluated	Operated
Assisted	Examined	Organized
Authored	Expanded	Oversaw
Budgeted	Expedited	Performed
Built	Extracted	Recommended
Calculated	Facilitated	Recruited
Cataloged	Fashioned	Regulated
Chaired	Granted	Remodeled
Classified	Forecasted	Reported
Coached	Formulated	Restored
Collected	Founded	Reversed
Compiled	Generated	Reviewed
Computed	Guided	Saved
Conducted	Identified	Scheduled
Contracted	Illustrated	Solved
Controlled	Improved	Strengthened
Coordinated	Increased	Summarized
Counseled	Influenced	Supervised
Created	Informed	Trained
Critiqued	Initiated	Translated
Delegated	Inspected	Trimmed
Demonstrated	Installed	Tutored
Designated	Instituted	Upgraded
Designed	Instructed	Validated
Developed	Integrated	Worked
Devised	Interviewed	Wrote
Diagnosed	Invented	

IRM Link and Discussion Prompt:
Discuss with students the importance of using verbs to describe their accomplishments. Ask them to review the words on this list and share the list in the IM—Teaching the Text, Career Module, Section VIII.

The same rules hold for the second element of Part II of your Career Portfolio, your cover letter, which we discuss next. Before moving on, though, get a start on creating a résumé by completing Try It 4 on page C-18.

Cover Letter Although your résumé is the centerpiece of your presentation to potential employers, your cover letter is no less important. It shows that you can string words together into well-crafted sentences, and it gives you the opportunity to bring life to the list of qualifications on your résumé. It also gives you the opportunity to say how enthusiastic you are about the job for which you're applying and to illustrate how well your qualifications match the job requirements.

In writing a cover letter, keep in mind the perspective of the person who is reading it. Potential employers have a problem that they need to solve: identifying someone to do work that they need done so much that they're willing to pay someone to do it. The better you can provide them with a solution to this problem, the more attractive you will be.

What this means is that your cover letter should be oriented toward helping employers solve *their* problem, not toward how the job will solve *your* problems. Consequently, don't talk about how you think the job will fulfill you as a person or how much you need it to pay your bills. Instead, orient your letter toward describing how well your own unique qualifications match the specific job requirements.

Although every cover letter should be tailor-written to a specific position (see the two sample letters in Figure C.2 on pp. C-20–C-21), they typically contain the following elements:

- **Introduction: Catching the reader.** Describe why you are writing, how you learned about the job, and why you are interested in it. Emphasize the connection between the position requirements and your qualifications.

- **Letter body: Drawing in the reader.** Here's where you describe, in very brief terms, who you are and what makes you unique. Highlight major accomplishments and qualifications from your personal history, making the argument that your skills are a close match to the job. Show enthusiasm!

  You can also include information that does not appear on your résumé; for instance, if you paid for your education entirely on your own, mention that fact. In addition, you can write about what you hope to accomplish on the job.

  Finally, show that you know something about the organization to which you are applying. Do some homework to learn about the employer, and state specifically what you find attractive about them.

- **Conclusion: A call for action.** End the letter by restating your interest in the position and suggesting that you would like to discuss the position further. State that you are available to meet for an interview. Thank the employer for considering your application.

Like your résumé, the letter should read well and look good. Before you send it, be sure to proofread it carefully.

The point of including a sample cover letter in your Career Portfolio is to be ready at a moment's notice to revise the sample and send it off. Job opportunities sometimes appear unexpectedly, and it will be much easier for you to respond quickly, and respond well, if you already have a sample letter on file.

Unless you are certain of the job you'll be seeking in the future, you might want to prepare several cover letters, targeted at the different job possibilities you are considering. In addition, the act of writing cover letters for a variety of professions may actually help you come to a decision regarding the path you ultimately choose to follow.

One final note about your Career Portfolio: Keep in mind that it is a work in progress, a living document that is meant to be revised as your interests

Creating a Résumé

It's time to use some of the pieces you have been thinking about and working on to create a résumé. You have explored your ideas about your ideal job (Try It 1) and your occupational goals (Try It 2), and you have gathered important elements of your personal history (Try It 3). Now put the pieces together by filling in the worksheet below. Then use the worksheet to create a clean, one-page résumé that you can have reviewed and proofread.

Contact Information:
Your name, address, phone number(s), and e-mail address.

Job Objective:
Use your ideas about your ideal job and your list of occupational goals. Write one statement, beginning with the word "To," that sums up your goals. Be specific ONLY if you are applying for a job you understand and want to focus on; otherwise, state your goals broadly and generally.

Education:
List any colleges attended, including your current college, starting with the most recent. If you have taken college courses without being formally enrolled, list those too.

Awards and Honors (Optional):
List any honors you have received. Academic honors are of primary importance, but honors and awards from social, religious, and community groups (e.g., 4-H, Red Cross, Rotary Club) may be worth including if they testify to personal characteristics that may help you gain employment, such as leadership, perseverance, or a sense of civic duty.

Campus and Community Activities (Optional):
List any clubs, teams, or activities in which you participated in college. Include high school activities only if they were significant and are related to your career goals. Also list community activities in which you have participated, especially those in which you had a leadership role.

Professional Memberships (Optional):

List any professional organizations related to your career goals of which you are or have been a member. Professional organizations are groups such as the Modern Language Association; any of a number of national honor societies; the National Student Speech, Language, and Hearing Association; National Art Education Association; Student Sports Medicine Association; and the like.

Work Experience (If You've Had Any):

List all jobs you have had, including paid jobs (on campus and off), apprenticeships, internships, and similar "real" jobs. List your most recent work experience first and work backward through time. Include the title of the job, organization for which you worked, dates of work, and major responsibilities. Understand that you may be asked about any of the jobs you list, including your reasons for moving to the next job.

Particular Skills (Optional):

List anything you are particularly good at that might transfer to a work setting, including academic skills (e.g., excellent writing ability, ability to speak Russian), work skills (e.g., ability to fix computer hardware problems, write and debug software programs, repair engines, create Web sites, speak publicly), and even recreational skills and hobbies (e.g., unusual ability to complete or write crossword puzzles; proven ability to write creatively—meaning you have been published; ability to build and program robots, etc.).

References:

Available on request.

July 29, 2006

Mr. Reginald Pelly
Assistant Vice President
WorldWide Publishing Corp
New York, NY 10011

Dear Mr. Pelly:

Jennifer Windsor, Director of Editorial Development at WorldWide
Publishing, advised me of an opening in your company for an entry-level
trade book editor. From my enclosed résumé, you will find that both my
experience and my education fully meet the requirements you have
outlined for the position.

My current position as a copy editor at a medium-sized daily newspaper
has given me experience in dealing with deadlines and working closely
with others. Having served as a reporter for six years, I can relate to the
needs of writers as well. My colleagues consider me both outgoing and
diplomatic, traits that have served me well in my work as an editor.

I will contact you Monday to learn when we can meet for an interview.

Sincerely,

Martina L. Veschova

Enclosure: Résumé

FIGURE C.2
Two Sample Cover Letters

and aspirations change. That's why it may be a good idea to keep your Career
Portfolio in virtual form, rather than as a hard copy. By keeping your Portfolio in a computer file, you will be able to make revisions easily. Keeping the
Portfolio in virtual form also simplifies the process of producing your résumé
and cover letter for an actual job opening. If you do go the virtual route, just
make sure you have a backup copy.

Martin L. Chen

14A Orchard Street
Boise, Idaho 83702   email: marlchen@mrnr.com   Phone: 207 889-3763

July 29, 2006

Ms. Arlene Washington
Director, Human Services
Mercy General Hospital
18 Medical Plaza
Chicago, IL 60604

Dear Ms. Washington:

I am writing in response to the position advertised July 22, 2006, in the *Chicago Tribune* seeking a
Lead Cost Analyst Accountant. My professional experience and education match well with the
position requirements listed. Enclosed is my résumé.

In addition to being self-motivated, I work well under pressure and welcome new challenges and
opportunities. Among some of my accomplishments are the following:

- Analyzed, defined, and produced appropriate budgets for wages and salary
  costs, materials, expenses, and workload.
- Provided extensive, timely, and appropriate reporting for all aspects of the
  various budgets.
- Investigated variations from budget.
- Performed cost benefit analyses and assisted with capital expenditure proposals.

My experience in supervising a team of four co-workers has taught me patience and has
strengthened my organizational skills. My greatest satisfaction in a job comes from selecting,
training, and motivating personnel. I believe I have the qualities that can help a department
become more efficient and productive.

I am familiar with Mercy General Hospital from news stories on breakthrough cancer research
conducted there, and I have further researched your hospital and its contributions to medicine. I
feel there is a good fit between my career goals and your needs. I welcome the opportunity to
discuss the position further, and look forward to hearing from you soon. Thank you for your
consideration.

Yours truly,

Martin L. Chen

Enclosure

FIGURE C.2
Two Sample Cover Letters *(continued)*

E VALUATE: Getting Feedback on Your Résumé and Cover Letter

After you have created the key elements of your Career Portfolio—your
résumé and cover letter—it's time to evaluate their effectiveness. Start by asking a trusted person, such as one of your course instructors or someone on the

staff of your college's career center, to review what you've created. Ask them to provide honest and concrete suggestions, because the more feedback you receive, the better the finished product will be.

Once you've received an initial review, one of the best strategies is to ask individuals working in the field in which you're interested to review your résumé and cover letter. Requesting feedback from one or two people who are already working in your desired profession, particularly if they have hired people in the past, serves several purposes. First, your reviewers will be in the best position to know what employers are looking for, and they can tell you how to present yourself most effectively. Not only can they help you say the right things, but they can also help you avoid saying the wrong thing.

But there's an extra bonus from seeking advice from someone currently working in the field: You become a known quantity to them, and at some point in the future they may have a job opening and you may spring to mind. Or if you contact them in the future, they may be able to steer you to a job opening.

R ETHINK: Reconsidering Your Career Choices

Going through the process of identifying your skills and resources, researching careers, and building a Career Portfolio may lead you to solidify your ideas about which occupation you'd like to pursue. That's great—that's the point of career exploration.

But even if you are sure about what you intend to do professionally, it's important to take some time to reconsider your choices. Consider these questions:

- Does the occupation you've chosen take advantage of your skills and strengths?
- Have you been diligent in carrying out research about alternative careers?
- Are you excited about your choice?
- Does the job fit closely with your values and aspirations?

The most important thing is to avoid what psychologists call "foreclosure." Foreclosure is making a premature decision and sticking with it so persistently that you ignore other possibilities, even ones that hold considerable promise. Keeping an open mind by reconsidering your choices will help you be sure that you've made the best decisions.

What if you haven't been able to narrow things down? What if you're still completely up in the air about what career you'd like to pursue? First, realize that often it is absolutely fine to delay making a decision. If you're just starting college and don't know what you want to do, you're similar to millions of other first-year students who have no idea about their future careers. As you move through college and become exposed to new ideas and subject areas, you may move in professional directions that you can't even contemplate now. So relax for the moment, and don't feel pressured into making a decision.

On the other hand, if you're close to the point where you need to start work, and you still don't have a clue about what you want to do, then maybe you need to rethink your approach. Assuming you've considered various possibilities, you may want to reconsider the career-planning strategies you've been using. Ask yourself these questions:

- Have you been too restrictive or too selective in considering possibilities?
- Have you done sufficient research?
- Have you rejected professions that seem somewhat interesting without carefully considering what they have to offer?
- Have you underestimated (or overestimated) your skills?
- Have you taken full advantage of all the resources your college offers in terms of career planning?

By retracing the steps you took when you began the career process (see the P.O.W.E.R. Plan), you may find there are things that you could do to bring you closer to a decision. Finally, don't despair if you haven't identified something that you want to do for the rest of your life. Remember that most people change jobs multiple times during their working lives. If your first job doesn't work out, you've got many years to find something that works better for you. Like career planning itself, your career is an unfolding process.

> "Your true pilot cares nothing about anything on earth but the river, and his pride in his occupation surpasses the pride of kings."
>
> Mark Twain, author,
> *Life on the Mississippi*, 1883

Your References: Who Says What about You

Getting the job you want sometimes can hinge less on what you say about yourself and more on what others say about you. A good reference can make the difference between getting a job and getting passed over. A bad reference can destroy your chances of being offered a position.

CAREER CONNECTIONS

Starting Over: Once You Have a Job You Want

What's the best time to start looking for a job? When you already have one and don't need to find a new position.

Even if you feel happy and secure in your job, it makes sense to be prepared for the unexpected. Perhaps you'll get a new boss whom you can't work with, or your current job's activities and requirements change for the worse. Or maybe the company will downsize or be merged with another corporation, causing widespread layoffs.

For a variety of reasons, then, you'll want to keep your résumé and Career Portfolio updated, even if you've just started a new job. You will want to stay in contact with the people who have provided you with references in the past.

Above all, take every opportunity to learn new skills. As the economy and technology change, you'll want to have cutting-edge skills that will allow you to compete effectively.

In short: Be prepared!

That's why finding just the right people to supply potential employers with a reference can be the key to obtaining the job you want. That's why it's critical to identify people who are willing to speak on your behalf well before you face a deadline.

Identifying People to Provide References

Several categories of individuals can provide you references, including:

- Former job supervisors
- Colleagues in previous positions
- Class instructors
- Community service supervisors
- Coaches, club advisors, or heads of professional groups to which you belong
- People who can provide character references (e.g., clergy)

Student Alert and IRM Link:
See Teaching the Text, Career Module, Section IV; we suggest interviewing upperclassmen as part of career exploration. This is also a group to consider as references. Peer references can be informative and very different from those mentioned here.

The most effective references come from people who know you well—very well—and can speak to your skills, abilities, accomplishments, motivation, and character. In addition, people who can speak to the specific requirements of the job you're seeking (especially those who have worked with you in environments similar to that of the potential job) are highly effective.

The least effective references are those from family members or friends or, even worse, friends of friends. For instance, a reference from someone famous who happens to play tennis occasionally with your uncle will rarely be helpful, unless that person knows you well. Remember a key rule of references: The ability of a reference provider to describe in detail *your* strengths and *your* accomplishments is considerably more important than the identity of the reference provider, whatever *his or her* strengths and accomplishments.

What if you're seeking a position straight out of college, and you have no relevant work experience? That's fine. Potential employers understand that you've been in school, and they don't expect you to provide a reference from someone in a field in which you've never worked. On the other hand, if you have done an internship that is relevant to the field, a reference from your supervisor can be extremely helpful.

Asking for a Reference

When choosing someone to be a reference, **always ask permission.** Never give out the names of people who you think will provide references without asking them beforehand. Not only is seeking permission common courtesy, but asking first avoids violating another rule of references: *No reference is better than a bad reference.* You need to check that the reference someone provides will be an explicitly positive one.

Although you can't directly ask someone if they can provide a positive reference (it's very hard for someone to tell you straight out that they can't), you can approach the issue indirectly. When asking someone to serve as a reference, ask them if they have any reservations. If they do, no matter how minor, turn to someone else to provide the recommendation.

You should also offer some guidelines for those providing recommendations. Let them know why you're asking them in particular, and remind them of the context in which they've known you. If there is something you'd like them to specifically address in providing you with a reference—such as, for example, the unusual creativity you showed in a previous position or the fact that you wrote exceptionally good research papers in a class—let them know. The more explicit information you can provide them, the better.

The best time to request references from people is when their experience with you is fresh in their minds. For example, you should ask for a reference from an instructor at the end of a course or from an internship advisor when the internship is completed. Request a general letter, and add it to your Career Portfolio.

In addition, your college may have a career center that can maintain a file of letters of recommendation for you. These letters can then be sent to potential employers upon your request. The advantage is that such letters can be confidential—you won't get to see them—and potential employers may place greater weight on them because they'll be viewed as potentially more candid than nonconfidential letters.

Teaching Tip:
Many college career centers now offer online services to students; you can review job postings of employers who have a relationship with your institution. Does your institution have this service?

Teaching Tip:
Some Web sites are more complex than others. Consider your audience. If you are teaching freshmen, make sure the intricacies of the site are not discouraging. A class activity would include how to search different sites.

■ Using the Internet in Your Job Hunt

The Internet has changed some of the rules for conducting a job search. It permits you to post your résumé and have the potential for thousands of possible employers to screen it. It also permits employers to post their job needs and have the potential for thousands of possible employees to see them. You can even apply for jobs online. Internet services can help you to conduct automated searches, exposing you to job listings in your chosen field and receiving e-mails containing job postings that fit your skills.

The advantages of electronic job searches—such as the potentially wide exposure of your résumé—come at some potential costs. First, your résumé quite likely will be "read" by a computer. That means you must be extremely precise and follow some specific stylistic rules to avoid its being misread or ignored. Second, there are security issues, since you never know who may be reading your résumé.

In using the Internet for a job search, you need to cast your net widely. Although general interest job sites such as **monster.com** and **careerbuilder. com** post millions of jobs each year, there are more focused boards that can help you identify possible jobs in specific industries (see Table C.3). In addition, most large companies post job openings on their own Web sites.

TABLE C.3	Finding the Right Site on the Web[1]
Specific Sites	
www.HigherEdJobs.com	Teaching
www.EngineerJobs.com	Engineering
www.ShowBizJobs.com	Acting
www.Medzilla.com	Doctors, nurses
www.RXCareerCenter.com	Pharmaceuticals
www.HR.com	Human resources
www.dice.com	Information technology
www.LegalStaff.com	Legal
www.AgCareers.com	Agriculture

There are several general guidelines to follow when posting your résumé on an online employment site:

- Be very precise in the words you employ. For example, use action verbs and other words that are standard within an industry.
- Use simple type styles, such as Arial or Times New Roman.
- Avoid elaborate formatting, such as tabs or italics.
- Use a standard 80 characters per line.
- As always, proofread, proofread, proofread. A typographical error is more than embarrassing: Computers screening your résumé may reject your application before a human ever sees it because they do not recognize a misspelled word.

Job Interviews: Putting Your Best Foot Forward

For a potential employer who has never met you, a job interview puts a face to what has previously been an impression based on mere words written on a page. The interview is your chance to show who you are, to demonstrate your enthusiasm for a potential position, and to exhibit what you can bring to a position.

The fact that interviews are so important may make them seem intimidating and overwhelming. However, remember that the mere fact that you've been invited to an interview means you've overcome some of the highest hurdles already. Furthermore, there are a variety of concrete strategies you can follow to ensure that you maximize the opportunity an interview presents. Among the most important are the following.

Before the Interview

Teaching Tip:
This is an excellent place to bring role play into the classroom. Pair students as employers and interviewees. See Try It 5 for suggestions.

- **Learn about the potential employer.** It's important to learn as much as you can about the position and the company that is offering it. Go to the potential employer's Web site and find out as much as you can about the organization's management style and company culture. Then try to find magazine and newspaper articles to gain a sense of the success and effectiveness of the organization. The bottom line: If an interviewer asks, "What do you know about our organization," be prepared to answer, "Quite a bit, because I've researched it thoroughly."

- **Prepare with questions.** Come to the interview prepared with questions. Think up a set of questions and write them down so you can remember them—it's perfectly fine to refer to them during the interview. Having targeted questions shows that you've spent time thinking about the position. (Don't ask about salary during the interview; salary issues are usually addressed if you get an actual job offer.)

- **Prepare answers.** Finally, come prepared with answers to likely questions. For instance, it shouldn't be a surprise if an interviewer asks you to "tell me about yourself." So have an answer ready, a two- or three-minute response that touches on these aspects of who you are:

1. Your career goals and interests, and what led you to develop them.
2. Your intellectual and people skills.
3. Your previous experiences that are relevant to the job, including major accomplishments.
4. Your values.
5. Something personal about you, such as a hobby or unusual skill, that may be irrelevant to the job but gives the interviewer a sense of you as a person.

Student Alert:
Prepare questions for your interview. This is an excellent way to demonstrate that you did your homework and you are engaged in knowing more about the potential employer.

Obviously, this is a lot to cover in just a few minutes, so practice it until you can do it comfortably within that short time frame. Going longer than three minutes runs the risk of boring your interviewer. Furthermore, don't just practice it by yourself. Have someone else listen to it and give you feedback.

Other favorite interview questions include "What are your major strengths and weaknesses?" "Why do you want to leave your current position?" "What are your major qualifications?" "What are your short-term and long-range goals?" and "Why should I hire you?" Although you can't prepare for every possible question in advance, thinking through some of the most likely possibilities will help you feel more confident and ready to deliver polished responses.

During the Interview

IRM Link:
Teaching the Text, Career Module, Section VIII, Mock Interview activity.

■ **Be punctual.** Allow yourself enough time to arrive well ahead of the scheduled interview. That will help you find a parking space, locate the building and room, and generally get composed.

■ **Dress appropriately.** Wear the right clothes for the interview. Stop by beforehand to see how people dress. If you're unsure of how formal to be, keep in mind that it's almost always better to be overdressed than to be underdressed. This is not the time to make a fashion statement. You want to look professional.

■ **Use your social skills effectively.** Shake hands firmly, and look the interviewer in the eye. Show that you're interested in the interviewer as a fellow human being, not just as someone who might give you a job. Listen attentively to what he or she has to say, and be responsive. Above all, try to think confidently. Thinking positive, confident thoughts will help you appear positive and confident.

■ **Ask questions.** If you have prepared for the interview, you've got some questions to ask about the organization with which you're

Arrive at your interview on time, prepared, and confident. Do your homework and find out as much as you can about the company. Bring questions that demonstrate you are knowledgeable about the organization and are highly interested in the position.

> **"Rule No. 1: Just be yourself. Unless, of course, you're sloppy, lazy or otherwise undesirable, in which case, be someone else. Be ready to humbly sell yourself, and if someone asks about your weak points, say, 'Occasionally I just work too hard.' "**
>
> Rainbow Rowell, the *Daily Nebraskan*[2]

looking for a job. Be sure to ask them. Interviewers almost always ask if you have any questions, but if they don't, try to work them in when you sense that the interview is almost over. It's also a good idea to ask about the hiring process the employer is using. Ask how long it will be before they will be making a decision and when you will be hearing from them again.

- **Above all, be yourself and be honest.** You do yourself no favor by pretending to be someone other than who you are. Getting a job under false pretenses virtually guarantees that neither you nor your employer ultimately will be satisfied with your job performance. You may end up doing things you don't like to do and may not be very good at, and neither you nor your employer will find that acceptable for very long. (To get experience interviewing, complete Try It 5.)

After the Interview

Teaching Tip:
Again, your institution may offer important resources in a career resource or development center. Does the center conduct mock interviews? Can they videotape the session?

You may heave a sigh of relief at the end of your interview, but the interviewing process is not over yet. In fact, what you do after the interview is as important as what you do during the interview.

Interview follow-up consists of several steps, each of which can make the difference between whether you get the job or not:

- **Evaluate your interview performance.** Are you pleased with how you presented yourself in the interview? What did you do particularly well? What things could you have done better? Are there things you forgot to say? Were there out-of-the-ordinary questions that surprised you? Did you prepare sufficiently for the interview? What could you have done to be better prepared before you walked in the door?

  Jot down your impressions of the interview while they're still fresh in your mind and place them in your Career Portfolio. These notes will be valuable when you prepare for future interviews.

- **Consider if you still want the position.** Suppose, for a moment, you were actually offered the job. Do you really want it?

  It's important to ask yourself whether, given what you learned about the position, you would accept it if it were actually offered to you. You probably found out things about the position that interested you, and others that may be worrisome. Evaluate the job, and if there are too many negatives, rethink whether you'd actually want it.

  However, unless there are so many negatives that you're certain that under no circumstances would you take the job, don't withdraw your application. It may be that if you are offered the job, you could negotiate with your potential employer to eliminate the factors that you find undesirable.

- **Write a thank-you note.** It's common courtesy to thank someone for giving you his or her time during an interview.

  It's also strategically important. It shows that you are polite and can be counted on to do the right thing. It demonstrates your interest in the job. And it gives you one more opportunity to show you have the "right stuff."

5

TRY IT!

Interviewing

Nothing will prepare you better for an upcoming interview than a number of prior interviews. To get practice interviewing, ask an instructor, a person who has had experience in hiring, or even a fellow student to role-play an interview with you in which they will interview you, the potential job applicant. Tell them that you will prepare for your role carefully and that you will treat the practice interview seriously.

Follow these steps:

- Choose a company or organization that you would like to work for, and provide the person who will interview you with some details about it, such as information from the company Web site.
- You should also research your chosen company as a potential interviewee would, to gain enough knowledge to answer potential interview questions well.
- Hold the interview. You should be serious and try to play your role well. If you like, you can "dress the part" to help you set the right tone. You may also want to tape-record the session.
- After you've concluded the interview, ask your interviewer for a critique of your performance. Ask the interviewer to make as candid a judgment as he or she can as to which category you would fit into based solely on the interview: (A) Offer a job; (B) Don't offer a job; or (C) Call back for another interview to follow up with additional questions.

After you've completed the steps outlined above, answer the following questions:

1. What did you learn from the interview?

2. Critically assess your performance as an interviewee. What was your greatest strength as an interviewee? Your greatest weakness?

3. What would you do differently during an actual interview?

4. How can you better prepare for an actual interview in the future?

Although you shouldn't turn your thank-you note into a sales pitch, do indicate your continued interest in the position. Write about the aspects of the job that were of particular interest to you and explain how you can see yourself fitting in well with the company.

It doesn't hurt to write two thank-you notes, one sent via e-mail right after the interview and one that is a more traditional written note, mailed (via regular mail) to arrive about a week after the interview.

- **Follow up.** If you haven't heard from the employer in a few weeks, and it's past the point where you were told you'd be contacted, it's perfectly reasonable to e-mail or call. The purpose is not to badger the employer into hiring you—that's not going to work—but to simply check up on where the process stands. Of course, it also serves another purpose: to remind a potential employer of your continued interest in the position. You can also use the opportunity to provide additional information or to inform the employer of another job offer.

SPEAKING OF Success

Name: James S. Cook

School: Art Institute of Houston, Houston, Texas

James Cook readily admits he wasn't a very diligent student when in high school, skipping classes and not working very hard. He felt he would never make it to college.

His outlook would have almost become a reality if it were not for his love of art.

"I've always been an artistic person and had an eye for design," Cook said. "I started out doing graffiti on buildings, but I knew that I had to put my skills into an actual profession where I could succeed and not be the starving artist."

To further his education, he enrolled in the Art Institute of Houston, pursing a degree in graphic design. But he was not able to focus on his studies.

"I still had fuzzy goals, and I was stuck in trying to be social, instead of academic," he noted. "I wanted to succeed, but I wasn't fully engaged. If a class met three days a week, I'd be there for two and a half days."

He fell further and further behind, and became involved in activities that eventually led to a run-in with the law, causing Cook to drop out of college temporarily. However, it led Cook to turn his life around.

"I grew up and put away my childish ways," Cook said. "I hoped to return to the Art Institute, but I wasn't sure if they would let me back in."

Through the efforts of two administrators who saw his promise, Cook did return, with a new major in multimedia and Web design and, more important, with a new set of goals.

"The major thing I did was set a goal," he explained. "I said to myself that I'm going to graduate, and I'm going to do it on time. I also set little goals for myself along the way, helping me to know that I was on the right path.

"One of my main goals is to bring up my grade point average, which is now 3.1, to where I will qualify for the National Vocational Technical Honor Society, and I expect to do that the next quarter," he added. "Another goal is to use my hardheadedness within the system instead of against it."

Cook has kept busy. To support himself financially he has waited tables and has started a business designing Web sites and producing multimedia presentations. For spiritual support, he has become a youth leader in his church's youth ministry—in addition to carrying close to a full load of courses.

"Once I got back into school, my goals and focus were clear," Cook said. "I saw I could reach those goals. I knew I had to study and work hard in class."

How do I identify my ideal career and job?

■ Careful and systematic research is the key to identifying possible careers.

■ Books, Web sites, interest and personality assessments, and informational interviews provide useful information about careers.

■ A Career Portfolio can document a person's skills, capabilities, achievements, and goals, as well as provide a place to keep notes and research findings relating to jobs. It also includes one's résumé and cover letter.

What are the best strategies for finding and getting a job?

■ It is important to find appropriate references.

■ The Internet not only provides substantial information about potential jobs and companies but also can play an important role in getting a job.

How can I maximize my job interviewing skills?

■ Job interviews require a significant amount of preparation.

■ Useful interview strategies include being punctual, dressing appropriately, using social skills effectively, asking questions, being oneself, and being honest.

■ After an interview, follow up with the interviewer.

KEY TERMS AND CONCEPTS

Career Portfolio (p. C–9)

RESOURCES

On Campus

Your campus almost certainly has an office devoted to career planning. In addition, your college library, as well as any public library, will surely have books that can help you decide on a career and find a job.

In Print

There are thousands of books that can help you with career planning. One classic is Richard Bolles's *What Color Is Your Parachute* (Ten Speed Press, 2005), which comes out in a new edition almost every year.

Another useful guide is Frank Satterthwaite and Gary D'Orsi's *The Career Portfolio Workbook* (McGraw-Hill, 2003).

Finally, *Interviewing for Success,* by Arthur Bell and Dayle Smith (Prentice Hall, 2004), provides a great variety of interview strategies.

On the Web

The following sites on the World Wide Web provide opportunities to extend your learning about the material in this chapter. (Although the Web addresses were accurate at the time the book was printed, check the P.O.W.E.R. Learning Web site [**www.mhhe.com/power**] for any changes that may have occurred.)

■ The Planning a Career section of Mapping Your Future's Web site (**www.mapping-your-future.org/planning/**) discusses everything from developing a career plan to writing a résumé. It offers an abundance of other information related to students and schooling as well.

- Welcome to Resumania (**www.resumania.com/**). A fun, but practical look at those things you shouldn't put into a résumé. The term "Resumania" was coined by Robert Half, founder of the specialized staffing firm Robert Half International Inc. (RHI), to describe errors made by job seekers on résumés, applications, and cover letters.
- From the University of Toledo, Ohio (**www.buscareer.utoledo.edu/interviewing. asp**), this site offers a comprehensive outline on successful interviewing. It provides dozens of tips on various topics including how to research a company, frequently asked interview questions, and types of interviews.

TAKING IT TO THE NET

1. Use the Internet to identify two companies that work in one field that is of potential career interest to you (e.g., using the HotJobs section of **www.yahoo. com**). Find out what you can about the companies, trying to go beyond the public relations statements that you will find on their Web sites. Write down your impressions about such features as their location, current financial situation, history, work setting and atmosphere, dress code, and benefits, as well as your need for prior experience in the field, your chances for advancement, and anything else of interest to you. Note similarities and differences between the two companies. Can you tell enough about the two companies to prefer one over the other? Would your preparation for an interview with each company be different?

2. Explore at least two Web sites that offer advice about interviewing. See if you can find sample questions that are often asked at interviews (including both traditional questions and brainteasers), tips on what to do and not do at an interview, hints for making a good impression and improving your chances of success, and other advice. Write down the names of the Web sites you found helpful and take notes on the advice they offer.

NOTES

1. Farquharson, L. (2003, September 15). Find a job. *The Wall Street Journal,* p. R8.
2. Combs, P. (1998). *Major success.* Berkeley, CA: Ten Speed Press, p. 103.

PHOTO CREDITS

Page C–1: © Rob Melnychuk/Getty Images
Page C–2: © Siede Preis/Getty Images
Page C–8: © PhotoDisc/Getty Images
Page C–27: © Keith Brofsky/Getty Images

THE CASE OF...
The Job That Got Away

It should have been a slam-dunk interview.

At least that's what AJ Watts thought the day before he was scheduled to talk with a senior manager at the Luce Company. He felt he was perfect for the sales position Luce had been advertising on their Web site—he was good with people and certainly could talk a good game. Sure, he had no experience except for the painting jobs he held in college. But he figured what he lacked in experience he could make up in charm—it was sales, after all. Even though he didn't really know all that much about the company because the ad hadn't said much, the salary and benefits were terrific. It had all the makings of a dream job.

However, the day of the interview, everything went wrong. First his car wouldn't start, and he had to borrow a friend's, setting him back a half hour. Then he got lost getting to the Luce headquarters. By the time he arrived, he was 20 minutes late. He ran into the building from the parking lot, and because it was a hot day, he was short of breath and sweating profusely when he finally found the correct office.

Although he thought things couldn't get much worse, they did. The interviewer was visibly annoyed at AJ's tardiness, and he showed his anger by asking a series of tough questions. AJ, after trying his best to calm down, eventually began to get angry himself. When the interviewer asked AJ if he had any questions about the position, AJ couldn't think of one. The interview ended on a chilly note, with the interviewer snapping that if the company were interested in pursuing AJ as an employee, he'd let him know in the next few weeks.

So much for my dream job, thought AJ, as he made his way back to the parking lot.

1. Was AJ adequately prepared for the interview? What steps could he have taken before the interview to ready himself?

2. Is there anything AJ could have done to avoid being late? Once he realized he was going to be late, what could AJ have done to minimize the effects of his tardiness?

3. After the interview, what could AJ have done to try to remedy the situation? What steps should he take immediately? What could he do later?

4. Can you suggest ways that AJ could have prevented the interview from going so badly?

CHAPTER T

Transfer Strategies: Making the Leap from Community College to a Four-Year School

Alicia Martinez's campus visit had not gotten off to a great start. After driving two hours from home just to get to the Florida State campus, she drove around for another 10 minutes looking for a parking space. Compared to her community college campus, which had only a few buildings, the State campus was huge.

By the time she finally parked and found the Admissions office, her scheduled campus tour had already left, but the secretary in the office told her she could catch up with the tour. Alicia sprinted out of the office, looking for the tour group. To her relief, she soon found it and began walking around campus with the group.

As soon as she calmed down, Alicia found herself enjoying the tour. The library was amazing, and the campus student center looked like an upscale hotel. The large lecture hall they visited—so big the professor needed a microphone to be heard—was intimidating, but she figured she could manage.

In fact, as she saw more and more of the campus, she became more convinced that this was the right move for her. It would be a big transition from a small community college to a large university, but she was prepared for the challenge.

P.O.W.E.R. UP:
Use the questions in Try It 1.
It is a comprehensive, reflective approach to the issues a transfer student should consider.

LOOKING AHEAD >>>

The transition that Alicia was contemplating—transferring from a two-year community college to a four-year college or university—is one that millions of students make each year. That doesn't make it any easier, though. Transferring from one school to another is challenging, no less challenging than the move from high school to college.

But it's a challenge that can be met. With careful thought, preparation, and work, transferring can produce benefits that will help you for the rest of your life, both personally and professionally.

In this chapter we consider the transfer process. We address strategies for maximizing the credit you'll receive from your prior educational experiences. In addition we consider the application process and how to make choices among different educational institutions. Finally, we discuss ways of avoiding "transfer shock" when you move to a new college or university.

After reading this chapter, you'll be able to answer these questions:

- **What are the strategies for choosing a specific college or university to transfer to?**

- **How do I transfer credits?**

- **How can I adjust to a new college?**

Mastering the Transfer Process

Transferring from one school to another is not just a matter of credits, units, and courses. It is a process that will have an impact on your life in significant ways.

Although it is a complicated process, transferring can be broken down into a series of steps that will help you navigate your way.

P REPARE: Making the Decision to Transfer

Deciding whether to continue your education should not be taken lightly. You'll need to consider a variety of factors, including academic, financial, and social considerations. However, in some ways the most important part of the process is considering the reasons why you may be thinking of transferring in the first place.

Why Transfer?

There are many good reasons to transfer—and some bad ones. Let's start with the good reasons for continuing your college education at a four-year institution:

- **You will have more career opportunities.** Graduates of four-year schools have more opportunities in the job market and are more likely to get jobs that require sophisticated skills.

- **Your salary will be higher.** Graduates of four-year schools make on average $8,400 more annually than graduates of two-year schools (see Figure T.1). Over your lifetime, that's a big difference. In addition, unemployment rates differ: The unemployment rate for people with a bachelor's degree is lower by more than half a percentage point than for those with only an associate's degree.[1]

- **You will be better educated, understanding more about the world around you.** At its most basic level, college is about gaining an education, and the more college courses you take, the better educated you'll be. Don't underestimate the value of the knowledge you will gain if you continue your

Student Alert:
Not all career choices require a four-year degree. It is important for students to truly assess their educational needs in light of the career they hope to pursue.

PREPARE
Make the decision transfer

ORGANIZE
Get it together: Determine where you should transfer to

WORK
Apply to four-year schools

EVALUATE
Assess your options

RETHINK
Reconsider your choices

P.O.W.E.R. Plan

Educational Degree Attained	Median Earnings	Unemployment Rate
Less than high school grad	$19,700	7.10%
High school grad	$26,000	4.00
Some college, no degree	$30,400	3.20
Associate's degree	$31,700	2.50
Bachelor's degree	$40,100	1.90
Master's degree	$50,000	1.60
Doctorate	$62,000	1.40
Professional degree	$72,700	1.30

FIGURE T.1
Those Who Learn More Earn More: Earnings by Educational Level, and Unemployment Rate

education. You will be better informed about the world, have more basic knowledge, and will have the opportunity to specialize in different areas.

- **You'll have more options.** By enrolling in a new school you may find a program of study that is not available at your present, two-year school. This will open new options and directions for your education. You may have more opportunities to take advantage of an internship, study abroad, or even put together your own program of study. In short, the school to which you transfer may meet your own needs more effectively than your current college (also see the Career Connections feature).

Ultimately, once you graduate from a four-year college, you'll have more options available to you. As a graduate of a four-year school, you'll have gained more knowledge, skills, and experiences to be better able to fit into and profit from a changing world—both professionally and socially. You'll be better able to adjust to the changes that will inevitably occur during your lifetime.

On the other hand, there are reasons for transferring that may not be so good. Wanting to transfer because you don't know what else to do, because your parents won't let you live at home anymore unless you enroll, or because your boyfriend or girlfriend is enrolling and you don't want to be away from them are all questionable reasons for transferring.

However, even these less-than-optimal reasons may have value if they at least get you thinking about the possibility of continuing your education. To delve into the reasons—pro and con—for transferring, complete Try It 1 on page T-6.

Choosing Not to Transfer

In some cases, choosing *not* to continue your education is the right choice. For example, if you have had considerable academic difficulties, you may think twice about moving to a four-year school, where often the academic challenges are

Teaching Tip:
Ask the class to generate a list of possible internship sites or opportunities in the area to assist them in making better choices about their future work environment.

CAREER CONNECTIONS

Internships

Want to find out firsthand what it's like working in, say, public relations, human services, or government? One way to do it—and earn college credit at the same time—is to participate in an internship.

Internships are off-campus, temporary work situations that permit you to obtain experience in a particular field. They are not always paid, but in many cases can substitute for a course. For example, you might be able to receive three college credits for spending 10 hours a week at a work site during the course of a term.

Internships are an excellent way to learn about a profession, up close and personal. Working as an intern will let you know the kinds of things employees do on a day-to-day basis and the responsibilities and duties of the profession you're interested in. You can

gain experiences that you would not be able to get on campus.

Before signing up for an internship, make sure you have a clear agreement with your on-site supervisor about the type of work you'll be doing. If it consists of standing in front of a copy machine all day, you're not going to learn very much. Be clear that you are looking for valuable learning experiences during your internship.

You will also need to have your internship approved by your college, which will require documentation that the internship will provide experience that can reasonably substitute for a course. Undoubtedly, there will be forms to complete and signatures to obtain. This documentation will be important if you transfer to another college.

Be certain that you are assured of receiving credit before you begin your internship. That way you will have the best of both worlds: a career-enhancing experience and a chance to earn college credit at the same time.

even greater than you're currently experiencing. Furthermore, if you have little academic motivation and continually have to force yourself to be academically engaged, transferring to a four-year institution may not be the right choice.

Also, depending on your area of study (such as a trade profession), a two-year program may be the wisest choice. You may also need a more flexible schedule, which may be more difficult to obtain at a four-year institution.

Keep in mind that choosing *not* to continue your education is not an irreversible decision. You could work for a few years and then go back to college. "It's never too late to learn" is an accurate statement, and you may later decide that the time is right.

Whatever choice you make, be sure that it is *your* choice—a thoughtful, reasoned, and logical decision that takes account of your needs and preferences. Don't just do something because everyone else is doing it. The more you think about your choices—which you can explore further in the Journal Reflections—the more committed you will be about your ultimate decision.

O R G A N I Z E : Getting It Together: Determining Where You Should Transfer To

Once you've made the decision to transfer to a four-year institution, you'll need to determine *how* to do it and decide what schools you're interested in applying to. Although it's never simple to transfer—you're dealing not just with the

Journal REFLECTIONS

Should I Transfer?

Contemplate the reasons why you might want to transfer by considering the pluses and minuses of your current college.

1. What are the things you like best about your current college experience?

2. What aspects of your current college experience do you like least?

3. What are the things that you would miss most if you complete your schooling at your current school?

4. What might you gain if you transfer to a new college to continue your education?

5. What would be the drawbacks of transferring to a new college?

Why Consider a Transfer?

Examine your reasons for considering a transfer at this time by answering the questions below. Jot down notes in response to each question. Some reasons may seem more serious than others, but the purpose of this exercise is not to judge yourself, but to know yourself.

You may want to complete this exercise with the help of other people whose opinions you respect (such as fellow students, friends, parents, siblings, other relatives). If you are comfortable with this approach, you may find that varied ideas, suggestions, and feedback can really help you sharpen your focus and identify your strongest reasons for considering a transfer.

I. Academics:

- Does your current institution offer enough courses that you are interested in?
- Are there specific courses that you would like to look for elsewhere?
- Is there an entire area of study (i.e., a major) that you would like to pursue in another institution?
- Do the courses you have taken seem too limiting or too easy?
- Have you not done well academically and think you might do better or find better teachers at another institution?
- Have the courses you've taken sparked an interest that you would like to pursue in a four-year college?
- Have you discovered that you are a more serious student and more interested in learning than you thought you were?

II. Extracurricular Activities:

- Does your current institution offer enough extracurricular activities?
- Are there particular sports, clubs, organizations, or other activities that you would like to try out, whether at a competitive level or a less formal level, that are not offered at your current institution?
- Are you interested in experiencing, even just as a spectator, a higher level of student sports or performances?

III. Career Reasons:

IRM Link:
Visiting campuses is essential. See Teaching the Text, Section V, for a way to accomplish this step.

bureaucracy of your current institution but also with the one that you're seeking to transfer to—there are things you can do to simplify the process.

Begin with your own campus advisor. Almost all two-year colleges have a designated transfer advisor who can provide guidance. Even if there is no specific individual charged with providing transfer help, you can be sure that you'll find written material, on the Web and in brochures and catalogs, that can help you out.

A transfer advisor can help you identify four-year institutions with which your present college has existing relationships. Those institutions are the schools that should be at the top of your list of most likely transfer possibilities. Why? Because agreements between colleges will make the most of what you've already accomplished, giving you academic credit for more, or even most, of the courses you've already taken. (We'll talk more about the specific types of agreements later in the chapter.)

- Are you thinking of a career that is different from (e.g., more demanding or stimulating) the ones that a two-year degree will enable you to pursue?
- Have you identified a specific career that you can't pursue any further at your current institution?
- Are you interested in a career that promises to pay better than the ones available with a two-year degree?
- Have you been looking for a job and found nothing that is right for you?
- Are you simply not ready to start a career, but don't yet know what you want to do?
- Are you trying to expand your career choices by educating yourself further?

IV. Social Reasons:

- Do you feel that you have "used up" or exhausted the social possibilities available at your current institution?
- Do you want a more active, campus-centered social experience than what's found at your current institution?
- Are you interested in meeting a greater number of students from different states, regions, countries, and/or cultural backgrounds?
- Do you simply feel that you need a "bigger pond" to swim in?

V. Other Reasons:

- Are you simply looking to make a fresh start in a different place?
- Are you considering a change for geographical reasons (e.g., different climate, different region)?
- Are you considering a change to a different setting (e.g., a switch from an urban environment to a more rural one, or vice versa)?
- Are you trying to get away from someone or something in your current school or neighborhood?
- Are you pursuing someone who is at the institution you are considering transferring to?
- Are you being pressured (e.g., by parents) to transfer to a four-year college?
- Can you identify any other reasons why you are considering a transfer?

Transferring to Four-Year Institutions That Don't Have Formal Arrangements

Don't limit your choices of transfer schools only to those with formal arrangements. Although it clearly will be easier to transfer to a four-year institution that has a formal agreement with your current school, almost every four-year school accepts community college transfers. It may be harder, and you may be forced to take some extra courses, but the trade-offs may be well worth it. Why should you consider transferring to a school that lacks an agreement with your current community college? There are several good reasons:

- **You may be seeking a specialized major that only certain colleges offer.** If you have well-established career goals that involve specific course work or a

Teaching Tip:
Consider inviting an academic advisor or transfer specialist from your campus or neighboring four-year institution to class to answer questions.

Student Alert:
Transfer students who enter a campus with a substantial number of credits may be subject to different retention policies or academic standards than students who entered the institution as freshmen.

specialized course of study, you may be limited in the four-year institutions that provide what you want.

- **You may wish to continue your education in another state or geographic locality.** Because formal agreements are usually arranged between state-supported institutions within the same state, you're unlikely to find four-year colleges with agreements in locations that are distant from your current school.

- **You are seeking new academic challenges.** Perhaps you have done well in your current school, but you feel you haven't been challenged. Transferring to an institution that is highly selective in its admissions requirements may give you the opportunity to take on more academic challenges.

- **You are seeking a college that is very different from your current institution.** You may currently be attending a small school, with a student body that is not very diverse and classes where you know everyone. Maybe, though, for the rest of your college career, you'd like to experience a much larger campus, with a more diverse student body and classes in which you hear a broader range of opinions.

Narrowing the Choices

Once you've done the background research on which four-year schools best fit your academic needs, you may have a fairly long list of possibilities. How do you narrow that list to a manageable few to which you will actually apply? Here are some things to take into consideration:

Location and setting of a new school may be important factors to you. You may be looking for something entirely different than your current surroundings. Available housing or commuting time might also weigh heavily on your decision.

- **Where do you want to live?** There are four-year colleges and universities throughout the United States and Canada that can provide you with a fine education. You need to ask yourself whether location is an important consideration. How close to your family and friends do you want to be? Do you enjoy large cities, with their great cultural resources and sense of excitement, or do you prefer quieter, more rural areas where you can more easily enjoy natural resources? Do you intend to live at home and commute, or do you wish to live in a residence hall?

- **What is the philosophy and mission of the college?** Although every school has the basic goal of educating students, there are other aspects to the mission that differ significantly from one college to the next. You'll find a statement of the philosophy and mission of most schools on the Web or in a catalog. Use it to get a sense of what is important: Is the school oriented more to research than to teaching? Is there a religious affiliation? Is there an emphasis on student choice and freedom, or are there so many requirements that there is little room for experimentation?

- **How large is the college or university?** Schools vary significantly in size. The smallest four-year institutions have fewer than 1,000 students, and the largest over 50,000. Size matters: It sets the tone of the institution. Smaller schools offer more individual attention, and often classes are smaller than at larger schools.

At smaller schools, courses are typically taught only by faculty, but in larger universities with graduate programs, graduate students may do much of the teaching.

On the other hand, larger institutions may offer more courses in a greater variety of disciplines and often provide more services. Furthermore, even if their classes tend to be larger—and sometimes huge—the classes may break down into smaller sections with individual attention. If you are interested in specialized fields that require considerable equipment and facilities, a larger school may be better equipped to meet your needs.

Ultimately, there are trade-offs between colleges of different sizes, and no size fits all. You'll need to weigh the pros and cons based on your particular needs.

- **What is the student body like?** There are vast differences in the makeup of the student body of different colleges. You might want to consider the male–female ratio, the ethnic and racial composition of the students who attend, the number of foreign students, and the proportion of out-of-state to in-state students. You'll also want to check out the number of transfer students on campus and the number accepted each year. Finally, especially if you're an older student, you should check out the average age of the undergraduate student body on campus.

- **What extracurricular activities can you participate in?** Even if you haven't been a regular participant in activities outside the classroom at your current institution, you may wish to get more involved after you transfer. Consequently, determine what extracurricular activities are available at the schools you are considering. The possibilities can be staggering, including intramural sports, service organizations, student government, religious groups, theater and other arts groups, and campus publications.

- **Is student housing available?** One of the primary questions you need to ask yourself is where you intend to live. If you are thinking about living on campus, you'll need to know the options available to you. In addition to traditional residence halls, where you will probably have a double or triple room with the bathroom down the hall, many schools also have suites and apartments that you can share with only a few other students.

- **How much will it cost?** There are vast differences in the costs of different four-year schools. Public, state-supported schools are almost always less expensive than private colleges. However, even public four-year schools are usually more expensive than public two-year schools. Although financial aid packages at four-year schools may ease the sticker shock, you are still likely to end up paying more at a four-year college than you pay at a two-year school.

- **What is the school's reputation?** Although you won't find it in the school's promotional literature, try to find out something about the school's reputation. Among questions to ask: Are graduates highly regarded by employers? Are graduates readily admitted to graduate schools?

The only way to find answers to such questions is by asking as many knowledgeable people as possible. For example, your community college transfer counselor will have a good idea of the reputation of nearby four-year schools. Your instructors might also have some suggestions. Finally, you can consult college guidebooks (such as the *Fiske Guide to Colleges*) or the *U.S. News & World Report* annual rankings of colleges, which usually provide a fairly accurate picture of the strengths and weaknesses of four-year schools.

> **"'Tis education forms the common mind, Just as the twig is bent, the tree's inclined."**
>
> Alexander Pope, author (1688–1744)

Discussion Prompt:
Transfer students will (theoretically) spend less time on a campus than those who entered as freshmen. Ask your students to discuss what is gained and lost by making the decision to move to another campus.

Student Alert:
Ask students to determine if their intended transfer institution has a special orientation session for transfers or other ways to bring transfer students together. If not, encourage them to begin such an effort.

IRM Link:
Nothing replaces a campus visit when making a decision to transfer to another school (Teaching the Text, Transfer Module, Section V) but the next best plan is to encourage your students to engage in an e-mail conversation with a faculty member, academic advisor, or student at the transfer institution. If you have colleagues at a nearby institution that is a popular transfer site, invite those individuals to your class for a question and answer session.

■ **What is your own personal take on the school?** There is nothing like a campus visit to get a sense of what a college is like. If you can, take the time to visit the schools in which you are interested. Take a tour, talk to students, and get a general feel for the campus.

Don't be swayed by first impressions and irrelevant aspects of the visit—potential students tend to be less enthusiastic about a school if they visit on a cloudy, rainy day than if it's sunny and bright. At the same time, listen to your gut feelings. If you end up feeling that a school just isn't right for you, it probably isn't.

■ **Will the four-year school accept me?** In making your decision about which schools to apply to, be sure to consider whether it is likely that you'll be accepted. Although some four-year colleges have formal agreements that they will accept every graduate of certain two-year schools who are in good academic standing and have a certain number of credits, most schools do not have such an arrangement.

Every college will evaluate your academic credentials before they accept you. You need to examine a college's degree of selectivity and realistically consider your chances of getting in. Some colleges have minimum standards for prior academic performance which they state up front; others apply some type of standards but don't explicitly say what they are. In any case, your prior academic performance (including your high school grades) will be taken into consideration.

Does this mean you should avoid taking a risk and rule out applying to a school that you'd really like to attend? Absolutely not. You lose nothing—except the application fee—by applying to a college even if you believe it's a toss-up as to whether you'll be accepted. The important thing is to apply to other schools as well, ranging from those where you're nearly certain you'll be accepted to those that are a stretch.

After you've examined the options, try to narrow down your choices to no more than five. If you pick a range of schools—some relatively sure bets, some that are good possibilities, and perhaps a "stretch" school—you should be in good shape when admissions letters are sent out.

It's also important to create a backup plan in the event that none of your applications are successful. Be prepared to take action by rethinking your choices of schools. In addition, you might consider working for a year and reapplying or taking an additional class or two to improve your academic record. Preparing in advance for any eventuality is important.

To help you decide on the four-year school that you'd like to apply to, complete Try It 2.

W ORK: Applying to Four-Year Schools

Teaching Tip:
Not only can some applications be downloaded, completed, and mailed in, some institutions provide students with the opportunity to submit applications online. Hold class in a computer lab and show students the different options.

If you've prepared and organized yourself adequately, you're now ready to apply. In some ways, applying is the easiest part of the process of transferring, since in essence all you're doing is filling in the blanks on a variety of forms. Still, it's not simple, because there are quite a few steps you'll need to follow:

1. **Obtain an application from the colleges to which you are applying.** Sometimes you can download the forms from the Web, while in other cases you will have to ask the school to mail you an application. It is even possible that your current college may have applications available.

2

Your Transfer Preferences

The questions below should help you define your preferences and narrow your options.

1. What are the two or three main reasons why you are considering a transfer? (Use the list of reasons you generated as part of Try It 1.)
2. Where do you want to live? What country, region, state, city, or area?
3. What type of setting do you prefer (i.e., urban, suburban, rural)?
4. How large a school do you want to attend (e.g., fewer than 5,000 students, between 5,000 and 10,000 students, or more than 10,000 students)?
5. What sort of student body do you prefer in terms of diversity, gender mix, geographical origins, etc.?
6. What potential major(s) are you considering?
7. What sort of academic standards and difficulty level do you want in a four-year college (high, moderate, relaxed)?
8. How much money are you prepared to pay each year? How large a loan are you willing to carry?
9. What other needs do you have (e.g., sports programs, religious affiliation, art or performance opportunities, student housing, handicapped accessibility, laboratory facilities, library, etc.)?

Use your answers to these questions to find four-year colleges that will meet your needs. You can do this by discussing your needs with a counselor at your current institution and/or by using a Web-based college search tool, such as the one at **furtheryoureducation.com** or **collegeboard.com**. If you find a school in your immediate area (i.e., commuting distance) or in your state, remember to find out if it has any kind of transfer arrangement with your current institution.

2. **Make a list of the application deadlines.** Schools have deadlines for receiving all your materials. Sometimes there is a priority period, during which your application will get preferential treatment. Miss the priority period, and you may lose your preference. In other cases, schools have a "rolling" admissions process, which means the earlier you get your application in, the earlier you will learn about whether you have been accepted.

3. **Identify individuals who can provide you with a recommendation.** Because most schools require several recommendations, you will need to identify several people who can provide you with strong references. Look back over your academic career and think of the courses in which your performance was strongest or the classes in which an instructor took special notice of your talents. You can also ask counselors, employers, or members of the clergy who know you well to write a letter. Good recommendations can also be provided by high school teachers who knew you.

   Be sure to ask people if they are willing to write a recommendation well before any deadlines, and give them any forms provided by the college to which you are applying. Also include a stamped, addressed envelope to make it easy for them to return the recommendation.

4. **Arrange for transcripts and test scores to be sent.** You will need to send an official college transcript, listing the courses you have taken and your grades, to the colleges and universities to which you are applying (also see the accompanying Course Connections feature). In some cases they may also want a copy of your high school transcript.

You also may need to send a copy of your standardized test scores, such as the SAT or ACT. You won't need to retake these examinations if you have already taken them; just arrange for the testing service to have them sent directly to the schools to which you are applying.

5. **Complete the applications.** Filling out forms is not fun. It takes effort and concentration. But it is important to complete the application carefully and legibly. You are providing a first impression that can make an impact, even in a small way, on the person deciding on your admission.

The application will undoubtedly ask for a variety of information, including your name, social security number, addresses, educational history, residency status, languages spoken, and so forth. Not only should you be clear in your answers, but you must follow the cardinal rules of applications: Be yourself, and be honest.

If an application requires an essay, leave yourself plenty of time to write it. After you compose a first draft of the essay, it is perfectly acceptable to run it by others who are good writers to get their feedback. Use their com-

Teaching Tip:
The transfer process requires planning and is an excellent opportunity for reinforcing time management lessons.

COURSE CONNECTIONS

Documenting Your Courses

While you are gathering the information that you need to send to the colleges to which you are applying, there's one more step in the process: Gather documentation for every course that you have taken. What that means is to collect as full a description as possible of each course that you have completed (or in which you are currently enrolled).

There are several good reasons for documenting your courses. Some time in the future, you may wish to take a course at your new institution that requires that you've already taken a prerequisite (a particular course that must be completed before one can enroll in the new course). For instance, you may want to take an abnormal psychology class that requires that you've already had an introductory psychology class. You may need to provide evidence not just that you've taken a course called "Introductory Psychology," but what the course consisted of.

In other cases, there may be a required course at the college to which you transfer that you've already taken. Having full documentation of the course content will make getting excused from the required course at your new institution considerably easier.

To document your prior courses, put together a separate folder for every course you've taken. At the very least, it should contain a syllabus for the course showing the course description and goals, textbook name, and topics covered. You can also include in the folder any papers or tests you've completed in the course.

Think of your course documentation in the same way you think of a medical insurance policy. You may never need to use it, but if you do need to, you'll be awfully glad you have it.

ments to improve your essay. Remember that the essays are less a test of writing mechanics—although they do matter a lot—and more a way for the college to get a sense of who you are. Let your personality show through.

The last three steps in completing your applications are proofread, proofread, and proofread. You need to be sure that you have answered all the questions, that you've checked your spelling, and that everything is legible. Don't forget to sign the application, and then send it off—and wait!

Use the checklist in Try It 3 on page T-14 to keep track of your work.

Student Alert:
Remind students not to skip any required steps when applying to another institution. It will delay their acceptance.

E VALUATE: Assessing Your Options

At some point down the road—it may be as soon as a month or so, or as long as six months later—you will know how successful you have been. Whatever the outcome, you'll need to deal with your options.

If you've been accepted by most, or even all, of the schools to which you have applied, consider yourself lucky. But you still face some tough decisions, since each school will have specific benefits and drawbacks.

Although you probably considered the pros and cons of the colleges before applying, you are likely to have gained some new information from your letter of admission. Specifically, you may have learned how many of your prior credits will be accepted for transfer. Comparing what the different schools will permit you to transfer can help you make an informed decision.

Financial Aid Packages

Your acceptance letter may have brought another piece of information, this in the form of a number: the amount of financial support you are being offered. If financial aid makes a difference to you—and it most likely will—you must then carefully evaluate the different financial packages.

Financial aid packages are not written in stone. You have nothing to lose by attempting to negotiate a better package, and there are two strong reasons for trying. First, financial aid is generally made up of several components, including direct scholarships, loans, and campus job earnings. The greater the direct scholarship offered, the better, since there is no payback or work required. Second, the overall size of the financial aid package can make the difference between whether you can afford to attend the school or not. Thus, it makes sense to try to ask for a larger overall package.

Although negotiating may seem daunting, it's important to make the effort. Here are the steps to follow:

- Call to make an appointment to speak with a financial aid officer.

- Prepare a case that shows why you need a better package. Remember that you can ask for a larger package overall and/or ask for a change in the specific components of the package. Justify what you are asking for by showing how the current financial aid offer is too small to allow you to afford attending the college.

- If your desired school's offer is smaller than that of another college, mention that. A college that knows you will definitely attend if they can provide a better offer has a greater incentive to provide more aid.

- Be polite as you present your case. Heavy-handed tactics will not work. You want the financial aid officer to do everything possible to permit you to attend the college.

Teaching Tip:
There is a difference between campus-based and federal/FAFSA-based financial aid packages. Tell students not to assume that an aid package from one school will look like the aid package from another school. Also, financial aid information is not shared by institutions; it is the student's responsibility to apply and send information to *each* campus.

Following the Application Trail

Use the running checklist below to keep track of the steps you will take in applying for admission to four-year colleges.

Application Step	Notes	Step Begun (date)	In Progress	Step Completed (date)
1. Obtain applications (enter college names)	Enter application deadlines below			
College 1:				
College 2:				
College 3:				
College 4:				
College 5:				
College 6:				
2. Identify and ask for references (enter name of each reference below)	Enter addresses, phone numbers, e-mail addresses below			
Reference 1:				
Reference 2:				
Reference 3:				
Reference 4:				
Reference 5:				
3. Follow up on references	Enter a check (✓) if letter of recommendation has been sent			
Reference 1:				
Reference 2:				
Reference 3:				
Reference 4:				
Reference 5:				
4. Arrange transcript(s)	Enter contact information to obtain transcript (usually Registrar's Office)			
Transcript 1:				
Transcript 2:				
Transcript 3:				
5. Complete applications (fill out form, complete essay, proofread, mail)	Enter F for form, E for essay, P for proofread, and M for mail			
College 1:				
College 2:				
College 3:				
College 4:				
College 5:				
College 6:				
6. Keep track of results	Accepted? Financial aid?			
College 1:				
College 2:				
College 3:				
College 4:				
College 5:				
College 6:				

To help you assess your options among several colleges that have accepted you for enrollment, complete Try It 4 on page T-16.

R ETHINK: Reconsidering Your Choices

If you've been accepted to a four-year school, the decision to attend takes on a life of its own. Before you enroll, though, take a moment to reassess your decision. Are you continuing your education for the right reasons? Are you doing it for yourself or to please someone else? Does the thought of taking more classes, spending late nights writing papers, and studying for tests fill you with dread and anxiety?

Unless you are fully committed to attending college, you should reconsider your decision to transfer. In most cases, you'll probably conclude that your decision to pursue a transfer to a four-year school was the right one. But if you are not sure, then systematically review your choices. For instance, you might want to work for a period before continuing your schooling. Many colleges will permit you to defer admission for a year, and that might be the right option for you to take at that point in time.

(To review the steps in transferring, see the P.O.W.E.R. Plan on page T-3.)

■ Making the Most of Your Transfer Credits

Perhaps you are moving straight from a two-year college to a four-year school. Or perhaps your route has been a little more roundabout, and your earlier educational progress has come in fits and starts. Maybe you've had to suddenly leave college because of a business transfer or the need to take care of an ailing relative, and you have accumulated college credits from a number of schools.

Whether the route has been straight or winding, having your college credits evaluated to determine how many will be accepted for transfer to a four-year college is central to transferring. The outcome of this process is crucial, and it can determine how many and what courses you will need to take in the future. It can also save—or cost—you thousands of dollars.

Getting Credit Where Credit Is Due

The process of determining how much credit you will receive is complicated and the outcome can be affected by several factors, including:

- **Where you earned the credits.** Unless a school is accredited (approved) by the appropriate state or regional authorities, courses will not be accepted for transfer. Although most two-year schools are accredited, if you have any doubts, you should check before beginning the process of transferring. Similarly, if you took a course through a continuing education program, the credits you earned may not count as college-level work (even if you received "continuing education credit" for them).

- **The grades you received in the course.** Many four-year colleges require a grade of C or better in order to accept a course.

Student Alert:
Remind students that the question "Will my credits transfer?" is different from "How do my credits transfer?" Students may receive 30 transfer credits, but only 10 of these credits may be used toward the specific program of study or major they hope to pursue.

Teaching Tip:
Remind students to explore credit for out-of-class experiences they might have under their belts—travel abroad, service learning opportunities, leadership roles, internships, etc.

Assessing Your Options

If you have several options to consider, complete this Try It to organize your thoughts and weigh the options.

1. How closely does each college match the preferences you identified in Try It 2? Use a scale of 1 to 4 to rate each college, where "1" = Not a close match and "4" = A very close match. Then add the ratings in each column.

Your Preferences	Ratings (1 to 4, Higher Is Better)		
	College 1	College 2	College 3
1. Your main reasons for transferring: Reason 1			
Reason 2			
Reason 3			
2. Where you want to live			
3. Setting of school			
4. Size of school			
5. Student body			
6. Major(s)			
7. Academic standards			
8. Cost			
9. Other needs			
Total Preference Rating (highest possible rating is 44)			

2. Now look more closely at the cost of attending each college. Use the categories below to estimate what it would cost **per year** to attend each one. Then, in the last row, enter a "3" for the highest cost college, a "2" for the next lowest, and a "1" for the lowest (assuming you are rating three colleges).

Your Preferences	College 1	College 2	College 3
Estimated Costs			
Tuition			
Room and board			
Textbooks and supplies			
Transportation			
Other expenses			
Total costs			

Your Preferences	College 1 _____	College 2 _____	College 3 _____
Estimated Available Funds			
Savings or help from home			
Scholarships			
Loans			
College work programs			
Other work			
Other income			
Total funds available			
Costs minus funds			
Cost Rating (1 to 3, assuming three colleges; higher number corresponds to lower cost)			

3. Next consider how many credits from your current institution you will be permitted to transfer to each college. In the last row enter a "3" for the greatest number of transferable credits, a "2" for the next lowest, and a "1" for the lowest (assuming you are rating three colleges).

Your Preferences	College 1 _____	College 2 _____	College 3 _____
Number of credits transferable			
Credit Transfer Rating (1 to 3, assuming three colleges; higher number corresponds to more credits transferable)			

4. Now consider your overall impression of each college, based on visits you have made or on other information. Rate each college on a scale from 1 to 4, where "1" = very unfavorable impression and "4" = very favorable impression.

Your Preferences	College 1 _____	College 2 _____	College 3 _____
Overall Impression Rating (1 to 4, higher is better)			

5. Finally add up your four separate ratings to produce a Total Rating for each college.

Your Preferences	College 1 _____	College 2 _____	College 3 _____
Total Rating (= Total Preference Rating + Cost Rating + Credit Transfer Rating + Overall Impression Rating. Higher is better; highest possible rating is 54.)			

While you may use these ratings any way you want, or even ignore them, they may help you decide among your options.

- **When the credits were earned.** If the credits were earned many years earlier, some colleges will not accept them. This is especially true of programs in which there have been significant advances, such as computer technology and genetics.
- **The level of the courses.** In order to graduate from a four-year program, you will need to take a variety of lower- and higher-level courses. Some four-year programs will accept only a limited number of lower-level courses and will require you to take more upper-level courses when you transfer.
- **Residency requirements.** Virtually all schools require that you earn a certain number of credits on their campus. Consequently, the need to fit in the required number of courses at the new college may cause some previous credits to be disallowed.

All these factors, and many more depending on a particular college's regulations, enter into decisions about whether your prior credits can be transferred. Happily, though, matters can be much simpler if the college you wish to transfer to has a special arrangement with your current school. As we discuss next, such agreements can ease the transition significantly.

Transfer Agreements

In some cases, schools have done much of the work of transferring credits for you by entering into transfer agreements. Among the most common arrangements are the following:

Articulation agreements
Formal arrangements with four-year colleges that will automatically accept certain courses or credits taken at your current institution

Teaching Tip:
Many public institutions have an online resource page that gives information about how specific two-year institution courses will be counted at four-year institutions.

2 + 2 plans
A formal agreement between a community college and a four-year institution that permits students to transfer courses into a specific major or specialty program

- **Articulation agreements.** Most community colleges have **articulation agreements,** formal arrangements with selected four-year colleges that will automatically accept certain courses or credits taken at your current institution. Articulation agreements may even spell out what groups or blocks of courses will be accepted, as a set, by a four-year college to which you're considering applying.

  For example, an articulation agreement might specify that English 1 at a community college is the equivalent of English 100 at a particular college covered by the agreement, and that History 2 is the equivalent of History 101. If you have taken one of the courses covered by the articulation agreement and achieved some specified minimum grade, credit for that course will automatically transfer to the four-year college.

  Articulation agreements are often complicated and difficult to understand, but it's worth the time and effort to decipher what they say. They can save you literally hundreds of hours, permitting you to avoid repeating courses similar to ones you have already taken or scrambling to complete requirements at your new college.

  In most cases, articulation agreements cover basic, general education courses. They typically do not cover more specialized, advanced courses counted toward a future major at the four-year institution to which you are transferring. There is an exception to this general rule, however: 2 + 2 plans.

- **2 + 2 plans.** Many state higher education systems have what are called 2 + 2 plans. A **2 + 2 plan** is a formal agreement between a community college and a four-year institution that permits students to transfer courses into a specific major or specialty program.

  Courses a student takes at the community college level are applied not only to general education requirements at the new institution but also to a major or other specific program. In most cases, 2 + 2 plans are restricted to only a few selected majors, such as human services, nursing, computer technology, or engineering.

The main advantage of 2 + 2 plans is clear: They can provide you with a real head start after your transfer. The downside of a 2 + 2 plan is that it may tie you to a specific major earlier than you may want. Unless you are quite sure of what you want to specialize in, 2 + 2 plans may lead you to make a choice before you are ready to make it.

- **Priority enrollment plans.** Even if there is no formal agreement between a community college and a four-year state school to accept particular courses, some state four-year colleges have priority enrollment plans. In a **priority enrollment plan,** a four-year school gives preference to students from community colleges within the state when it considers which students to admit as junior-year transfers. Although priority enrollment does not guarantee admission, it provides potential transfer students from state community colleges with an advantage over other applicants.

Priority enrollment plan
A plan that gives preference to students from community colleges within the state when it considers which students to admit as junior-year transfers

The Appeal Process: When No May Not Mean No

You've completed Psychology 1, "Introduction to Psychology," at your community college, but the university to which you are transferring hasn't given you credit for it. What should you do?

Although you may think your hands are tied, you generally do have some options. Remember, transfer credit decisions are not made by a college, but by a person who works for that college. That person can be rushed, can make a bad decision, or may just plain be in a bad mood when evaluating your previous courses.

If you feel that a mistake has been made, you probably have the right to appeal the decision. Don't appeal it lightly or without considerable deliberation, but also don't be reluctant. You won't be seen as a troublemaker, but as a serious student who wants to right a possible academic wrong.

The first thing to do is to try for an informal resolution. E-mail or call the office where the decision was made, contacting the person who made the initial decision. Ask if the decision can be reviewed, and be ready to show why you should be granted the credit.

If the informal route is ineffective, then you may be able to file a formal appeal. An appeal may consist of a form, or it may be a letter stating your case. Find out what the specific process is, and be prepared for a lengthy procedure. Your appeal may be evaluated by a committee of faculty and administrators. Keep it brief and to the point and, as always, be sure you carefully proofread the document before you send it.

What arguments are most persuasive? The best is to clearly demonstrate that the course you have taken is, in fact, very similar to the one offered at your new institution. You can demonstrate the similarity by showing that the course syllabus and textbooks used in the two courses cover similar material. If the syllabus from the course you took does not show a significant course component that was actually included in the course, enclose additional handouts from the course, or ask the original course instructor to provide a "To Whom It May Concern" letter that states that the seemingly missing component was, in fact, covered in the course.

Teaching Tip:
Remind students to "be polite, be persistent, and provide documentation" when seeking specific recognition of credit.

Teaching Tip:
When making an appeal for course credit, remind students to offer realistic substitutions and explanations. It seldom helps to be angry or become overly emotional in an appeal process.

> "Knowledge comes, but wisdom lingers."
>
> Alfred Tennyson, author (1809–1892)

Making the Move: Mastering the Transition from Old to New College

You've done it!

You've made the move from your previous school to your new one. However, your feelings of elation at being accepted may turn to anxiety and concern as you face the prospect of starting over. How you manage the transition can have repercussions for the rest of your college career.

Transfer Shock

Student Alert:
It is easy, particularly in the beginning, to criticize a new institution because it is different from what has already been experienced.

Many students experience what has been called *transfer shock*, the feeling that their new college is so different from their old one that they will be unable to adjust. Students experiencing transfer shock may feel lonely and unhappy, and they may question their decision to transfer.

Why might you face transfer shock? There are a number of challenges posed by a transfer to a new college, including these:

- **Time management issues.** Every college operates on a slightly different schedule and time frame. Your old college may have started the term in August and finished before the end-of-year holidays. Your new college may start later and finish the term after the first of the year.

  The two schools may even have different term lengths. You might be changing from a semester system, in which the term consisted of 15 weeks, to a quarter system, in which terms last 10 weeks. What that means is the rhythm of the terms will be completely different. For example, in a quarter system, the term is nearly over at the same point in a semester system where you've just reached the midpoint of the course. Such changes in the timing of a course can be disorienting, and you need to prepare yourself for them by paying special attention to time management strategies.

- **Academic requirements may be more stringent.** Your courses may be more rigorous, requiring greater effort. You may be reading and writing more than you were used to. Assignments may call for more higher-order thinking, and courses may present concepts that are more abstract. You also may have to take classes in technical subject areas in which you have little interest or natural ability.

  If your classes are large, you may have to take multiple-choice exams, bubbling in your answers on machine-scored forms just like you did when you took the SAT or ACT standardized tests.

  In addition, your classes may require the use of technology in significant ways. Course assignments may be posted on a course Web site, and you may do homework online. You will need to develop new technology skills and have access to a computer.

- **Financial demands.** Four-year institutions are often more expensive than two-year colleges. Even if you have received a generous financial package from your new school, you still may face difficulties in making ends meet. In

Discussion Prompt:
Invite students to make a list of their strengths and weaknesses as a brainstorming exercise in class. Many transfer students experience a drop in their grade point average the first semester of transfer work but improve in subsequent semesters. Remind them that their experience makes them more mature learners which should lead them to seek additional support earlier.

addition, if the courses are more challenging than you've previously faced, you may have less time to work at a part-time job to help support yourself.

- **Roommate challenges.** If you previously lived at home and commuted to college, becoming a residential student will offer a stark contrast. You may live in a small room with two, three, or sometimes even four other students with whom you may have little in common. You'll share a bathroom with people you don't know and whose concerns about cleanliness and neatness may be very different from your own.

- **Commuting issues.** If you are a nonresidential commuter, you will have your own set of challenges that residential students don't need to worry about. For example, your new college may be farther away from home than your old one, requiring a longer commute. In addition, once you arrive on campus, you may encounter parking problems. On some campuses, finding a parking space close to where your classes are will be a challenge.

  If you are commuting to a school where most other students live on campus, you'll face other issues, as well. For example, scheduling times to work on a group project will be more difficult. If you forget to pick up a book at the library, it may mean you need to make a long trek back to campus.

Student Alert: Residential campuses seldom have the same level of parking that commuter campuses have—remind students that they may need to adjust their expectations about transportation options.

- **College size differences.** If your new school is larger than your old one, you'll face other challenges. Bigger colleges mean more students, larger classes, and a bigger library. You will probably have to stand in longer lines. In large classes, there may be hundreds more students sitting with you in a huge lecture room than you've experienced before. The only thing smaller will be your view of the professor, who may be so far away from where you are sitting that you can barely see him or her.

  On the other hand, that doesn't mean that the skills you have developed in your earlier years of college are suddenly useless. If you have learned to use a computerized library catalog and find a book in the stacks at your old school, you'll undoubtedly quickly manage to do the same thing at your new school. Similarly, taking lecture notes in large classes requires much the same set of skills as taking notes in small ones.

- **Diversity issues.** The student body of your community college might have been relatively homogeneous, consisting of students who grew up in the same geographic area and having little ethnic and racial diversity. Moving to a new four-year school may mean a more diverse student body, which can be challenging, but can also be a great learning experience.

  For example, you may find yourself uncomfortable with the political attitudes advocated by classmates in your courses. You may hear speeches by people whose views you find puzzling or even objectionable. You may be assigned a residence hall roommate whose habits and customs you don't understand. Other classmates may practice religions that you've never even heard of.

  All this means is that you have to be open to people who are different from you. Realize that they have had experiences that are very different from the ones you've had, and that their perspective on the world may be quite dissimilar from yours. However, opening yourself to people who are different from you will enrich both your college experience and your education as a whole.

In addition to facing these challenges, you will undoubtedly encounter challenges that are specific to your own situation. Use Try It 5 to consider the factors that might have the most impact on you.

TRY IT!

5

Absorbing the Shock of a Transfer

Once you have decided to transfer to a four-year college, you can expect to feel some degree of transfer shock. A good way to lessen the effects of transfer shock is to prepare in advance for the shocks that you are most likely to experience and to be ready to do something about them. Use this Try It to consider likely shocks and prepare to absorb them.

In the first column, consider the most likely sources of discomfort under each category that applies to you. If you don't think you will experience any shock in that category, move on to the next. Then in the second column, try to come up with creative ways to deal with each possible shock.

This is an exercise that you may want to complete with a group of friends. It helps to put a lot of creativity and imagination from more than one mind to work in thinking up effective "shock absorbers" to call on in your first months at your new school.

Source of Potential Shock	What Can I Do about It?
Time management issues: • Different term schedule at new college? • Courses meet at different times of day? • Assignments due on shorter time line? • Need to do part-time work to afford new college? • Less time structure and more responsibility to manage own time? • Other time issues?	
Academic issues: • Harder courses at new college? • Courses move at faster pace? • More reading and writing? • Need to spend more time in library? • Different types of tests? • Greater use of technology? • Other academic issues?	
Financial issues: • Hard to pay tuition and fees? • Worries about student loans? • Higher transportation costs? • More expensive books, and more of them? • Higher entertainment costs? • Higher cost for clothing and food? • Other financial issues?	

Roommate issues: • Not used to living with others? • Worried about not liking roommates? • Pressure to spend money and time to fit in with roommates' lifestyle? • Different standards of cleanliness, privacy, noise, and so forth? • Other roommate issues?	
Commuting issues: • Longer commuting time? • Parking problems? • Feeling left out of campus life? • Hard to make good friends? • Hard to schedule group study time with others? • Other commuting issues?	
College size issues: • Hard to find things? • Longer lines and waits? • Hard to pay attention or ask questions in large classes? • Large library hard to understand? • Confusing array of entertainment and social events? • Generally feeling lost and ignored? • Other size issues?	
Diversity issues: • Hard to understand other people's ideas, dress, habits? • Hard to relate to different backgrounds and experiences? • Hard to accept unusual ideas and practices? • Feeling that others are looking down on you? • Other diversity issues?	

Getting involved in extracurricular activities, such as intramural sports, can help alleviate transfer shock by providing opportunities to meet people with similar interests.

Student Alert:
Even though transfer students have already attended at least one orientation, it is essential for them to attend the orientation program at their new institution. This is a great time to meet other students and to solve problems before classes begin.

Overcoming Transfer Shock

Although there are clearly many challenges in a successful transfer experience, there are several strategies you can use to diminish and even avoid the consequences of transfer shock. Consider these:

■ **Knowledge is power.** Find out as much as you can about your new college before you get there. Read the information on the school Web site and in the catalog. Understand what is expected of you academically and the kinds of courses you need to take. Learn about the extracurricular activities and campus organizations that are available to you. Understand the technology resources that are available, such as where you can have access to a computer and how the library functions. The more you know about your school, the less anxiety you'll have.

■ **Attend orientation.** Virtually all schools have an orientation program for new students. Don't ignore it even though you probably went through an orientation at your previous school. You'll receive valuable information, and you will meet transfer counselors who can give you advice on which courses to take. You will be introduced to the college's resources, and you'll find out how to sign up for courses. If you're living on campus, you'll also receive information about your residence hall.

■ **Meet with your advisor.** At some point after you are accepted into your new college, you will be assigned an advisor. Meet this person as soon as possible, because he or she holds several keys to your academic future.

Your advisor will help you navigate through the maze of requirements that you will need to fulfill. He or she will help you choose courses, assist you in filling any gaps in your background, and generally advise you on the things you need to do to have a successful academic career. Good advisors can not only help you understand the things you need to do but also give guidance on the things you *shouldn't* do.

■ **Seek out other transfer students.** Having friends who are going through the same thing you are can make the transfer experience much more manageable. Seek out other transfer students, because they will provide a sounding board for what you are going through and can also be a source of information you may have missed.

■ **Find a mentor.** Get to know your instructors. Remember, they went into teaching because they enjoy interacting with and getting to know students. Even if you are in a large class with hundreds of other students, your instructor will enjoy meeting you. Choose an instructor who seems most approachable and likable, and stop by his or her office at the beginning of the term. Periodically drop in, just to say hello or to discuss an academic issue. You'll soon find yourself building a relationship with that individual. If you do that every term, you will develop a valuable network of instructors who will keep you feeling like you are a part of the academic community of the school.

■ **Remember that you have done it before.** Keep in mind that this is not the first time you have started college. You did it several years earlier, and you were successful enough to be accepted by your current school. You're also older than most typical beginning students, so you probably have a degree of maturity not seen in the average first-year college student. You know what college is like.

Your prior experiences and successes put you several steps ahead of most beginning students on the campus to which you have transferred. That doesn't mean the transition will be easy or stress-free. It does mean, though, that you can be more confident that you will master this new transition and be successful.

SPEAKING OF
Success

Name: Elese Washines

School: University of Washington at Seattle; double major in Mathematics and American Indian Studies

After having excelled at Yakima Valley Community College, a two-year school in the state of Washington, Elese Washines had the opportunity to transfer to some of the best colleges in the country, including Harvard, Purdue, and Dartmouth. However, after much thought, she decided to stay much closer to home and enrolled at the University of Washington in Seattle.

Washines, a member of the Yakama Nation, felt that the offer of a full academic scholarship, a strong mathematics department, and a strong diverse student population at the University of Washington made her decision easier.

Another important factor in her decision was meeting with members of the school's Student Outreach Ambassadors program, a group of diverse students who work to recruit new students.

"I really liked the message they gave. And when one student introduced himself to me in his native language and described being a Pacific Islander, I knew I could be involved with my culture and still pursue the education I wanted," she added.

Making the decision to attend the University of Washington, which was almost 10 times larger than her community college, was easier than actually going there.

"I had traveled a lot, and I thought I was experienced in being away from home," Washines noted, "but once I got to the University of Washington, I was homesick a lot. I really missed being around my tribe and family, and I even considered dropping out."

One of the things that helped her overcome the homesickness was to become more involved with other native students.

"All the native students found each other in the student groups and it became our family away from home," she added.

Ultimately, transferring to a much larger institution worked out well for Washines, who plans to teach at the Yakama Nation Tribal School. "I didn't find it intimidating. I just saw it as offering more options. It becomes what you make of it."

What are the strategies for choosing a specific college or university to transfer to?

■ To *prepare* to transfer, consider the reasons why you should (or shouldn't) transfer.

■ The *organization* step in the transfer process involves identifying schools to which you might consider transferring.

■ The *work* of transferring involves the actual application process.

■ To *evaluate* your options, consider the positive and negative aspects of schools to which you have been accepted, including the amount of financial aid that has been offered.

■ It's also important to *rethink* your choices to ensure you've made the right decisions.

How do I transfer credits?

■ Determining which credits will transfer is a central issue for transferring students.

■ Many schools have articulation agreements, formal arrangements that determine which courses or credits will automatically transfer.

■ Many states have 2 + 2 plans that permit students to transfer into specific majors or programs.

How can I adjust to a new college?

■ Some students face transfer shock, which impedes the transition to their new college.

■ Among the steps to combat transfer shock are getting as much information as possible, attending orientation, seeking out other transfer students, and finding a mentor.

KEY TERMS AND CONCEPTS

Articulation agreements (p. T–18)
2 + 2 plans (p. T–18)

Priority enrollment plan (p. T–19)

RESOURCES

On Campus

To help plan a transfer from a two-year college to a four-year school, seek out your transfer advising office. Staff in that office will be well equipped to give you advice and information about the schools to which most students transfer. In addition, you can call or visit the transfer office at the schools to which you are thinking about transferring.

In Print

A variety of books provide useful information about the transfer process. Nadine Koch and K. William Wasson's *The Transfer Student's Guide to the College Experience* (Houghton Mifflin, 2002) is a good place to start.

In addition, Eric Freedman's *How to Transfer to the College of Your Choice* (Ten Speed Press, 2001) and Carey Harbin's *Your Transfer Planner* (Wadsworth, 1995) provide a variety of strategies to help master the transfer process.

On the Web

The following sites on the World Wide Web provide opportunities to extend your learning about the material in this chapter. (Although the Web addresses were accurate at the time the book was printed, check the P.O.W.E.R. Learning Web site [**www.mhhe.com/power**] for any changes that may have occurred.)

- The benefits of transferring to a four-year college are explored at **www.intstudy. com/study_abroad/livfiles/saww6a14.htm**. From the International Education Site, this link provides an in-depth feature on how the advantages of transferring to a four-year institution far outweigh the difficulties of the potentially lengthy and sometimes confusing transfer process. Many links are given to overseas colleges and universities, and alternative professions.

- Further Your Education.com (**www.furtheryoureducation.com/transfer/ nontraditional-college-student-resource/transfer-college-student.shtml**). The title of this site says it all. It provides extensive infomation on all aspects of transferring to four-year institutions and offers important information geared toward the nontraditional student in a step-by-step guide.

- The British Columbia Council on Admissions & Transfer offers this comprehensive site on transferring to another academic institution: **http://www.bccat.bc.ca/tips/ index.html**. Dozens of tips and a nice section on dealing with Transfer Shock.

- At **www.ccc.edu/co/main_articagree.shtml** you will find a comprehensive look at the articulation agreements of City Colleges of Chicago that encompass 209 programs at 52 senior institutions. This example is followed by hundreds of other institutions of higher learning across the country.

TAKING IT TO THE NET

1 Finances are often one of the main considerations students face when transferring from a community college to a four-year school. In order to explore this issue, visit several college Web sites and learn about their financial aid policies. Review the approaches used by different colleges offering aid. Do most offer scholarships? What about work-study? Are low-interest loans an option?

2 Use the Internet to find information on the steps to follow and issues to consider when transferring to a four-year school. Go to Google (**www. google.com**) and Yahoo! (**www.yahoo.com**) and enter "transferring to a four year college." Many of the sites are for community colleges that offer a multitude of tips and suggestions on preparing for a transfer. Review a number of them and consider the strategies that you might use.

NOTES

1. Based on data from the Bureau of Labor Statistics, 2003.

PHOTO CREDITS

Page T–1: © CORBIS
Page T–2: © F. Schussler/PhotoLink/Getty Images
Page T–8:© Patrick Clark/Getty Images
Page T–24: © PhotoDisc/Getty Images

Three courses at Foothill Community College, one of which produced a grade of F. A course started, but then dropped, at Nassau Community College. Two online courses from eArmyU while in the military service. Finally—and more recently—a semester's worth of courses at Holyoke Community College.

Not a very coherent picture, thought Perry Washington. It's not that he set out to build such a checkered record. It's just that his military service, his marriage and subsequent divorce, and his job kept him moving around.

Despite his past, Perry was actually quite proud of his current stint at Holyoke Community College. He was doing well, with a solid B average. This time, he thought, he would stick it out and earn his associate's degree.

Still, Perry was surprised when one of his instructors asked him if he intended to transfer once he completed his associate's degree. With such a blemished academic record, was it even possible to think of transferring to a four-year school? Could he overcome his background? Was it even worth thinking about obtaining a bachelor's degree?

1. What advice would you give Perry about the possibility of transferring to a four-year school?

2. What would be the advantages of continuing his education beyond an associate's degree?

3. What are the first steps Perry should take to consider transferring?

4. What should Perry do to determine if his credits might transfer?

5. How should Perry identify schools he might transfer to?

ROBERT S. FELDMAN

P.O.W.E.R. LEARNING, Third Edition

STUDENT TEXTBOOK SURVEY

INSTRUCTIONS FOR SENDING IN YOUR RESPONSE BY MAIL:

Please fill out this survey, detach, affix stamp and drop in the mail. Your comments will help Robert S. Feldman and McGraw-Hill improve this textbook in future editions.

... OR, YOU MAY SEND IN YOUR SURVEY RESPONSE _ONLINE_ AT: *www.mhhe.com/powersurvey*

Thank you for your participation!

◄— REMOVE TOP PORTION BEFORE SENDING —►

ROBERT S. FELDMAN

P.O.W.E.R. LEARNING, Third Edition

STUDENT TEXTBOOK SURVEY

NAME: _____ SCHOOL: _____

E-MAIL: _____ PHONE: _____

COURSE TITLE & NUMBER: _____ TEXT(Author/Title): **Feldman, P.O.W.E.R. Learning, 3/e**

1. Is the course required for all first-year students at your institution? ❏ yes ❏ no

   If "no," please explain who takes the course: _____

   _____

2. How long have you been with your current text? _____

3. When is your next text evaluation? _____

4. Explain your text evaluation process: _____

   _____

   _____

5. Do you currently or have you ever used a custom text for the Student Success course?

   _____

6. What topics do you cover? ❏ Study Skills ❏ Life Skills ❏ Both

7. Is Your Student Success Course part of a Learning Community? ❏ yes ❏ no

8. Do you offer sections for special populations, such as student athletes? ❏ yes ❏ no

9. What assessments do you use? _____

   What would you like to add/change about your assessments? _____

   _____

10. What technology, if any, do you currently use in this course? _____

    _____

    _____

11. What faculty development/instructor training do you have in place? _____

    _____

    _____

12. McGraw-Hill offers a variety of workshops in student success. Would like to be notified of workshops in your area?

    _____

13. What changes do you envision for this course? Please use the space provided to share unique aspects of the course/program at your institution.

    _____

    _____

    _____

PLACE
STAMP
HERE

McGraw-Hill Higher Education
Two Penn Plaza
New York, New York   10121

Attn: Maria Romano, 20th Floor